# Sweet Freedom's Song

# Sweet Freedom's Song

*How Music of Patriotism, Protest, and
Persistence Shapes American Identity*

Michael Lasser

BLOOMSBURY ACADEMIC
NEW YORK • LONDON • OXFORD • NEW DELHI • SYDNEY

BLOOMSBURY ACADEMIC

Bloomsbury Publishing Inc, 1359 Broadway, New York, NY 10018, USA
Bloomsbury Publishing Plc, 50 Bedford Square, London, WC1B 3DP, UK
Bloomsbury Publishing Ireland, 29 Earlsfort Terrace, Dublin 2, D02 AY28, Ireland

BLOOMSBURY, BLOOMSBURY ACADEMIC and the Diana logo are trademarks of Bloomsbury Publishing Plc

First published in the United States of America 2025

Copyright © Michael Lasser, 2025

Cover design: Sally Rinehart

All rights reserved. No part of this publication may be: i) reproduced or transmitted in any form, electronic or mechanical, including photocopying, recording or by means of any information storage or retrieval system without prior permission in writing from the publishers; or ii) used or reproduced in any way for the training, development or operation of artificial intelligence (AI) technologies, including generative AI technologies. The rights holders expressly reserve this publication from the text and data mining exception as per Article 4(3) of the Digital Single Market Directive (EU) 2019/790.

Bloomsbury Publishing Inc does not have any control over, or responsibility for, any third-party websites referred to or in this book. All internet addresses given in this book were correct at the time of going to press. The author and publisher regret any inconvenience caused if addresses have changed or sites have ceased to exist, but can accept no responsibility for any such changes.

Library of Congress Cataloging-in-Publication Data
Names: Lasser, Michael, 1936- author
Title: Sweet freedom's song : how music of patriotism, protest, and persistence shapes American identity / Michael Lasser.
Description: New York : Bloomsbury Publishing, 2025. | Includes index.
Identifiers: LCCN 2025013839 (print) | LCCN 2025013840 (ebook) | ISBN 9798765149157 hardback | ISBN 9798765149164 pdf | ISBN 9798765149171 epub
Subjects: LCSH: Songs—United States—History and criticism | Popular music—United States—History and criticism | Popular music—Social aspects—United States—History | Popular music—Political aspects—United States—History
Classification: LCC ML3477 .L3805 2025 (print) | LCC ML3477 (ebook) | DDC 782.421640973—dc23/eng/20250514
LC record available at https://lccn.loc.gov/2025013839
LC ebook record available at https://lccn.loc.gov/2025013840

ISBN: HB: 979-8-7651-4915-7
ePub: 979-8-7651-4917-1
ePDF: 979-8-7651-4916-4

Typeset by Deanta Global Publishing Services, Chennai, India
Printed and bound in the United States of America

For product safety related questions contact productsafety@bloomsbury.com.

To find out more about our authors and books visit www.bloomsbury.com and sign up for our newsletters.

# Contents

| | | |
|---|---|---|
| Introduction: Songs Are the Pulse of a Nation's Heart | | 1 |
| 1 | An *American* Character | 16 |
| 2 | A Yankee Doodle Dandy | 36 |
| 3 | The Faces of Patriotism | 47 |
| 4 | Fight for Love and Liberty | 55 |
| 5 | Attuned to the Needs of the Nation | 65 |
| 6 | Protest as Patriotism: African Americans, Letting the People Go | 82 |
| 7 | The Mingling of Black and White | 99 |
| 8 | African Americans, Acts of Desegregation | 112 |
| 9 | Women and the Nineteenth Amendment | 126 |
| 10 | "Ragging and Nagging in Politics" | 138 |
| 11 | Racist Songs and African Americans | 148 |
| 12 | "I'll Be Down to Get You in a Taxi, Honey" | 158 |
| 13 | Come On and Hear! | 168 |
| 14 | "The Sweetest Taste of Freedom for My Soul" | 181 |
| 15 | "They're All Good American Names" | 188 |
| 16 | "There She Lies, the Great Melting Pot—Listen!" | 203 |
| 17 | His Immigration Rose | 214 |
| 18 | Feasting on the Stereotypes | 227 |
| 19 | More Than Fifteen Million Immigrants | 236 |
| 20 | The Urge to Roam | 246 |
| 21 | Thousands of Miles from Home | 257 |
| 22 | Hard Travelin' | 267 |
| 23 | Wandering and Returning | 274 |
| 24 | Longing for My Homeland | 282 |
| Epilogue | | 291 |
| Notes | | 293 |
| Index | | 313 |

# Introduction

## Songs Are the Pulse of a Nation's Heart

It's an odd time to be affirming patriotism. We divide down the middle, sometimes brutally so. We have politicized everything, even the receiving of a vaccine to save our lives and the lives of others. I may be naive, but I can't think of a better time to do it, especially by relying on something we have in common, even though we sometimes fail to pay it a lot of serious attention. No one, regardless of point of view, gets to take the nation, its symbols, or its ideals from the rest of us. Nearly all of us embrace the virtue of patriotism, even though we may interpret the word differently. I'm going to try to stretch the limits, often by implication, especially in the face of doubt in the best of us and the near-violent confrontations between too many of us. I'm going to be writing about songs.

In response to the politicizing of so much of American life and the deep divisions within the country, a number of writers, ranging from the former CBS newsman Dan Rather and his collaborator Elliot Kirschner to the Yale University professor of political science and philosophy Steven B. Smith, have taken a new look at patriotism that considers the past as it must and considers its implications for the future. Rather and Kirschner write:

> Patriotism . . . takes work. It takes knowledge, engagement with those who are different from you, and fairness in law and opportunity, It takes coming together for good causes. . . . We are a nation not only of dreamers, but also of fixers. We have looked at our land and people, and said, time and time again, "This is not good enough; we can do better."[1]

At the same time, Smith sets out to "reclaim patriotism . . . as the most fundamental political virtue." He calls it "a due regard for our collective values, what we look up to as a people. It is an expression of our highest ideals and commitments, not only to what we are, but also to what we might be. It is devotion to the republic and the way of life for which it stands."[2] And then the great, ragged, unending democratic argument continues.

Smith makes an essential distinction between patriotism and nationalism. Patriotism, he writes, is inclusive; nationalism, exclusive. A successful popular song potentially includes everyone who hears it, if only for a short time. In so unlikely a nation as ours, we have to take what we can get and struggle to expand what we have.

So many of our greatest songs are dark. They dwell on betrayal and obsess over lost love. They find the future bleak and unrelenting. In these songs, hope is what you turn to when you have nothing else to hold on to. Yet at the same time, as John Wilmerding explains, "There is a sense of self-reliance, of our natural resilience and of our undercurrents of optimism. These are beliefs and attributes that have always stood us well."[3] A great authority on American art, Wilmerding found them in such artists as Winslow Homer and Gilbert Stuart, but the same applies to such songwriters as Jerome Kern and Oscar Hammerstein, Harold Arlen and Johnny Mercer, and the Gershwins.

Their songs express a lingering sense of American wanderlust, no matter how far we remove ourselves from the frontier. Americans have always been, at heart and in their sense of themselves, a people on the move.

The author Washington Irving was one of the first to use the American landscape in his writing. In one of his most famous stories, "Rip Van Winkle" from 1819, he wrote about the Kaatskill Mountains,

> swelling up to a noble height, and lording it over the surrounding country. Every change of season, every change of weather, indeed, every hour of the day produces some change in the magical hues and shapes of these mountains; and they are regarded by all the good wives, far and near, as perfect barometers.[4]

A decade and a half later, Irving traveled west, including a month spent largely on horseback in what would later become Oklahoma. He wrote when he returned that the land was "vast and beautiful" and "boundless and fertile." He saw in it the future of America.[5]

In the early years of the Republic, the citizens of the new nation turned to nature as "a source of national pride."⁶ It thrilled Europeans as much as it did Americans for its size and diversity. We went east to west mainly, but we could also trace the size of a burgeoning nation from the five northern inland seas to the tropical marshes of the Deep South.

Like Irving, the painter Thomas Cole went west in the 1830s. Another believer in American exceptionalism, he wrote that America had features "unknown to Europe." When he returned, he began a series of paintings in upstate New York that defined the Hudson River School in its depiction of a distinctively American landscape. At the same time, Albert Bierstadt, another Hudson River School painter, went west to depict the great crests and cataracts of the Rockies.⁷

§ § §

Rufus E. Miles coined Miles's Law in 1948: "Where you stand depends on where you sit." Commitment to the common good doesn't mean we don't also have loyalties based on where we live as well as on family, race, gender, and religion. We juggle any number of identities at the same time. They affect our grasp of the common good, for, as the poet Walt Whitman intuited, we "contain multitudes." Yet large numbers of us like the same movie, TV show, or song at the same time. Does this transitory common affection for something so small affect our ties to the nation? We do not have a single voice; far from it. Are we a single varied people in need of any social and cultural glue we can find, or is that nothing more than another form of self-serving national myth? Despite our troubled past and present, and what is bound to be a vexing future, the sense of the people arising from vigorous debate is essential for the health and survival of a democratic republic. Steven B. Smith asserts that America, since its founding, "has contained a deliberative and self-questioning character. . . . To be an American is to be continually engaged in asking what it means to be an American."⁸

Including popular songs as part of the conversation sounds absurd—or does it? Smith makes an essential distinction between patriotism and nationalism. A successful popular song potentially includes everyone who hears it for as long as it persists.

The substance of a song is largely emotional, yet taken together, popular songs suggest something about what it means to be in love in all its possibilities. They may not always bind the nation, but they touch many individuals within the nation. In their small but engaging way, they speak to us and for us. It's not what Lincoln had in mind, but in their transitory way, they reach for the better angels of our nature. They bring to bear the kinds of emotions that patriotic songs also express, though in significantly different ways and for obviously different purposes. Patriotic songs are *significant*, while popular songs are *merely* about love. And yet these popular miniatures, often limited to speaking for one person in love with someone else, help to shape our emotional identity. Because they set out purposely to be popular, they are the voice of the people in the most intimate ways. They speak to the many, but they do so one by one. Patriotic and popular are two chambers of the same heart, ultimately inseparable no matter how different they may appear to be.

Smith continues, "Patriotism or loyalty to country is ultimately a species of care, and care requires a degree of empathy. We care about things to which we feel an emotional attachment because we feel them worthy of our care."[9] If I didn't know that he was writing about patriotism, I might think that in a way he had popular songs in mind. We see and hear ourselves in songs. Perhaps it's not too far a reach to add that we feel ourselves in them. They require no action on our part except to pay attention, respond, and find ourselves there. That's their great limitation, but also an indication of how they mirror and give expression to American lives. It suggests that they matter as a vivid piece of the American fabric.

Despite everything, I hope that an open-eyed patriotism might be part of us as Americans, but aside from such obvious titles as "America the Beautiful" and "God Bless America," what does all this have to do with a book about songs? The historian Sarah J. Purcell writes about patriotic songs during the American Revolution and the early years of the Republic as:

> a public culture, including memories of a shared past, [that] allowed people to create images of their "communion" as they imagined their connections with one another to form national allegiances.[10]

Music, especially directly patriotic songs, "shaped Americans' visions of the nation." It "helped form a national identity and national consciousness."[11] Irving Berlin said, "Songs make history, and history makes songs."[12] But it gets more personal than that. Songs reach for an audience of millions, but the encounter is with one person at a time. Even in a one-thousand-seat theater, each individual hears it for himself or herself. This embrace of songs and what they say contributes to the shaping of American identity despite the vagaries of popularity. Yet the stuff of popular culture appears again and again in lyrics, everything from trains to autos to jet planes, the waltz to the jitterbug and the twist, lunch at the Automat to dinner at Schrafft's.

On a deeper level, similar points of view persist into the twenty-first century. Echoing Abraham Lincoln's civic religion, author David Lehman says about songwriters from the Great American Songbook, "What the artist finds as a substitute for religion in America is America itself, in part because America itself is a work in progress . . . and you can create it as you go along."[13] An authority on American popular music, Jeff Melnick adds about the songwriters, "These are city artists who are willing to use everything,"[14] including a scene in a barn in the Marx Brothers' movie *A Day at the Races* (1937). After some no-holds-barred Lindy Hopping—a distinctively American dance—by African Americans, Harpo Marx grabs a pitchfork as if it's a drum major's baton and leads the dancers in a grand march to John Philip Sousa's "The Stars and Stripes Forever." Meanwhile, Groucho and Chico, desperate to avoid three men who are pursuing them, don blackface so they can join the parade of Black people and disappear. We find the scene offensive, but in its time it was comic and improvisational, as well as socially telling: Americans hiding by turning themselves into Black people. It was also an attack on authority by African Americans allied with a couple of anarchic Jewish performers.

More recently, and in a more personal way, the lyricist E. Y. Harburg explained:

> Songs are the pulse of a nation's heart. A fever chart of its health. Are we at peace? Are we floundering? Are we in trouble? Do we feel beautiful? Do we feel ugly? . . . Listen to our songs. . . . The lyricist, like any artist, cannot be neutral. He should be committed to the side of humanity.[15]

Harburg's assertion remains true even in love songs that seem to have nothing to do with patriotism, yet each one affirms some small aspect of American identity. We are bound by common emotion if not political outlook. Through their deep commitment to a cause, American folk songs may be intensely political, mainstream popular music much less so, yet they connect us implicitly through what we believe or desire.

Americans sing. Even in the most contentious times, songs help to get us through. We sing slow ballads and jive tunes, ragtime and the blues, folk songs and gospel, R&B and rock, Western Swing and sentimental ballads, lullabies and rap. We sing old songs and new as we give voice to many of the things we live through, delight in, and endure. We sing about fads and fashions, war and peace, and the news of the day. We romanticize "sleigh bells in the snow" and "Christmas time in the city." We "climb every mountain" and "gather at the river." We sing about the West, Midwest, and South; San Francisco, Chicago, and New Orleans; and we sing more songs about New York City than any other place.

We conjure up memories of the past and dreams of the future as we sing about love of country and, most of the time, love itself—romance and sex, the ethereal and earthly, discovery and loss, ecstasy and despair.

From 1900 on, most of these songs came from professional songwriters in Tin Pan Alley, Hollywood, Harlem, and Nashville, and on Broadway. The songs they wrote limn the lives we've led as individuals and Americans. They overflow with allusions to everyday life that change because the times and our lives change. In 1892, a successful courtship led to an idyllic image of a young man's bride looking "sweet / On the seat / Of a bicycle built for two!" (Harry Dacre, "Daisy Bell," 1892). In 1905, when owning an automobile probably meant that a young man was financially independent, he could propose to his sweetheart while they rode in his Oldsmobile: "Down the road of life we'll fly, / Automobubbling you and I" (Gus Edwards and Vincent Bryan, "In My Merry Oldsmobile," 1905). By the early 1970s, a teenage couple drove to a drive-in movie for whatever happened next. Imagine the horror of breaking up and being there alone: "I'm all alone / At the drive-in movie, / It's a feelin' that ain't too groovy." Is there anything worse for this devastated teenager than "watchin' werewolves without you" (Jim Jacobs and Warren Casey, "Alone at a Drive-In Movie," *Grease*, 1971)?

Yet during the first half of the twentieth century, and before and after as well, we sang love songs that reflected truths we believed were permanent. We also sang about moving to the city from the farm, silent movies when they were new, and Lindbergh's flight in 1927. We even sang about such baseball stars as Joe DiMaggio, Jackie Robinson, and Mickey Mantle. We sang naively optimistic Pollyanna songs in the 1920s because so many of us were carefree; we sang them in the 1930s because so many more of us needed their optimism and encouragement:

> Grab your coat, and get your hat,
> Leave your worry on the doorstep.
> 
> (Jimmy McHugh and Dorothy Fields, "On the Sunny Side of the Street," *Lew Leslie's International Revue*, 1930)

We sang with an urban sensibility about taxicabs, joints that never closed, and women making it on their own. Fields and villages in songs were places to delight in, but just as often to leave and remember. City songs found their drive in jazz and an eye to the future; country songs, in nostalgia. We sang new songs in new styles, but we also remembered the songs our parents and grandparents had sung and taught us. As America shaped us and we shaped ourselves as Americans, our songs gave us an idealized mirror of who we were and what we felt. If it was on our minds or in our hearts, it soon ended up in a popular song. Beliefs and styles came and went, but sentiment remained.

I'm suggesting that many songs that have nothing to do with the flag or the Fourth of July affirm, at least implicitly, the norms of a still-free country even when their subject matter may appear to be frivolous—an invitation to a dance, for instance, or an automobile ride for an afternoon in the country. Other songs from early in the twentieth century set out to broaden these norms by persuading white America that Black people merited full citizenship. Like the immigrants from Eastern and Southern Europe, they redefined American identity. Unlike the immigrants, African American songwriters and performers set out to do it consciously. When African Americans wrote a song or sang it onstage, they had a sense of purpose that included entertainment but often reached beyond it.

It's debatable in such a contentious time as ours, but earlier writers have asserted, despite the scoundrels who wrap themselves in patriotism's cloak, "Patriotism remains the cement that binds any society together. Without patriotism a society becomes unstuck."[16] Who knows where we go next in the third decade of the twenty-first century, but for nearly three centuries so far, songs in their own way have helped us stay stuck together. Although ideas about patriotism and American identity have changed over the years, popular songs continue to face the issue, often indirectly.

The *New York Times* critic Stephen Holden wrote about Irving Berlin's achievement a few years before Berlin's death at 101: "Patriotic razzle-dazzle, sophisticated melancholy and humble sentiments: Berlin's songs span the emotional terrain of America with a thoroughness that others may have equaled but none have surpassed."[17] "The emotional terrain of America": Holden got it just right, even though Berlin was not alone in doing it. He did do it, though, more broadly and more often than his fellow songwriters. That spanning of America's emotional terrain becomes as much a part of us as settling the West had been.

Berlin's eagerness to write—sometimes as many as forty songs a year—reflected his deep desire to be recognized and accepted as an American: an outsider finally at home. Berlin's drive to remake himself served as an unarticulated subtext in many of his songs, regardless of the subject matter. Writing about love became the pathway to the future and home.

Many popular songs align with our history by articulating the sentiments and behavior of their time. Others extend beyond their time to speak to the future as well. We hear a good song, and we recognize ourselves. Even though we don't think of many of these songs as immediately patriotic, they helped to shape a nation and its people and to sharpen their sense of identity. The shaping was often suggestive or metaphorical rather than literal. It could be reactive rather than formative, and anecdotal rather than measured. Because songs have always relied so heavily on sentiment, they reflect not reality, but what William H. A. Williams calls "the public *discourse* about reality."[18] The response of the people gives them their importance and, sometimes, authority.

For a long time, new arrivals were Americans because they landed here and said they were. Sometime after that, those who were here before them moved over a little and made some room. It wasn't easy or simple.

Songs confirmed what Americans felt or believed or wanted to believe, yet at the same time, they were inseparable from commerce. Professional songwriters have always sought a large buying public by choosing subjects with broad appeal. The successful songs spread in popularity across the nation; a few of them also extended through the generations.

We still sing "Battle Hymn of the Republic" and "God Bless America," and many of us can sing at least some of the words to "Alexander's Ragtime Band" (Irving Berlin, 1911) and probably all of "Over the Rainbow" (Harold Arlen and E. Y. Harburg, "Over the Rainbow," *Wizard of Oz*, 1939). Sometimes nothing more than a title or a line or two ("Come on and hear" or "Somewhere over the rainbow / Way up high") is enough to lend a song a particular aura. Each of these songs plays a part in how a song reflects and shapes us simultaneously. They are, in their way, patriotic. We hear them filtered through a varied but necessarily American sensibility.

Learning to sing "Over the Rainbow" with my mother is one of my earliest memories. Many years later, the lyricist E. Y. Harburg's son, Ernie, told me a story about an off-the-beaten-track vacation that he and his wife, Deena Rosenberg, had taken in the South American *altiplano*. They were riding at one point on a rickety bus filled with local people of Indian stock who spoke either Spanish or Quechua, the language of the Incas. Rosenberg spoke fluent Spanish, so she and Ernie were doing fine.

The other passengers welcomed their new American friends and began to sing their songs to them. Eventually, Deena turned to Ernie to say, "We should sing them an American song." He answered, "One of Yip's." Everyone, including Ernie, called Harburg Yip. They settled on "Over the Rainbow." Within a few bars, everybody on the bus—in Spanish, Quechua, or English— was singing. Perhaps they all knew it because TV stations show *The Wizard of Oz* worldwide year after year. Ernie prefers to believe that it's become the universal American song.

The song's melancholy during the Great Depression gave even its inkling of hope something that people took hold of. It spoke to their fears and their reluctance to dream. It was an American anthem for its time that still resonates more than eighty years later. Americans test their resilience again and again with mixed results. We continue to dream America's dream. We carry "Over the Rainbow" just under our skin.

So many songs played essential roles in our coming of age. I can still hear the voices of Martin Block and then William B. Williams on WNEW in New York, and I remember discovering the likes of Rosemary Clooney, Lena Horne, Benny Goodman, Ella Fitzgerald, Frank Sinatra, Peggy Lee, and Nat King Cole because Block and Williams played their recordings. They provided the soundtrack to my adolescence and young manhood. Many thousands of others were also listening to those same singers and songs.

Hundreds of songs, from the patriotic to the romantic, play an essential role in America's collective memory. People learned songs from sheet music but eventually heard them on radios and recordings. They sang along at pianos in their parlors and whistled them in the shower. They heard them performed in minstrel shows, vaudeville houses, and nightclubs; on Broadway stages and in Pops concerts; and in the only movie theater in a small town. If they had the means in the 1930s, they hopped a cab or took the A train to Harlem to hear something new and jazzy at the Cotton Club or Connie's Inn.

There was a time when three generations of a family could stand around a piano and spend an hour or two singing the same songs. Each of them knew songs the others didn't, but they also had a large number of songs in common. The songs were as familiar as nursery rhymes, and Americans of all ages sang them—relied upon them—with confidence and delight. To this day, you can't have Christmas without "White Christmas" (1942), the Fourth of July without "God Bless America" (1918, revised 1938), or a seventh-inning stretch without "Take Me Out to the Ballgame" (1908).

Each of these songs is patriotic in its own way. "White Christmas," for instance, uses an idealized view of an American holiday set in a rural, snow-blanketed New England to combine childhood memories with the melancholy of separation. In simplified form, it confirms our mixed feelings about Christmas but still manages to affirm, "May your days be merry and bright." Beyond that, it creates a climate for songs that also dwell on the sad side of what we wish were only joyful, especially "I'll Be Home for Christmas" and

"Have Yourself a Merry Little Christmas." Written during a worldwide war, these songs touched something true in Americans' sense of themselves; more than seventy-five years later, they continue to do just that.

We have always been a people on the move; we arrive from somewhere else to settle and build. As eager as we are to set out, we also have an urge to shape a clearing in the wilderness or settle near a wide place in the river. We like both the rootlessness and the putting down of roots. We settle ourselves in a new place, at least for now. If we're later arrivals, we probably choose neighborhoods already populated by others of our kind. Wherever Americans have gone within the fifty states, we have remembered and re-created home. In the aftermath of the First World War, we sang, "We'll build a sweet little nest somewhere in the west, / And let the rest of the world go by" (Ernest R. Ball and J. Keirn Brennan, "Let the Rest of the World Go By," 1919). We anticipated the end of the Second World War by singing, "I'm going to settle down and never more roam / And make the San Fernando Valley my home" (Gordon Jenkins, "San Fernando Valley," 1944).

More than a century before that, Americans had first sung, "Be it ever so humble, there's no place like home" (Henry Bishop and John Howard Payne, "Home! Sweet Home!" 1843). The song is English, but Americans have long since adopted it. Despite our passion for progress, we are great borrowers and appropriators; we especially absorb from those who arrive with their own music in hand. Nothing was more important to the task of crafting a distinctively American popular music than African American song forms, and no one was more important than the recently arrived Irish and Jewish songwriters of early Tin Pan Alley who "translated" them into American, everything from ragtime to jazz to the blues. Josh Kun, director of the University of Southern California's Popular Music Project, says, "If you go through the history of American popular music, what you see over and over again are moments when music serves as a kind of bridge, of encounter, exchange, and negotiation between different cultural groups."[19]

The joining of people and places, lovers and locales, is an essential part of our popular music, where lovers discover one another and move toward marriage and the making of a home. Nothing was more important to the shaping of these songs than an urban sensibility, especially in the first half of the twentieth century. Most of the thousands of popular songs from the time came from Tin Pan Alley, Broadway, and Harlem, all located on the West Side of Manhattan. Tin Pan Alley songwriters stole from everybody and everything: from Black songwriters who had limited access to music publishers, from the music of European immigrants who arrived in great waves beginning in the 1850s, and from ragtime and the blues to reinvent as ragtime songs and blues songs, thirty-two bars at a time. In one very real sense, the Alley's entire output was one huge pastiche, much like the country itself. But it wasn't the whole story—not by a long shot.

Affirming the elemental Americanism of jazz and the blues, the jazz trumpeter Wynton Marsalis told an interviewer that improvisation "is our kind of individuality. We have rights and freedoms that are about the individual." Elsewhere in the interview, he said that jazz "gives you tremendous pride in America." He called it "nonpredatory": "You can be as rich as you want to be in jazz and nobody else has to be poor."[20] He added that within the individuality of jazz, swing is about "nurturing common ground."[21] The music historian John Edward Hasse wrote, "To swing means to play with the feeling of forward thrust, the propulsive rhythmic quality heard in much African-rooted music." He cited something that Duke Ellington had said. Swing is "that part of rhythm that causes a bouncing, buoyant, terpsichorean urge."[22] As the Ellington trumpet player Bubber Miley put it, "If it ain't got that swing, it ain't worth playin.'"[23]

In the same interview, Marsalis described the blues as "an optimism that's not naive. It implies an acuity. That's a democratic thing." Many blues are about betrayal, but at a basic level, they're about survival, about the narrator's ability to articulate melancholy and, by the 1920s, utter a cry of joyful sexual defiance:

> He's got to get it, bring it, and put it right here
> Or else he's gonna keep it out there.
> (Eddie Green, "Put It Right Here [Or Keep It Out There]," 1917)

Rose Rosengard Subotnik suggests that the Tin Pan Alley song embodies something Americans want to believe about themselves. It exemplified, promoted, or celebrated . . . an optimistic belief in the efficacy of action. Thus, far from stifling an individual's power to stake out a meaningful life in a depersonalizing society, such songs . . . offered an important source of empowerment to ordinary people. In terms of performance, the livelier songs said, "Get out there and keep rolling." Laugh and be clever. Don't whine, but if you do whine, said the ballads, whine with style.[24]

She locates the Tin Pan Alley song's optimism not only in its subject matter, but also in "the strength that the pleasure, humor, and sweetness of the Tin Pan Alley song lent to people of all ages in the ordinary moments of their lives."[25]

This book begins with the one place we have in common: the nation, the land, the United States, no matter how fractious and flawed. Then it ranges from city to countryside, using song lyrics to carry the reader through regions, states, cities, and towns, down rivers, and along highways. Song lyrics parallel our lives by setting lovers in places both imagined and real, from the "land where the good songs go" to "Chicago, that toddlin' town." They connect the lovers and, by extension, us to places of meaning—a national past, family histories, personal memories, today and tomorrow, and home.

I've written elsewhere about the ways that cities and city life define the Great American Songbook,[26] but I've also come to see that popular music's urban sensibility during those decades is part of a larger story that weaves together people and places into a singular popular music. Ellen Harper writes, "No matter how much Americans tried to segregate themselves, the music ignored boundaries and slipped in and out of parochial communities, creating something bigger than the sum of its parts."[27] She happens to be writing about folk music and its effect on how we see ourselves as Americans, but what she says is true of every kind of American song.

America is an unlikely place, born of an idea about liberty and personal freedom, tested and given new form by the many different peoples who kept arriving over two and a half centuries. We were adaptable whether we liked it or not. At its best, America's genius lay in compromise and reconciliation, essential in so varied a population: the forging of a nation from thirteen disparate colonies and the recognition that a free people has "a more perfect union" yet to build. At its worst, compromise led to the perpetuation of slavery and its reemergence in Jim Crow after the failure of Reconstruction. Rather and Kirschner write, "I have seen how a nation can pick itself up and make progress, even at divisive and dysfunctional political moments like the present when we seem to be spinning backwards.... I see my love of country imbued with a responsibility to bear witness to its faults."[28]

When it worked, it could lead to a deeper connection between different groups of Americans, and between Americans and the nation. The Melting Pot of the late nineteenth and early twentieth centuries, despite its many injustices, led after generations of struggle to the broad acceptance and assimilation of immigrants from Eastern Europe and Asia. All too often, though, the Melting Pot led first to discrimination and exclusion, while Jim Crow perpetuated the undermining of human dignity and led to violent subjugation. It amounted to slavery in a different form.

To offer an alternative, Catherine T. Hodges wrote recently,

> When one imagines a melting pot, one sees that all of the ingredients to the pot have melded... to become one. Yet I contend that we are not a melting pot; we are a stew pot. The stew is delicious with all of its ingredients, but all of them are allowed to keep their own identity while they all combine to make the whole "pot" better.[29]

It's a persuasive argument, but there's more to say. America is so unlikely a nation in its capacity to absorb so many immigrant groups, so many customs, so many opinions, and so many different kinds of music. A song we all know because it's old and familiar or because it's new and popular reaches large numbers of Americans, a small thing to have in common in an enormously diverse country. Yet when we sing together, differences may fade for a moment as we enact, however slightly, the grand idea of "We, the people."

Many Americans confuse nationalism with patriotism; they accuse those who disagree of disloyalty, even treason. Nationalism excludes; that need to exclude extends to a variety of group identities within the nation. Patriotism, at its best, makes room for disagreement but clings to a belief in unifying goals—our noblest dreams of ourselves and the nation.

That distinction makes a song like Berlin's "Alexander's Ragtime Band" patriotic rather than nationalistic. It includes rather than separates. It invites everyone. Berlin wrote, "that idea of inviting *every* receptive auditor ['Come on and hear'] within shouting distance . . . —an idea pounded in again and again throughout the song in various ways—was the secret of the song's tremendous success."[30]

The sentiments they express will be familiar, their subjects and themes recognizable. They're defined more, though, by the way similar subjects and themes appear and reappear, persist and change, at different times and in different circumstances. The themes reverberate through our history. The overlapping is constant and essential. I am not a poet or a songwriter, but at its heart, this book draws upon the underlying awareness of America that animates Benet's poem and Silverstein's song. In its own way, it sets out to achieve much the same thing.

# 1

# An *American* Character

By January 1777, George Washington, a prosperous slave-holding Virginia planter with military experience in the French and Indian War, had commanded America's Continental Army for just over a year and a half. After being routed again and again by British regulars and Hessians, the army had eventually won victories at Trenton and Princeton. More importantly, the bond between the leader and the troops had deepened. Rick Atkinson observes that in Washington's remarks to his men, he "spoke to them affectionately, not as military underlings and social inferiors, but as fellow republicans."[1] The historian David Hackett Fischer had previously recognized in Washington "a new idea of honor, which was not defined by rank or status or gender, but by a principle of human dignity and decency."[2]

Washington also believed in the new nation as a hallmark of individual identity. The political scientist Virginia L. Arbury wrote that in his Farewell Address, he invited "his fellow citizens to view themselves now as American . . . out of their love for the truth of liberty." "In a word," Washington wrote to Patrick Henry, "I want an *American* character."[3] Washington was no fool. He deplored political parties, but he also saw their rise during his presidency. He understood that there were differences and disputes between individuals, groups, and entire states, sometimes rancorous. People lived different lives and held different views, but he hoped that the idea of an American character would provide the glue for an American nation.

Alexis de Tocqueville arrived from France in 1831 to work as a surveyor but soon found a larger sense of purpose. He began to travel around the country to observe the state of American society and, just as important, the Americans. But *Democracy in America* was the work of an acute foreign observer. John Hector St. John, born Michel Guillaume Jean de Crevecoeur in 1735 in

Normandy, became an American. He settled first in New France and served during the French and Indian War. After the British defeated the French in 1759, he moved to New York, where he Americanized his name to John Hector St. John and, in 1770, married an American woman.

He became a citizen. He bought a farm in Orange County in upstate New York. It prospered, but he often traveled to serve as a surveyor. It was during these trips that he started to write about life in the American colonies and a new breed of person, the American. In 1782, he published a series of essays entitled *Letters from an American Farmer*. The title page names him as J. Hector St. John Crevecoeur. He had lived as an American for more than two decades when the book appeared. Crevecoeur discerned a distinctively American character half a century before de Tocqueville.

Crevecoeur is wise to differences within the colonies, and between town dwellers, farmers, and woodsmen, but he also sees something stronger that binds them despite disagreements and tensions. In one of his letters entitled "What Is an American?" he writes about what he calls "a new man." He describes a single family: the grandfather was English, the grandmother Dutch. Their son married a Frenchwoman, and their four sons married women who came from four different European countries. "*He is* an American," Crevecoeur writes,

> who leaving behind him all his ancient prejudices and manners, received new ones from the new mode of life he has embraced, the new government he obeys, and the new rank he holds. He becomes an American by being received in the broad lap of our *Alma Mater*. Here individuals of all kinds are melted into a new race of men. . . . The American is a new man, who acts upon new principles; he must therefore entertain new ideas, and form new opinions. . . . —This is an American.[4]

Crevecoeur's attitudes, like Washington's, remain essential to the democratic norms that came to gird up the often-frustrating pursuit of "a more perfect Union." These same assumptions eventually (and surprisingly) found expression in simplified form in popular songs. They are "republican" songs, designed to appeal to the broadest popular audience, not because they are directly patriotic, but because they reflect the attitudes of a people. In addition to the ennobling embrace of such songs as "America" and "America the Beautiful," we tell truths in songs, often optimistic but sometimes troubling, about ourselves as Americans—idealized and simplified but truths nevertheless. We also leave out a lot because these songs usually affirm the values and successes of a nation rather than its failures. Together, they express the attitudes and assumptions that underscore what Washington called "an *American* character." The songs came from cotton fields and factory yards as well as Tin Pan Alley and Broadway—acts of loyalty, love, and patriotism, usually thirty-two bars at a time. They are part of the mix that has helped to shape and reflect American identity. As the historian Peter Ackroyd wrote, "History is about longing and belonging. It is about the need for permanence and the perception of continuity. It concerns the atavistic desire to find deep sources of identity."[5] I'm not sure how deeply songs take us, but I am sure that they are part of the search whether we realize it or not.

Melodrama was the most popular American theatrical form of the nineteenth century. The musical counterpart to melodrama was the sentimental ballad, the most popular song form of the century. It elevated the beloved in romantic melodies whose hyperbolic lyrics were formal and literary. In one of his most beautiful songs, Stephen Foster wrote a dramatic monologue to a beloved who is unaware of worldly intrusions: "Beautiful Dreamer, wake unto me, / Starlight and dew drops are waiting for thee!" (Stephen Foster, "Beautiful Dreamer," 1864). More than a century and a half later, it's impossible to imagine someone actually speaking these words. They express an attitude toward women and their relationships with men that was idealized but suffocating.

In the three decades between the Civil War and the coming of ragtime, the sentimental ballad peaked in popularity and importance. Yet for decades after 1865, every form of expression responded, consciously or not, to the carnage of the war. Darkness was everywhere in our art, literature, and music. In an online interview, Eleanor J. Harvey, senior curator at the Smithsonian American Art Museum, said that for the 2011 art exhibition, *The Civil War and American Art*, she set out to "unearth the Civil War-related layer of meaning that resides in some of the finest works of art made during those turbulent years."[6] It was not a matter of subject but of sensibility, an intuitive grasp of the time the artists were living through.

The death of someone young and innocent—a young woman about to marry or a child—became the great subject of the sentimental ballad during these same years. A maiden will die before she marries; she will go to her grave in a state of virginal purity. Several of these songs are variations on the theme. In one of the most popular, a man sees his fiancée kissing another man. He breaks off the engagement and never marries. Years later, after the woman dies, he explains to his niece that he never knew she had been kissing her brother:

> One day a letter came from that man,
> He was her brother the letter ran.
> That's why I'm lonely, no home at all;
> I broke her heart, pet, after the ball.
>
> (Charles K. Harris, "After the Ball," 1891)

By the time the early Tin Pan Alley stalwarts Harry Von Tilzer and Arthur J. Lamb wrote "Bird in a Gilded Cage" in 1900, the musical world was changing; it is one of the last important sentimental ballads. It tells the melodramatic story of a beautiful young woman who avoids death but marries for wealth rather than love. She lives an unhappy life in her "gilded cage."

Post–Civil War sentimental ballads also portray the deaths of children. In this dramatic monologue, a little boy who knows that he is about to die offers comfort to his beloved mother. The generosity of the child in his final moments is both melodramatic and sentimental, just the sort of thing guaranteed to pluck the heartstrings of nineteenth-century audiences:

> Give them all my toys, but Mother,
> Put my little shoes away.
>
> (Charles E. Pratt and Sam'l. N Mitchell, "Put My Little Shoes Away," 1873)

In act 2 of *Show Boat*, Magnolia desperately seeks work after separating from her dashing husband, Gaylord Ravenal. For the scene in which she auditions for a job as a singer in a nightclub, Jerome Kern and Oscar Hammerstein II decided against writing a new song in a period style. Instead, they revived "After the Ball."

The song had sold more than two million copies of sheet music in 1892, unheard of at the time. Its success convinced Harris to move from his home in Milwaukee to New York City, where he became one of the first music publishers in what people were beginning to call Tin Pan Alley. In the early years, the publishers put the songwriters under contract. Tin Pan Alley's songs soon blanketed the country, thanks in large part to the railroads. They carried traveling vaudevillians and touring companies of Broadway hits led by the stars of the original productions. Eventually, radio and recordings accelerated the spread. In the 1920s, country music grew up largely in the rural South and Southwest, but even there, the songs of Tin Pan Alley made their way. These songs fed Americans' desires, shaped their tastes, and gave them a body of common experience, no matter where they lived.

The nineteenth century's patriotic songs were melodramatic and sentimental. They shared a similar language and common ways of seeing the world. They reflected a view of the United States as unique among the nations. They used a language of praise that rose to the level of exceptionalism and triumphalism. These qualities paralleled the excessive emotionalism of melodrama and the elevated romanticism of the sentimental ballad. They were part of the same American cultural stew.

At the same time, reverence for nature served as an inspiring counterpoint. The bounteous land fulfilled the Myth of the Garden and underpinned the nation's sense of triumphalism. As Americans first pushed west in the late eighteenth and early nineteenth centuries, they discovered the continent's rich grasslands. The Great Plains seemed never to end. It would be theirs for the taking as soon as they could remove the indigenous peoples who had been there for centuries, for whom ownership of the land was an alien concept.

The Myth of the Garden combined Western migration, agriculture, and the capacity of the land to feed a growing free people. It soon merged with Manifest Destiny, in which the practical matter of settling the continent and building towns came wrapped in a spiritual cloak.[7] It also cloaked the genocide of the Native tribes. At its worst, patriotism became mere jingoism, though there were often people to counter it. In 1871, when Senator Matthew Hale Carpenter (R-WI) said on the floor of the U.S. Senate, "My country right or wrong," fellow Republican Senator Carl Schurz (R-MO) countered, "My country, right or wrong; if right, to be kept right; and if wrong, to be set right."[8]

As immigrants arrived from Western Europe, and later from Eastern and Southern Europe, patriotic songs reaffirmed the preciousness of liberty and freedom and the need to defend them. American patriotism burgeoned. We had established a nation and ratified a Constitution. Despite the deep, persistent stain of slavery and its aftermath, we had elected a president and passed power to his successors peacefully. The songs of the time affirmed love of country in straightforward but impassioned ways. Although we need to face the fact that slaves built the White House, we can still be glad that it stands. It resulted from the degradations of slavery, but it remains the people's house, an image of a unique democratic republic.

Francis Scott Key's poem, "Defense of Fort McHenry," became the words to "The Star-Spangled Banner" when they were set to "To Anacreon in Heaven," at first the official song of a London gentlemen's club, the Anacreontic Society. It's where the members went to carouse, carry on, and sing their song. Key's poem celebrates in triumphalist terms the British fleet's all-night bombardment of Fort McHenry near Baltimore during the War of 1812. Its final lines affirm America's idealized view of itself: "O say does that star-spangled banner yet wave / O'er the land of the free and the home of the brave." America was not only free and courageous; it was indomitable. Key wrote the poem when he was a prisoner on a British warship from which he saw the fort hold out. Although Maryland did not secede during the Civil War, it was a slave-holding state. It did not dawn on Key to consider the plight of African Americans as he praised the "land of the free." Why would he when he had been a slaveholder since 1800 and opposed abolition?[9]

America has a number of other songs that qualify as unofficial anthems because of the chords they strike with the people. Their popularity and appeal never flag: "America the Beautiful," "America," "God Bless America," "This Land Is Your Land," and one that differs from the others, "Lift Every Voice and Sing."

Many patriotic songs combine love of country with a prayer. Like "My Country, 'Tis of Thee" and "America the Beautiful" before it, "Lift Every Voice and Sing" is a patriotic anthem in the form of a hymn. These songs frequently call on God to bless the nation through times of danger, tribulation, and war. "Lift Every Voice and Sing" is different because it combines African Americans' agonizing past with their deep faith in the future. The writer, activist, and sometime song lyricist James Weldon Johnson wrote it as a poem in 1900. His brother, J. Rosamond Johnson, then set it to music.

In 1919, the National Association for the Advancement of Colored People first called "Lift Every Voice and Sing" the "Negro national anthem." Black schoolchildren in the South continued to sing it until it became part of the Civil Rights Movement of the 1960s. James Weldon Johnson wrote, "The lines of this song repay me in an elation, almost of exquisite anguish, whenever I hear them sung by Negro children."[10]

The song doesn't turn aside from the experiences of the past, but it insists on hope. Its use of the imperative in the opening stanza is a command to be optimistic and insistent about what will come:

> Sing a song full of the faith that the dark past has taught us,
> Sing a song full of the hope that the present has brought us.
> (James Weldon Johnson and J. Rosamond Johnson, "Lift Every Voice and Sing," 1900)

This is no Pollyanna song, though. It describes the "stony" road and the "chastening rod" of the past, and it knows that the remaining journey will require determination, stamina, courage, and faith:

> We have come over a way that with tears has been watered,
> We have come, treading our path through the blood of the slaughtered, ...
> Thou who hast by Thy might
> Led us into the light,
> Keep us forever in the path, we pray ...
> May we forever stand.
> True to our God,
> True to our native land.

Weldon Johnson's allusion to America's civic religion lights the way from slavery and its remembered burdens through a clear-eyed present to a difficult but ultimately fulfilling future—a historical and spiritual journey, not unlike the Exodus, which is so important in so many spirituals. This profound sense of hope makes the song's final lines perhaps its most powerful. Always the land, the nation, and its promise, however unfulfilled. It is a stirring example of the faith in the future that lies at the heart of American patriotism.

In the aftermath of the American Revolution, patriotic songs affirmed the triumphalism that would last at least into the late twentieth century in a song like the country singer Lee Greenwood's "God Bless the U.S.A." (1984). When the nation was still small and weak, its people and their songs bragged "as lustily as chanticleer in the morning"[11] about its uniqueness and pride in liberty. It was the clarion call of a new people and their independence. As early as 1789, Philip Phile wrote "The President's March" for George Washington's inauguration. When Joseph Hopkinson added words in 1798, he changed its name to "Hail, Columbia."[12] Written not very long after the Battle of Yorktown, it was easy to remember and praise the "heav'n born band, / Who fought and bled in freedom's cause." The words call on the people to stand "firm, united let us be, / Rallying round our liberty." If we remain true as a "band of brothers," we shall find the "peace and safety" we seek (Philip Phile and Joseph Hopkinson, "Hail, Columbia," 1789, 1798). Although the words are largely militaristic, the reference to "peace and safety" suggests a second theme that would emerge in some of these songs through the nineteenth century and beyond.[13]

Exactly one hundred years before an act of Congress established "The Star-Spangled Banner" as the national anthem, Samuel Francis Smith set words to a melody he had heard as part of Muzio Clementi's Symphony No. 3. He entitled his work "America," though Americans often prefer to call it "My Country, 'Tis of Thee." It was first performed here in 1831. Great Britain had adopted "God Save the King," set to the same melody, as its unofficial national anthem; the English had first sung it in 1745.

"My Country, 'Tis of Thee" finds great satisfaction in the diversity of the land. The "land of liberty" is sweet. The citizen who speaks in the lyric loves "thy rocks and rills, / Thy woods and templed hills," but at the song's heart lies a triumphalist affirmation of the "Land where my fathers died, / Land of the pilgrims' pride," as it calls upon the mountainside to echo the refrain, "Let freedom ring." Then, in the final stanza, this hymn-like song becomes a prayer to the "author of liberty": "Long may our land be bright, / With freedom's holy light" (Samuel Francis Smith, "America," 1831).

As I write this chapter, Americans confront wars in Ukraine and the Middle East, still-troubling inflation, an extremely nasty presidential election, and an inability to find common ground. Dave Frishberg transforms "My Country, 'Tis of Thee" into a protest song, "My Country Used to Be," in which he describes a nation he could pledge allegiance to and "the values for which it stood / . . . / 'Cause while it lasted, well, it sure felt good." Now he sees that we pledge allegiance to "mighty corporations," "the airport search," wiretaps, and warfare. He concludes:

> I hope my children live to see
> The way my country used to be.
> (Dave Frishberg, "My Country Used to Be," before 2004)

Americans still sing "My Country, 'Tis of Thee," but "Hail, Columbia" (1798) and "Columbia, the Gem of the Ocean" (1843) have largely disappeared from memory, even though all three served as unofficial national anthems until "The Star-Spangled Banner" replaced them by an act of Congress.

Whether or not Robert E. Lee ever said, "I do not think we can have an army without music,"[14] the line rings true despite its hyperbole. Union and Confederate armies sang on the march and in bivouac, and people at home soon picked up the same songs. A song begun in one army might find its way to the other, though often with altered words. The two armies would serenade each other across the lines at night and slaughter one another in the morning.

Aside from "Yankee Doodle" and "The Star-Spangled Banner," many of the songs of wartime that we remember come down to us from the Civil War, especially from the Union side. One Confederate officer told his Yankee counterparts after Lee surrendered to Ulysses S. Grant, "If we'd had your music, sir, we'd have whipped you out of your boots."[15] The armies sang sentimental ballads and great, inspiring anthems. Ballads were about the experiences of ordinary people, about dreams and hopes; the anthems were about a cause. Both helped to shape the attitudes of a nation and linked Americans to the refounding of that nation in blood. It discovered its new founding document in Lincoln's "Gettysburg Address."

Many Civil War songs feel remote a century and a half later, but some can still stir us. They resonate if we can make our way past the styles and rhetoric of another time. These songs influence and reflect the intense emotions of a people aroused but shaken by civil war. Some of the best of them come in the first year and a half after the firing on Fort Sumter. The sentimental ballads of those years were preparing us for what was to come. They affected their audience but without the profoundly dark emotions that would soon permeate the nation. It would take a while before the exhaustion and dread pervaded the country on both sides. Many of these songs re-created everyday life at home and in the army. Ballads might typically describe the relationship between a young son about to face combat and a mother waiting tearfully at home.

Nearly a century later, songs from the Second World War often spoke for and to the wife or sweetheart left behind, but the songs of the Civil War were likelier to take a soldier's point of view, one soldier and one family at a time. They illuminated the upheavals in family life in wartime. This sentimental ballad is a letter from a son who writes the night before a battle. Because it takes form as a letter—"Just before the battle, Mother, / I am thinking most of you"—it frees the soldier to speak intimately, without the bravado of young men. He describes his comrades, "Fill'd with tho'ts of home and God," because they know they may die in the morning. In his mix of fear and duty, he longs to return to his mother and home, but honor requires him to stay, and then the bugles sound. The song's most personal lines are in the chorus. He expresses his worst fears as he bids his mother farewell:

> Farewell, Mother, you may never
> Press me to your heart again;
> O, you'll not forget me, Mother,
> If I'm numbered with the slain.
>
> (George Frederick Root, "Just Before the Battle, Mother," 1862)

A young soldier writes home to his mother, but in his fearful determination to fight, the personal and patriotic mingle in a single popular song.

The Union's growing sense that it had engaged in a great moral crusade to preserve the nation and end slavery introduced a spiritual element to the songs. When Henry S. Washburn visited the family of a young officer who had died in battle just before he was to return home for Thanksgiving, he turned the irony of the eighteen-year-old's death at a festive time into a poem. The earliest settlers from Europe had gathered to offer thanks to God at harvesttime. It was a custom long before Abraham Lincoln formally proclaimed it a holiday in 1863. The composer George Frederick Root soon set Washburn's poem to a hymn-like melody that lent the song a spiritual aura but also deepened its despair. Family members confront an empty chair at the dining room table and turn their mutual grief into a form of grace-saying. The word "meet" suggests the gathering of the family around the dining room table, the center of the home and its inhabitants, but also a religious meeting, a gathering akin to the familiar hymn, "Shall We Gather at the River?"

> We shall meet, but we shall miss him
> There will be one vacant chair;
> We shall linger to caress him
> While we breathe our evening prayer.
> (George Frederick Root and Henry S. Washburn, "The Vacant Chair," 1861)

Through the rest of the song, the family takes pride in the son's courage to "uphold our country's honor." Their belief that "wreaths of glory / Ever more will deck his brow" provides only passing comfort, as they link his death and their grief to the response of the natural world: "Dirges from the pine and cypress / Mingle with the tears we shed." As the number of dead rose in both armies, people in the Confederacy also adopted the song. For the duration of the war, it served as an American song.

"The Battle Hymn of the Republic," the most important song of the Civil War, had a roundabout beginning. Northern abolitionists had been writing songs to express their hatred of slavery for at least half a century before the Civil War began. In the summer of 1861, troops in the 12th Massachusetts were improvising a camp song they called "John Brown's Body." It had nothing to do with the notorious John Brown, whose raid on the arsenal at Harper's Ferry in 1859 led to his arrest and eventual execution. He was a religious zealot and radical patriot who believed that his God was leading him to abolish slavery. The lesser-known John Brown was a sergeant whose men used to make up verses about him to the tune of an old Methodist hymn. When the song became popular, people assumed that it meant the firebrand John Brown.

George Kimball, who was in the same unit as Sergeant Brown, wrote forty years later:

> We had a jovial Scotchman in the battalion, named John Brown . . . as he happened to bear the identical name of the old hero of Harper's Ferry, he became at once the butt of his comrades.[16]

Eventually, the soldiers set what they had invented spontaneously to the melody of a familiar hymn, although African American soldiers after Emancipation added some words of their own: "We're done with hoeing cotton, we're done with hoeing corn / We're colored Yankee soldiers just as sure as you were born."

There's an irony beyond the confusion sown by the two John Browns. In the early years of the war, Lincoln made it clear that its single purpose was to preserve the Union. Widespread attitudes toward Black people would have made it nearly impossible to convince soldiers to march south to end slavery until "John Brown's Body" affected people's beliefs.

Near the end of the same year, Julia Ward Howe, an abolitionist, suffragette, and aspiring poet, visited Washington, D.C., with her husband and a clergyman friend named James Freeman Clarke to watch a military review. They were returning to their lodgings when Union guards, fearing an attack, forced them to stop. As an act of defiant patriotism, the threesome sang "John Brown's Body," and the soldiers guarding them sang along. Although her husband was part of a group that had helped to fund John Brown's crusade, Howe responded eagerly to Clarke's suggestion that she set better words to the stirring melody.

Many members of the rising middle class were drawn to high inspiration. The expansive emotionalism of melodrama drew them in, as did the supposed truths of spiritualism and dreams. Howe later reported that the song's first line—"Mine eyes have seen the glory of the coming of the Lord"—came to her in the early hours after midnight. She spent what remained of the night in her nightgown, writing by candlelight. I have no reason to doubt her testimony, although it matches descriptions by other nineteenth-century songwriters' mix of moral fervor and apparently spontaneous creativity:

> I awoke . . . in the gray of the early dawn, and to my astonishment found that the wished-for lines were arranging themselves in my brain. I lay quite still

until the last verse had completed itself in my thoughts, then hastily arose, saying to myself, "I shall lose this if I don't write it down immediately."[17]

She sent the words as a poem to the *Atlantic Monthly*, where it appeared on the magazine's front page in February 1862. The editor named it "Battle Hymn of the Republic" and sent her a check for four dollars.

The "Battle Hymn" matches the fervor of a hymn like "Onward Christian Soldiers" and even of John Brown himself. It calls for a muscular rooting out of evil in the name of right. It is moralistic and judgmental, but no one can deny its power, conviction, or authority. In what Dominic Tierney calls its "vivid portrait of sacred violence,"[18] it is an anthem for a holy war:

> Mine eyes have seen the glory of the coming of the Lord:
> He is trampling out the vintage where the grapes of wrath are stored.
> (Trad. Melody and Julia Ward Howe, "Battle Hymn of the Republic, 1861)

Lincoln, who liked martial music but who understood what he was asking of the American people, is said to have wept when he first heard it. It's hard not to believe that he recognized it as our great hymn for the struggle for freedom, even though he was unable to say so in the first years of the war. What began as a war to preserve the Union would, with inspiration from this song's embrace of a holy mission, become a moral crusade to preserve the Union and end slavery. It remains the great anthem of Lincoln's (and America's) civic religion in which "this nation, under God, shall have a new birth of freedom."

Those who came of age in the era of Vietnam or Afghanistan may find it hard to believe that earlier wars inspired great patriotic anthems to rally the nation. By 1862, enthusiasm for the war had worn off, and enlistments had dropped. Lincoln called for the drafting of 300,000 men. A man could avoid the draft by paying someone to serve in his place or by paying $300 to void his obligation. Having a way to buy your way out enraged immigrants who lived in Northern cities and could afford neither. The following year, two weeks after the Battle of Gettysburg, draft riots erupted in New York City.[19]

A poem by James Gibbons, a Quaker abolitionist and supporter of Lincoln, sets its belief in the draft to the language of triumphalism. Someone named Luther Emerson set it to music. The song describes leaving home and marching South as the younger children learn "how to reap and sow against their country's needs." Ultimately, the song lifts Lincoln to the level of a biblical patriarch:

> We are coming, we are coming, our Union to restore;
> We are coming, Father Abra'am, with three hundred thousand more.
> (Luther Emerson and James S. Gibbons, "We Are Coming, Father Abra'am," 1862)

Following Lincoln's call for additional troops, George Frederick Root responded with a new song whose effect on the army and the public was electric. Root was one of the major songwriters of the nineteenth century, although his name has largely faded. After a series of defeats that had demoralized Union soldiers, his new song lifted their spirits. Lincoln wrote to Root, "You have done more than a thousand generals and a thousand orators." Root wrote, "If I could not shoulder a musket in defense of my country, I could serve her in this way."[20] Henry Stone, a Union veteran writing in the 1880s, remembered that Root's song "ran through the camp like wildfire" and added, "I shall never forget how the men rolled out the line, 'And although he may be poor, he shall never be a slave.'"[21]

In May 1864, Confederate soldiers had broken through a Union line and were pursuing their enemies. As the Union troops fled for their lives, above the tumult of cannons, rifle fire, and the cries of the wounded, one soldier began to sing Root's "Battle Cry of Freedom." It stopped the retreat as the Union side regrouped and then charged the enemy. The assault inspired by the song led to a Union victory.[22]

The song's lyric defines the break between North and South by combining a call for the preservation of the Union with a denunciation of secession and slavery, but it treats the war's two great causes—the Union and abolition—evenhandedly. It calls for "the Union forever," but the battle cry that Root's lyric shouts is "Freedom." In the context of the war, historian Christian L. McWhirter writes that Root "clearly meant to suggest some degree of abolitionism."[23]

> The Union forever, Hurrah boys, hurrah!
> Down with the Traitor,

> Up with the Star;
> While we rally round the flag, boys,
> Rally once again,
> Shouting the battle cry of Freedom.
>
> (George Frederick Root, "Battle Cry of Freedom," 1862)

The best songs of the Civil War take their listeners past the easy jingoism of wartime. Unlike high-flying anthems or domestic ballads of parting, fearfulness, and pride, Walter Kittredge's "Tenting on the Old Camp Ground" is a uniquely melancholy ballad that eventually appealed to both armies. Kittredge was a draftee who never did a day of soldiering. Army surgeons rejected him because he had had rheumatic fever as a child. That close call inspired him to write what became one of the major songs of the Civil War.

At first, anthems urged the Union on, but they gave way to songs of sorrow and loss. Ballads about the miseries of military life were popular around the fires in camp and back home, especially as the war persisted and casualty lists lengthened. Kittredge turned what might have been a conventional ballad of parting into a yearning for peace. It confirmed the attitudes of those who already served. The lyric imagines looking out at an encampment to capture soldiers' feelings about the war: separation from those they love, exhaustion from marching and fighting, and endurance after the death of friends.

> Many are the hearts that are weary tonight,
> Wishing for the war to cease;
> Many are the hearts looking for the right
> To see the dawn of peace.
>
> (Walter Kittredge, "Tenting on the Old Camp Ground," 1863)

Kittredge wrote one of the nation's early protest songs when he turned his sentimental ballad into an anti-war song. He showed it to the Hutchinson Family Singers, with whom he'd previously toured. When they introduced it, it became an immediate success.

The songs of the Civil War come from a time before ragtime and jazz, before the completion of the transcontinental railroad, before the automobile, before the explosive growth of our cities and the arrival of millions of immigrants from Eastern and Southern Europe, long before women could vote. They are the sound of a different America, but an America that shaped our own. They still speak with passion and conviction and, more than a century and a half later, map the emotional terrain of a singular, defining event in American history.

American expansion exploded in the nineteenth century. It began with the Louisiana Purchase in 1803, when Thomas Jefferson was president, and continued as Americans pushed farther west. The inflated patriotism of the time matched our sense of inevitability. It found an outlet in the Battle for the Alamo (1836), fought by brave men whose leaders had also been slave owners and even slave traders; the American-Mexican War (1846–1848); and ultimately the Spanish-American War (1898), which established the United States as an imperial power. The nation came away from its last nineteenth-century war with control of the Philippines, Guam, and Puerto Rico.

"America the Beautiful," the most moving patriotic song of the nineteenth century, takes a different approach to the celebration of America. Extending beyond "Hail, Columbia's" passing reference to "peace and safety" and "My Country, 'Tis of Thee's" linking of the continent's natural beauty to triumphalist sentiment, it largely replaces triumphalism with imagery of nature's bounty. That bounty will lead not only to prosperity but to the crowning of American goodness with a brotherhood that stretches from one coast to another. In its merging of the material with the visionary, the Myth of the Garden with Manifest Destiny, it is as much a hymn as a patriotic song. It uses the language of devotion to aspire to a just, egalitarian nation.

The song began as a poem by Katherine Lee Bates. Its heart lies in Bates's ability to transform her personal experience into her love for America and her deep commitment to what it might yet become—she anticipates the achievement of "a more perfect Union." In 1893, when she was a thirty-three-year-old professor of English literature at Wellesley College, she took the railroad west to Colorado Springs to teach for the summer at Colorado College. When the term ended, she and some fellow teachers celebrated with a trip to the top of Pikes Peak. Some of the women felt faint at the top, so everyone returned after only half an hour. Nevertheless, the view had a profound effect on Bates. "Near the top," she later wrote, "we had to leave the wagon and go the rest of the way on mules. I was very tired. But when I saw the view, I felt great joy. All the wonders of America seemed displayed there, with the sea-like expanse."[24]

That same summer, she hastily jotted down a version of the poem. It first appeared in print in 1895 and then again after she revised it in 1904. She wrote an expanded version—the version we sing—in 1911. It was set to several different melodies before it became permanently linked to the hymn, "Materna," written by Samuel A. Ward in 1882.

On the return from Pikes Peak, Bates told her friends that such countries as England had failed because, while they may have been great, they had not been good: "Unless we are willing to crown our greatness with goodness and our bounty with brotherhood, our beloved America may go the same way."[25] You can already hear the beginnings of what she would write. The poem combines in verse what she saw from the train west and her day atop Pikes Peak. She expressed her love of country by writing about the wheat fields of the great open plains that she saw as the train steamed through Kansas; the majestic Rockies, which she had just climbed; and the Great White City that she had seen at the World's Columbian Exposition in Chicago, but she did so in a way that encompassed the nation by including its land and its people. It is much more than another exercise in triumphalism (Samuel A. Ward and Katherine Lee Bates, "America the Beautiful," 1910).

Bates had originally begun her poem, "Oh, beautiful for halcyon skies." I like the word; it fits well with "amber," "purple," and "fruited." I also like her eventual choice of "spacious." Despite its abstraction, it helps to set up the rest of the poem by underscoring the vastness and variety of the American land and suggesting a spiritual dimension to its natural wonder. From Pikes Peak, we can see an open, expansive nation; certainly, we can imagine it. "Spacious" is also an allusion to the West, where the sky is "big" and, in the American myth, the dream of a continental nation reaches its fulfillment.

Bates grounds her patriotism in an America defined by "the spacious skies," but also in the "patriot dream" of alabaster cities "undimmed by human tears," and in the equality of the people and the spiritual dimension our writers have often discerned in the American land. When she draws her conclusion, she turns to prayer. The poem asks God to "shed His grace" on America, although it remains a nation yet to be bound by brotherhood, and calls on it "to mend thine every flaw." Like so many other patriotic songs, it links love of country to religious devotion—the land, its history, and the hope for what is to come.

Beyond writing poetry and teaching, Bates was a social activist who had witnessed the poverty and injustice of the Industrial Revolution. She was committed to an all-inclusive egalitarian America. She wrote the poem's first version during a severe economic depression: "America! America! / God shed His grace on thee / Till selfish gain no longer stain, / The banner of the free" (1893). By the final version, the poem asks God to "shed His grace on thee / And crown thy good with brotherhood / From sea to shining sea" (1910). This version is more directly spiritual and less political, but it makes the same point implicitly. The most important word in the chorus is "brotherhood."

The transformation of patriotic anthems by African American singers broadens and deepens our understanding of the promise of the nation. That hope somehow abides in our most oppressed citizens. When African American singers perform patriotic songs, it is as if they are portraying the America for which they hope rather than the America in which they live. In 1972, Ray Charles first recorded a version of "America the Beautiful" unlike any we had heard before. His approach made him the embodiment of American music, an African American singer and piano player whose singing combined soul, the blues, R&B, gospel, rock, and country. Here he rearranges stanzas, alters lines, and invents new lines to turn a stately hymn into an equally powerful combination of gospel and blues. Every performance is potentially different; every performance finds its way intuitively to the heart of the song. His version echoes with the fervent improvisational singing of the Black church and brings it closer to spontaneity and speech. It also evokes the emergence of jazz at the end of the nineteenth century: loose, but not in the sense of sloppy, rather of freedom within a structure—in this case, a song. This is part of the lyric as Charles sang it on television in 1972:

> But look here, I'm talking about
> America, sweet America,
> You know, God done shed his grace on thee.
> He crowned thy good, yes he did, in brotherhood
> From sea to shining sea.
> ("'America the Beautiful' by Ray Charles," YouTube, February 13, 2009)

A decade or two earlier, Jeffrey Melnick writes, the Jewish songwriters of Tin Pan Alley first figured out "how to use the sounds of blackness as the basis of their own creations."[26] They were New York songwriters who loved living in New York. They spoke not about America but about the city, and the rest of the country bought it. George Gershwin embodied this point of view. He said in the 1920s that he wanted to "write an opera of the melting pot, of New York City, itself, which is the symbolic and actual blend of their native and immigrant strains. This would allow for any kind of music, Black and white, Eastern and Western, and would aim for a style that should achieve, out of this diversity, an artistic and aesthetic unity."[27] In other words, he would craft it into something authentically American. As the child of immigrants, it was something he understood and felt deeply.

Forty years before Katharine Lee Bates wrote her first draft of "America the Beautiful," Stephen Foster wrote "Hard Times Come Again No More." He intended it as a parlor ballad, a song written to be sung in the parlors of newly affluent members of the rising middle class. They could now afford to live decorously; that often meant buying a piano for the parlor. After dinner, guests would gather around it to sing. Parlor songs were the music of choice. Songwriters had begun to write them specifically to be sung in parlors, including Foster's "Come with Thy Sweet Voice Again," "Ah! May the Red Rose Live Alway," and "Hard Times Come Again No More." "Hard Times" relies on contrast as it calls on the well-fed to note the plight of those less fortunate:

> While we seek mirth and beauty and music light and gay,
> There are frail forms fainting at the door;
> Though their voices are silent, their pleading looks will say
> Oh! Hard times come again no more.
>
> (Stephen Foster, "Hard Times Come Again No More," 1854)

This is an unusual subject for a parlor ballad. On one hand, Foster captures the suffering of those who have no recourse; on the other, he asks little more of the singers in the parlor than awareness. The final line of every verse and the chorus is identical; Foster imagines an unspoken plea or prayer for release. From a different angle, though, the line breaks near the end. "Hard times come again" is rooted in bleak memories and a recognition that hard times always return. The last two words, "no more," are both a cry against pain and a statement of defiance. The first part looks to the past, the second to the future.

Parlor ballads were similar to sentimental ballads; in fact, they were often one and the same. They couched deeply felt emotion in formal rhetoric but limited themselves to the emotions suitable for a proper parlor, particularly the depth of love and, equally, the depth of sorrow brought on by separation or death—such songs as "Just Awearyin' for You," "The Old Arm Chair," "The Lost Chord," and "When the Swallows Homeward Fly":

> Thou, my heart, must find relief,
> Yielding to these words belief;
> I shall see thy form again,
> Though today we part in pain.
> (Franz Abt, "When the Swallows Homeward Fly," 1860)

Like Ray Charles before her, Mavis Staples, an African American R&B and gospel singer, transforms "Hard Times" without sacrificing its original sentiment. Nevertheless, her phrasing and the African American subtext she finds in the lyric turn a parlor ballad into a gospel song. No longer a ballad designed to have respectable whites take note of those less fortunate, it becomes an uplifting song that recognizes the unavoidability of hard times but insists on the future, now rooted implicitly in the memory and experience of Black people:

> 'Tis the song, the sign of the weary;
> Hard times. hard times, come again no more.

# 2

# A Yankee Doodle Dandy

George M. Cohan was the quintessential Broadway guy—theater owner, producer, director, playwright, composer, lyricist, actor, dancer, and singer. Between 1901 and 1904, when he was still in his twenties, he interpolated songs, wrote scores, and appeared in four Broadway musicals. They all flopped. Next, he wrote the book, music, and lyrics for *Little Johnny Jones*, an American musical from the get-go: the story, the characters, the feel of the music, and the sound of the lyrics were ours. Some have called it the first truly American musical. Irving Berlin's biographer Philip Furia calls its songs "a refreshing antidote to the Viennese schmaltz of Franz Lehar and Victor Herbert."[1] Many shows in the years before the First World War adapted London's West End hits for American audiences. Not Cohan. He was a New Yorker, the son of Irish immigrants, and an American patriot rolled up in one. How else to explain the way he moved? His dancing held his upper body straight and stiff as he clogged with a kind of strutting joy in his own being there on stage to sing and dance about Broadway and the United States.

Cohan starred as brash, flag-waving Johnny Jones, a jockey who sails to England to ride his horse, Yankee Doodle, in the English Derby. He's accused of taking a bribe to throw the race but is eventually cleared. Near the end of the first act, he shows English well-wishers that he's the "Yankee Doodle Dandy" come to win the English Derby. The song is inseparable from Cohan's mastery of punchy, pugnacious Yankee jabber[2] and Jones's (and Cohan's) cock-of-the-walk manner. In his lyrics, patriotism was taking form as entertainment. Like Teddy Roosevelt, only a generation older than he, Cohan flexed America's muscles and announced to the rest of the world that the United States had arrived. We come closest to the moment by watching James Cagney re-create Cohan's style in the 1942 movie biography *Yankee Doodle Dandy*:

> I'm a Yankee Doodle Dandy
> A Yankee Doodle, do or die;
> A real live nephew of my Uncle Sam's
> Born on the Fourth of July.
> I've got a Yankee Doodle sweetheart,
> She's my Yankee Doodle joy.
> Yankee Doodle came to London,
> Just to ride the ponies;
> I am that Yankee Doodle boy.
> (George M. Cohan, "Yankee Doodle Boy," *Little Johnny Jones*, 1904)

The show and the song were naturals for Cohan. Back in his vaudeville days, he had billed himself as the "Yankee Doodle Comedian." When Jones calls himself a "Yankee Doodle Dandy" and his girl a "Yankee Doodle sweetheart," and then quotes a couple of lines from the original eighteenth-century "Yankee Doodle," he provides a neat segue back to America's longest-running patriotic song. Although American soldiers appropriated it from the British army during the American Revolution, it sure doesn't sound like a patriotic song, even though its nonsense line ("Put a feather in his cap and called it macaroni") made sense once upon a time. The Redcoats were insulting the Americans by suggesting that Yankee Doodles were gay. The "macaronis" were flamboyantly foppish British gentlemen in the mid-eighteenth century.

Once the ragtag American soldiers began to win, first skirmishes and then the occasional battle, the more they celebrated with "Yankee Doodle." When they won the Battle of Saratoga in September 1777, they serenaded the defeated Brits with it as they marched down to take their surrender. They had turned a song meant to be insulting into an anthem.[3] To this day, we teach it to our children so they can laugh at its silly words.

The narrator in the lyric, probably male in 1904, takes Sousa over Wagner any time because, with a touch of overstatement and a bit of playfulness, he identifies himself as "the original cranky, Yankee popular melody fool." The melody alternates between long melodic phrases and short, quick, staccato lines. For some of them, you wonder how Cohan could jam in all the words and still keep up with the tune. But it was the kind of peppy, confident flag-waver that linked patriotism to the effects of a song on the listener. The patriotic and the popular merge in Cohan's songs.

Compare the formality of such nineteenth-century patriotic songs as "Columbia, the Gem of the Ocean" and "My Country, 'Tis of Thee" with Cohan's "You're a Grand Old Rag." Its slang-filled conversational lyric is the perfect match for Cohan's rat-a-tat-tat musical style. You can imagine that you're watching the man bounce down the street as he shows off with a triple rhyme in the very first line: "There's a feeling comes a-stealing and it sets my brain a-reeling." A few lines later, he adds, "Any tune like 'Yankee Doodle' can set me off my noodle, / It's that patriotic something that no one can understand." The rest of the song adapts a phrase from "The Star-Spangled Banner" to praise "the emblem of / The land I love / The home of the free and the brave." It's easy to overlook the triumphalism in such a jaunty song (George M. Cohan, "You're a Grand Old Rag," *George Washington, Jr.*, 1906).

The opening-night audience cheered Cohan's new patriotic song, but the title got him into trouble almost immediately. He had written the song after an encounter with a veteran of the Civil War. The old man had fought on the Union side during Pickett's Charge at Gettysburg. As he told Cohan his story, he rubbed a worn old flag that he held in his lap. He had been the flag bearer during the battle and had carried that bullet-riddled flag ever since. By the end of their drive, Cohan had composed the first verse and the refrain.

Cohan had originally called the song "You're a Grand Old Rag" in tribute to the old man, his story, and his flag, but one reviewer complained about what he called Cohan's desecration of the flag. The resulting to-do in the newspapers convinced Cohan to change the title to "You're a Grand Old Flag," even though it weakens the song. "Flag" is predictable, but "rag" is surprising and, in the dramatic context, stirring. It adds humanity to an already-punchy lyric. In the first act of *George Washington, Jr.*, an old veteran comes onstage to hand the title character (played by Cohan) a tattered flag. George reacts, "Gee, it's a grand old rag, isn't it?" If that's not a cue for a song, what is?[4]

Although the First World War was two years old by 1916, some American songs managed to ignore it—largely, but not entirely. Dukes and earls, but also "warriors bold," pursue a "chic Yankee girl" who is traveling abroad as if everything in Europe is just fine. She rejects their advances and, in the chorus, explains her reason for returning home as she also pleads for national unity. The song merges flirtatiousness with patriotism:

> Just a Yankee Doodle Boy is good enough for me
> Just a son of Uncle Sammy from a land so free.
> (Will L. Livernash, "A Yankee Doodle Boy Is Good Enough for Me," 1916)

By the time the United States joined the war a year later, "Yankee Doodle" appeared in several of Tin Pan Alley's patriotic songs, not as the title of the original song but as a reference to the Americans who had sailed off to France. When America first entered the war, songs were optimistic to the point of cockiness. The Yankee Doodles were the doughboys who would teach the Kaiser a quick lesson and then sail home to the sweethearts they'd left behind. In "When Yankee Doodle Marches Thro' Berlin, There'll Be a Hot Time in the U.S.A.," written in 1917, the Yankee Doodles are brimming with confidence in a song whose sheet music cover could just as easily have served for "Over There." Long lines of troops, accompanied by horse-drawn cannons on caissons, march down a Paris boulevard. When an American in the crowd sees the doughboys parading, he cries out:

> And they'll win,
> Yes, they'll win,
> Then they'll flash the news to old Broadway.
> And when Yankee Doodle marches thro' Berlin,
> There'll be a hot time in the U.S.A.
> (Arthur Lange and Andrew B. Sterling, "When Yankee Doodle Marches Thro' Berlin, There'll Be a Hot Time in the U.S.A.," 1917)

Although the British originally meant "Yankee Doodle" as mockery, by the time Cohan wrote "Yankee Doodle Boy" in 1904, it had come to mean anything all-American. To top it off, Cohan, born on July 3, 1878, insisted throughout his life that he'd been born on the Fourth. During the jingoistic years that exploded with the Spanish-American War and lasted into the First World War, Cohan brought "Yankee Doodle" to Broadway and, with it, the revival of the word *Yankee*, although Southerners used it scornfully during the four years of the Confederacy.

Among the Yankee and "Yankee Doodle" songs that preceded and followed "Yankee Doodle Boy," Cohan's "Over There" (". . . the Yanks are coming, the Yanks are coming"), written soon after the United States entered the First World War in April 1917, is the most famous, although it's hardly alone. Fred L. Moreland wrote the instrumental march "Yankee Shuffle" in 1908, and both John Philip Sousa and Arthur Pryor recorded it with their famous bands. Sousa also used the melody of "Yankee Doodle" as counterpoint in his march, "America First."

John Edward Hasse calls Sousa "the nation's first musical superstar."[5] He grew up in Washington, D.C., during the Civil War and played in the U.S. Marine Band before becoming its conductor when he was twenty-five. A national passion for marching bands was one result of the war. Sousa and the Marine Band soon became the best-known musical ensemble in late nineteenth- and early twentieth-century America. He wrote, arranged, and performed marches—a total of 136 of them. He and his band gave concerts but also marched in parades to lift the spirits of the thousands who watched them pass by. It was a time of burgeoning, even imperialistic, patriotism, and such marches as "Washington Post," "Semper Fidelis," and "The Stars and Stripes Forever" embodied the national mood.

Sousa's and Pryor's bands, in concert or marching down the avenue, played with the drive of a march lightened by a touch of syncopation. They were performing music that amounted to ragtime's cousin, but with more emphasis on the march than the ragging.

The title of "Yankee Shuffle" also links it to the popular, but degrading, "coon songs" of the day because the shuffle was a dance done by Black people.[6] "Coon songs," popular Tin Pan Alley fare between roughly 1890 and 1920, were bluntly racist responses to the arrival of African Americans in Northern cities to escape the South's Jim Crow laws and the violence they encouraged. Earlier songs, heard mainly in minstrel shows, portrayed Black people as playful children in need of supervision—the clowning of the End Men in blackface played off against Mr. Interlocutor, dressed in white and often seated a step higher than the rest of the performers. The arrangement suggests the power structure of a rural plantation during slavery.

"Coon songs," the direct descendants of minstrel songs, moved to town when African Americans moved north. Set primarily in cities, "coon songs" added the urban image of the razor to rural images of watermelon and chicken stealing. Minstrel songs see African Americans as foolish, lazy, and not very bright, but "coon song" lyrics portray them as coarse, vulgar, and dangerous. The more money Black people in these songs earn, the more ridiculous, "uppity," and threatening they become[7] (see chapter 5).

By the early 1920s, the blues was becoming a national music rather than a regional African American music, thanks in good part to its becoming a performance music, most significantly by Gertrude "Ma" Rainey and Bessie Smith. Just as important was the African American blues singer Mamie Smith's recording of "Crazy Blues" in 1921. Smith recorded it for Black Swan Records, the first recording company owned by African Americans. They marketed 78-rpm releases aimed mainly at an African American audience.

"Crazy Blues" was an exception because it sold hundreds of thousands of copies to both Black and white people. Soon, white songwriters in Tin Pan Alley and on Broadway began turning out songs with the word "blues" in the title and lyrics, whether or not they actually were the blues. Young George Gershwin was no exception. In 1922, two years before he and his brother Ira began the collaboration that ended only with George's death in 1937, he was working with the lyricists B. G. DeSylva and Irving Caesar. Among his and DeSylva's hits were the sexy "Do It Again" and the yearning, but still confident, "Somebody Loves Me" ("Somebody loves me, / I wonder who. / Maybe it's you").

In 1922, Gershwin, DeSylva, and Caesar collaborated on "Yankee Doodle Blues," a march about the blues, in which syncopation adds spice to patriotism.[8] The lyric cautions the traveler: the minute you leave the United States, you itch to return because you can't believe "how quick you get those Yankee Doodle Blues!" When you return, you burst into a patriotic song to celebrate America because only being here can make you lose the same "Yankee Doodle Blues." That old familiar "Yankee Doodle" melody means you're back where you belong:

> When I hear "Yankee Doodle," that melody keeps on ringin' in my ear.
> "Yankee Doodle," that melody makes me stand right up and cheer.
>
> (George Gershwin, B. G. DeSylva, and Irving Caesar, "Yankee Doodle Blues," *Spice of 1922*, 1922)

Five years later, in "Yankee Doodle Rhythm," Ira Gershwin's lyric takes the opposite stance: it describes not an American eager to return home, but foreigners affected by up-to-date American music, what Ira calls the "piping of the jazzbo / Real American." Like a lot of songs from the late 1910s and well into the 1920s, the common subject was American music itself. In Ira Gershwin's lyric, Americans can stay home, but their music travels the world. Walter Rimler, author of *A Gershwin Companion*, describes the music as "stuttering, syncopated."[9] The rhythm is so "insidious," it makes "the universe dance." When the Spanish, Eskimos, Greeks, Japanese, and Mexicans dance to "that ticklish tempo, / Everything else is passé" (George Gershwin and Ira Gershwin, "Yankee Doodle Rhythm," *Strike Up the Band*, 1927).

Both of these songs helped to perpetuate "Yankee Doodle" as an affectionately slangy way to identify Americans or America. Both songs must have felt irresistibly up-to-date when they were new, but neither of them stirs the heart the way that a true patriotic anthem can. Both of George Gershwin's songs, however, balance out his and his brother's earlier work, "The Real American Folksong (Is a Rag)," interpolated in *Ladies First* in 1918. Instead of having Americans leave the country or foreigners affected by American music, this time the Americans stay put because the best music is already here. "The Real American Folk Song" is a ragtime song about ragtime rather than a march about marching or a rhythm tune about rhythm. It is also Ira Gershwin's first contribution to a musical score.

When George learned that a producer had a spot for an interpolation in a musical opening in Chicago, Ira chose to use a pseudonym because he feared that the producer might take a skeptical view of collaboration between brothers. He chose to write as Arthur Francis, the first names of his younger brother and sister. When the producer asked who this Francis was, George answered, "Oh, he's a clever college boy with lots of talent."[10] Ira used his own name for the first time when he and George collaborated on what would be their first successful Broadway show, *Lady, Be Good!*, in 1924.

The music and lyrics to "Real American Folk Song" are syncopated and snappy. While the folk songs of every nation give each "a creative vein / Originating a native strain / . . . / American folk songs, I feel, / Have a much stronger appeal." The American folk song, Ira Gershwin asserts, "is a rag— / A mental jag— / A rhythmic tonic for the chronic blues." You can lose the blues by staying home with ragtime (George Gershwin and Arthur Francis, "The Real American Folk Song Is a Rag," *Ladies First*, 1918).

These three songs by George Gershwin fit with his style at the time; they're syncopated and percussive, helped along by Ira Gershwin's use of slang and his ability to fit words to George's tripping melodic lines. Without sacrificing cleverness, they assert a patriotic but still inventive view of the country.

At the start of the First World War and the Second World War, Tin Pan Alley and Broadway produced a lot of patriotic popular songs, from Irving Berlin, Edgar Leslie, and George W. Meyer's "Let's All Be Americans Now" (1917) and George M. Cohan's "Over There" (1917) to Jimmy McHugh and Harold Adamson's "Comin' in on a Wing and a Prayer" (1943).

When America declared war on Germany on April 6, 1917, the conflict had already been underway in Europe for three years. We were going to send the doughboys to France to teach the Kaiser not to fool with the United States. People felt a great burst of enthusiasm for songs about the doughboys and the confidence we had in them. Americans marched into our first war in Europe, driven by patriotism and innocence. After a year and a half in the trenches, we slogged back out to reject the League of Nations and, within a few years, began a party called the Jazz Age that we were sure would last forever.

The public in the Second World War was much less interested in these kinds of songs. Such quick jingoistic affirmations as "We Did It Before" and "Remember Pearl Harbor" (both published within a few weeks of the Japanese attack) weren't very good, although they did stir the public's patriotism. Americans were as loyal as ever, but they had just endured the privations of the Great Depression and were still in shock after the surprise bombing of Pearl Harbor on December 7, 1941.

American audiences during the First World War were much more responsive to patriotic popular songs, but during the Second World War, they quickly fell out of favor. Women on the home front much preferred such mournful love ballads as "I Don't Want to Walk without You" and "I'll Walk Alone," which mirrored their own emotions.[11]

A reference to "Yankee Doodle" appears at least twice in the songs of the Great Depression. Not surprisingly, neither smacks of anything resembling jingoism. It was a time for satire and social criticism. Three years earlier, in one of his first songs, the lyricist E. Y. Harburg, along with the composer Jay Gorney, wrote the towering but bitter Depression protest anthem, "Brother, Can You Spare a Dime?" Harburg told an interviewer, "I didn't make a maudlin lyric of a guy begging. I made it into a commentary. It was about the fellow who works, the fellow who builds, who makes railroads and houses—and he's left empty-handed. This is a man proud of what he has done but bewildered that his country with its dream could do this to him."[12]

The song's single character ("They called me Al, / It was Al all the time") sees himself "building a dream." He had fought in the Great War, plowed the nation's fields, and then worked hard to build the railroads and "a tower up to the sun," yet he now finds himself begging on a street corner. He recalls his patriotic pride during the war: "Once in khaki suits / Gee, we looked swell, / Full of that Yankee-Doodle-de-dum." The lines affirm the eagerness of young men in uniform, but the nonsense syllables, "Doodle-de-dum," create a coating of irony. All that remains of the spirit is mockery, confusion, and bitterness.

The next year, for *Gold Diggers of 1933*, composer Harry Warren and lyricist Al Dubin wrote "Remember My Forgotten Man" (Harry Warren and Al Dubin, "Remember My Forgotten Man," *Gold Diggers of 1933*, 1933). Its similarity to "Brother, Can You Spare a Dime" is unmistakable, but its point of view is different. Rather than an out-of-work man begging on a street corner, a woman pleads for us to remember her man, and all the other men, who fought in the First World War and are now lost in despair. To encounter this kind of confrontation of the American government and American values in a popular song is striking. Yet the character who sings "My Forgotten Man" speaks freely and sympathetically about an American failure. In its way, it is an act of patriotism and protest driven by desperate need.

Busby Berkeley, who directed the film's musical sequences, drew inspiration from the Bonus March, a protest by seventeen thousand First World War veterans in Washington, D.C., the previous year. Most of them had been out of work since the onset of the Great Depression. They and their families set up a tent city and demanded early payment of service pensions not due legally until 1945. After some violence on both sides, President Herbert Hoover ordered a unit of the US Army infantry and cavalry led by Gen. Douglas MacArthur to remove the desperate protesters from all federal property. They did their job with brutal effectiveness.

"Remember My Forgotten Man" ends the movie on a deeply pessimistic note.[13] Its torchy, blues-like melody has a measured, ominous pace that also feels like something between a march and a dirge as it exhorts us to remember those who suffer. The scene begins with the character played by Joan Blondell, forced by poverty to work as a prostitute. She is hard-boiled but honest in her feelings. Her man went off to war, "but look at him today"; he's become the "forgotten man" she sings about. The two of them were happy and in love until "they" sent him off to war. She needs him back, she says, because "Forgetting him means you're forgetting me."

The scene changes from a close-up of Blondell leaning against a lamppost to soldiers marching off to cheers and then slogging through a downpour as wounded soldiers march dispiritedly back from the front. They stare vacantly ahead and lead us to images of men, implicitly the same men who were in the war, moving through bread lines, their collars turned up against the cold. Their eyes are empty. At the end of this performance number, supposedly in a theater, the audience sees three tiers of soldiers marching while, in front of them, the forgotten but determined veterans march toward the camera. The scene ends with a return to the song's individual story as the prostitute remembers again that her man loved her and begs for his return.

After the 1960s, the Kennedy and King assassinations, and the Vietnam War, and six years after Bruce Springsteen wrote "Born in the U.S.A."—also in a similar vein to "Brother, Can You Spare a Dime?"—Charles Strouse and Stephen Schwartz wrote the score for *Rags*, a Broadway musical that closed after only four performances. Borrowing an idea from E. L. Doctorow's novel *Ragtime*, Joseph Stein, the writer of the musical's book, tells a more conventional but often dark story of Jewish immigrants to New York. Rebecca Hershkowitz comes with her son to find her lost husband, Nathan. She is one of the millions of what Doctorow's novel called "the rags," the endless numbers of Europeans—especially Jews, Italians, Russians, and the cast-offs of Austria-Hungary—who fled poverty and persecution to make a new life in America. *Ragtime* sets its stories against this background—the *time* of the *rags*.

When the couple in *Rags* eventually reunites, Nathan explains in "Yankee Boy" how during his six years in America, he worked his way up from the Lower East Side to a better life. He aspires to what George M. Cohan's Johnny Jones has already achieved, a place in America and the success that comes with it. Within a few years, "Like every Yank you ever knew, / I'll own a bank and when I do, / I'm gonna be a Yankee boy" (Charles Strouse and Stephen Schwartz, "Yankee Boy," *Rags*, 1986).

"Yankee Boy" replays the American myths of "a nation of immigrants," "the land of opportunity," and "a self-made man." In the 1986 revue, *Tintypes*, five actors portray a working-class woman, a proper middle-class woman (who will eventually portray the Broadway star Anna Held), an African American woman, a prosperous middle-class man (who will become Teddy Roosevelt), and a Jewish immigrant. The score consists of songs from the first fifteen years of the twentieth century. The show begins with the immigrant, singing in a heavy Yiddish accent, "I'm a Yenkee Doodle dendy, / Ah Yenkee Doodle, do or die." He sings it, not as Johnny Jones did, as an expression of identity or achievement, but as aspiration. He has come to America, and so he will become an American, with all that seems to promise on his first day in the land where the streets are supposed to be paved with gold.

Some "Yankee Doodle" songs were popular for a few minutes and then disappeared, while others became standards. A very few lasted for decades or even centuries. A single odd title that we claimed during the American Revolution has carried us from patriotic anthem to racist screed, from marches to the blues, and on to an affirmation of the immigrants who helped to shape America.

3

# The Faces of Patriotism

Between the publication of Katharine Lee Bates's poem in 1893 and that of Samuel Ward and Bates's song in 1910, many white Americans heard ragtime, jazz, and the blues for the first time. All three soon became essentially American. All three are also the music of an oppressed people and happened to emerge in cities: ragtime in St. Louis and jazz in New Orleans. The story of the blues is more complicated. As always, Tin Pan Alley songwriters took from what they heard around them—anything to turn out another hit. When ragtime spread across the nation, Americans took to it, but when Tin Pan Alley took its syncopation for what the music publishers were calling "ragtime songs," it became a national craze that lasted for more than two decades. People went looking for syncopated music to dance to, and they found it.

In 1915, four years after Irving Berlin's "Alexander's Ragtime Band" gave ragtime songs a new lease on life, Berlin wrote a song called "Ev'rything in America Is Ragtime." America, he said, was "a million acres / Of shoulder shakers" as Tin Pan Alley songwriters turned out hundreds of ragtime songs to sway to, snap your fingers to, tap your feet to, and, especially, dance to in startlingly sexual ways. People were learning a new way—an American way—to move. It was off the beat and syncopated, the first popular musical sound of the modern era. As America sharpened its imperialistic elbows at the turn of the twentieth century, its music showed signs of conquering the world. The English and French couldn't get enough of it.

For a nation long devoted to Calvinist restraint, ragtime and ragtime songs helped to shape Americans' sense of pleasure for its own sake. The flapper perfected that sort of thing in the 1920s, but it began with ragtime and then jazz, and defined a new and up-to-date America. Berlin wrote in the same song, "The U.S.A. is a land of syncopation" (Irving Berlin, "Everything in America Is Ragtime," *Stop! Look! Listen!*, 1915). He was right.

In the early years of the twentieth century, the songwriters of Tin Pan Alley emphasized African American stereotypes because their behavior and identity were perceived "to be characteristically American."[1] Charles Hamm, in his book about Irving Berlin's early songs, wrote, "Syncopated dance music represented a new, brash, dynamic sensibility that Americans found refreshing and exciting."[2] Berlin himself called ragtime "a necessary element of American life. . . . The country speeded up."[3] Telephones, automobiles, and ragtime—we were laying claim to modernism.

In the 1920s, though, when America's heart rate increased and its temperature rose, Berlin also slowed the country down. He was very good at being counterintuitive and making it pay off. He was very much a traditionalist. He saw minstrel shows as an essential part of American entertainment but was blind to their offensiveness as attitudes changed. He also kept a picture of Stephen Foster on his office wall. Yet he rarely gets credit as a major innovator, even though that's what he was. He also believed that originality wasn't as important as getting it right. If a song was original, so much the better, but writing a good song was of first importance, original or not. During the rampaging 1920s, he wrote a series of melancholy slow ballads in, of all things, waltz time after the one-step and about the same time as the Charleston. Three of these songs became standards—"What'll I Do?" (1923), "All Alone" (1924), and "Remember" (1925). He also contributed a song for the March 1927 opening of Samuel L. Rothafel's huge Roxy Theatre. With seating for 5,920 people, it was only forty seats smaller than Radio City Music Hall, which would eventually open in 1932.

For an extravagant opening night at the Roxy, Berlin wrote a tender lullaby performed by Douglas Stanbury, a baritone in the male chorus. You might expect a song full of brass and blare for big-name stars or a line of women with long legs and tap shoes. Instead, Berlin wrote a lullaby that became a patriotic song just as it ended. He rooted it not in arrival or achievement, but in the dream of America. A friend, on hearing it for the first time, told me that it made her think of the Statue of Liberty. Ironically, by 1927, the ports of immigration were no longer welcoming Central European immigrants.

In the song, a mother gazes down tenderly at her baby. Every night she will "croon / A Russian lullaby" (Irving Berlin, "Russian Lullaby," 1927). The tune is plaintive and comforting, and shaped ultimately by the mother's love for her infant and, at the end, her dream of finding "A land that's free for you and me / And a Russian lullaby." A mother's crooning to her baby becomes a determination to find a better life in America for both of them. Berlin rarely wrote songs that were in any way autobiographical, but this one had to have drifted up from his childhood memory of coming from Russia to Manhattan when he was five. Or perhaps he responded indirectly to the lullabies his mother had sung to him and the stories he heard his parents tell. They certainly would have resonated in someone who saw himself as American but who had grown up amid the *Yiddishkeit* of the Lower East Side.

Many Tin Pan Alley songs drew on ragtime's syncopation, though not its formal structure. Most of these ragtime songs were still thirty-two bars long, but their lyrics sang about syncopation and the new syncopated dances everybody was doing: the Camel Walk, the Kangaroo Hop, and the Grizzly Bear, among many others. They were songs about themselves. Through the roughly thirty years of the Great American Songbook, songs took syncopation from ragtime, a deeper melancholy from the blues, and more inventive rhythms from jazz.

Cabaret and jazz singers throughout the twentieth century and into the twenty-first continue to perform jazz-inflected standards from the Great American Songbook. Jazz appeared in songs at the same time as the First World War, before anybody quite figured out what it was—a musical revolution. Jazz first tapped its toes in New Orleans's Tenderloin as a new kind of ensemble music with improvised solos at about the same time that ragtime first tickled the ivories in St. Louis sporting houses along the Mississippi. In Chicago in the early 1920s, Louis Armstrong redefined jazz as a solo rather than an ensemble music, and a syncopated music as well. Armstrong made it hot.

What made jazz feel so American was its soloists' eagerness to show off and its emphasis on the individual musician who also remains part of the group (much as baseball, the National Game, does). Even more, it was the soloists' reliance on improvisation, on making it up as you went along, of using a song to strike out in new directions. You weren't casting yourself loose because you were building from the song's original chords. You knew where what you were doing came from. You weren't faking it; you were winging it.

Jazz was the discovery of a musical *terra incognita*. It was a sublime, if unrecognized, metaphor for the way we settled the nation and held it together. It was effective more than efficient, and sometimes ruthless in the process, but always essentially American. Even Huck Finn, determined to avoid Aunt Sally's efforts "to adopt me and civilize me," decides "to light out for the territory ahead of the rest."[4] He may not be eager to run, but at least, like Jim, his companion on the river, he gets to live free. Jazz, in its own way, also lit out for the territory.

Like ragtime and the blues, jazz became a common subject of popular songs with influence that continues to the present. Many of the songs of the 1910s and 1920s were not jazz, but they had the jazzy rhythms that provoked a kind of looseness in the performing that felt distinctively American. What could have been more American in the early twentieth century than the jazzy singing of a jazzy song about jazz? References to jazz kept popping up in song titles but were most prevalent when people first began to notice the music. Tin Pan Alley has always been very good at sensing what was on the public's mind.

Most observers take the position that jazz became so popular so quickly in New York City because of the growth of the recording industry; the arrival of African Americans, thanks to the Great Migration; and the arrival of Black musicians everywhere because Prohibition closed the bars and clubs where they worked. They fled to someplace wide open, like Manhattan. Yet large numbers of Black musicians were already in the city, providing the dance music and the ragtime that New Yorkers had been feasting on for nearly two decades. The newcomers quickly adapted to the newest music of the day.[5]

The year 1917 marked a time of great change. As ragtime grew tired, jazz suddenly became all the rage. Before 1920, people were listening to "That

Jazzbo Jungle Band," "I'm Just Simply Full of Jazz," and "Take Me to That Land of Jazz." These songs are pretty much alike: the music is irresistible, you have to move and dance to it, and it changes you as you cast off restraint, not unlike the ragtime songs that preceded them. The word *jazz* itself suggested something up-to-date, hot, sexy, and inescapably American. The fact that Black musicians were serving it up also made it feel just a little bit dangerous. It gave us a musical accompaniment to the world in which we wanted to live. As we moved in large numbers to big cities, it provided the imperative call: *Don't just sit there, move.*

You could hear the music everywhere: "You can see it, so they say at most any cabaret, / At all the dancing halls, / Even society balls, they're crazy about it." The lyric watches people affected by jazz; the music drives them out of their minds, and the madness finds expression in dancing:

> When they see me shake, it makes them shiver,
> When I do a break it makes them quiver,
> But I'm not insane. I'm not to blame, . . .
> I ain't crazy, I'm just full of jazz, jazz, jazz,
> Simply full of jazz.
>
> (Eubie Blake and Noble Sissle, "I'm Just Simply Full of Jazz," 1919, in *Shuffle Along*, 1921)

The people in these songs upend convention and find delight in being wicked as the music and behavior wrench them away from the nation's Puritan past. It was part of America's redefinition of itself in the twentieth century. In yet another way, we were remaking the nation. Hear the call of jazz at its most provocative:

> Went down to the river, stood on the bank,
> Shook my shoulders and the boats all sank,
> For I'm the meanest kind of jazz vampire,
> I'm the wicked vampire of jazz.
>
> (Arthur Swanstrom and Lewis B. Alter, "I'm a Jazz Vampire," 1921)

The blues has a more roundabout history. An indigenous African American folk music, it grew out of spirituals and work songs, mainly in the Mississippi Delta. As freed African Americans moved to Northern cities to escape Jim Crow, and continued to do so during the Great Migration, they took their music with them, including the blues. The blues changed in these new places. The urban blues sometimes kept its traditional structure of three-line stanzas: a statement, a repeated or altered version of that statement, and then a new line to advance the story:

> Backwater rising, Southern peoples can't make no time.
> I said, backwater rising, Southern people can't make no time
> And I can't get no hearing from that Memphis girl of mine.
> (Blind Lemon Jefferson, "Rising High Water Blues," 1927)

The subject matter of the blues also broadened under city lights. The loss of love and betrayal will always be its essential themes, but now the blues turned despair into defiance along with a combination of bawdy humor, heated emotion, and independence. That strain of defiance spread beyond the blues to affect Tin Pan Alley songs as well.

When women sang the blues in the 1920s and beyond, that defiance turned sexual, as in Bessie Smith's performance of "Empty Bed Blues":

> He boiled my fresh cabbage and he made it awful hot
> When he put in the bacon it overflowed the pot.
> (Alphonso Johnson, "Empty Bed Blues," 1928)

Often expressed in sexual terms, and despite the suffering at its core, the blues celebrate. The songs are jubilant. Yet despite their bawdy delights, no other music exemplifies American loneliness better than the blues. It captures the vast desolate spaces and the empty beds, the individualism that can collapse into despair, and the idealism into cynicism. More than anything, an American way of feeling penetrates to the bone.

Together, ragtime, jazz, and the blues created a sound that was essentially American—syncopated, off the beat, and blue. They taught Americans how to sing and dance in new ways, how to move free and easy. Instead of holding one another at a distance to do the waltz, we took Irving Berlin's advice to "hug up close to your baby." We shook our shoulders and wiggled our hips to ragtime songs in the teens. We trucked on down and added a jittery step to jazz. We swayed our shoulders and ground our hips to the blues. How we danced became as natural as walking. As Berlin wrote elsewhere, "No one gives a damn if it's music or not" (Irving Berlin, "Pack Up Your Sins," 1921).

Just over a decade later, George Gershwin, very much a New Yorker, wrote that the sound of America is "all colors and souls unified in the great melting pot of the world. Its dominant note is vibrant syncopation."[6] The songwriters of the Jazz Age, including Gershwin, learned from what they were hearing. They borrowed, appropriated, and downright stole. No songwriter of his time was more influenced by jazz than Gershwin or more by the blues than Harold Arlen. Arlen never wrote a blues, but the blues was everywhere in his music. Instead, he transformed it into blues songs: blues-influenced melodies that grew up in Tin Pan Alley.

Arlen and lyricist Johnny Mercer wrote what just might be the greatest of all the blues songs, "Blues in the Night." Its deep melancholy finds its home late at night in an otherwise-deserted house somewhere in the vast open land. The narrator in the song, alone in the house, tries to sleep but hears in the distance the mournful wail of a freight train cutting through the night. As the lonely character confronts the truth, the train whistle carries the person deeper into memory and regret:

> Hear that lonesome whistle
> Blowin' 'cross the trestle.

Once the narrator insists on the need to listen, he bursts into a perfect imitation of a blues-like whistle spreading across the open land:

> Whoo-ee (my mama done tol' me)
> A whoo-ee-duh-whoo-ee, ol' clickety clack's
> A-echoin' back the blues in the night.
> (Harold Arlen and Johnny Mercer, "Blues in the Night," Blues in the Night, 1941)

Americans like to think of themselves as optimistic, but few songs come closer to America's dark side: the empty land, the isolation, and always the penetrating cry of the train. It is the opposite of the American wanderlust that we romanticize. The prospect of escape has rarely seemed so bleak.

When I hear "Blues in the Night," I often think of the painter Edward Hopper, especially his urban paintings. He is the great portrayer of American solitude. Although he died in 1967, he reveals our existential isolation in ways that pertain before, during, and after a pandemic. Although he painted on Cape Cod and in the Southwest, his most characteristic paintings are urban. He sets most of these works in indoor places: movie theaters, diners and restaurants, and unwelcoming houses, dark with their shades drawn. He captures the isolation of a woman sitting alone in a Chinese restaurant or a man nursing a cup of coffee in a diner sometime after midnight. He depicts the crushing desolation of an empty room made of nothing but walls, angles, and light—not impressionistic, liquid and fleeting, but American light, solid and unrelenting. He is our great painter of American loneliness. He would have understood the line from the poet E. E. Cummings: "nothing is more exactly terrible than to be alone in the house."[7]

Aloneness is Hopper's great subject in a nation that is only abstractly a nation. Hopper could not have developed as he did in any other place. His subjects are specific to his time, but his mature art stands beyond time, deeply American, unsettling yet unable to turn away from. At the same time, how do you stop listening to "Blues in the Night"? Paintings and song tell a similar story.

# 4

# Fight for Love and Liberty

By the time the final version of "America the Beautiful" appeared in 1910, the popular music business was flourishing in New York City. Who would have thought that commercial popular songs would affect the way we sing about America? Our songwriters have always known how to write about love, usually relying on a harmonious mix of melody and words to inveigle us into buying sheet music and recordings, and then singing along. When songs turned to patriotic sentiments, the lyricists kept the language of hyperbole and praise, but managed to link it to the vigor of American speech.

In the nineteenth century, many of the songwriters who wrote patriotic anthems were amateurs. In the twentieth, professional songwriters who knew how to write about love sometimes turned their eye—and their craft—to songs about America, especially during wartime, reflecting what they believed the nation at its best stood for. People of color and recent arrivals were usually the exceptions. More often than not, they were subjects of disdain or mockery.

Within a decade, the Great War had begun, but the United States was determined to stay out of it. It finally drew us in nearly three years after it started. Once Americans joined the fighting, Tin Pan Alley churned out dozens of commonplace patriotic sentiments, along with one major song we still sing. "Over There" remains America's most important martial anthem. George M. Cohan wrote it almost immediately after Congress declared war on April 6, 1917. He locked himself in his office at home and emerged after an all-night session with a new song. He said that he borrowed its melody from a bugle call. Cohan then rearranged the living room furniture so all the chairs were facing in the same direction, brought in his wife and children, donned a pot for a helmet, and carried a broomstick on his shoulder. He marched back and forth singing the words: "And we won't come back till it's over over there"[1] (George M. Cohan, "Over There," 1917).

Eventually, we had had enough of the marching songs and jingoistic anthems you expect to hear in a country at war, but the songs also relied on the conversational language of love songs to affirm the nobler side of America's history and what it believed about itself. "America, I Love You" devotes a stanza to the American Revolution ("It's now quite a nation / Of wond'rous population, / And free from ev'ry King"). The second verse merges the welcoming of immigrants with the concept of law:

> From all sorts of places,
> They welcomed all the races
> To settle on their shore . . .
> To give them protection
> By popular election,
> A set of laws that chose,
> They're your laws and my laws,
> For your cause and my cause
> That's why this country rose.
>
> (Archie Gottler and Edgar Leslie, "America, I Love You," 1915)

The same chorus follows both verses. The narrator in the song loves an America that resembles "a sweetheart of mine, / From ocean to ocean, / For you my devotion, is touching each bound'ry line." The love quickly extends to the country and its people: "America, I love you, / And there's a hundred million others like me." Gottler wrote in march time, but Leslie's lyrics adapted what he knew about writing love lyrics to a patriotic sentiment.

Songs that combined patriotism with romance were generally more popular than straightforward patriotic popular songs, such as Irving Berlin's "For Your Country and My Country" (1917) and "We're on Our Way to France" (*Yip Yip Yaphank*, 1917).

Tin Pan Alley's merging of patriotism and romance was actually pretty easy. Most of the songs were dramatic monologues or duets in which the lovers manage a few moments alone to bid one another farewell. Actually, they are love songs set in a wartime context, just before the young man sails to France to fight the Hun. He comforts her and then explains what he must do. In this case, where the urge to fight is stronger than the love that binds them, at least for now, Irving Berlin wove both strains together. A departing soldier says to his beloved, "I've got to fight for love and liberty" (Irving Berlin, "The Ragtime Soldier Man," 1917).

Typically, the soldier's departure in these songs creates dramatic tension between the sadness of the girl and the determination of the boy to do his duty, coupled with her promise to remain faithful and his to return safely. His commitment to his patriotic duty provides the underpinning for the songs' romantic emotions. The lyric makes room for the four major themes of wartime songs: parting, separation, loneliness and longing, and the dream of return. He asks her to write and promises that when he returns, no matter how long he's away, "We will build a little home for you / Then we'll settle down, dear, for life / Far away from care and strife." Their vision of life beyond the war is idyllic. The lyric never mentions the war to end all wars, but the theme runs beneath many of these songs. The soldier reassures the girl he loves by merging his love with his sense of duty:

> And I'll be just as true to you
> As to the Red, White and Blue
> Though I'm gone for a long, long time.
>
> (Albert Von Tilzer and Lew Brown, "I May Be Gone for a Long, Long Time," 1917)

In other songs, a soldier in France dreams about his beloved back home or imagines that he's speaking to her. The songs range from the formal, fanciful "Wander with a peaceful mind / In the land of fancy with the girl you left behind" (Irving Berlin and Jean Havez, "Dream On, Little Soldier Boy," *Rilla of Green Gables*, 1917) to a chatty letter a soldier writes from France. He reminds her to send the sweater she made as he sends her a goodnight kiss (Albert Von Tilzer and Lew Brown, "I May Stay Away a Little Longer," 1918).

Perhaps the best of these songs written from a soldier's point of view is Irving Berlin's "I'm Gonna Pin a Medal on the Girl I Left Behind." It's distinctive because "Johnny's" patriotism is more than talk. He has fought bravely and earned a medal. He also understands the loneliness of the girl he loves: "You should have seen her try to keep away the tears that blind / A braver hero / Would be hard to find." The medal makes him happy because:

> I'm gonna pin my medal on the girl I left behind.
> She deserves it more than I
> For the way she said "Goodbye."
>
> > (Irving Berlin, "I'm Gonna Pin a Medal on the Girl I Left Behind,"
> > *Ziegfeld Follies of 1918*, 1918)

Songs from the sweethearts left behind express the same sentiments but from a woman's point of view. A young woman knows from her sweetheart's letters that he's in the fighting but has promised to return:

> Could I see him, I'd tell him that I love him
> And I'd put all my heart in one fond glance . . .
> My sweetheart is somewhere in France.
>
> > (Mary Earl, "My Sweetheart Is Somewhere in France," 1918)

Some of these songs are no less loving although the lyricist's approach is comic: "And if he fights like he can love / Why, then, it's good night Germany!" (George W. Meyer, Grant Clarke, and Howard E. Rogers, "If He Can Fight Like He Can Love, Good Night Germany!" 1918). The girl in "I'm Going to Follow the Boys" says that she misses the dancing and kissing. "If they start a suffrage regiment," she adds, "I'd hurry to enlist." The song mixes the comic and the romantic, but ultimately she combines her eagerness to be back with "Bill, Jack and Harry" with a patriotic commitment:

> But I'm strong to do my bit,
> And if one little kiss or more
> Can help them win the war,
> Why I'm going to follow the boys!
>
> > (James V. Monaco and Howard Rogers,
> > "I'm Going to Follow the Boys," 1917)

"K-K-K-Katy" and "Till We Meet Again" are among the best-known songs from the First World War. "Katy" is also the most important of the "stuttering songs," popular in the first decades of the century, and "Till We Meet Again" is the most important American love song of the war. Both portray a last moment before parting, but "K-K-K-Katy" lacks any trace of melancholy. It's a lively little song about Kate and Jimmy, "a soldier brave and bold." He has bought a wedding ring, but first "he's off to France. . . . See if he could make the Kaiser dance." Before he leaves, he makes a promise born of confidence and innocence: "When the m-m-m-m-moon shines / Over the cowshed, / I'll be waiting at the k-k-k-kitchen door" (Geoffrey O'Hara, "K-K-K-Katy," 1918).

The lyricist Raymond B. Egan blends the same four themes in "Till We Meet Again" to mix melancholy at parting, a sense of longing even before the young soldier leaves, and hope in the promise of return "when the clouds roll by" (Richard A. Whiting and Raymond B. Egan, "Till We Meet Again," 1918). He promises that "Wedding bells will sing so merrily / Ev'ry tear will be a memory" and asks her to pray for him, "Till we meet again." The lyrics never mention the war or the man's patriotic duty; the indirect allusion lies in his departure. Even so, the melancholy tone persists in Richard A. Whiting's melody. The sheet music cover of lovers holding one another close creates the mood before you hear a single note.

Popular songs about patriotism may sound frivolous, but in a diverse nation that proclaims its devotion to freedom, equality, and opportunity, songs affirm at least implicitly that love is the ultimate democratic emotion. Everybody, regardless of social standing or bank account, gets to topple head over heels, often urged along by a song's unlikely combination of sentiment and wit. In a Broadway musical from the Great Depression, you could even run for president on it.

In George and Ira Gershwin, George S. Kaufman, and Morrie Ryskind's *Of Thee I Sing*, a musical lampooning of American politics, John P. Wintergreen runs for president on the Love ticket. His humorous campaign song, "Love Is Sweeping the Country," stirs audiences from one end of the nation to the other: "All the sexes / From Maine to Texas / Have never known such love before." In addition to its up-tempo drive, the song's confidence is infectious (George Gershwin and Ira Gershwin, "Love Is Sweeping the Country," *Of Thee I Sing*, 1933).

As part of turning romance into a presidential campaign song, Ira Gershwin recast patriotic slogans as love songs. Once the Gershwins borrowed their title and title song from the stately anthem "America," George wrote a jazzy march to which Ira set snappy, colloquial lyrics. The usually caustic playwright George S. Kaufman objected to the irreverent but affectionate juxtaposition in the first line of the song's chorus, "Of thee I sing, baby." In five words, it sweeps from stately to slangy. Kaufman urged the brothers to write a straightforward love duet instead. They stuck with what they had. They must have understood that the collision between formality and slang, sentiment and wit, could have great appeal in a song. They also had to understand that the line paved the way for what was to come. This duet between Wintergreen and Mary, the woman he loves, starts with familiar images of silver linings and blue skies, but they're a setup for the emotional yet clever ending that lifts the spirit in the middle of the Great Depression. It feels almost as patriotic as it does romantic. Mary, Wintergreen sings, is

> Shining star and inspiration,
> Worthy of a mighty nation—
> Of thee I sing!
>
> (George Gershwin and Ira Gershwin,
> "Of Thee I Sing," *Of Thee I Sing*, 1931)

Two years later, the composer Ralph Rainger and the lyricist Leo Robin borrowed Patrick Henry's famous line from the Second Virginia Convention, just a few weeks before the Battles of Concord and Lexington. They used it as the title line for a blues-flavored torch song entitled "Give Me Liberty or Give Me Love." In the 1933 tearjerker *Torch Song*, Claudette Colbert plays an unwed mother who can't support her two-year-old daughter. She puts the child up for adoption to pursue a career as a torch singer. The father has sailed off to China without knowing that he has a daughter. Later, working in a nightclub, Colbert's character sings the weary torch singer's lament. The dismal woman within the song raises no eyebrows and causes no laughter when she uses Henry's famous line to demand fidelity. By then, you're attuned to her point of view. The monosyllabic lines trudge forward until the three-syllable "liberty" provides a linguistic and emotional climax:

> You can have me if you want me
> But you must be mine alone,
> Give me liberty or give me love.
>
> (Ralph Rainger and Leo Robin,
> "Give Me Liberty or Give Me Love," *Torch Song*, 1933)

The Gershwins weren't the only songwriters to twit presidents. In *I'd Rather Be Right*, Richard Rodgers and Lorenz Hart collaborated with the playwrights George S. Kaufman and Moss Hart to turn a conventional musical comedy plot into a political satire that cast the Broadway legend George M. Cohan as Franklin Delano Roosevelt. The plot is no weightier than a fellow's need for a raise so he can afford to marry his girl. His boss won't agree until Congress and the president balance the budget. Young man Phil dreams that he and fiancée, Peggy, meet FDR sitting on a park bench; he offers to help out. When his efforts fail, he suggests that they marry anyway. Phil wakes up and decides to take the president's advice.

Rodgers and Hart wrote two songs for Cohan to sing and dance to. Hart's lyrics for the singing president give Roosevelt the chance to make fun of himself: "I'm really quite the hero / I only have to say 'My friends . . .' / And stocks go down to zero" (Richard Rodgers and Lorenz Hart, "Off the Record," *I'd Rather Be Right*, 1937). Nobody seemed to mind; the show opened on November 2, 1937, and ran for 290 performances, a decent run in the middle of the Depression.

In 1948, after a lot of soldiers had returned from the Second World War and taken jobs back from the women who had been filling them, Olive Oyl runs for president in a Popeye cartoon. Her stump speech imagines what life would be like if she, a woman, ran the country. The humorous lyric ranges from playful fantasy to the issues of the day, from "An all-day ice cream cone would cost a cent / If I were President" to the more topical "Apartments would once again be for rent / If I were President" (Winston Sharples and Buddy Kay, "If I Were President," *Olive Oyl for President*, 1948).

Right from the start, presidential aspirants have had campaign songs. They reflect partisanship rather than patriotism, or perhaps the line between them isn't especially clear. Thomas Jefferson began the practice with "Jefferson and Liberty" in his 1800 run against John Adams. Thereafter, you could count on them to arrive for every presidential election. Among them was "Tippecanoe and Tyler Too" for William Henry Harrison in 1840. He won the race but died after thirty-one days in office. Rutherford B. Hayes, an abolitionist before the war who, as president, ended Reconstruction, relied on E. W. Foster's "Hurrah for Hayes and Honest Ways." In "Lincoln and Liberty," one of the best of these songs, Jesse Hutchinson Jr. set countrified conversational words to a familiar tune, "Old Rosin the Bow." It was common to set new words to well-known tunes to encourage people to sing along:

> We'll go for the son of Kentucky
> The hero of Hoosierdom through
> The pride of the suckers, so lucky
> For Lincoln and Liberty, too.
>
> (Jesse Hutchinson Jr., "Lincoln and Liberty, Too," 1860)

The practice of campaign songs showed signs of wearing thin when Franklin D. Roosevelt chose a hit song for his 1932 campaign, Milton Ager and Jack Yellen's "Happy Days Are Here Again." It was one of the Pollyanna songs so welcome during the Great Depression: "Your cares and troubles are gone, / There'll be no more from now on" (Milton Ager and Jack Yellen, "Happy Days Are Here Again," *Chasing Rainbows*, 1929).

Ager and Yellen had intended the song for a scene in an early talkie that celebrated the end of the First World War, but the movie was so bad that MGM kept delaying its release. Finally, the songwriters decided to release the song on their own. They took it to the society bandleader George Olsen, who premiered it that night at the Hotel Pennsylvania across from Penn Station in New York City. Unfortunately, the date was October 28, 1929, a few hours after the Wall Street Crash that led to the Great Depression. The audience mocked the song, a kind of graveyard humor, but it caught on as the Depression's first major Pollyanna song. It remained the Democratic Party's campaign song for presidential elections through John F. Kennedy's 1960 run. In recent years, campaigns have chosen contemporary popular songs to blare at rallies as the candidates enter.

Fortunately, we're not stuck with only campaign songs, most of which are serviceable boilerplate and disappear as soon as the campaign ends. We do have some songs about presidents that are worth remembering for their diversity and underlying patriotism. Not surprisingly, a nineteenth-century song settles for triumphalism and exceptionalism. After praising Washington for our independence and Lincoln for setting a people free, it turns to a universal future. Henry Clay Work probably wrote it as a campaign song for Lincoln in 1864, although it rises above the level of most of the others:

Earth's weary bondmen shall listen with cheer—
Tyrants shall tremble, and traitors shall fear—
When, in its fullness of glory, they hear
The story of Washington and Lincoln.
(Henry Clay Work, "Washington and Lincoln," 1864)

Americans were determined to avoid war after hostilities broke out in 1914 between Germany on one side and Great Britain and France on the other. The streak of isolationism ran wide and deep in the American grain. Besides, we had no particular love for the English: we'd fought them off in the Revolution, they'd burned the White House during the War of 1812, and they'd sided with the Confederacy during the Civil War. We liked the German U-boats' attacks on shipping even less. President Woodrow Wilson was determined not to lead the nation into war until he had to face the sinking of the *Lusitania* and the rapid change in American attitudes toward Germany.

In 1945, near the end of another war, the songwriter and folk singer Woody Guthrie wrote a letter in song to Eleanor Roosevelt soon after the death of her husband. It summarizes FDR's life in a series of brief stanzas, from his birth "in a money family on that Hudson's rocky shore" to his helping "to build my union hall" to fighting the Axis in the Second World War. Guthrie's lyric urges Mrs. Roosevelt not to cry because "his good work fills the sky" (Woody Guthrie, "Dear Mrs. Roosevelt," 1945). Guthrie, who held leftist political convictions, had been against the war until the *Wehrmacht* invaded Russia.

Several revues that opened on Broadway in the years right after the Second World War reflected the lives of ordinary Americans. Their titles give us their points of view and the underlying patriotism of their approach. *Call Me Mister*, the first important hit of the 1946–1947 season, could not have been timelier. Its upbeat approach overlooked some of the more troubling aspects of life right after the war, as it used song, dance, and comedy to celebrate the return of servicemen to civilian life. All the male actors were veterans, and all the female actors had appeared in USO shows to entertain the troops.

The show opens with GIs on a train anticipating their return home. Composer/lyricist Harold Rome sets their growing excitement to rhythms that combine African American spirituals (and the image of home) with the drive of a railroad train: "This train is a going home train / This train" (Harold Rome, "Going Home Train," *Call Me Mister*, 1946). The first act finale portrays the ways in which the newly returned veteran, now a civilian, reacts to being in civvies at last: "Just call me mister from now on" (Harold Rome, "Call Me Mister," *Call Me Mister*, 1946).

# 5

# Attuned to the Needs of the Nation

Folk music couldn't be much farther from a Broadway musical if it tried. Although protest is often its bread and butter, it has a capacity for patriotism when the times call for it. Protesters were patriots with a gripe, but patriots nevertheless. In 1941, the Bonneville Power Administration hired Woody Guthrie to write songs and narrate a documentary film about the construction of dams in the Pacific Northwest. He wrote a total of twenty-six songs, including "Roll On, Columbia" and "Pastures of Plenty," but the administration never made the movie.

"The Biggest Thing That Man Has Ever Done," also known as "The Great Historical Bum," is one of the major songs from what later became known as the Columbia River Ballads. It includes many of the recurring themes in Guthrie's writing: a love for the land and its people, but disdain for the injustices imposed by those with wealth and power. What's unusual, though, is that the ballads contain no sign of protest. With a wife and small children to support, Guthrie needed money desperately and had signed a contract for one month to do the writing. He continued to add new songs into 1942. Always strongly anti-fascist, Guthrie now expressed a new patriotic eagerness to destroy Hitler and the Nazis without surrendering his leftist politics. It helped that Hitler had broken his nonaggression pact with Joseph Stalin by attacking Russia from the West.

In the song's unusually broad approach to history, a single narrator journeys through space and time to describe all that he's seen and done over the centuries. Its hyperbole is comic, but Guthrie's intent is serious: "I'm just a lonesome traveler, The Great Historical Bum. / Highly educated from history I come" (Woody Guthrie, "Biggest Thing That Man Has Ever Done," 1942). The narrator builds the Rock of Ages, works in the Garden of

Eden, oversees the building of the pyramids, and defeats conquering armies from the Romans to Kaiser Bill. He never claims to be God, though, just a "lonesome traveler" who keeps stepping into world history to make things happen. He is much more than an observer. The song's second half covers American history from the Revolution and the abolition of slavery to the Dust Bowl and Guthrie's faith in the destruction of Nazi Germany. During the war, he shipped out in the merchant marine and eventually joined the US Army.

Guthrie must have seen himself enlarged in the character he created. He'd always had wanderlust. Again and again, he took to the open road, walking and hitchhiking from coast to coast to write songs about what he saw and sing them to anyone who'd listen. Here, Guthrie tells about a chronological trek that includes his commitment to left-wing causes and the labor union movement: "I worked in the Garden of Eden, that was the year of two, / Joined the apple pickers union, I always paid my due." His general outlook and his purposely ungrammatical speech are essentially rural, an image of authenticity. Or so he believed. He later wrote in his introduction to the Columbia River Songbook, "I pulled my shoes on and walked out of every one of these Pacific Northwest Mountain towns drawing pictures in my mind and listening to poems and songs and words faster to come and dance in my ears than I could ever get them wrote down."[1]

At the same time, technology fascinated him, everything from the Grand Coulee Dam and the Empire State Building to the Golden Gate Bridge. He also includes the coming of the immigrants by comparing them implicitly to the Children of Israel, also a common trope in spirituals during slavery: "I opened up the ocean let the migrant children through."

The song merges Guthrie's personal experience and his politics with myth, history, and patriotism. Ultimately, he praises America with humor, though without irony. He writes about his "freedom wife" and the "big land we built": "Our kids are several millions now; they run from sun to sun." For a stanza or two, the line blurs between the wanderer and the nation he wanders. Is he somehow the embodiment of the nation? He doesn't work out the theme in any logical way, but it crops up from time to time, often helped along by hyperbole: "Coulee is the biggest thing that man has ever done."

Many of Guthrie's songs tell stories about his roaming and his politics. He praises the building of the great dams in the Pacific Northwest because they will help ordinary people, and in the midst of the war, he looks ahead to a peaceful world. At the end, he reclaims his role as the Great Historical Bum, who may also be the embodiment of the nation at its best: "I'm about the biggest thing that man has ever done."

"Pastures of Plenty," another song from the Columbia River Ballads, begins in protest. It takes a while before it turns to patriotism. The character who tells the story describes his life as a farmer: "It's a mighty hard row that my poor hands have hoed." He persists until the Dust Bowl forces him West: "I worked in your orchards of peaches and prunes," but he knows his life has become ever-shifting: "We come with the dust and we go with the wind" (Woody Guthrie, "Pastures of Plenty," 1941). In the song's final two choruses, the outlook changes. As the migrant farmer moves from farm to orchard, from state to state, he recognizes the plenty in the midst of the desert. It justifies his hard work:

> Every state in this Union us migrants have been
> We'll work in this fight and we'll fight till we win.

When Guthrie wrote "Pastures of Plenty," the Second World War was nearly two years old in Europe and four in Asia. He had begun to think about the war still to come for America. In the last of five choruses, the farmer sees himself connected to the land through his labors and reaffirms his commitment to the nation: "My land I'll defend with my life if it be / 'Cause my pastures of plenty must always be free."

The year before he started to work on the Columbia River Ballads, Guthrie had set new words to a Carter Family song called "When the World's on Fire." Its performance by Pete Seeger and many other folk singers, and its eventual acceptance in thousands of classrooms across the country (and then in their families), made it one of America's unofficial national anthems. Most of us are at the very least familiar with its chorus. Its overarching view of the country calls up distant echoes of "America the Beautiful."

> This land is your land, this land is my land
> From California to the New York island,
> From the redwood forests to the Gulf Stream waters;
> This land was made for you and me.
>
> (Woody Guthrie, "This Land Is Your Land," 1940)

Guthrie wrote the song, stowed it away, and pretty much forgot about it for four years. In addition to "the ribbon of highway," "that endless skyway," and "her diamond deserts," he had also written two stanzas that looked back to the Great Depression, even though things were booming on the home front during the war. The version printed on the Guthrie website (woodyguthrie.org/Lyrics/This_Land.htm) includes a stanza that Guthrie dropped when he first recorded the song in 1944. In it, he describes those on relief and wonders about the nation:

> As they stood there hungry, I stood there asking,
> Is that land made for you and me?

Guthrie attempts to reconcile the song's different themes in his final verse because he loves the country's open expanses and the rural people who inhabit them. He is adamant as he freely takes to the road, claiming the land for himself and us:

> Nobody living can ever make me turn back
> This land was made for you and me.

Yet even a song as easy to take as Guthrie's has faced criticism. A musician and member of the Native American Abenaki tribe named Mali Obomsawin wrote,

> In the context of America, a nation-state built by settler colonialism, Woody Guthrie's protest anthem exemplifies the particular blind spot that Americans have in regard to Natives: American patriotism erases us, even if it comes in the form of a leftist protest song. Why? Because this land "was" our land. Through genocide, broken treaties, and a legal system created by and for the colonial interest, this land "became" American land.[2]

The Native Genocide first came to wide attention only in the 1960s and 1970s, helped along by folk singer Buffy Sainte-Marie's "Bury My Heart at Wounded

Knee" and Dee Brown's seminal work, *Bury My Heart at Wounded Knee: An Indian History of the American West*, in 1970. The title comes from "American Names" by Stephen Vincent Benet. Sainte-Marie's lyric is about Anna Mae Aquash, a Native activist found murdered in 1976, possibly by federal agents, and Leonard Peltier, another Native activist serving a life sentence in federal prison. Sainte-Marie also wrote "Now That the Buffalo's Gone," about what she described as "the building of the Kinzua Dam [in Pennsylvania in 1961], breaking one of the oldest treaties in American history, authorized by George Washington."[3] The song is direct to the point of bluntness, as Sainte-Marie's lyric raises a series of unanswered questions whose answers are obvious:

> Has a change come about my dear man
> Or are you really still taking our lands?
> (Buffy Sainte-Marie, "Now That the Buffalo's Gone," 1964)

During the Second World War, Guthrie attached a sign to his guitar, "This machine kills fascists," as he rallied to America's cause after Adolf Hitler invaded Russia. The lines that he deleted in "This Land Is My Land" also expressed his political convictions as a man of the left who often associated with Communist groups but never joined the party. Guthrie's inspiration for the song was much less idealistic than that. He wrote it because he was sick and tired of hearing Irving Berlin's "God Bless America" on car radios as he hitchhiked from Oklahoma to New York City.

Berlin had not set out to write a patriotic song as Europe careened toward the Second World War. He had first written "God Bless America" in 1918, during the First World War, though its tone was different from what he would publish two decades later. Originally, it was to be a martial song for his all-soldier revue, *Yip Yip Yaphank*. The revue's goal was to raise as much money as possible for Army Relief, to help the families of those killed in combat. For the finale, the entire cast in uniform with helmets and rifles was to march up the aisle as if they were leaving for France, singing "God Bless America."

When his musical secretary, Harry Ruby, heard the song for the first time, he blurted out, "Geez, Irvy, another patriotic song?" That was all the insecure Berlin had to hear. He replaced it with a new song, "We're on Our Way to

France." Sometime after that, Berlin said that having soldiers ask for God's blessing as they leave for combat was gilding the lily.

Twenty years after *Yip Yip Yaphank*, Berlin was returning from England, where he happened to be when Neville Chamberlain and Adolf Hitler signed the Munich Pact. As his ship sailed toward New York, he realized that war was coming. He determined to write a song about peace—his own small protest against another war. He made three or four stabs at it, but nothing satisfied him. Then he remembered that song from the First World War. He cabled his staff to locate the unpublished sheet music.

It took them days to find it, but when he arrived at his New York office, it was waiting for him. He saw immediately that he'd have to change the words, and that might require some changes in the music as well. He had originally written, "Stand beside her and guide her to the right with a light from above." By the late 1930s, the use of "right" could signify a political point of view. The line had to go. He changed it to "through the night with a light from above." He had also written a more warlike line: "Make her victorious on land and foam." That soon became the all-inclusive "From the mountains, to the prairies, to the oceans white with foam," not unlike Guthrie's chorus. Finally, he links the song's embrace of the nation and its vastness "to a prayerful but familiar domestic image at the heart of America's view of itself."[4] "God bless America, my home sweet home." It is a gentle reminder of the role played by spiritual resolve in Americans' patriotic view of themselves and their nation (Irving Berlin, "God Bless America," 1918, 1938).

Berlin also added a verse that the popular singer Kate Smith always included, although many singers have dropped it over the years. It alludes to the coming war, declares allegiance to "a land that's free," and calls on all Americans to "raise our voices in a solemn prayer."

Smith had sensed a change in the country's mood in the late 1930s. Isolationism remained strong. We wanted to stay out of the war, but we were not immune to what was happening in Europe. Smith wanted something that would both stir and reassure her large radio audience. She went to Irving Berlin to ask him for a new patriotic song. Legend says that he took the revised "God Bless America" out of his drawer, tossed it on the desk, and said, "You can have this if you want it." She wanted it. She first sang it on Armistice Day (now called Veterans Day) in November 1938 and sang it repeatedly through the war. It became an image of American unity through four years of struggle in Europe and the Pacific. Beyond that, when Berlin sang it, his daughter wrote, "No other singer . . . could give it quite that conviction. He meant every word. . . . It was his home sweet home. He, the immigrant who had made good, was saying thank you."[5]

We now sing it during seventh-inning stretches in ballparks, just before "Take Me Out to the Ball Game." We also turn to it in times of terrible tragedy. After 9/11, it became the anthem we sang again and again. When performers sang it from the stage in the months after the attack, audiences often stood without prompting to sing along. Groups on opposite sides of issues have also used it, including Christian evangelists in the 1960s in their opposition to people against the war in Vietnam. Protesters sang it during the early days of the civil rights movement and often at union rallies. Not everyone appreciated it, though. The Ku Klux Klan protested against its use because its writer was a Jewish immigrant.[6]

Its title, a familiar phrase, also became a universal password of sorts. When Secretary of State Anthony Blinken was speaking after then–president elect Biden announced his appointment, he talked about his grandfather who had survived four years in a Nazi concentration camp. He was on a death march from one camp to another near the end of the war when he was able to dash into the woods to try to escape. He suddenly heard a tank approaching, but rather than a swastika on its side, he saw a five-pointed white star. He fell to his knees as an African American soldier stood up from the hatch and recited the only three English words he knew, "God bless America."

What got Woody Guthrie so annoyed at the song, aside from its constant playing on the radio? It so irritated him that he wrote a retort, sarcastically titled "God Blessed America for Me." He wrote it in his room in a fleabag in Manhattan after he had arrived from Oklahoma. He thought that Berlin's song was jingoistic and ignorant of the plight of many Americans during the Depression. Guthrie often wore his politics on his sleeve. He eventually named his song "This Land Was Made for You and Me" to remove anything spiritual from the lyric, but turned to the passive voice instead. We never learned who made the land. Its emphasis, though, is on the experience of the land as someone—probably Guthrie himself—"roamed and rambled" from coast to coast. It was something he had done more than once in his life. Yet Guthrie, so much a man of the people, missed something in "God Bless America." Stephen Holden wrote that its introduction "enshrines a strain of official patriotism intertwined with a religious faith that runs deep in the American psyche," much as "America the Beautiful" did before it.[7]

Berlin's song is a prayer, while Guthrie's focuses on the inclusion and equality of all Americans: "This land was made for you and me." It lacks Berlin's spiritual aspirations but feels inviting and familiar as someone takes us around the country. It also becomes a forum for Guthrie's political opinions, something Berlin, rooted in Tin Pan Alley, would have been much less likely to do.

Even so, Berlin took gentle shots at politics in 1932 and again in 1950. First, he and librettist Moss Hart found humor in the Great Depression in *Face the Music*, their spoof of political and police corruption. The score originally included "Two Cheers Instead of Three," but it was cut before opening night. It's a jaunty march with a playful lyric. It urges us to be thrifty in hard times, even when we "cheer the colors we prize": "Just give two cheers instead of three / For the land of the brave and the free." Berlin manages to make fun and be patriotic at the same time.

Eighteen years later, in 1950, he wrote *Call Me Madam*, in which he and librettists Howard Lindsay and Russel Crouse crafted a spoof of politics and foreign policy. President Harry S. Truman appoints the inexperienced Sally Adams as his ambassador to the fictional country of Lichtenberg. She is a fictionalized version of Perle Mesta, who had a reputation for throwing lavish bipartisan parties in Washington, D.C., during the Truman and Eisenhower administrations, and became Truman's ambassador to the tiny country of Lichtenstein. The satire took aim at the United States's habit of lending billions of dollars to rebuild Europe and counter the Soviet Union during the early years of the Cold War. As was often the case, a Broadway musical treated a serious matter with humor.

Although Berlin usually avoided political commentary, the plot of *Call Me Madam* notes that the 1952 presidential election is approaching. Even though the Democrats have held the White House for nearly twenty years, the American people liked Dwight Eisenhower, who eventually became the Republican candidate and won the election in a landslide. For now, though, two senators and a congressman speculate about the future: "But Harry won't consent, / They'll get a sock on the jaw. / Republican President? / That's against the law" (Irving Berlin, "They Like Ike," *Call Me Madam*, 1950).

During 1942, America's first full year at war after Pearl Harbor, the military situation was bleak, and the songs were unusually dark. After a brief spurt of Tin Pan Alley jingoism right after Pearl Harbor, songwriters settled into writing love songs—what they did best—for the next four years. The songs were different from those that preceded them, though. They limited themselves again and again to the same four themes, singly or in combination: parting, separation, loneliness and longing, and the dream of return.

In 1942, when the emotions felt new, the songs, many of them melancholy, dwelt on loneliness and longing; return felt very far away, especially in such titles as "Don't Get Around Much Anymore" and "I Don't Want to Walk Without You." They don't sound patriotic, but they were attuned to the needs of the nation in one of its most perilous times. They recognized what people on the home front needed, and they provided it. They mirrored the emotions of millions of women to provide both an outlet and reassurance. The songwriters wrote not for brass bands and parades, but for the quiet times when the workday was over and a woman could settle down to confront her loneliness and dread. They provided not reality, but what I noted earlier as "the public *discourse* about reality,"[8] one of the great tasks of popular songs.

There are several contradictory stories about how Berlin wrote "White Christmas," and it's hard to know exactly which facts are true. What's clear, though, is that he did not write it for the movie *Holiday Inn* in 1942. He might have written it four years earlier and intended it to be sung sarcastically by a group of New York sophisticates. Fortunately, that project never came to fruition. The most romantic version of its composition says that he wrote it while working in Hollywood, unable to get home for the holiday. He was Jewish, but his wife was Roman Catholic, and he had become very fond of Christmas as a family holiday. Perhaps feeling a little sorry for himself, the insomniac songwriter stayed up all night to finish the song before calling his musical secretary in the morning: "Grab your pen and take down this song. I just wrote the best song I've ever written—hell, I just wrote the best song that anybody's ever written!"

A pretty ballad called "Be Careful, It's My Heart" was supposed to be the big hit from *Holiday Inn*, but the public, including men in combat on Guadalcanal, took "White Christmas" to heart, intuiting its appeal when the war was just about a year old—during the first Christmas when large numbers of Americans were in peril. The song's conjuring up of childhood memories and idyllic New England winters transformed it into a comforting vision of home for Americans frightened and bewildered by the demands of wartime. It also set a pattern for Christmas songs for years to come.

When Berlin realized that circumstances had changed "White Christmas" from a holiday song into a war song (or what he preferred to call "a peace song"), he gave orders to drop its verse from the sheet music. No more lines like "the orange and palm trees sway" and no more references to "Beverly Hills." He had come to see that servicemen in combat on a distant island in the Pacific had recognized an image of home. Berlin was also a very canny businessman.

Today, as we stand around a piano, bellowing out "Deck the Halls" and "God Rest Ye Merry, Gentlemen" and then "White Christmas," most of us are far removed from the emotions of those who heard the song when it was new. Despite its idyllic imagery of sleigh bells and glistening treetops, the song's melancholy melody touched a deep emotional chord—and still does for those who truly listen. The second chorus has someone writing on a Christmas card, "May your days be merry and bright, / And may all your Christmases be white" (Irving Berlin, "White Christmas," *Holiday Inn*, 1942). The wishes are genuine, but what's missing is any promise of return. It is as upbeat as a song without hope can be.

Americans have two Christmases. One celebrates the birth of Christ, the other the coming of Santa Claus, the decorating of trees, and the gathering of families. Berlin's simple song has nothing to do with religious belief; it is the great anthem of America's secular Christmas. An anthem does more than sing about its subject; somehow it illuminates, elevates, and embodies it so that subject and song become one. No one had a keener feel for what Americans believed, knew, remembered, hoped, and dreamed than Irving Berlin. In songs like "God Bless America," "Alexander's Ragtime Band," and, of course, "White Christmas," Berlin spoke for all of us. Having lived out a quintessentially American story, he felt a deep love for his adopted country. In return, he provided the musical accompaniment for a half century of American life—and beyond.

After "White Christmas," New England in winter became the setting for Christmas songs, augmented by all the trimmings—bells, trees, lights, snow, and perhaps a sleigh—images reminiscent of Currier and Ives prints and Grandma Moses paintings. During the war years especially, "White Christmas" inspired a number of other songs that became standards. The first of them, "I'll Be Home for Christmas," is one of several songs from a soldier's point of view. In a letter home, he promises that he'll be home for Christmas and asks the letter's recipient to ready the celebration. He asks for snow, mistletoe, and gifts, only to end with a dramatically ironic turn that deepens the melancholy, as nostalgia becomes immediacy: "I'll be home for Christmas / If only in my dreams" (Walter Kent and Kim Gannon, "I'll Be Home for Christmas," 1943).

In 1944, in the movie musical *Meet Me in St. Louis,* Esther, played by Judy Garland, sings "Have Yourself a Merry Little Christmas" to her younger sister, Tootie, played by the child star Margaret O'Brien. The family has just learned that Father has received a promotion, which requires that he and his family leave St. Louis, the only home his children have ever known. The family has also set its heart on seeing the St. Louis World's Fair to celebrate the 1903 centennial of the Louisiana Purchase. Now they'll have to miss it. Tootie is inconsolable on their last Christmas in St. Louis. To calm and reassure her, Garland sings "Have Yourself a Merry Little Christmas," even more mournful than "White Christmas" in its sense of impending loss (Hugh Martin and Ralph Blane, "Have Yourself a Merry Little Christmas," *Meet Me in St. Louis*, 1944).

The song is heartbreaking, but actually less dark than songwriters Hugh Martin and Ralph Blane's original version. After visiting wounded soldiers in military hospitals, Garland said she wouldn't be able to sing the song's most hopeless lines. It needed to offer something to those young men she had seen. "Have yourself a merry little Christmas," it said originally, because "it may be your last / Next year we may all be living in the past."

Martin resisted making any changes but eventually agreed. The lines now read, "Let your heart be light, / From now on our troubles will be out of sight." To comfort her sister, Esther gives the distressed child a promise for the future, but the song's unyieldingly sad melody and its use of "little" to describe Christmas confirm its lingering melancholy even in the changed lyric. This melancholy lifted it from a song about characters in a story to one that resonated with the American people.

These songs may not have been written with patriotism in mind, but their composers and lyricists understood their primary audience: women at home alone. It was a time of social upheaval and raw emotion. These songs gave voice to what these wives and sweethearts felt; they served the nation by helping people endure.

A lot of songs have "America" or "U.S.A." in the title. You look at the title and think you know what's coming: yet another patriotic anthem. But some of these songs turn out to be surprising. They don't portray the America we expect to find in a song. Often, they unsettle us. Like Woody Guthrie's earlier "This Land Is Your Land" and "The Biggest Thing That Man Has Ever Done," Paul Simon's "America" derives from personal experience. His songs about America put a character on the road, an essential American image of searching. In the process, he rediscovers America for himself. In 1964, Simon and his girlfriend Cathy Chitty spent five days driving across the country. The song, written two years later, grew from that trip. Its lyric portrays two lovers who take an impromptu bus trip, fortified with cigarettes and Mrs. Wagner's pies. Eventually, the song focuses on the man who sets out to find America and himself. Like so many American stories, it begins in optimism ("Let us be lovers, we'll marry our fortunes together") and becomes progressively darker. Patriotism and truth-telling are two of the ways we endure life's complexities and disappointments.

Along the way, the two of them play games, smoke, and make up stories about their fellow passengers. Once he knows that she is sleeping, he speaks to her, "Cathy, I'm lost . . . / And I'm empty and aching and I don't know why" (Paul Simon, "America," 1966). The dark side of the 1960s suddenly surfaces—its uprootedness, its loss of a reliable history, and its sense of unfocused longing. The young man feels a sudden kinship with all the other Americans out there in their cars on the New Jersey Turnpike, all of them like him, "All come to look for America" and themselves. Marc Eliot writes that the narrator, like the other people he observes, has been searching "for a literal and physical America that seems to have disappeared."[9] The frayed connection to the nation offers little comfort. In the middle of the 1960s, this is patriotism at its most anguished.

In Simon's "American Tune," an even more reflective song about the state of the Union, the character tries to understand what he's seen and what he and others have had to bear. The line between patriotism and despair seems to blur. He admits to struggle, mistakes, and confusion, and to feeling forsaken, but he insists in a line that quickly turns on itself: "But I'm all right, I'm all right / I'm just weary to my bones" (Paul Simon, "American Tune," 1973). The repetition makes his assertion suspect, but everything becomes clear when he pulls himself up short. His confession of weariness gives the lyric the feel of spontaneity, especially in a song that begins in personal testimony but expands until nearly the end.

The character's weariness deepens his understanding as he realizes that he doesn't know anyone "who's not been battered." As he looks out on the nation, he raises an elemental question: "I wonder what's gone wrong." Only then does he ground the song's inwardness in a witty but dark metaphoric America. The Statue of Liberty sails away to sea while the *Mayflower* sails to Plymouth but also over the moon. The times are uncertain, tomorrow's another day of work, and then the terrible truth at last: "You can't be forever blessed" as either an individual or a nation. The song feels personal, but Simon also holds the entire country in his hands. Facing the truth, he ends quietly, as if the rumination has come at night while he tries to fall asleep.

When an interviewer asked Simon about political references in his songs, he replied: "I don't write overtly political songs, although 'American Tune' comes pretty close, as it was written just after Nixon was elected."[10] More lyrical than strident, more personal than political, Simon achieves an equilibrium between personal experience and patriotism that grows from suffering and a deepening awareness of loss for himself and the nation.

Different settings and points of view for different kinds of songs, all with "America" or "U.S.A." in the title: Leonard Bernstein and Stephen Sondheim's effervescent "America" from *West Side Story* (1957), Sammy Johns's affirmative but questioning "America" sung by country star Waylon Jennings (1973), and Bruce Springsteen's double-edged "Born in the U.S.A." (1981). The list is far from complete, but it suggests the emotional range of these songs in the second half of the twentieth century. They recognize the nation's flaws and urge improvement, but they also affirm their commitment to its ideals. They are not the kind of patriotic songs that their titles suggest, but they are patriotic nevertheless.

"America" from *West Side Story* is a fiery debate in song and dance about the lives of Puerto Rican immigrants in Manhattan. Some embrace their new lives; others long to return to San Juan. The lyrics are barbed and satiric, and nobody comes off without a bump or bruise. The character of Bernardo is the leader of the Sharks, a Puerto Rican gang in conflict with the Jets, a native-born gang. Anita is his woman. Anita loves America; Rosalia, also Puerto Rican, prefers San Juan. Anita gets the better of the argument, but this song, which praises America, is set, ironically, to an electrifying Latino beat. Rosalia praises life in San Juan, but Anita always has a humorous topper at the ready:

> *Rosalia:* I'll bring a TV to San Juan.
> *Anita:* Is there a current to turn on!
>
> (Leonard Bernstein and Stephen Sondheim,
> "America," *West Side Story*, 1957)

When all the Puerto Ricans join in a chorus, they praise America with humor as they sing about the large numbers of Puerto Ricans who live in New York and the better life they find here despite their relative poverty. It's as if Stephen Sondheim wrote the lyric with an arched eyebrow.

> Immigrant goes to America . . .
> Puerto Rico's in America!

The country music singer and songwriter Sammy Johns wrote "America" in 1973, but his fellow country singer Waylon Jennings had the hit recording in 1985. Jennings had found the 1984 Olympics inspiring but failed to write anything about them that satisfied him. He said, "Everything I had was too corny." That's when he remembered "America," a song he'd carried with him for years but had never sung. "It wasn't just flag-waving," Jennings added, "It was talking about the ideals we had fought for and the blunders committed in their name and the honor that lay behind our national character. I found the song again and listened to it with a decade's distance."[11]

Jennings understood the song. He saw that the observer is of two minds about America. He deplores the treatment of the downtrodden but also "celebrates those things that make America unique."[12] The song's view of the nation is ultimately an affirmation. As in many patriotic songs, someone roams the country, learning from the wandering and from the hospitality he encounters: "Well I come from down around Tennessee / But the people in California / Are nice to me, America" (Sammy Johns, "America," 1973). I wonder about that word, "America," at the end of the line. The song is a dramatic monologue in which he speaks to America. He doesn't turn aside from the need to make things better, but he finds a way to link it to his hope for the nation:

> And my brothers are all black and white, yellow too
> And the red man is right, to expect a little from you
> Promise and then follow through, America.

When Bruce Springsteen sings the refrain to "Born in the U.S.A.," many in his audiences stand, cheering and clapping, their hands over their heads, thousands of them as one, as if they have suddenly discovered the revealed truth of American patriotism. Yet from the time Springsteen first worked on the song in 1981 until he recorded it in 1984 and it became an essential part of his performances, it never felt entirely finished to him. As Lauren Onkey, the music director for National Public Radio, explained, "It took time for Springsteen himself to figure out just what the song was meant to say."[13] Steve Inskeep added, "In the version that became the title track on his 1984 smash album, Springsteen made one more change: turning up the volume and shouting out the lyrics almost as if for joy. Rarely has a man with nowhere to go sounded so triumphant."[14]

The refrain repeats the simple mantra that the character was born in the United States. But it's actually more complicated than that. Springsteen had struggled to say in song what he felt about the war in Vietnam. Initially, he wrote a song he called "Vietnam," in which a father speaks to his son:

> Ain't nothin' for you here.
> From the assembly line to the front line . . .
> You died in Vietnam.
>
> (Bruce Springsteen, "Vietnam," 1981)

In its next version, Springsteen added the celebratory chorus. Its repetition carries it close in feeling to the call-and-response singing in African American churches. Drawn to Springsteen's cranked-up performing style and the easily remembered lines of the refrain, many of his fans must have assumed that he was expressing full-throated praise for America. The chorus is so ardent and insistent that it can drown out the verses. President Ronald Reagan was among those who failed to get it: "America's future . . . rests in the message of hope in songs of a man so many young Americans admire, New Jersey's own Bruce Springsteen."[15]

Yet Springsteen devotes most of the song to defiance rooted in need—a failure of America. His young, working-class character lives in the kind of town where Springsteen had grown up, "a dead-end town" where you cower "like a dog that's been beat too much." It's a place without hope. The young man gets into trouble and winds up in the army in Vietnam. When he returns, he can't find a job, and the VA offers no help. He's lost. The *New York Times* critic Jon Pareles calls it "a holler of impotent desperation."[16]

Springsteen follows each step in the vet's story with the chorus. Is it meant ironically? Is he consciously creating a paradox? Is he suggesting something about America's damaged promise that somehow manages to survive? He once told the NPR interviewer Terry Gross, "In my songs, the spiritual part, the hope part, is in the choruses. The blues and your daily realities are in the details of the verses."[17] The song never mentions Vietnam or the shabby way we treated the returning veterans, but it embodies Springsteen's lover's quarrel with America. He's proud of the nation's ideals, but, using Vietnam as an object lesson, he urges the nation to live closer to them—a step toward the more perfect union.

Springsteen called "Born in the U.S.A." a protest song: "It was a GI blues, the verses an accounting, the choruses a declaration of the one sure thing that could not be denied . . . birthplace. Birthplace, and the right to all that blood, confusion, blessings and grace that come with it."[18] Jim Cullen observes, "The grit and determination the song exudes is far more obvious than the lament at its core."[19] In this single song, Springsteen creates the ground where protest and patriotism meet.

Patriotic songs, which began in the new republic with a triumphal celebration of American exceptionalism, have taken many turns over the last two and a half centuries. They've celebrated military might but deplored wars; celebrated the nation's freedom but also felt the intimacy and loss in one family; and marched down the boulevard to the blare of a brass band but also attuned themselves to the introspection of a single American in times of doubt. The longer the republic survives, the more we press to improve on the compromises that ensured the passage of the Constitution as well as the failures that roiled the nation over the years. Some of the decisions of those who once held power changed things for the better but were often slow in coming. Others, still uncorrected, range in our eyes from the foolish to the reprehensible. To this day, whenever we see leaders make decisions that deepen the troubles of those who already suffer, some of us turn to protest. We demonstrate our patriotism by marching and singing.

6

# Protest as Patriotism

## African Americans, Letting the People Go

*[Protest songs have covered a wide range of issues over the last century or two, as James Sullivan shows in his recent book,* Which Side Are You On? 20th Century American History in 100 Protest Songs. *He provides historical context but emphasizes the last seventy-five years: civil rights, women's rights, the union movement, the environment, free speech, gay pride, immigration, and disarmament. Despite their importance, protest songs are not the primary subject of this book. To make the case for their being a form of patriotism, I've chosen to focus on two of the many possibilities: African American songs from slavery into the 1920s and women's suffrage songs from the mid-nineteenth century until the ratification of the Nineteenth Amendment. ML]*

We choose to believe in our national motto—*e pluribus unum*—even though it's not always true, certainly not always complete. Patriotic songs affirm unity to celebrate what they believe we have in common and inspire us to a sense of nationhood, even though we may disagree about nearly everything else.

I heard the author and former newspaper columnist and TV commentator Chris Matthews repeat an anecdote several times when he was the host of the MSNBC program *Hard Ball*. He said that when he returned home from serving in the Peace Corps, he wanted a career in Washington politics. The only job he could find at first was working as a uniformed US Capitol police officer. Most of his coworkers were middle-aged men with families; none but Matthews had been to college. They understood that this job, this life, was it. They also understood that Matthews would soon move on because he would have opportunities they never had. He recounted what they told him: "We don't have a lot of money or an education or great prospects. You know what holds us together? The country. We love the country." He used the story to underscore the people's intuitive grasp of what America means.

Despite Matthews's good intentions, a decade ago the historian Collin Woodward wrote presciently, "We are very different Americas, each with different origin stories and value sets. They led to a Civil War in the past and are a potentially incendiary force in the future."[1] The *New Yorker* columnist Robin Wright added, "The American promise has not delivered for many Blacks, Jews, Latinos, Asian Americans, myriad immigrant groups, and even some whites as well."[2] Just maybe our patriotic songs are so important to us because what binds us together, however strong, is also fragile—a lesson we relearned on January 6, 2021.

Many who consider themselves loyal Americans would insist that when songs protest against injustice, they are no less patriotic than "America the Beautiful" or "God Bless America." Their task is to point out America's flaws and failures, as they try to inspire us to make things better than they are. Most of them pull no punches. Their approaches may vary from advocacy to accusation, but inspiration is their common currency. They may confront the nation, but they are reformist by nature. They point the way to what they believe is a better America. The truest patriotism may lie in our capacity to balance a love for the country with the many differences that divide us. It doesn't always work.

Yet protest and its songs can seek to diminish injustice and, in the process, try to ease the divisions between us by region, race, gender, and class. Fueled by freedom of speech, the struggle "to form a more perfect union" is neverending. A determination to broaden freedom and deepen justice stands beneath nearly all these protests. It weaves its way erratically to Martin Luther King Jr.'s belief that "the arc of the moral universe is long, but it bends toward justice."[3]

Protest is the lifeblood of folk music. As the singer Morrissey said in 1985, "I thought that if you had an acoustic guitar, it meant that you were a protest singer."[4] Folk songs usually categorize: protest over here, storytelling over there, love songs in a third place. They only occasionally mix together. When they protest, they rouse up support for everything from women agitating for the vote to union members on strike to marchers for civil rights. They tell stories to entertain and encourage.

Folk songs are often political; they take sides on issues that they hope large numbers of people will take seriously. They sometimes urge people to action, but more often than not, I suspect, they sing to those who already agree with them. The anti-war songs of young protesters against the war in Vietnam are an exception. Their demonstrations, urged on in part by songs, persuaded many in their parents' generation to reconsider their initial support of the war: "All we are saying is give peace a chance" (John Lennon and Yoko Ono, "Give Peace a Chance," 1969).

Unlike popular songs, which seek a large market, folk songs feed on confrontation. Popular songs usually soften controversial subjects with humor, ignore them altogether, or find a way to blend them into a love song. Tin Pan Alley, like Broadway, is essentially conservative; it doesn't tackle a difficult subject unless it thinks the public will be responsive.

Occasionally, folk songs may also mix something of a love story with loyalty to a cause. A militant feminist named Ina Wood once scolded Woody Guthrie and his new sidekick, a young folk singer named Pete Seeger, for not singing about women in the union movement. That night, Guthrie set new words to the familiar melody of "Red Wing" for a song he called "Union Maid." A short time later, Seeger, about to record the song with the other members of the Almanac Singers (Guthrie, Millard Lampell, and Lee Hayes), decided that it was uneven and cut several stanzas. Now it was too short. Lampell said, "Give me twenty minutes"[5] and added the chorus that shifts the song in the direction of love with a touch of humor and without losing its commitment to the union cause. Quite the contrary:

> You gals who want to be free, just take a tip from me,
> Get you a man who's a union man and join the ladies' auxiliary.
> (Woody Guthrie and Millard Lampell, "Union Maid," 1940)

Most folk songs address issues from the left of center. They denounce the lack of social justice and agitate for greater freedom. More than one of these songs first appeared as a spiritual during slavery and then reappeared as part of the union movement in the 1930s and civil rights protests three decades later. Each time, verses were dropped, added, and revised to fit the needs of the moment. Originally, the chorus to this spiritual affirmed one's unshakable faith in God. In the hands of others, it became a song of determination and defiance:

> Just like a tree that's standing by the water
> We shall not be moved.
>
> (Songwriter unknown, "We Shall Not Be Moved," date unknown)

As times and causes changed, the first line of the verse began, "The union is behind us" or "We're fighting for our freedom," among others.[6] That same defiance appears in spirituals during slavery. It was one of the slaves' few weapons as long as they spoke in a hidden language of protest that the overseers could not translate. Exuberance and defiance by using spirituals to shout back at the powerful in spirituals. Underlying the mockery is a serious question framed initially by the African American theologian Howard Thurman. A slave might wonder, do the oppressors get to heaven? One spiritual tells us that "I got wings, you got wings, all God's children got wings," but later it says with a mix of defiance and mockery, "Everybody talking 'bout Heaven ain't going there." You can feel the unexpressed laughter. In the hands of slaves, heaven becomes a democratic promise.[7] As the lyric ends, it becomes giddy with delight:

> Heaven, Heaven,
> Everybody talking 'bout Heaven ain't going there;
> Heaven, Heaven,
> I'm going to shout all over God's Heaven.
>
> (Songwriter unknown, "All God's Chillun Got Wings," date unknown)

And then there are the protest songs that don't quite protest. Rather, they observe, but from a particular point of view. None of these songs is more important (or was more successful) than Don McLean's "American Pie" (Don McLean, "American Pie," c1971). The story has been told many times about McLean's refusal to explain his allusions and indirect storytelling. He wrote the song in 1971 but finally released his notes in 2015. By that time, speculators and critics had solved at least some of the lyric's mysteries. Yes, it is about the death of important early rock-and-roll performers Buddy Holly, the Big

Bopper, and Ritchie Valens in a plane crash in 1959. McLean was neither the first nor the last to see the violent deaths of three of the heroes of the first generation of rock and roll as an image of innocence lost.

The song then expands to include the loss of something essential in America. Not its innocence; we'd already been through too much in the twentieth century to be able to claim that for ourselves. But rather, a loss of confidence in the nation and in its people. McLean links Holly to himself; he heard the news when he was thirteen years old. From young McLean to Holly to an adult McLean who can look with clearer eyes at what the nation had become in the face of Vietnam. The point of view in the song and the combination of the personal and the patriotic are hardly unfamiliar, but McLean writes with a kind of allusiveness that only adds to the song's authority. McLean's biographer, Alan Howard, writes, "The image of America evolving from a savior of the free world during World War II, to a bullying military giant in Vietnam, meant to McLean, and to many of his generation, that his country was most definitely lost."[8]

By the time Africans arrived in the United States in chains, they had been torn from their families and villages, beaten and shackled, marched miles to a ship, and made to endure the Atlantic crossing in unspeakable conditions. "America," writes poet and author Nikki Giovanni, "while extolling the rights of man in language more fluid and forceful than ever before was, because of the slavery of Africans and the genocide of indigenous peoples, along with a failure to heed the advice of Abigail Adams to 'remember the ladies,' is on the verge of moral bankruptcy."[9]

As the years passed, Black people, both in bondage and after Emancipation, developed a music of their own; what began mainly in Western Africa evolved into new forms in the United States—spirituals, work songs, ragtime, jazz, and the blues. To a significant degree, African American music derived from the experience of an enslaved people. Their songs combined history with hope, misery with determination. They defined the Black experience in America. As James H. Cone writes, "Black music is unifying because it confronts the individual with the truth of black existence and affirms that being black is possible only in a communal context."[10] To affirm the common humanity of

African Americans and seek justice in their claim of acceptance in America are not new ideas. They take us back, most importantly, to W. E. B. Du Bois a century ago. He was the first to call spirituals "sorrow songs," but he also discerned something affirming in them: "Through all of the sorrow of the Sorrow Songs there breathes a hope—a faith in the ultimate justice of things."[11] These songs combine long memories of tribulation and affliction with a refusal not to dream. Nothing gave this double view of Black experience fuller expression than the religious faith at the heart of the spiritual.

Roughly six hundred thousand Africans reached the United States as slaves. After their arrival, the first generations continued to practice their own religions. They had to worship in secret because their owners considered their drumming and dancing forms of idolatry. Free African Americans eventually formed separate Christian churches in the North. Only after Nat Turner's rebellion in 1831 did slave owners decide that Christianity might help to prevent uprisings. By that time, African American and white Christian worship had begun to merge spontaneously. The combination gave rise to a new African American song form, the spiritual. It did more than vary familiar Christian hymns; it reinvented them through the use of changed melodies and words, and new singing styles to create something that was essentially African American but would also in time become essentially American. The African American sociologist Alain Locke wrote in the middle of the Harlem Renaissance:

> The spirituals are really the most characteristic product of the race genius as yet in America. But the very elements which make them deeply expressive of the Negro make them at the same time deeply representative of the soil that produced them. Thus, as unique spiritual products of American life, they become nationally as well as racially characteristic.[12]

That the music of one group of people could spread throughout the nation to change the taste, behavior, and understanding of the America they lived in gives them a patriotic purpose beyond their beginnings in slavery or, centuries later, their adaptation in Tin Pan Alley or on Broadway. Americans tend to take what they need where they can find it. That doesn't make the task any easier.

Spirituals soon combined belief in a heavenly reward with the sorrows of life and hopes for a better future, if only by crossing the River Jordan. They joined faith with protest. Most spirituals do not protest, but those that do sound an even more urgent cry in their use of secret messages that only the slaves would understand. The Jordan River became a central image of heavenly salvation but also an expression of the escape to freedom. Numerous spirituals turn to the Old Testament, especially Exodus and the story of Moses, for an overriding statement of faith that ranges from protest to calls for rebellion to calls for escape. The one necessity: the masters must not understand the hidden message. The slaves saw Exodus—the enslaved Children of Israel and their liberation by Moses before he leads them to the Promised Land—as a narrative that paralleled their plight and hope:

> Go down Moses
> Way down in Egypt land
> Tell old pharaoh to
> Let my people go.
> 
> (Songwriter unknown, "Go Down, Moses," date unknown)

"Go Down, Moses" pleads in a way that borders on prayer, a muted, disguised cry of desperation, but "Song of the Free," sung to the tune of "Oh! Susannah," is more pressing. The character in the lyric describes his escape to Canada as he lives through it. He will live as a free man despite the dangers of the journey or he will die. Only after we hear what he's up against does he turn to prayer. What begins as need and fear culminates in qualified hope:

> I'm on my way to Canada,
> That cold and dreary land,
> The dire effects of slavery
> I can no longer stand,
> My soul is vexed within me more
> To think that I'm a slave,
> I'm now resolved to strike the blow
> For freedom, or the grave.
> Oh, righteous father, wilt thou not pity me,
> And aid me on to Canada, where colored men are free.
> 
> (Songwriter unknown, "Song of the Free," 1860)

Once he was free and safe in the North, the former slave, abolitionist, author, and orator Frederick Douglass raised the hope that spirituals might have a stronger and more lasting effect on white listeners: "I have sometimes thought that the mere hearing of these songs would do more to impress some minds with the horrible character of slavery, than the reading of whole volumes of philosophy on the subject might do."[13]

The Underground Railroad was a secret network of white abolitionists and free or escaped African Americans who helped small groups of slaves reach safety. Guided by Harriet Tubman and others, they found their way to the Northern states or Canada: "O Great Father! Do Thou pity me, / And help me on to Canada where the panting slave is free!" (G. N. Allen, "The Underground Railcar (Song of the Fugitive)," 1854). Several spirituals were supposedly sung along the way North. The message is always tacit; the spirituals often refer in biblical terms to going to heaven, but the combination of allusion and imagery may suggest something more immediate.

In recent years, some have questioned the assumptions about secret messages in spirituals, but Harriet Tubman reported that she and her parties of escaping slaves sang several of them as she led them to freedom. Because the songs are part of the oral tradition, it's impossible to know for sure. One of the spirituals in question is the well-known "Swing Low, Sweet Chariot." Those who believe that it was a call to escape see in the chariot an allusion to the Underground Railroad, which swings low—to the South—to carry them North to home. Tubman told her first biographer, Sarah H. Bradford, that she sometimes sang the spiritual "Dark and Thorny Is the Desert" to let the escaping slaves know that the time had come. She then recited the words to Bradford:[14]

> Dark and thorny is de desert
> Through de pilgrims makes his ways;
> Yet beyon' dis vale of sorrow,
> Lie de fiel's of endless days.
>
> (Songwriter unknown, "Dark and Thorny Is the Desert," date unknown)

Frederick Douglass, born a slave, wrote that the hope of reaching Canaan or arriving in heaven also symbolized the dream of freedom: "A keen observer might have detected in our repeated singing of 'O Canaan, sweet Canaan, I am bound for the land of Canaan,' something more than a hope of reaching heaven. We meant to reach the North, and the North was our Canaan."[15]

Douglass also recounted his memory of spirituals when he was still a slave:

> They were tones, loud, long and deep, breathing the prayer and complaint of souls boiling over with the bitterest anguish. Every tone was a testimony against slavery, and a prayer to God for deliverance from chains. The hearing of those wild notes always depressed my spirits, and filled my heart with ineffable sadness.... To those songs I trace my first glimmering conceptions of the dehumanizing character of slavery. I can never get rid of that conception. Those songs still follow me, to deepen my hatred of slavery, and quicken my sympathies for my brethren in bonds.[16]

In addition to helping finance and run the Underground Railroad, some white abolitionists wrote lyrics, usually set to familiar hymns, to convince their fellow citizens of the evils of slavery. As more abolitionist societies formed in the first half of the nineteenth century, antislavery songs and sheet music reached a broader public. The Hutchinsons were New Hampshire natives who wrote songs in support of abolition, temperance, workers' rights, and women's rights:

> Liberty is our motto, Liberty is our motto
> Equal liberty is our motto from the Old Granite State
> We despise oppression, We despise oppression
> We despise oppression and we cannot be enslaved.
> (Hutchinson Family, "The Old Granite State," 1843)

They called themselves the Hutchinson Family Singers and traveled the country to sing their songs, mainly in the 1840s. One of their most popular abolition songs uses the contemporary image of the railroad to underscore the force behind the ending of slavery:

> Ho! the car Emancipation
> Rides majestic thro' the nation,
> Bearing on its train the story
> Liberty! A nation's glory.
> Roll it along, thro' the nation,
> Freedom's car, Emancipation!
>
> (Jesse Hutchinson, "Get Off the Track," 1844)

A decade later, Judson Joseph Hutchinson called on legislatures to end slavery so that former slaves could live with hope "this side of Jordan," but he also recognized how difficult the task would be in a continuing allusion to labor, borrowed perhaps from the work songs of the slaves: "Then take off coats and roll up sleeves, / O, Slavery is a hard foe to battle!" (Judson Joseph Hutchinson, "Slavery Is a Hard Foe to Battle," 1855).

Harriet Tubman made her own escape from slavery single-handedly. She needed to remain secretive, but she also needed to bid farewell to her family and friends. She used the hidden meaning of a well-known spiritual:

> I'll meet you in the mornin',
> I'm bound for de promised land,
> On the oder side of Jordan,
> Boun' for de promised land.
> (Songwriter unknown, "Boun' for de Promised Land," date unknown)

During her flight, when she realized that she had finally crossed the geographical line from bondage to freedom, she later said, "I looked to my hands to see if I was de same pusson. There was such a glory over ebery ting; de sun came like gold through the trees, and ober the fields, and I felt like I was in Heaben."[17] Within a few years, with help from abolitionists, she returned to the South again and again to lead small bands of slaves to freedom. As Bradford wrote, "Well has she been called 'Moses' for she has been a leader and deliverer unto hundreds of her people."[18]

Because Tubman needed to alert those she was rescuing that it was time for their escape, she sometimes sang "Boun' for De Promised Land." On other occasions, she used "Steal Away Home": "Steal away, steal away, steal away to Jesus / Steal away, steal away home / I ain't got long to stay here" (Songwriter unknown, "Steal Away to Jesus," date unknown). At still other times, her gathering song was "The Old Ship of Zion": "'Tis the old ship of Zion, / Get on board! Get on board!" (Songwriter unknown, "The Old Ship of Zion," date unknown).

Morning in these lyrics is metaphoric: a time of awakening and reawakening, reaching heaven or freedom. But the escaping slaves had to travel during the day. Giovanni writes, "A black man at night on the road was a dead man. The only way to run was during the day,"[19] from plantation to plantation, where other slaves would protect him overnight.

Work songs relied on their strong rhythmic drive to keep the men and women working steadily from dawn to dusk and as a way to avoid punishment. Their subject matter ranged widely: reminders of the homes they had lost, especially in the early days of slavery, and as a way to endure suffering and express anger and resistance through metaphor and allusion. In particular, the work songs of female slaves "centered around resistance and self-care. . . . [They] helped to pass down information about the lived experience of enslaved people to their communities and families."[20]

The subject of a work song doesn't always sound like an expression of protest, however guarded, but context matters. Corn was a frequent image in these songs because it was a staple of the slaves' diet. They sang about it year-round, but especially when planters would bring their harvested crops and their slaves to a single plantation for shucking, rolling logs, and threshing rice. These days were called corn-shucking jubilees. An ex-slave named William Wells Brown was the first to write down one of these call-and-response songs. The song accompanied the work done under the supervision of the overseer and his lash.[21] The lines of the call describe the pleasures of the day, while the repeated response reasserts the unceasing hard work that precedes them:

> All them pretty gals will be there,
> Shuck that corn before you eat;
> They will fix it for us rare,
> Shuck that corn before you eat.
> I know that supper will be big,
> Shuck that corn before you eat;
> I think I smell a fine roast pig,
> Shuck that corn before you eat.
>
> (Songwriter unknown, "Shuck That Corn Before You Eat," date unknown)

Work songs persisted after Emancipation because African Americans continued to perform arduous tasks for long hours. Once again, the songs helped to pace the labor while sending hidden messages that the overseers and bosses would not understand. Often, the songs were call-and-response, with a leader choosing a song to fit the work that needed doing and varying the rhythms and inventing new content. Tilford Brooks writes, "Improvisation is utilized extensively in Black folk songs that employ call-and-response pattern . . . the leader has license to improvise on the melody."[22] They are among America's first examples of improvisation, decades before jazz.

After the Civil War, prison workers, mostly Black, did the hard work that slaves had previously done. Prisons in the South leased them out for unpaid forced labor in mines and on railroads. They built the levees, labored on chain gangs, and toiled on huge plantation-like prison farms. You can hear the blues' sense of betrayal and its groans against oppression in a pre-blues song like "We Don't Have No Payday Now." A recording made by collector John A. Lomax at the Raiford Penitentiary in Florida includes beats for the labor, whether the striking of rocks or the chopping down of trees.[23]

A more daring song also performed by African American convicts in the South, "Take This Hammer," anticipated the widely known folk song "John Henry." After it emerged, probably in the 1870s, the words would change depending on the work the men were doing.[24] In every version, though, its protest appears in its crowing about escape:

> If he asks you was I runnin'
> Tell him I was flyin'
> Tell him I was flyin'.
>
> (Songwriter unknown, "Take This Hammer," 1870s?)

Not every blues-influenced song is a work song, but it's a natural linkage. Not every one of them laid out the rhythms for a long day of toil, but it still joined the sorrow and weariness of the blues with the miseries of forced labor. "I Heard What You Said About Me" complains not about slavery, but about false accusations and having to work in the mines, which usually had the worst working conditions. The lyrics are less about self-pity than a sense of oppression:

> I don't do nothin', Jesus
> But they hates me just the same . . .

> But somehow or other, O Lord,
> They 'bukes me jes' the same.
>
> (Songwriter unknown, "I Heard What You Said About Me," date unknown)

The link between spirituals and the blues may not appear obvious at first, but worry and heartbreak permeate both of them, as does an undertone of defiance. James H. Cone points to such spirituals as "Nobody Knows the Trouble I've Seen" and "Sometimes I Feel Like a Motherless Child" as precursors of what he calls the "worried blues."[25] Huddie Ledbetter, known as Leadbelly, wrote, "Blues was composed up by the Negro people when they was under slavery they was worried."[26] In effect, the blues consists of what C. Eric Lincoln calls "secular spirituals."[27] Both express the deep truth of African American experience, one during slavery, the other afterward—one seeking escape, liberty, and freedom, the other protesting against racial subjugation.

After Reconstruction ended in the 1870s, state governments in the South restored white supremacy and limited the rights of Black people, even though the Fourteenth Amendment affirmed their full citizenship. The police in the South routinely arrested African American men who were out of work. These "vagrants" spent years in prison separated from their families. The victim in "Worried Man Blues" wakes up one morning to find shackles on his legs. When he asks about his fine, the judge tells him, "Twenty-one years on the RC Mountain line." He explains as he tells his story, "It takes a worried man to sing a worried song" (Songwriter unknown, "Worried Man Blues," date unknown).

"The Bourgeois Blues," written and recorded by Leadbelly in 1937, rails against the discrimination he encountered as he traveled to Washington, D.C., and then in the Capitol when he arrived:

> Home of the brave, land of the free
> I don't wanna be mistreated by no bourgeoisie.
>
> (Leadbelly, "The Bourgeois Blues," 1937)

Unlike spirituals, which look to a heavenly reward as they cry out for escape from bondage, the blues focuses on this life, on the inescapability of history and memory, and the immediacy of Black experience, "the laments of folk

Negroes over hard luck, 'careless' or unrequited love, broken family life, or general dissatisfaction with a cold and trouble-filled life."[28]

The protest was rarely as outspoken as later folk singers such as Pete Seeger, Bob Dylan, and Joan Baez made it. It was a more personal response to suppression.[29] The blues singer John Lee Hooker explained, "It's not that I had the hardships that a lot of people had throughout the South and other cities throughout the country. . . . It's not only what happened to you—it's what happened to your foreparents and other people. And that's what makes the blues."[30]

Often disguised as a lament for lost or betrayed love, the blues' depth of loss becomes the cry of an oppressed people. Rather than being sung by groups of workers in the fields or mines, the blues is the unrelenting call of a single individual. The playwright and poet Amiri Baraka writes, "The blues was conceived by freedmen and ex-slaves—if not as a result of a personal or intellectual experience, at least as an emotional confirmation of, and reaction to, the way in which most Negroes were still forced to exist in the United States."[31] He's speaking about the blues in totality, but each blues bears witness; it is an implicit protest regardless of subject matter. How do we understand the blues without rooting it in African American identity and survival? It is about lost love but also *appears* to be about lost love. The surface shifts as the dramatic but mournful quality of the blue notes makes each blues distinctive yet communal.

Bearing witness in the blues can also take form as a combination of defiance and affirmation. In 1927, Gertrude "Ma" Rainey wrote and performed "Prove It on Me," a blues song that leaves no doubt about her sexuality. An undercurrent of humor only strengthens her insistence that she be seen for who she is. It is an assertion of identity that refuses to bow the head or bend the knee. It crows in self-awareness and acceptance:

> They say I do it, ain't nobody caught me
> Sure got to prove it on me;
> Went out last night with a crowd of my friends,
> They must've been women, 'cause I don't like no men.
> (Gertrude "Ma" Rainey, "Prove It on Me," 1927)

Even when professional songwriters wrote the blues, they sometimes feel unpolished, even raw. Clarence Williams was a traveling vaudevillian, music publisher, and songwriter. He was something of a wheeler-dealer, but he once explained how he first grasped what the blues is: "Why, I'd never have written the blues if I had been white," he said. He had been lying in a swamp in Louisiana, hiding for hours from white men who were trying to track him down. He said, "I began to hum a tune—you know like this. . . . Jes as blue as a tree—an old willow tree—nobody 'round here, just nobody but me."[32] And so began a blues as a spontaneous emotional response to a moment in a life recognizable to so many others.

Professional performers of the blues first appeared in significant numbers in the 1920s. This is the decade when the subject matter of the blues broadened. It became a national music by becoming a performance music. In its defining combination of despair and protest, the blues exposes the tribulations of life. In Blind Lemon Jefferson's "Tin Cup Blues," you can hear the anger beneath the despair:

> I stood on the corner and almost bust my head.
> I couldn't earn enough money to buy me a loaf of bread.
> 
> (Blind Lemon Jefferson, "Tin Cup Blues," 1929)

Nothing in the blues is more insistent than the refusal to let the world break your spirit. Somehow, hope survives and, at times, flourishes for a passing moment. You never let go of it as you face the past, present, and future, sometimes with a caustic sense of humor:

> People is ravin' 'bout hard times, I don't know why they should.
> If some people was like me, they didn't have no money when times was good.
> 
> (Lonnie Johnson, "Hard Times Ain't Gone Nowhere," date unknown)

At the same time, the blues sung by professional performers appealed more to white people because the subject matter was more familiar and often more concrete than singing about hard times. It re-created the experience of both Black and white people. The African American songwriter Porter Grainger, best known for "'Tain't Nobody's Business If I Do," also wrote the double-entendre blues, "Put It Right Here (Or Keep It Out There)," recorded by Bessie Smith[33] in 1928, although it was probably written earlier in the decade:

He must get it, and bring it, and put it right here,
Or else he's goin' to keep it out there.

(Porter Grainger, "Put It Right There
[Or Keep It Out There]," 1922?)

The blues singer Mamie Smith's recording of Perry Bradford's "Crazy Blues" is an essential work of American popular song. More than any single work, it established the blues as a national American music, appealing to Black and white people alike (although some whites always found Black music objectionable). David Hajdu says, correctly, that it "prepared the way for a century of Black expression in the fiery core of American music."[34]

Bradford and Smith entered a New York studio on August 10, 1920, to record "Crazy Blues." Some say that it was the first song by an African American heard on a recording.[35] In fact, the public had first become aware of the blues in the previous decade, and singers had recorded many songs with the word "blues" in the title, whether or not the song was actually a blues. But Smith's recording of "Crazy Blues" was the first true blues to become a major success. Bradford also claimed that his revue, *Made in Harlem*, was the first stage production to perform the blues for Northern white audiences.[36] Bradford wrote other songs that were momentarily popular, but none of them became standards; his name is largely forgotten.

In the space of a month, "Crazy Blues" sold seventy-five thousand copies. Sales eventually reached an estimated two million. Black families gave the 78-rpm disc pride of place in their living rooms. For the first time, recording companies began to release songs and performances directed at an African American audience.[37] Yet the song's power does not emerge from reading the lyrics; except for a very few lines, they do not prepare you for what you hear on Smith's recording (Perry Bradford, "Crazy Blues," 1920).

The song lands somewhere between a traditional and an urban blues. Its structure is a variation on a typical Tin Pan Alley tune, complete with a repeated melody in each of the choruses plus a release (*AABA*). At the same time, it's a good deal longer than a typical 32-bar popular song of the day. It begins with the conventional subject of a blues: a woman bemoaning the departure of the low-down man she loves:

> I can't sleep at night
> I can't eat a bite
> 'Cause the man I love
> He don't treat me right.

Not until the sixth stanza does the desperate woman turn in a darker direction that combines her sense of betrayal with deepening rage:

> Now the doctor's gonna do all that he can
> But what you're gonna need is an undertaker man
> I ain't got nothin' but bad news
> Now I got the crazy blues.

She even considers suicide, but her anger saves her in the song's troubling conclusion:

> I'm gonna do like a Chinaman
> Go and get some hop
> Get myself a gun, and shoot myself a cop
> I ain't got nothin' but bad news
> Now I've got the crazy blues.

Hajdu argues that Smith's recording is a "boisterous cry of outrage" aimed at Black listeners who had been "ravaged by race-hate groups, the police, and military forces during the preceding year—the notorious 'Red Summer' of 1919."[38] It's widely understood by now that the blues, ostensibly about lost love, is actually a cry of protest by an oppressed people. It uses, in Hajdu's words, "the language of domestic strife to tell a story of violence and subjugation"[39] that African Americans understood all too well.

In the decade after Mamie Smith's recording, a new generation of blues singers emerged. Most of the great ones were female, and their songs often reflected the ways in which many African Americans had become city dwellers rather than field hands. When Black people moved North, they took their music with them. The traditional blues became the urban blues. The betrayal of love and the misery it causes would always be central, but the blues also reinvented itself in a new time and place. Sung by such women as Gertrude "Ma" Rainey, Bessie Smith, Trixie Smith, Ida Cox, young Ethel Waters, and younger Alberta Hunter, it became both defiant and bawdy. These women expected good sex from their daddies. They also expected to be treated as equals.

# 7

# The Mingling of Black and White

Using the blues for protest wasn't limited to African Americans. As the blues became a national music and then the Great Depression threw people out of work, hoboes rode the rails, and desperate people sought work as migrant workers in California. Woody Guthrie grew up in rural Oklahoma and spent much of his life on the road, exploring the city streets and country lanes across the nation. He felt a strong bond with those who lost everything in the Dust Bowl that struck the Southern Plains, also during the 1930s. "The Talking Dust Bowl Blues" was among the Dust Bowl Ballads he wrote to report what he had seen and affirm that kinship. It combines a rambling first-person narrative about an Okie family moving West, their rhythmic speech slathered with irony. With an eye on the "mighty thin stew" his wife prepares for the family, Guthrie wonders if it had been any thinner:

> Some of these here politicians
> Coulda seen through it.
>
> (Woody Guthrie, "Talking Dust Bowl Blues," 1940)

Christopher Allen Bouchillon wrote the first talking blues in 1926. It begins, "Well, if you want to get to heaven, / Let me tell you what to do, / Got to grease your feet into little mutton stew" (Christopher Allen Bouchillon, "Talking Blues," 1926). Folk singers soon found that the form's strong rhythm, rolling melody, clear narrative line, and humorous commentary made it easily adaptable to many different causes. Guthrie was one of the first to see its potential. He wrote eleven different talking blues.

During the unsettled years at the end of the Second World War, five years after Guthrie's "Talking Dust Bowl Blues," millions of troops returned home, manufacturing switched back to peacetime goods, workers struck for higher wages, the cost of living increased, and people felt anxious about nuclear power, the beginnings of the Cold War, and Communist infiltrators at home. In such a world, Americans endured a surge of antisemitic and racist feeling. In a blues song entitled "Black, Brown and White" by Big Bill Broonzy, the character recognizes the discrimination, mainly in the workplace:

> Me and a man was working side by side . . .
> They was payin' him a dollar an hour,
> They was payin' me fifty cents.
> 
> (Big Bill Broonzy, "Black, Brown and White," 1945)

Most of the song is a loose narrative that recounts the character's experience. He reminds his white listener that he helped to build the country and "fought for it too." He seems to be running out of patience as he concludes with a confrontation: "Now I want you to tell me, brother, / What you goin' to do about the old Jim Crow?"

Tin Pan Alley abutted the Tenderloin, a raffish area on the West Side of Manhattan where most Black New Yorkers lived in poverty at the turn of the twentieth century, along with pockets of Irish, German, and Jewish immigrants. It ran roughly from West 24th Street to West 53rd Street and from Sixth Avenue to Ninth, and it was one tough neighborhood. A police department captain named A. S. "Clubber" Williams gave it its name in 1876, when he was transferred there. Anticipating a shower of payoff money, he said, "I've been having chuck steak ever since I've been on the force, and now I'm going to have a bit of tenderloin."[1]

The Tenderloin especially attracted African American composers, lyricists, and performers to the Black-owned Hotel Marshall, where they lived or hung out to talk about their own futures and the future of African American music. Their conversations may have been about show business, but they were setting out to undermine the supremacy of white people. It was a radical protest as cleverly disguised as the message of spirituals that it was time to escape North. They saw ragtime as the key. Without fully realizing it, they were also laying the foundation for the next century of American popular song. They served the country so well that syncopation became the hallmark of songs linked to New York in the first half of the twentieth century. These were syncopated ballads. The Marshall was also the place where white women met their African American lovers.²

All through the Tenderloin ran a perpetual party of pimps, hookers, songwriters, and entertainers in juke joints, saloons, and cabarets. Audiences feasted on ragtime as the composers, lyricists, and performers built on an authentic African American music—not white ideas about music from minstrel shows, but something truly their own. And then the Alleymen borrowed what they heard coming from the Tenderloin's bars and clubs where African Americans performed. They were the translators to an eager American public.

Irish and Jewish songwriters led the way in Tin Pan Alley. Their grandparents and parents, and sometimes they themselves, were part of a great cultural shift that turned such immigrants and their offspring, from George M. Cohan to Irving Berlin, into deeply committed patriots whose loyalty took form in songs. America was becoming a Melting Pot or a stew; take your pick. And now there was room for the zest added by African Americans. The nineteenth century's sentimental ballad had become a moldy fig.

Ragtime was irresistible. How could you not drum the tabletop and shrug your shoulders—first this one and then the other—to the percussive beat of a piano and the syncopation in the tune? The first time that Duke Ellington heard the great ragtime and stride piano player, Willie "the Lion" Smith, he suddenly realized that "everybody and everything seemed to be doing whatever they were doing in the tempo the Lion's group was laying down. . . . The waiters served in that tempo; everybody who had to walk in or out, or around the place, walked with a beat."³

White people got one of their first tastes of mingling with African Americans as musicians and singers performed the first popular Black music since the colossally inauthentic minstrel shows that were finally dying out in the new century. The music that audiences heard was largely European in origin. At the same time, its themes, sentiments, and diction were American, while its instruments—the banjo, the fiddle, and the bones—were African American.⁴ Minstrel shows were so popular for so long because they gave white audiences a look at what Black people were "really" like, even though the performers were white people in blackface. With their songs and broad comedy, minstrel shows persuaded white people who had little exposure to African Americans that Black people were basically different and probably inferior. Stereotypes of African Americans as lazy, dishonest, and ignorant ran riot on the minstrel shows' many stages.[5] Companies abounded in large cities while smaller touring troupes would arrive for a night or a week in any town large enough to have its own theater. Ironically, minstrelsy's continuing popularity for nearly a half century after Emancipation gave African American songwriters and performers opportunities they might otherwise not have had. The shows, writes Saidiya Hartman, shaped an image of blackness that "aroused pity and fear, desire and revulsion, and terror and pleasure."[6] They reconfirmed the paradox of race in America within the safe confinements of performances by Black people who were actually white people in blackface. They made the contradictions palatable and reassuring.

Black songwriters wrote echoes of minstrel songs and cranked out blatantly racist "coon songs." Black performers borrowed some of the trappings of minstrelsy because white audiences recognized and liked them. Yet these songwriters and entertainers were also introducing Black rhythms and ways of syncopating and singing that were their own—in the Tenderloin, eventually the Broadway theater, and later during the Harlem Renaissance in the 1920s and 1930s. Ragtime, early jazz, and the first professionally written blues were recasting American popular music. At the same time, some Black performers added spirituals to their performances—genuine African American songs for largely white audiences.

While all this was happening, white audiences were also embracing jazz by turning it into a white music. "Real jazz was hot and unapologetically sexual,"[7] writes James Kaplan. Much of what passed for "white jazz" cooled down the temperature. Such white musicians as Bix Beiderbecke, Eddie Lang, and Frank Trumbauer aligned themselves with Black jazz musicians, but Paul Whiteman's Orchestra and the Original Dixieland Jazz Band played little that resembled the real thing. Whiteman argued in favor of jazz, but he played a sweet, watered-down version that was easy to dance to. He thought his brand of music would be the jazz of the future. The emergence of swing in the 1930s, played most successfully by such white bands as Benny Goodman, Artie Shaw, and Woody Herman, suggests that he had a point. The all-Black bands of Fletcher Henderson, Duke Ellington, Jimmie Lunceford, and Count Basie suggest that the mix was more complex than Whiteman anticipated. For his famous 1938 Carnegie Hall concert, Goodman augmented his band with sidemen from Duke Ellington's band: an integrated band of white and Black musicians playing together in the 1930s.

People liked what African Americans first called "jass" even if they didn't exactly know what it was, just as the Original Dixieland Jass Band didn't exactly play it either. No matter; the ODJB was the first popular "jazz band," partly because the musicians were white people and partly because their style, unusual for the time, persuaded people that it was the sound of the real thing. Nick LaRocca, who was the leader and played cornet, claimed that the band was the first to make *commercial* jazz records, including "Tiger Rag" and "Livery Stable Blues" in 1917. It was the first jazz (or pseudo-jazz) record ever released. Their recordings were so popular that the ODJB soon began to call itself the Creators of Jazz, as if the music that Black musicians first created in New Orleans was irrelevant, as if such musicians as Jelly Roll Morton, King Oliver, and Louis Armstrong didn't matter. A few months before the record's release, the band opened at Reisenweber's "400 Club" Café on West 58th Street in Manhattan. One reviewer devoted one sentence to what he heard: "Its weird music must be heard to be appreciated."[8]

By the late 1890s, Blacks had begun to appear in otherwise all-white vaudeville, although they had to wear the blackface that white audiences expected. Some of them pushed harder against the stereotypes than others. One of the first successful examples of understated but determined undermining of minstrelsy's requirements was the all-Black *The Creole Show*, a revue from 1890. It looked like a minstrel show, but the performers did not wear blackface and some of them were women, a departure from two of minstrelsy's sturdiest conventions. The women in the cast were attractive and elegantly costumed and were treated in a dignified way.[9]

African American songwriters had to navigate an ever-shifting line. By the 1920s, they were free to identify themselves as Black people or let the sheet music and recordings stand on their own. The first was a matter of pride and identity, but the second gave a song a better chance for success. The goal was to have a popular white singer record a new song, someone like Marion Harris, because she was popular and had a feel for jazz and the blues. In 1916, she became the first to record the Black songwriters Spencer Williams and Roger A. Graham's "I Ain't Got Nobody (Much and Nobody Cares for Me)."

At the turn of the twentieth century, a number of African Americans thrived on Broadway before Jim Crow sent nearly all of them packing. Intentionally or not, they performed a patriotic task despite the different kinds of songs they wrote. They also protested against the limitations imposed on African Americans by the Broadway theater. Marvin McAllister provides context: "After performing in blackface minstrel companies, vaudeville houses, and colored road shows controlled by white producers, most Negro artists had a definite idea of what America's class- and race-coded theatrical industry had to offer them."[10]

Virtually no Black people wrote or performed on Broadway between 1910 and 1920, with the exception of the *Ziegfeld Follies* star Bert Williams. Williams and his songwriting and performing partner George Walker worked in the early years of the new century along with composer Will Marion Cook, composer Bob Cole, lyricist James Weldon Johnson, and composer and lyricist J. Rosamond Johnson. At the same time, the composer and conductor James Reese Europe appeared everywhere from Carnegie Hall to the Sans Souci, a nightclub where its founders, the dancers Vernon and Irene Castle, performed. These men endured racism but found an outlet in protest expressed subtly and indirectly; they knew what they were doing. They entertained white audiences while affirming Black identity and the value of Black music in the songs they wrote and performed. They tried to narrow the gap between Black and white people by demonstrating the American-ness of African American song.

The major compromises they had to make in the kinds of songs they wrote and performed gave them access to Broadway but also diminished the effect of their songs. They had to be both daring and cautious. It was a fine line to walk. The more familiar to white people the language and style was, the more popular their songs were and the harder it became to make their larger point. This tricky balancing act that began with all-Black minstrel shows after

Emancipation lasted for decades to come. When white minstrel companies refused to hire Black people, African Americans formed their own companies, complete with blackface. As always, it's hard to talk about race in America without a sense of irony.

Modernism and industrialism shaped the early years of the twentieth century as millions of new immigrants arrived to transform American identity. The nation's assumptions about race, class, and modernity changed (or at least were challenged) in the hands of those African American composers, lyricists, and singers who had the creativity and savvy to argue for what was new. They worked everywhere, from rowdy joints where they sang the blues to Broadway theaters.[11] Americans were working out a revolution of sorts as Black composers drew upon the Black music that preceded them. They found something alive and authentic in it. In the process, ragtime became the sound of African American modernity, and white dancers happily shook their shoulders as they followed along.

After having trouble finding work as a classically trained African American violinist, Will Marion Cook decided to write for the popular theater. From that point on, he borrowed European harmonies for his blending of ragtime with slave melodies. David Gilbert writes, "Cook imagined one of the first American fusions of the arts—and anticipated an entire twentieth century of American music making."[12] He chose ragtime because he believed that its roots lay in African American life and music. His success opened Broadway to more Black performers, helped to make this modern music commercially appealing to white audiences, and led to a new acceptance of Black music across the culture. He said that the music's ragged quality—a way of describing its heavy use of syncopation—"offered unique rhythms, curious groupings of words and melodies which gave the zest of unexpectedness."[13]

He and the African American poet and lyricist Paul Laurence Dunbar collaborated on their first show in 1898. *Clorindy, or the Origin of the Cakewalk* grew from Cook's idea to dramatize the history of the African American dance, the cakewalk, which flourished on Southern plantations in the mid-nineteenth century as a mockery of the dancing styles of the white gentry and their ladies.

The two men wrote the entire score in a single ten-hour session, including such "coon songs" as "Darktown Is Out Tonight," "Hottest Coon in Dixie," and "Who Dat Say Chicken in Dis Crowd." When Cook's mother heard the songs they had written, she was distraught. "Oh, Will! Will!" she cried. "I've sent you all over the world to study and become a great musician and you return such a nigger!"[14] Neither of his college-educated, middle-class parents understood what he was setting out to do. He had come to believe that ragtime was the direct descendant of call-and-response spirituals. It was, he thought, an authentic African American music waiting to be discovered by a national audience. His success on Broadway helped to make it happen.

Yet Mrs. Cook was on to something. Her son's theater scores consisted largely of ragtime songs, many of which were also "coon songs." African Americans detested them, but white audiences loved them. With the best of intentions, Cook wrote songs that sought to create an authentic Black music in America but also promoted the grotesque distortions of minstrelsy. That paradox appeared and reappeared in the work of early African American composers and lyricists, and also helps to understand the dilemma of freed slaves who founded their own Black minstrel companies. In her splendid book about Stephen Foster's "My Old Kentucky Home," Emily Bingham refers often to what she calls the "authentically inauthentic." She is referring to white songwriters like Foster, who wrote for white performers in blackface to sing for minstrel shows' white audiences.

When Cook could not find a producer for *Clorindy*, he approached Isadore Witmark, a major song publisher, and offered to give him publication rights to all the songs in the score if he would help him find one. Witmark told him he was mad to think that a white Broadway audience would want to hear Blacks perform songs by Black songwriters.[15] Undeterred, Cook got some help from the white orchestra conductor at the Casino Roof Garden, the first of many rooftop theaters in the days before air-conditioning. The audition arranged by the conductor was successful.

*Clorindy*, with a cast of twenty-six African Americans, opened on July 5, 1898. Gerald Bordman calls it "the first full-length musical written and played by Blacks to be performed at a major Broadway house."[16] It wowed its white audience. When the first performance began, about fifty people were in the seats. When the audience members downstairs were leaving the main show, they heard the singing on the roof and raced up to see what it was. By the end of the opening chorus, the house was full, and the audience rose for a ten-minute ovation[17]—at a time when standing ovations were still something you had to earn. Cook said later with some irony, "Negroes at last were on Broadway and there to stay.... We were artists and we were going a long way. ... Nothing could stop us and nothing did for a decade."[18]

Before *Clorindy*, only white writers of musical books and songs created Black stage characters. Everything was secondhand, as inauthentic as minstrel shows. Another Black theater composer, Bob Cole, wanted to compete with white songwriters by showing that Black people could successfully write the same kinds of songs, but Cook believed that they should create their own style. Yet Cook also wrote "coon songs" because audiences demanded them. On one hand, Cook advanced the cause of Black people in Broadway theater by demonstrating that an African American could write the kinds of songs that white people successfully wrote. At the same time, he also tried to develop an authentic African American music deriving from spirituals and ragtime. If writing "coon songs" was the price he had to pay, then so be it.

*In Dahomey* was Cook and Dunbar's most important show together. Despite its brief run of only fifty-eight performances, it drew enthusiastic audiences. Despite its historical importance, the score included "coon songs," among them "Dat Gal of Mine" and "When Sousa Comes to Coontown." Bert Williams played a character named Shylock Homestead and introduced a third "coon song," "The Jonah Man." The Jonah Man soon became the sympathetic comic character that Williams created onstage for the rest of his career. In some ways, the compromises were paying off.

Bob Cole's protest was a little more direct than Cook's. At first, though, he wanted to compete directly with white songwriters. Between the late 1890s and his eventual death (possibly suicide) from tertiary syphilis in 1911, Cole was one of the most important composers for all-Black Broadway musicals. In 1900, Cole, James Weldon Johnson, and J. Rosamond Johnson wrote a song for the notorious "coon shouter," May Irwin. It was exactly the kind of song that they would eventually refuse to write:

Bein' a convenience for dese dead broke coons will put me on de shelf
I'm gwine to cultivate other 'sociates so I can borrow, now and then, myself.
(Bob Cole, J. W. Johnson, and Rosamond Johnson,
"I've Got Troubles of My Own," 1900)

In 1898, before Cole began to write with the Johnsons, he and fellow songwriter Billy Johnson wrote and produced *A Trip to Coontown*, Cole's first major work on Broadway and the first New York musical written, performed, and directed by African Americans. The score included such titles as "The Christening of a Little Black Coon," "The Wedding of the Chinee and the Coon," and "A Coontown Frolic."

The musical's book also relied on stereotypes that dated back to minstrelsy. The story wasn't much: Jimmy Flimflammer tries to con an old man out of his pension and fails. The show had trouble opening because the white men who controlled Broadway had the power to blacklist any writer or performer. Trying to keep the show alive, Cole and Johnson took it to a number of lesser theaters around the country. They were then boycotted in New York because they had produced the show on their own. Finally, one of the major theater bookers in New York City opened *A Trip to Coontown* at the Third Avenue Theater. Cole and Johnson's determination to stick with it is sufficient to call *A Trip to Coontown* an act of protest.

Although the original manuscript disappeared years ago, some of the songs survive. One in particular, "The Wedding of the Chinee and the Coon," demonstrates the kind of racist song that Cole and Billy Johnson were willing to write, but it also goes to the heart of the protest. The tongue-in-cheek lyric anticipates the problems in the relationships between the bride and groom and their families. They quarrel over whether to use a Chinese or Black clergyman to perform the ceremony, and an African American cuts off the queue of the Chinese preacher. Yet the end of the song holds out the possibility of more interracial marriages in the future.

This is a daring song in its way. Krystyn R. Moon, David Krasner, and Thomas L. Riis write, "To address interracial marriage in a period when African American men were lynched for merely looking at European American women, 'The Wedding of the Chinee and the Coon' is a bold political statement that celebrates a future where interracial marriage is commonplace."[19] Getting there would be a struggle:

> This strange amalgamation twixt
> These two funny nations
> gwine to cause an awful jumble soon
> Twill cause a great sensation
> over the whole creation
> The wedding of the Chinee and the Coon.
> (Bob Cole and Billy Johnson, "The Wedding of the Chinee and the Coon,"
> *A Trip to Chinatown*, 1898)

Cole soon became known for "his theatrical skills, comedic gifts, dancing ability, and directorial savvy."[20] After 1899, he collaborated with the two brothers who wrote the lyrics to most of his melodies, James Weldon Johnson, better known later as a poet, social critic, and activist, and J. Rosamond Johnson, who was also a composer. Cole sometimes collaborated with one, sometimes the other, sometimes both. In addition to their work for Broadway, the Johnsons are best known for "Lift Every Voice and Sing," which eventually became known as the Black national anthem. Cole and the Johnsons wrote more than 150 songs together.

The threesome eventually set out to change depictions of African Americans by eliminating the demeaning content of "coon songs" and restoring dignity to African Americans. White producers knew what sold tickets, and white audiences responded to the old insulting tropes, but Cole also wanted to attract a more broad-minded audience. He also knew that the African American audiences for whom they sometimes performed had grown sick and tired of what Thomas L. Riis calls "the grotesque stereotypes."[21]

After writing so many successful songs but having limited success with their own attempts to write and stage Broadway shows, Cole and Rosamond Johnson returned to vaudeville. They appeared in formal evening wear as they portrayed young men about town on their way to a party. They turned completely away from songs that featured Black men with hidden razors. Riis writes, "The directness and wit of [Cole's] early songs contrast markedly with the suave, cute, but un-'cooney' lyrics and polished, harmonically rich textures of his songs written in the decade following 1899."[22]

James Weldon Johnson described "coon songs" as "crude, raucous, bawdy, [and] obscene."[23] He, his brother, and Cole were determined to change that, but they still relied on widely acceptable dialect as they substituted "dat" for that and "ribber" for river. In 1901, they were still writing:

> Now aint dat scan'lous!
> For to act dat way!
> Now ain't dat awful!
> Well I should say!
>
> (Rosamond Johnson, Bob Cole, and J. W. Johnson,<br>"Ain't Dat Scan'lous," 1901)

They refused to use the most egregious stereotypes as they turned to more romantic songs and sometimes wrote in defiance of the widely held assumption that African Americans were incapable of what white Americans thought of as the higher emotions. That kind of song by African American songwriters was, in itself, an act of protest.

A more direct protest appears in Cole and James Weldon Johnson's "Gimme de Leavin's," performed by Bert Williams (Bob Cole and James Weldon Johnson, "Gimme the Leavin's," 1904). It is an important example of a Jonah song. A Jonah Man is the unluckiest person in the world. No matter what he tries, it backfires. Because the Jonah Man in songs is almost always a Black person, these apparently racist songs become a shrewd but careful commentary on white people and their view of African Americans. An audience might think it's just another "coon song" unless it listens carefully.

The narrator describes his circumstances with a subdued sense of humor that never points directly to the oppression that lies beneath it—oppression dating back to slavery and continuing through Jim Crow: "Somehow the good things, all run out before they get to me." He's aware of the irony, but he feels perplexed because he dare not show anger: "The stronger I reach for a thing, the farther it gits away." If an opportunity comes along, "den, as usual, it pass me by." Throughout the song, the character speaks about himself, but in the chorus, he turns to his amused white listeners. In comic terms, he accepts his plight and what appears to be his destiny: "Gimme de leavin's," he tells them, "when you get through."

Cole wrote his most famous and longest-lasting song with J. Rosamond Johnson in 1902. It first appeared as an interpolation in an otherwise-while

Broadway musical, *Sally in Our Alley*. Forty years after that, Judy Garland and Margaret O'Brien revived it for a cakewalk in *Meet Me in St. Louis* in 1944 (Bob Cole and J. Rosamond Johnson, "Under the Bamboo Tree," *Sally in Our Alley*, 1902).

The song's structure is simple and familiar: verse, chorus, second verse, repeat chorus, and so on. Johnson's verses tell a story without dialect and in fairly formal rhetoric. Even so, it's a coon song because the story is essentially comic and concerns natives in the jungle, a way to suggest African Americans' lack of civilization. The Zulu, after all, lives in a place with the nonsensical name of Matabooloo. To make the maid "of royal blood though dusky shade" only added to the comedy when it was new:

> Down in the jungle lived a maid
> Of royal blood though dusky shade,
> A marked impression once she made
> Upon a Zulu from Matabooloo;
> And ev'ry morning he would be
> Down underneath a bamboo tree,
> Awaiting there, his love to see.

In the chorus, Johnson writes in a mock native dialect that relates it to a "coon song." Its invented talk, bordering on the nonsensical, also mocks the racist dialect that "coon" characters speak: "I lak-a say, this very day, / I lak-a change your name."

# 8

# African Americans, Acts of Desegregation

James Reese Europe was a patriot. He was determined to create an authentic African American music to give expression to his race in ways that all Americans would accept. During his short lifetime, he was instrumental in moving the country toward an acceptance of African American performers and music. He succeeded in a white world without having to imitate popular song styles created by white writers and performers or present himself as a Black caricature. He brought a level of dignity to his place as the conductor of all-Black symphonic bands and as the musical director for the elegant dancers Vernon and Irene Castle, among the most famous entertainers of their day. The country was also aware of his service in the First World War. Six months after he and his military band had returned from fighting in the trenches for nearly two hundred days, a disgruntled musician stabbed him in the neck after a May 1919 audition. By the next day, he was dead at the age of thirty-eight.

As accomplished as he was, his life was more a matter of promise than achievement. He would almost certainly have become a major shaper of jazz in the 1920s and beyond. He had already played an essential role in the spread of ragtime by including it in concerts by the Clef Club Society Orchestra. What itinerant Black piano players had begun in St. Louis in the 1890s became an all-American music, thanks in important ways to Europe. He held out the same promise for jazz as well as for African American composers of symphonic music. Europe was not a man to be pigeonholed.

Born in Mobile, Alabama, in 1881 and raised in Washington, D.C., Europe moved to New York City when he was twenty-three. By 1912, he had formed the Clef Club, a social and professional organization for Black musicians. He soon formed an orchestra of more than one hundred members of the club and championed serious African American composers, including Harry Burleigh and Samuel Coleridge-Taylor. He also responded directly to criticism by asserting his determination to play music his own way: "We colored people have our own music that is part of us. It's the product of our souls; it's been created by the sufferings and miseries of our race."[1] A newspaper reviewer wrote, "He has been able to accomplish what white musicians said was impossible: the adaptation of negro music and musicians to symphonic purposes."[2] Twenty-six years before Benny Goodman's fabled 1938 jazz concert at Carnegie Hall, the Clef Club Orchestra gave several concerts on the Carnegie stage. He named the series "A Concert of Negro Music." With a mixed audience of Black and white people, the performances by 125 musicians were influential, even revolutionary, in their time. They faced down the status quo in American music (and American life) by letting the music speak for itself.

"The concert," David Gilbert wrote, "was to be a political act of desegregation, a cultural intervention into the sound and meaning of American music."[3] It didn't include jazz, but it moved in that direction. The composer, conductor, musician, and author Gunther Schuller wrote that Europe's Carnegie Hall concerts "had stormed the bastion of the white establishment and made many members of New York's cultural elite aware of Negro music for the first time."[4]

Neither the Clef Club Orchestra nor the Clef Club Society Orchestra was an early jazz outfit. They were large symphonic ensembles that drew white audiences who liked the music of such bandmasters as John Philip Sousa and Arthur Pryor. By the end of 1913, the Castles had become so impressed by Europe's Society Orchestra that they hired both Europe and his Orchestra as their exclusive accompanists, the sort of thing that was unheard of at the time.

Douglas Gilbert called Vernon "astonished, first at Europe's rhythms, then at the instrumental color of his band."[5] The Castles were elegant white dancers, he in a tuxedo and she often in light blue chiffon as they whirled to the music of a formally attired all-Black orchestra. Suddenly, Europe stood in the forefront of African American musicians. In 1913 and 1914, he and the Orchestra made a series of recordings for Victor, probably the first recordings of instrumentals by an African American orchestra and certainly the first to play music by African American composers.[6]

Europe and his band played an essential part in moving ragtime from the brothel to the bandstand, and from the saloon to the concert hall. New Yorkers especially—Black and white people alike—came to see ragtime as "a symbol of American urbanity and cosmopolitan U.S. modernity."[7] This up-to-date music pulsated with freshness and verve. The public's pulse beat to its off-center syncopation. Black musicians heard ragtime as the sound of American modernity, while many white audiences saw it as nothing more than a pleasurably thrilling form of African American primitivism.[8]

Europe wrote several syncopated numbers for the Castles to dance to and in the process change America, including the first fad for dieting among American women. The day of the hourglass figure was over. Collaborating with the ragtime pianist, composer, and arranger Ford Dabney, Europe wrote "The Castle Walk," "Castle Half and Half," and "The Castle House Trot," among others (all in 1914), as the Castles tamed the tango and danced the one-step, foxtrot, and maxixe.

During the First World War, Europe joined the 369th Infantry Regiment as bandmaster. In addition to leading the regimental band, the "Harlem Hellfighters," he, along with the band's members, saw combat. By then, the unit had been seconded to the French army because white doughboys did not want to fight next to them.[9] When the band played for British, French, and American troops, they often included such syncopated numbers as "The Memphis Blues" (W. C. Handy and George A. Norton, "The Memphis Blues," 1912). Noble Sissle, who later collaborated with Eubie Blake on the essential all-Black musical *Shuffle Along*, was a musician in that band for a while. He said later that it "started ragtimitis in France."[10]

By the end of the war, the word "ragtime" had fallen out of favor back home, only to be replaced by what many thought of as a new name for the same thing, "jazz." It wasn't, but in the band's European performances, the musicians made small changes to the arrangements to make them more immediate, more jazz-like—smears, slurs, syncopation, blue notes, changes in rhythm, and most importantly, improvisation in the breaks.[11] Europe was encouraging; he was edging up to jazz. As Gunther Schuller puts it in *Early Jazz*: "The music had a rough excitement and rhythmic momentum that simply carried its audience along physically.... Europe could take a polite salon piece and make it swing—in a rudimentary sort of way."[12]

After returning to the States in 1919, Europe said, "I have come from France more firmly convinced than ever that Negroes should write Negro music.... If we are to develop in America, we must develop along our own lines."[13] His postwar recordings were a departure from what he and the Orchestra had played before they went to France. In his later recordings, you can hear the influence of the blues and early jazz, especially in his version of the jazz instrumental "Clarinet Marmalade" (Larry Shields and Henry Ragas, "Clarinet Marmalade," 1918).

Unlike H. E. Krehbiel, music editor of the *New York Tribune*, Europe did not believe that that the "soul of black folks" was stuck in the past, unable to move forward. But he argued that "to write real negro music" in the present, "a negro must live with negroes. He must think and feel as they do," so the music "breathes the spirit of a race." This, he believed, was the source of its authenticity.[14] Gilbert adds, "As Europe maneuvered between the often-contradictory mandates of his audiences, he transformed black performance from a marginalized and largely stereotypical form of entertainment into a symbol of modern American culture."[15]

The trickster plays a role in cultures all over the world: Anansi the spider for the Ashanti people in what is now Ghana, the monkey in places as far apart as India and South America, and rabbits—both Br'er Rabbit and Bugs Bunny—in the United States. They bring the spirit of antic comedy, mockery, hyperbole, and truth-telling to outwit foes who are stronger and more powerful than themselves. They live by their wits and triumph at least for now. They must always be on their guard. And that takes us to Bert Williams, the great star of the early *Ziegfeld Follies* and probably the only African American to perform on Broadway between 1910 and 1921. It took his popularity and Florenz Ziegfeld's *chutzpah* to pull it off. Williams appeared as a leading figure in eight editions of the *Follies* between 1910 and 1919.

There Williams stood, a "darkey" trickster outfitted like a blacked-up clown, wearing a ragged coat, pants above his ankles, white gloves, oversized shoes, and a battered top hat. He appeared with fellow performer and songwriter George Walker until Walker took ill in 1909. The two men believed that only they and other African Americans could trade in blackness authentically by "grounding black performance in black bodies."[16] Yet they also adopted the manners of minstrelsy as a way of pointing out the minstrel shows' artificiality. They believed that sooner rather than later, "this slap-stick, bandanna handkerchief, bladder, and flour-in-the-face act with which all negro acting is associated ought to die."[17]

The struggle was to reach both Black and white audiences, although the two groups had different expectations. Williams and Walker first faced this problem early in their partnership, but Williams, with and without Walker, never fully resolved it. White people wanted the "coon," and Black people the "New Negro." At the same time that Williams seemed to be moving away from Black people by performing in the otherwise all-white *Follies*, the hallmarks of the New Negro at the start of the twentieth century included a determination by Blacks "to redefine themselves as a people. . . . Blacks wanted their true faces and experiences known and sought to do this by displaying the very best that Black America could be."[18]

Certainly, the enormously popular Williams was an example of what they had in mind as they set out to convince white people that they were a mature, intelligent, and principled people. The New Negro believed that the future they had in mind required them to discard parts of their history and culture, including slavery and minstrelsy.[19] They resembled the European immigrants of the nineteenth and early twentieth centuries, many of whom rejected their cultures and Americanized their names.

Many theaters did not admit Blacks, and Williams remained concerned that he might be distancing himself from the people he was determined to serve. He still portrayed a Jonah Man in raggedy clothes and blackface, but he believed that he was helping his people by reinventing the stereotype into someone sympathetic and recognizably human. Years later, he said,

> I am the "Jonah Man." The man who, even if it rained soup, would be found with a fork in his hand and no spoon. The man whose relatives come to visit him and whose head is always dented by the furniture they throw at one another. . . . If you sift them, you will find the same principle of human nature at the bottom of them all.[20]

As usual, he was trying to negotiate with America without alienating Black or white people.

When James Weldon Johnson first moved to New York City from his home in Jacksonville, he discovered the New Negro. Johnson lived at the elegant Black-owned Marshall Hotel in the Tenderloin, as did Williams. He wrote that he saw "crowds of well-dressed colored men and women lounging and chatting in the parlors, loitering over their coffee and cigarettes while they talked or listened to the music."[21] It was also a place where Black entertainers played before mixed audiences, and artists and performers (including Williams) gathered to discuss the future for themselves and their people.

After a career in largely all-Black shows, Williams joined the all-white *Ziegfeld Follies* in 1910. He explained his decision: "The colored show business—that is colored musical shows—is at a low ebb just now. I reached the conclusion last spring that I could better represent my race by doing pioneer work. It was far better to have joined a large white show than to have starred in a colored show, considering the consequence."[22]

Williams soon took command of his audience and his place within the spotlight. His biographer, Camille A. Forbes, describes his entrance after he became a solo act in the *Follies*:

> Beginning with curtains closed, a single spotlight trained on center stage. Bert crept his white-gloved hands through the opening of the curtains in hesitant movements. Little by little, taking his time, he revealed himself. His arm, his shoulder, then finally his entire body slowly and apprehensively pushed through the curtains.[23]

He moved slowly in the midst of the *Follies*' speed and glamour, surrounded by scenes with madcap comics and dozens of largely undressed white women. It was part of the shrewdness of his comedy and its relationship to his Black identity; he was different from everyone else onstage.

At the same time, he appeared to be a leftover from minstrelsy and thus a familiar figure to Ziegfeld's upscale white audiences. He seemed to be both safe and self-deprecating; he knew his place. But then he would begin to half talk and half sing such songs as "All Goin' Out and Nothin' Comin' In," "I Got De Headache Now: A Darkey Lamentation," and "I'm Tired of Eating in Restaurants." He lived up to the expectations of his white audiences while subtly skewering them at the same time.

Because Williams's performance had such a lightness of touch, many white audiences might never have noticed his character's understated protest and suppressed anger. Yet by continuing to portray a stereotype, despite the subtle ways in which he had deepened and humanized the character, Williams was also undermining his purpose.

He faced discrimination even after he had become famous. One night after a performance, he and his friend, *Follies* costar Eddie Cantor, agreed to have dinner together. As they parted, Williams, who lived in an upscale hotel, told him that he had to use the freight elevator in the rear. Cantor perceived a trace of bitterness in his voice. They stood in what Cantor called "understanding silence" until Williams said, with remarkable honesty, "It wouldn't be so bad, Eddie, if I didn't still hear the applause ringing in my ears."[24] The comedian W. C. Fields supposedly observed, "Bert Williams is the funniest man I ever saw and the saddest man I ever knew."[25] The man Bert Williams and the performer Bert Williams, like the performing "coon" who also asserts Black identity, required a hard-earned equilibrium.

When Williams performed, he had to be careful; he could go only so far. He stood alone on the white man's stage. He was fearless but not foolish. In song after song, he portrayed a plaintively comic Jonah Man, a figure of suffering, irony, and self-awareness—the opposite of the conventional minstrel show "darkey." "I Got De Headache Now," the earliest of Williams's major songs, performed in an all-Black show but for a white audience, is a finely tuned complaint about the Jonah Man's ceaseless bad luck rooted in poverty. Those amused white people who took the song in stride might never have felt the barb. Protest becomes a form of amusement:

> And ev'ry time I starts to think, my head begins to hurt;
> Da is so many things I want on this most precious earth.
> And when I think of money,
> Oh, I wonder where and how
> De white folks got so much of it!
> Oh, Oh, I got de headache now!
>
> (George Walker and Bert Williams, "I Got De Headache Now:<br>A Darkey Lamentation," 1900)

That final line is the punch line, the laugh line. Williams laid out his songs slowly and mournfully to underscore the confusion and melancholy that white audiences found so funny. It was what they expected to hear in a "coon song," but he did not sing conventional "coon songs." In another song by Williams and Walker, the character appears to be mocking a Black woman whose fiancé seems incapable of understanding the changes he sees in her. In reality, he also twits the white people whom she has begun to imitate:[26]

> I know when chicken was a luxury
> She'd eat 'em boiled or fried,
> Now she have a hummingbird's heart
> Or else she ain't satisfied.
>
> (Bert Williams and George Walker, "She's Getting Mo' Like the White Folks Every Day," 1901)

Williams's most famous song, "Nobody," is also his most powerful. The song became so important that an unusually wide range of singers recorded it over the years, including the crooners Bing Crosby and Perry Como, the comedian Carol Burnett, Billy Daniels, Nina Simone, the Four Lads, and the country stars Merle Haggard and Johnny Cash. Each one rendered it differently—a crooner's vocal polish, another crooner's awkward homage to Williams, a woman's soulless belting, and a country singer's deeply attuned melancholy. After Williams, Nina Simone comes closest to its heart, despite the slick arrangement.

In 1906, Williams and Walker appeared in *Abyssinia*, one of several all-Black musicals at the time. Although most of the score was by Will Marion Cook and Jesse A. Shipp, Williams and the lyricist Alex Rogers contributed "Nobody." The show set out to illuminate the long history of African civilization, especially the kingdom of Abyssinia. Unfortunately, no one associated with the show had ever been to Africa.

A lottery winner takes his dim-witted friend, Jasmine Johnson, to Abyssinia, the land of their forebears. Through a series of misadventures, they stand before a ruthless king, who will decide whether they live or die. Williams, who played Johnson, spoke in a typical "darkey" accent, while the African characters spoke standard English.

In some ways, "Nobody" takes advantage of the widely held white view of African Americans. Although its apparent comedy opens the way for Williams to speak hard truths, its serious undercurrent makes it an essential part of *Abyssinia*. The lyrics do not rely on dialect, except for the dropping of a final *g*, the use of *ain't*, and a few colloquial expressions. In fact, a few of the lines feel as if they derive from a long-forgotten sentimental ballad: "I am filled with naught but pain." No matter how bad the character feels, though, no matter how much he suffers in bad weather, no matter how hungry he is, no one offers help.

That recognition fuels his discontent. For the only time in Williams's songs, the rage threatens to boil over, but his performance style eases the effect of the words. Williams performed the song with a small notepad in one hand. Moistening his thumb to turn the pages, he seemed to be looking for something as he sang the Broadway musical's first great protest song. The small distraction freed him to tell a hard truth in public:

> I ain't never done nothin' to nobody;
> I ain't never got nothin' from nobody, no time:
> And until I get somethin' from somebody, sometime,
> I don't intend to do nothin' for nobody, no time!
>
> (Bert A. Williams and Alex Rogers, "Nobody," *Abyssinia*, 1905)

Not long after Bert Williams reached the height of his career, the songwriters and vaudevillians Eubie Blake and Noble Sissle appeared at an NAACP benefit. Waiting to go on, they started talking to two African American comedians they knew only slightly. Both Sissle and Blake, as well as Flournoy Miller and Aubrey Lyles, worked in white vaudeville, where white vaudeville bills never included more than one Black act. Miller and Lyles said that they wanted to restore Blacks to Broadway after a decade of exclusion. Sissle and Blake expressed interest.

Miller and Lyles hammered out a loose plot based on their comedy routines, while Sissle and Blake put together a score consisting of old and new songs. Their all-Black show, given the required racist name, *Shuffle Along*, opened on May 23, 1921, in a shabby, out-of-the-way theater on West 63rd Street. Word of mouth made it a hit; it ran for more than five hundred performances, a long run for the time. The plot concerns a three-sided political race between two dishonest pols and an honest man named Harry. Harry wins in the end—both the race and Jessie, the girl of his dreams. Lottie Gee, who played Jessie, also introduced the score's biggest hit, "I'm Just Wild About Harry." The show helped to launch the careers of such Black performers as Josephine Baker, Adelaide Hall, Florence Mills, and Paul Robeson.

*Shuffle Along* was both revolutionary and troublingly familiar. That it broke the color barrier after nearly a decade was enough to make it revolutionary, and its use of jazz-inflected songs performed by Blacks made it feel thrillingly modern just as the Harlem Renaissance was getting underway farther uptown. Sissle and Blake let audiences have what they expected from Blacks by the 1920s: a combination of jazz and heat, sex and the blues.

These songs ranged from the suggestive "If you've never been vamped by a brownskin, / You've never been vamped at all" (Eubie Blake and Noble Sissle, "If You've Never Been Vamped by a Brownskin," *Shuffle Along*, 1921) to a melancholy urban blues in the same year that Mamie Smith recorded "Crazy Blues": "It's not because I'm broke with all my clothes in pawn / But since the morn I woke up found my sweetie's gone" (Eubie Blake and Noble Sissle, "Low Down Blues," *Shuffle Along*, 1921).

Sissle and Blake also wrote two elevated romantic ballads for Black performers to sing, another innovation. They're not especially good. The lyrics are unusually stiff, but they matter anyway. James Weldon Johnson wrote in 1938, "The years have not been many since Negro players have dared to interpolate a love duet in a musical show to be witnessed by white people. The representation of romantic lovemaking by Negroes struck the white audience as somewhat ridiculous; Negroes were supposed to mate in a more primitive manner."[27]

The score also included such songs as "Bandana Days," "In Honeysuckle Time," and "Sing Me to Sleep, Mammy Dear." They conjure up memories of the recently departed minstrel shows to attract and reassure white audiences. They're appealing songs, but they're also a little too close to what the African American minstrel songwriter James A. Bland had been writing forty years earlier. It's a matter of balance, the same problem that turn-of-the-century African American songwriters and performers had had to face since the 1890s.

They were an essential part of white people's often ugly misunderstanding of what Black people were.

I can think of only one other song that equals the force and effectiveness of Bert Williams's "Nobody," although it took more courage to write. In 1929, two former butchers named Immerman opened a Harlem nightclub they called Connie's Inn, second only in importance to the Cotton Club during the Harlem Renaissance. They hired the composer and performer Thomas "Fats" Waller and the lyricist Andy Razaf to write the score for their latest lavish revue, *Connie's Hot Chocolates*. The score included "Honeysuckle Rose" and "Ain't Misbehavin'," and it was so successful that it soon opened on Broadway as well. It started at 8:40 downtown and again at midnight uptown. The Broadway run lasted 219 performances.

All the performers were Black, but unlike the Cotton Club, Connie's Inn did not restrict its audience to white people. The songwriters for the high-style revues in the major Harlem clubs—among them Dorothy Fields, Jimmy McHugh, Harold Arlen, and Ted Koehler at the Cotton Club—were all white. Being asked to write the score for a revue, and then having their songs on Broadway as well, was part of the 1920s breakthrough for Waller, Razaf, and other Black songwriters as well.

The song "Black and Blue" originated in intimidation and danger. Mobster Dutch Schultz was financing the show. A psychopath given to unpredictable brutal violence, he told Razaf that he thought it would be funny to have a scene in which a dark-skinned Black woman lies on white sheets in an all-white room. Razaf was to write a comic song in which the woman bemoaned her fate: she was too black to attract men who were more interested in lighter-skinned women. Razaf said he couldn't possibly write such a song. Schultz held a gun to his head and said, "You'll write it or you'll never write anything again."[28]

Although the encounter shook him, Razaf told Waller that he intended to write a song about racism. Waller picked up the spirit of Razaf's intent and wrote a mournful, blues-tinged melody that somehow feels spontaneous. Razaf then added a spare, elliptical lyric; what he wrote masterfully suggests what he doesn't say.

On opening night, Razaf was watching from the back of the room. Schultz came to stand next to him. As Edith Wilson began to perform the song, the crowd was laughing, and Schultz was smiling: "Gentlemen prefer them light / Browns and yellers have all the fellers." But then the song turned darker as she sang, "I'm so forlorn, life's just a thorn, / My heart is torn, why was I born?" (Thomas Waller and Andy Razaf, "Black and Blue," *Hot Chocolates*, 1929). Dutch stopped smiling. Razaf later said that he thought his life depended on the audience's reaction.[29] When Wilson finished, the room was silent before the audience stood and cheered. Schultz clapped Razaf on the back and walked away.

Razaf's lyric begins with what Schultz had ordered: a woman alone watches couples pass by in the street. He then deftly transforms her plight into a plaintive monologue about race from the point of view of one who's suffered from its burdens. The woman complains about her cold bed and its hard springs. She's so alone that even the mice have fled. Because she can't hide "what is on my face," she has spent her life being "black and blue." The song's implications carry the listener far beyond loneliness. She is an outsider, alone, the "other," facing laughter and scorn.

We have two great songs about lynching, both written by white men. Neither is a polemic, although they express their points of view with clarity and force. They share the same repugnance but are otherwise strikingly different. One is by a little-known poet and songwriter; the other is by one of the major figures in American music. One began as a poem by a left-wing schoolteacher and sometime poet named Abel Meeropol (writing as Lewis Allen). Irving Berlin wrote the other one in 1933 for *As Thousands Cheer*, the satirical Broadway revue he wrote with the playwright Moss Hart. One of the best and most successful revues of the 1930s, *As Thousands Cheer* ran for four hundred performances, a long run for a Depression-era musical.

Between 1890 and 1940, nearly four thousand people were lynched in the United States, mostly in the South. By the time Meeropol wrote "Strange Fruit" as a poem, lynchings had declined substantially. In fact, he never saw a lynching, but he may have written the poem after seeing a gruesome photograph of Thomas Shipp and Abram Smith, lynched in Indiana in 1930. Thirty years after he wrote it, Meeropol explained, "I wrote 'Strange Fruit' because I hate lynching and I hate injustice, and I hate the people who perpetuate it."[30]

Some months later, Meeropol and his wife, the singer Laura Duncan, set the poem to music. Billie Holiday was the first to sing it; her recording remains definitive. She was appearing at New York's Café Society, Barney Josephson's left-wing nightclub in Sheridan Square down in Greenwich Village. The patrons included "union officials, intellectuals, artists, jazz lovers, celebrities, and more. Performers and audiences alike were integrated."[31] When Meeropol first played it for Holiday, he said, "I don't think she felt very comfortable with the song, because it was so different from the songs to which she was accustomed."[32] When she agreed to sing it at Café Society, she worked on it for three weeks before she performed it.[33]

After Holiday sang it for the first time, she wrote, "There wasn't even a patter of applause when I finished. Then a lone person began to clap nervously. Then suddenly everyone was clapping."[34] Her record company, Columbia, refused to let her record it because it was too controversial. She eventually recorded it for Commodore, a small jazz label. Holiday later claimed that she wrote it.

Meeropol's song was as different as it could be from the other important songs of the year, among them "Over the Rainbow," "Moonlight Serenade," "God Bless America," and "Beer Barrel Polka." Its lyric relies on a sustained image of "strange fruit hanging from the poplar trees" to convey the narrator's revulsion at what he sees. He identifies a fruit fit for the crows,

> For the rain to gather, for the wind to suck
> For the sun to rot, for a tree to drop,
> Here is a strange and bitter crop.
>
> (Laura Duncan and Alex Meeropol, "Strange Fruit," 1939)

There is no way to turn away from what Meeropol is writing about or the grim force with which he writes it. The third line of the first verse grounds the metaphor in reality, laced with irony in the gentle image with which the line ends: "Black bodies swinging in the Southern breeze." The contrast between the genteel imagery we might associate with the South, including the scent of magnolias, and the monstrosity of the murder makes the effect even stronger.

Irving Berlin, however, was writing for the popular theater. He approached the same subject through the creation of a character in a dramatic setting. A

Black mother prepares dinner in a cabin in the South when she learns that a mob has lynched her husband. Imagine, an authoritative protest song in the midst of a largely comic Broadway revue. It took someone with the reputation and determination of Irving Berlin to make it happen.

For the most part, *As Thousands Cheer* satirized such prominent people as Gandhi, Noël Coward, John D. Rockefeller, and President Herbert Hoover. Then in the second act, amid such New York–centered songs as "Easter Parade," "Harlem on My Mind," and "Heat Wave," suddenly there was "Supper Time." Berlin and Hart organized the show's collection of diverse scenes around the headlines in the daily newspaper. A different headline preceded each scene: "Heat Wave Hits New York" led to the comic "Heat Wave," and "Unknown Negro Lynched by Angry Mob" led to a cabin in the rural South and "Supper Time."

Berlin had previously told Waters's agent, "We're going to try to inject a serious note in this musical." A series of lynchings in the South had appalled him. Years later, he said, "People told me I was crazy to write a dirge like that," but he believed that a revue about the news needed at least one serious song.[35] As Waters wrote in her autobiography:

> If one song can tell the whole tragic story of a race it was that song. In singing it, I was telling my comfortable, well-fed, well-dressed listeners about my people. . . . When I was through and that big, heavy curtain came down, I was called back again and again. I had stopped the show with a type of song never before heard in a revue.[36]

As the song's title suggests, Berlin limits his lyric to that single moment when the news and its immediate aftermath come crashing down. It mixes emotion with pressing questions, grief with a woman's never-ending role as a mother and wife. Her first worry is for her children:

> How'll I keep from cryin'
> When I bring their supper on?
> 
> (Irving Berlin, "Supper Time," *As Thousands Cheer*, 1933)

The song never mentions the lynching directly. Instead, it portrays its effect on a single family. It resolves nothing and offers no solution, only the moment itself.

# 9

# Women and the Nineteenth Amendment

In 1937, for the movie *On the Avenue*, Irving Berlin wrote a song in which the narrator urges people to take their protests to Park Avenue to confront the nabobs. Nobody's throwing bricks, but in the spirit of satire, he urges his listeners, "Let's go slumming, nose thumbing on Park Avenue" (Irving Berlin, "Slumming on Park Avenue," *On the Avenue*, 1937). It was the kind of gentle satire that kept showing up in the mainstream popular songs of the 1930s.

For seventy-five years before that, though, the suffragists did a lot more than thumb their noses. They marched and agitated. They picketed outside Woodrow Wilson's White House in 1917 and were arrested for it. The government imprisoned one of the protesters named Alice Paul, who "was kept in solitary confinement, force fed and placed in an insane asylum."[1] Her crime was organizing the White House demonstration in which women stood silently every day for months on end. Their banner read, "MR. PRESIDENT, WHAT WILL YOU DO FOR WOMAN SUFFRAGE?" Wilson was not sympathetic to civil rights or freedom of speech, and he approved of denying voting rights to half the population.[2]

Irwin Silber lists the ways in which the suffrage movement affected everyday life for decades:

> It is hard to realize that the issue of woman suffrage once wracked the nation from coast to coast. Riots, demonstrations, outraged sermons, indignant editorials, and frenzied emotional outbursts from all sides highlight the history of the long, uphill fight for woman's electoral rights.[3]

Rather than picket politely, some of the younger suffragists did throw bricks through windows, but all of them sang rally songs to advance the cause. They were polemics set to music. Many of the songwriters were amateurs who wrote for others as committed as they were but sometimes also reassured men who saw their world turning topsy-turvy.

At other times, the women roared ahead undaunted. They set new lyrics to familiar melodies and printed them on song sheets so people at rallies and marches could sing them immediately. "Goodnight, Ladies" became "Come Vote, Ladies," and "Dixie" became "Hurrah for Woman Suffrage Women's Song of Union," but a fair number were never published as sheet music and many were never recorded. The songwriters also rewrote hymns to define their cause as both patriotic and spiritual. The organized struggle lasted nearly seventy-five years, but the Nineteenth Amendment finally went into effect on August 26, 1920.

A concern for women's rights preceded the Women's Rights Convention in Seneca Falls, New York, in 1848. Although a number of conventions that focused on slavery and religion had also considered women's rights at least a decade earlier, the 1848 Convention marked the first time women had organized specifically to address those rights.[4] It began with a Declaration of Sentiments, written mainly by one of the most prominent suffragists, Elizabeth Cady Stanton. Stanton borrowed much of her language from the Declaration of Independence, but the changes she made matter.

It began, "When, in the course of human events, it becomes necessary for one portion of the family of man to assume among the people of the earth a position different from that which they have hitherto occupied" and asserted that "all men and women are created equal." She also added a fiery statement of her own: "The history of mankind is a history of repeated injuries and usurpations on the part of man toward woman, having in direct object the establishment of an absolute tyranny over her."[5]

Some who attended the conference, including the prominent Quaker Lucretia Mott, saw it as a step toward civil, social, and moral rights for women. Others, including Stanton, viewed it as a revolutionary beginning to the fight for complete equality under the law.[6] On the second of the convention's three days, controversy over the inclusion of suffrage in the Declaration threatened to split the three hundred women who were there. Only when Frederick Douglass argued in its favor did the opponents agree to go along.

According to Judith Wellman, a historian of the convention, the Declaration of Sentiments became "the single most important factor in spreading news of the women's rights movement around the country."[7] From that time forward, though, women and their male allies emphasized the fight for the vote. The convention gave it the impetus it needed.

Within a few years, suffrage appeared more and more often in songs. In 1871, the abolitionist William Lloyd Garrison lent his name to the struggle. He set new lyrics to Robert Burns's poem from 1795, "A Man's a Man for a' That," and borrowed the melody from a 1750 Jacobite song, "For a' That."[8] Protesters committed to abolition and improving working conditions also adopted it. Garrison chose well; Burns's poem expresses a belief in an egalitarian republic. Now, Garrison insisted, that principle requires that women must be the equal of men:

> Down with all barriers that prevent
> Her culture, growth, and a' that—
> Her rightful share in government,
> In Church and State, and a' that!
> For a' that, and a' that,
> "Her proper sphere," and a' that;
> Whatever right a man may claim,
> Belongs to her, for a' that!
>
> (William Lloyd Garrison, "Human Equality," 1871)

The commitment to full freedom for women was broader than suffrage alone. Its driving force combined zeal for reform with women's rights, but suffrage was the spearhead. Nothing was more important than the right to vote because it made other changes possible. It also extended beyond voting, sometimes in unpredictable ways. In the 1850s, suffragists Amelia Bloomer and Elizabeth Smith Miller argued that women should wear short skirts over loose trousers to the ankle. It would, they said, allow women to move as freely and easily as men. People found the idea shocking at first. It gave rise to at least one song that uses a light touch to defend the wearing of "bloomers" and mock the men who express horror:

> I wonder how often these men must be told
> When a woman a notion once seizes,

> However they ridicule, lecture or scold,
> She'll do, after all, as she pleases,
> She'll do, after all, as she pleases.
> They know very well that their own fashions change
> With each little change of the season,
> But Oh! it is "monstrous" and "dreadful" and "strange"
> And "out of all manner of reason,"
> And "out of all manner of reason."
> (Songwriter unknown, "The Bloomer's Complaint," 1850)

The arrival of the bicycle in the 1880s also meant that women needed clothing that would let them pedal easily and modestly. By 1892, bicycling became a way for a newly married couple to get around: "It won't be a stylish marriage / I can't afford a carriage, / But you'll look sweet / On the seat / Of a bicycle built for two" (Harry Dacre, "Daisy Bell," 1892). Six years later, Susan B. Anthony told the journalist Nellie Bly:

> I'll tell you what I think of bicycling. I think it has done more to emancipate woman than any one thing in the world. I rejoice every time I see a woman ride by on a wheel. It gives her a feeling of self-reliance and independence the moment she takes her seat; and away she goes, the picture of untrammeled womanhood.[9]

When songwriters chose to write about a controversial subject, they often turned to humor. What could be funnier, one antisuffrage song asked, than watching a woman who advocates the right to vote as she tries to manipulate a bicycle while she's wearing trousers? Dogs bark, and people shout, "Hi! Hi!" as she rides by, but she's also lost her beau, and her mother has stopped speaking to her. Her behavior is scandalous but leads to a mock serious concern for her well-being:

> Eliza dear, we sadly fear you have not started right;
> You will not see more liberty by being such a fright;
> Asylums yawn for you, my dear, and in the books we read,
> How bloomers that too early bloom soon fade and go to seed.
> (Winthrop Packard, "Eliza Jane," 1895)

The agitation for women's rights, and especially suffrage, expanded in the decade just before the Civil War and continued through Emancipation until the ratification of the Nineteenth Amendment. Because most of the women in the movement were white, they could argue more forcefully and openly than African Americans. Others might mock them, but they were not in the same kind of danger, especially in the South. After Emancipation, Black suffragists split over whether to support the Fifteenth Amendment because it gave only African American men the right to vote. The women chose to continue their work toward full citizenship and the right to vote for all African Americans.

Although many white suffragists considered themselves abolitionists before Emancipation, many of them also resented the Fifteenth Amendment. By the 1890s, the suffrage movement took a racist turn. Black men could vote, but white women couldn't. Jim Crow affected even those Americans who were allegedly fighting to expand the rights of all Americans. African American women had to organize and protest separately to continue their advocacy of enfranchisement.[10] Racism began to appear in suffrage songs, not often but there it was. Because women couldn't vote, this racist pro-suffrage song asks:

> Is it right for the Negro, the Jap, and the Chink,
> The tramp and the old whiskey bloat,
> To be hauled in a taxicab down to the polls
> And there be told how they must vote?
>
> (W. G. Fortney, "Is It Right?" 1911)

Another racist song, this time from 1913, is a wild mashing-together of themes and images. It includes a number of the beliefs that these respectable suffragists have raised in their songs as they reel from one to the next within a single stanza. It's a heady combination of racism, religion, patriotism, suffrage, and unjust taxation:

> We have no rights to call our own,
> Altho' of age and quite full grown;
> The intellects of "Chinks" and "Japs"
> is much preferred to ours, perhaps;
> But we shall preach and pray, and sing,
> And know someday the Lord will bring
> the women of our own fair land
> to Justice poor and good and grand,
> [Then we will not object to]
> Taxation without Representation.
>
> (Songwriter unknown, "Taxation without Representation," 1913)

It was common at the time to use "men" to mean all of humanity. The suffragists looked back to Jefferson's claim that all of humanity is "endowed by their Creator with certain unalienable rights." They saw liberty—and thus suffrage—as their birthright:

> Now's the day and now's the hour,
> To check unhallowed use of power,
> Secure to all their glorious dower,
> Of birthright liberty.
>
> (Songwriter unknown, "Strike for Liberty," 1884)

They argued in pamphlets, speeches, and songs that depriving them of the right to vote also deprived them of liberty and the full meaning of citizenship. They considered themselves at war with injustice and the powerful men who opposed what they believed. They wanted no more than what was fair and just, and they insisted on it with fervor. Their songs portray them as warriors for liberty and freedom. Miss F. E. M. Macauley set new words to the "Marseillaise":

> Arise! Ye daughters of a land
> That vaunts its liberty!
> May restless rulers understand
> That women must be free.
>
> (Miss F. E. M. Macauley, "The Women's Marseillaise," c1908)

These rally songs proliferated in the nineteenth century. Most of them spoke to other true believers to keep their spirits up. On May 6, 1911, the Women's Political Union sponsored a Woman's Suffrage Parade. The newspaper announcement read, in part, "To the beat of martial music women will show their faith in democracy, and their sense of obligation to the state."[11] They might have sung something like this anthem written to the familiar melody of "Men of Harlech":

> From the daughters of the nation
> Bursts a cry of indignation
> Breathes a sigh of consecration
> In a sacred cause.
> Those who share their country's burden
> Win no rights, receive no guerdon,
> Only bear the heavy burden

Of unrighteous laws. . . .
Leave unrighteous laws behind you,
Soon you shall be free!

(Songwriter unknown, "Shoulder to Shoulder,"
date unknown)

The songs of the movement echo the "Gettysburg Address." Suffragists found their guiding star in Lincoln's "new birth of freedom." It was for them "a great civil war" of another kind. The refounding of the nation in the address struck a chord of inspiration; its embrace of a distinctively American civic religion became their own. The ideas behind Lincoln's words stirred them—such words and phrases as "liberty," "created equal," "this nation under God," and "to be dedicated here to the unfinished work" of building a more perfect union, in their case through suffrage. These words, in one form or another, resounded in the songs they wrote and sang.

Most suffrage songs from the nineteenth century speak in the simplified, elevated language of true belief, but they also take on a complicated task. The songs merge love of country; the inseparability of suffrage, freedom, and full citizenship; a commitment to democracy and the nation; a battle against injustice; faith in the sacredness of their cause; and belief in their ultimate success. These themes become a single theme—the fight for suffrage in all its political, patriotic, and moral complexity.

Several songs see the goal in its entirety. Harriet H. Robinson's "Columbia's Daughters" is one of the best examples: confident, determined, and idealistic. Like Robinson, many of the composers and lyricists were amateurs, but they invested their songs with passion. If freedom and democracy are not to "perish from the earth," then every American must have the right to vote. Like so many rally songs, "Columbia's Daughters" borrowed a familiar melody. It began as a Civil War hymn called "Hold the Fort" but in 1888 added new lyrics that made it into a militant suffrage song: "Raise the flag and plant the standard" (Harriet H. Robinson, "Columbia's Daughters," 1888).

Suffrage posters from the nineteenth century through the First World War portray Columbia as a determined woman carrying the flag and bearing a sword. Sheet music covers typically link such iconic images as the flag and the

Liberty Bell with suffrage. Columbia usually wears a floor-length gown, but in some renderings, she stands tall, armed in a breastplate and helmet, carrying a standard. She is not someone to trifle with. I came upon a photograph of a woman named Frances F. Noyes posing as "Liberty" in a 1913 suffrage pageant. She embodies the women in "Columbia's Daughters." Yet as soon as the character in the lyric affirms her cause, she turns to men for help. With it, she says, women will become truly free. Beneath their idealism, the women also understood the importance of political persuasion:

> Hark the sound of myriad voices
> Rising in their might!
> 'Tis the daughters of Columbia
> Pleading for the right. . . .
> Brothers, we must share your freedom,
> Help us, and we will.

The word *pleading* surprised me. It appears in a number of other suffrage songs as well. Perhaps it's an attempt to soothe male egos and insecurities; perhaps, aside from their militancy over suffrage, many of these women were solidly middle class; perhaps, despite their determination, the word reflects the culture in which they lived. In the end, the song is an unlikely mix of traditional female roles and a demand for freedom. The women argue that their fight for the vote, their protest, is an act of patriotism that will give justice to their daughters. The song is forceful, unstinting, and generous of spirit. It embodies the interweaving of patriotism and protest:

> Great Republic to thy watchword
> Wouldst thou faithful be,
> All beneath thy starry banner,
> Must alike be free.

The lyrics argue for full freedom and democracy made possible only by citizenship for all. The fate of the nation hangs in the balance:

> O our country, glorious nation,
> Greatest of them all!
> Give unto thy daughters justice,
> Or thy pride will fall.

Theme and image often interweave within a single song, even within a single refrain. Many of the songs bask in a triumphalist view of America typical of the time but achievable only through suffrage and what follows it. When women win the right to vote, the nation will triumph:

> Thus evolves the greatest triumph of dual human race—
> Church and state, the home and school, and law and love embrace.
> We'll have a perfect nation, we'll march from near and far
> To glory 'neath the Stars and Stripes—it shall bear the woman's star.
> (William P. Adkinson, "The Suffrage Flag," 1884)

The lyric also argues that in the emotional and psychological aftermath of the Civil War, the coming of suffrage will lead to peace and an eagerness for reform. The lyric joins its faith in the future to the image of a roaring railroad train:

> This band is for all reforms, war shall be at an end,
> Bayonets and swords shall rust, we'll use the brain, the pen.
> Laden with precious freight now thunders on the progress car,
> As the headlight waves the suffrage flag that bears the woman's star.

Suffrage lyrics call on women to sing as they rally and march. Beyond the repetition of related themes, they also sing out in familiar images and allusions. Bells ring, trumpets blare, and dawn rises. These images and more give the movement its language of protest and determination. They fight for "freedom" despite the "mockery" of men and often see their fight as a war and themselves as warriors. Ultimately, there will be a national "awakening":

> We are coming from the mountains,
> We're coming from the plain,
> Singing our stirring songs of freedom,
> From the wild Pacific Hills
> To the rocky coast of Maine.
> (Julia Mills Dunn, "Rally for the Right," before 1862)

The list of images is long, and different images interweave in individual songs. They also recur in songs whose tone changes within their three or four verses. The moderate "Foremother's Hymn" begins with a "plea" from "supplicants" as they praise America but wonder how long they can tolerate "the chain." The message intensifies through three choruses until it identifies "freedom" as "mockery" until women win what they "crave."

A more confrontational rally song like William Hussey Macy's "Uncle Sam's Daughter," takes a common tack of speaking directly to the women engaged in the struggle (William Hussey Macy, "Uncle Sam's Daughter," date unknown). The differences between the two songs lie in language and tone. In Macy's lyric, the "sisters'" imperative is to "rouse the nation" and "inspire all hearts." They will "proclaim the truth" and challenge opponents, "Deny it if you can."

The themes stay the same—the cause, the vote, independence, justice, liberty, citizenship, and peace—and use the same related images to rally those already committed and persuade the unpersuaded. Songs speak of peaceful home lives and future generations of sons and daughters who will find their lives enriched by enfranchisement and equality.

The idea for women's rights traces back at least as far as 1792, when Mary Wollstonecraft, the English women's rights advocate, argued for educating men and women equally. She added, "For only by the jostlings of equality can we form a just opinion of ourselves."[12] More than a half century later, songs of suffrage pleaded with men to become brothers in the cause but also confronted men who opposed the movement. The women raised banners and fought to win the "battle" and the "war" that lasted seventy-five years in a cause they knew to be just and righteous. One anonymous song urges women to rise up to sing what it calls "a battle song":

> Rise up, women, for the fight is hard and long;
> Rise up in thousands singing loud a battle song.
> 
> (Songwriter unknown, "Rise Up Women!" date unknown)

In addition to men in general, suffrage songs rail at politicians in Congress. They cry out against taxation without representation. Because women had expanding but still limited property rights in the nineteenth and early twentieth centuries, governments could tax them, even though they had no say in governing. L. May Wheeler's lyric protests by reminding us of the heroic women of the American Revolution as she advocates for suffrage now:

> Who made Boston Bay and its waters
> All the tea of the Province to hold.
> Three cheers for the women of old!

> Three cheers for the women of old!
> Who planted the banner for freedom,
> Three cheers for the women of old. . . .
> Oh, shades of that "Bunker" hillside!
> Shine out in thy strength and thy might:
> And kill with thy sunlight, the tyrant
> Who fain would defraud us of right.
> Then rally, oh, men of the nation,
> Vote out this injustice to-day,
> And place in the hands of thy women,
> The ballot—forever and aye.
>
> (L. May Wheeler, "Taxation without Representation Is Tyranny," 1884)

Elsewhere, Wheeler again picks up the theme of the American Revolution. Suffragists saw themselves as inheritors of the fight against tyranny. The Declaration of Independence had enshrined the right to pursue liberty and, if necessary, fight for it. Just as the sentiments of the Gettysburg Address appeared in their songs, so did the Declaration's. These women saw themselves bound to those who broke away from tyranny a century earlier:

> Columbia's daughters saw it when their brothers sprang to arms
> They heard it in the blooming of battle's rude alarms,
> They read it in the shadows of th' dreary night's dead calms,
> That truth was marching on.
>
> (L. May Wheeler, "Hallelujah Song," 1884)

Pro-suffrage songs may rely on a mix of the same themes and images, but they also take different tacks. They plead with men but also confront them. They reassure men that they don't seek political power, but in some songs, they do:

> When women cast the ballot, with equal right and say
> For equality and justice, they'll wield a power some day.
> The blear eyed politician, the grafter and the bum
> Will find the day is over when they can rule with rum.
>
> (Benj. F. Nysewander, "When Women Cast the Ballot [The Important Question]," 1914)

In other songs, women won't cook dinner or tend the house, but they also affirm that suffrage will protect the home by creating equal partners. They are respectable revolutionaries who demand the vote and want to close saloons, protect their families, and bring peace to the world: "Spread the joyful news wherever man is found; / Women's vote will save the home" (Mrs. M. E. Balch, "Women's Ballot or 'Whosoever Will,'" 1884).

Their defense of home while pressing for suffrage also opened suffragists to the charge that the rough-and-tumble of polling places and politics was unsuitable for respectable wives and mothers. But women no longer saw themselves as demure and angelic. They argued back that their votes would reform politicians' behavior and advance causes of merit. They believed that they were already fighting against sin; politics was nothing more than a way to ensure that the fight for reform went forward. The women were determined but hardly naive:

> If the men should see the women going to the polls,
> To put down the liquor traffic,
> Need it vex their souls?
> If we're angels as they tell us, can we once suppose
> Then all the men would frown on us
> When going to the polls.
>
> (Julia B. Nelson, "Going to the Polls," 1884)

# 10

# "Ragging and Nagging in Politics"

From the beginning, women in the movement often wrapped their commitment to suffrage in a spiritual cloak. Soul and spirit infused their writing as they merged them with the fight for justice. They paralleled Lincoln's civic religion: "On freedom's altar now / Our hand is laid" (Elizabeth Boynton Herbert, "The New America," 1884). Yet many suffragists took matters of the spirit further than that. They believed that denying women the right to vote was not only reprehensible, but also sinful. Sometimes the lyrics deepened their determination with reverence and righteousness. In the songwriters' embrace of Christianity, they wrote lyrics as an expression of respectable nineteenth-century middle-class Protestantism. Those who sang them fought for the vote in the spirit of such hymns as "Onward, Christian Soldiers":

> No discharge have Christian women
> From the war with sin;
> At the polls with Gog and Magog
> Must the fight begin
> Since we've Bible marching-orders,
> Need it fright our souls,
> Though all the men should frown on us
> When going to the polls.

Like so many of the triumphalist patriotic songs of the nineteenth century, suffrage lyrics resemble hymns. Their sentiments align with Christian belief, not in a doctrinal way, but in their belief that God is a God of love, who will oversee the coming of justice. They see themselves in an alliance with the Almighty:

> Who's first in Christian life and love?
> Who makes the life of home?
> Who fights the "Demon of the Still"?

> Shall women here be dumb?
> An equal risk, an equal loss,
> Why not an equal gain?
> "The vote of woman must be felt
> Just as the vote of man."
>
> (Songwriter unknown, "The Woman's Cause Is Right," 1882)

Suffrage songwriters added new lyrics to familiar melodies all the time, none more often than "Battle Hymn of the Republic." Its combination of militancy and faith made it a perfect choice for the merging of suffrage and spiritual fervor:

> To "that more perfect union" foreshadowed by our sires,
> Not only for the Nation, but around our altar fires,
> The sacred source of Home's sweet love we'll trust in faith alway,
> And bless its hallowed sway.
>
> (Catharine F. Stebbins, "New Battle Hymn of the Republic," 1892)

In January 1920, the Eighteenth Amendment, banning the manufacture, distribution, and sale of alcohol, took effect. It was a victory for women in the suffrage movement and the conservative Women's Christian Temperance Union, who had joined forces in the cause of temperance. They forged an alliance that appeared in songs because the suffragists believed that giving women the vote was the best way to defend the home by stopping the devastating effects of alcohol on American families:

> When shall rise within us reason,
> As our Father has ordained;
> And the Women's Temperance Union,
> Shall the right of suffrage gain;
> Side by side with wives and sweethearts,
> We shall meet the foe someday,
> When we vote just as we pray.
>
> (Songwriter unknown, "Patriotic Voting," 1918)

References to temperance had appeared in suffrage songs as early as 1869. Soldiers had returned from the Civil War, and families were restored, but the scourge of drinking increased. In the middle of the century, the vote for women was the cure:

> Their first great vote to close shall be
> Those gilded haunts of infamy.
> The poor besotted wretch shall know
> That woman has shut the gate of woe.
> The light of truth shall shine again
> And Temp'rance on the earth shall reign,
> The night of darkness disappear
> The millenium [sic] sunshine bright and clear.
> (John W. Hutchinson, "Vote It Right Along," 1869)

Drinking appeared in anti-suffrage songs as well. Just as they did when Prohibition closed saloons all over the country (soon to reappear as speakeasies), men in the nineteenth century already bemoaned its possible effects: "It's good bye whiskey, beer and rum / If they let the women vote" (J. W. Holton and Jemmy Sayre, "Don't Let the Women Vote," 1892).

The most recent temperance songs appeared only two years before ratification and underscored the link between the suffrage movement and the WCTU. Set to the tune of the popular British First World War song "It's a Long Way to Tipperary," its first stanza concludes, "It's been a long, long way to Prohibition, / But we are almost there." The second stanza takes a similar stance: "It's been a long, long way to Woman's Suffrage, / But it is almost here" (Songwriter unknown, *Campaign Verses No. 34*, 1918).

In 1869, when it was still a territory, Wyoming granted women the right to vote. Before the ratification of the Nineteenth Amendment, another nine states, most of them west of the Mississippi, had granted universal suffrage. By the time Tin Pan Alley became the center of song publishing at the start of the twentieth century, full suffrage was increasingly on the nation's mind. Determined suffragists (but amateur songwriters) wrote most of the songs dating back to the 1850s, but the closer Congress came to passing the Nineteenth Amendment, the more likely Alley songwriters were to write songs about it. It was never a major subject for these songwriters. Most of them preferred to play it safe by writing anti-suffrage songs.

Al Piantadosi began his career as a composer by playing piano in a Chinatown dive just down the street from the Pelham Bay Café, where Irving

Berlin worked as a singing waiter. Lyricist Joe McCarthy went on to write such standards as "You Made Me Love You" and "I'm Always Chasing Rainbows." First, though, he and Piantadosi made fun of the women who wanted to vote by telling the comic tale of a young fellow who escapes marriage to a suffragist by the skin of his teeth:

> The sentence I had was a suffragette,
> The day of our wedding, I can't forget,
> I couldn't get married 'cause I was in debt.
> Then some other fellow he stole my pet.
> (Al Piantadosi and Jos. McCarthy, "I Just Met the Fellow Who Married the Girl That I Was Going to Get," 1911)

He learns years later that they had "six kids and maybe nine . . . / So let us give him three cheers."

Because suffrage was something that people were increasingly aware of, songs often mentioned it in passing so they felt up-to-date, as in George W. Meyer and Joe Goodwin's "We All Fall." On the sheet music cover, seven men offer gifts to a beautiful woman—a rich man, poor man, beggar man, thief, doctor, lawyer, and Indian chief. They never appear in the lyric, but there is this quick reference in the second verse: "City girl or suffragette, / Men look out she'll get you yet" (Geo. W. Meyer and Joe Goodwin, "We All Fall," 1911). The rest of the verse describes the dangers of wedded life regardless of the wife's political opinions.

The songwriters wrote in the style of the day. They were out to write hits, so they wrote everything from sweet ballads to ethnic songs to "coon songs." As millions of immigrants from Eastern and Southern Europe arrived between the Civil War and the First World War, songwriters both mocked and encouraged them. They made fun of their names, absurd accents, and customs, but they also urged them to adapt to America. They rarely advocated for votes for women.

The response to the immigrants was a new kind of song, the ethnic song that focused mainly on the Irish, Italian, and Jewish newcomers (see chapter 6). The songs preferred humor to rage, but like many of Tin Pan Alley's anti-suffrage songs, they worried about the role of men in the family and the larger world. Some songs combined the two.

An Italian immigrant finds that his wife lives on her own terms now that she's discovered suffrage. She no longer performs her wifely duties, and he is left with nothing but his own complaints and an Old World outlook. Gus Edwards and Will D. Cobb were well-established Tin Pan Alley songwriters. Together they wrote "By the Light of the Silvery Moon," "In My Merry Oldsmobile," "I Just Can't Make My Eyes Behave," and "School Days." What we find racist, people then found amusing:

> My heart is one-a shipwreck
> She wear-a da pants, dat kill da' romance;
> All day, daffy like a dilly, Poor old wop!
> To my eyes come da big tear drop,
> No more I eat da spagett' since my Margarette
> Become-a da suffragette.
>
> (Gus Edwards and Will D. Cobb, "Since My Margarette Become-a da Suffragette," 1913)

Suffrage rarely appeared in "coon songs," those offensive portraits of African Americans who had come North to escape Jim Crow and prosper. "Liza Johnson Joins De Sufferjets" is one of the few exceptions. A man lazes on a bench when suddenly Liza "lamm'd me wid a monkey wrench" to get his attention:

> Listen what I sez ter yer, coon,
> I'ze bound ter be a sufferjet soon;
> Ah might as well commence
> On yuh, so jump the fence . . .
> From now on Ahm de boss . . .
> 'Cause Ahm a real sufferjet.
>
> (A. De Chesney and Margaret Mountain, "Liza Johnson Joins De Sufferjets," 1913)

Despite Liza Jane's decision to take things into her own hands, most of these songs oppose votes for women. That was as true in Broadway musicals as it was in Tin Pan Alley. As far as I can tell, "As Far as I Can Tell" is the first song in a Broadway musical to mention suffrage even in passing. A group of girls sings to the audience as they point to their middle-aged chaperone, "We represent the suffragettes / Who sent us here from home / And he's the chaperone" (Benjamin Hapgood Burr, "As Far As I Can Tell," *They Loved a Lassie*, 1909).

The following year, Gustave Lauders and the then-well-known short story writer George Ade collaborated on *The Old Town*, a musical that ran for six months and included a suffrage song made distinctive by its colloquial lyric. It had none of the high-flying rhetoric of songs written so often within the movement. These are characters in a play talking and singing to one another. They need to sound like real people. A husband's gift to a wife might be an expression of affection, but in suffrage songs, it had also become a form of condescension, a way to keep wives in their place. A young woman lets her suitor know that gifts, even expensive gifts, won't do:

> You give us lovely pearls, in strings,
> You buy us rings and other things;
> I've even heard of wealthy chaps
> Who go as far as sable wraps;
> But when for ballots we insist,
> We'd rather not be hugged and kissed,
> Tho' once a little household pet,
> I'm now a fighting suffragette.
> (Gustave Lauders and George Ade, "Weak Little Woman, or the Militant Suffrage Song," *The Old Town*, 1910)

By 1913, suffrage was in the news and on the public's mind, so it was perfect for Florenz Ziegfeld, the producer of the *Ziegfeld Follies*, to tackle. He charged the highest prices on Broadway and catered to the carriage trade. Revues had started in Paris in the late nineteenth century as burlesques of popular plays and satiric commentaries on the news of the day. Ziegfeld and his Broadway competitors George White and Earl Carroll added extravagant sets and costumes, and parades of scantily clad showgirls, but never lost sight of current events. These Broadway visionaries remained very much attuned to what was on their audience's minds.

Ziegfeld was always out to entertain his audiences, not instruct them. His first stab at a suffrage song involves a breezy young woman who refuses to worry about anything. On the sheet music cover for Raymond Hubbell and Vincent Bryan's "I Should Worry and Get Wrinkles," a pretty girl opens a large hatbox from which other pretty girls emerge. Its lightness of heart feels Ziegfeldian. The song itself portrays a young woman who has to face the death of a rich elderly husband, a lawyer who's angling for a fee, and a suffragist who tries to enlist her in the cause—but always in comic terms. The woman's tone is devil-may-care regardless of the other people involved. The suffragist urges her on: "So go and get a piece of brick, / And throw it through some window quick, / Then all we women want of course we'll get." One of the first of the gold diggers, the young woman has her answer ready:

> I should worry and get wrinkles?
> I should care if women vote?
> Why I'd be off my trolley,
> When with just a little jolly,
> I can get [sic] another velvet opera coat,
> What care I for women's suffrage
> There's nothing that I want that it will buy . . .
> I should worry and wrinkle?
> Get away! not I.
>
> (Raymond Hubbell and Vincent Bryan, "I Should Worry and Get Wrinkles," *Ziegfeld Follies*, 1912)

Probably the most important of the Broadway anti-suffrage songs is "That Ragtime Suffragette" from the *Ziegfeld Follies of 1913*. When Ziegfeld added Nat D. Ayer and Harry Williams's new song to his score, he launched a comic attack on suffrage to appeal to his affluent audience. It's funny, but it also had to be unsettling for men. The lyric urges them to get their guns before the women attack and then take over:

> Ragging with bombshells and ragging with bricks,
> Ragging and nagging in politics . . .
> For Lordy while her husband's waiting home to dine,
> She's just raggin' up and down the line.
> Shouting votes, votes, votes, votes, votes for women,
> Oh, you ragtime suffragette.
>
> (Nat D. Ayer and Harry Williams, "That Ragtime Suffragette," *Ziegfeld Follies of 1913*, 1913)

The popular husband-and-wife team of vaudevillians and songwriters, Joe E. Howard and Emma Carus, wrote the score for (and starred in) *A Broadway Honeymoon* in 1913.[1] The song, "My Irish Suffragette," appears in a collection of songs from the score. On the cover sits a stylish, attractive couple out for a spin in their motorcar, but the lyric offers advice for young Irishwomen:

So girls I want to put you next don't trust the men in politics because they're Irish,
And they will fool you, and try to rule you, now you can bet.
Get their jobs and be a female cop, it's the only way to reach the top, and shout for the Irish suffragette.

(Joe E. Howard and Emma Carus, "The Irish Suffragette,"<br>
*A Broadway Honeymoon*, 1913)

A growing number of twentieth-century suffrage songs expressed concern about the effects of voting women on their families. Men feared that if women could vote, they would leave their husbands and children behind, or suffrage would create a climate in which men and women switched roles. The sheet music cover for "Mind the Baby, I Must Vote Today" (E. H. Webb, "Mind the Baby, I Must Vote Today," 1914) shows a well-dressed wife heading out the door, while her flummoxed husband sits in a rocker trying to figure out what to do with their screaming baby.

The lyric makes its case through fears and threats. It identifies the women as the ones who should cook, wash, clean, and make "home fit for habitation," but now they "want to run from Pres'dent down to Sheriff." The women conclude:

Women read and think the same as men
Why should they stay home just like a hen
Some day we will boss and run the show
Then your little baby will smile and say
Mind the baby I must vote today.

Some songs feel condescending to us even though they're pro-suffrage. Condescension was probably not the lyric's intent. It reflects its time and uses humor to soften the blow for men; women are becoming more independent and making their way in the world:

Better be nice to them now,
Oh! You'd better be nice to them now.
If you're married, then you needn't be afraid,
You'll never have to work if wifie learns a trade.
The girls have it all their own way.
They're more independent each day.
Say, don't be surprised if we have a lady "Cops" in time.

And if we do, the men will all commit some crime,
And when the cops get 'em, They'll love 'em and pet 'em,
You'd better be nice to them now. Now.

(William Tracey and Jack Stern, "You'd Better Be Nice to Them Now," 1918)

One of the best Tin Pan Alley pro-suffrage songs also faced men's fears that they would have to stay behind to raise the children and tend the house while women ran the nation. This song takes its stand for suffrage, but it also addresses men's concerns. It is insistent without being defiant, reassuring without giving in. For the first time, the woman on the sheet music cover is a respectable, perhaps affluent, wife and mother. She is one of the last in a long line of mothers who appear in suffrage songs. Suffrage songwriters recognized that references to mothers and their children made their cause more attractive to other women and to men:

Sing it with a spirit that shall
Start the cause along,
Sing it as we ought to sing it,
Cheerily and strong,
Giving the ballots to the mothers.

(Rebecca N. Hazard, "no title," 1888)

The mother in an even more recent song is youthful, attractive, and affectionate toward her child. Her smile is easy and inviting. She's not looking to create havoc or rebellion; she wants to make the world a better place by voting for laws that will protect her child as she also comforts her husband. If he values her as a wife and mother, how can he oppose her reasonable desire to vote? If he willingly turns the raising of his children over to her, how can he deny her full citizenship? It was perhaps the most popular of all the pro-suffrage songs, written only a few years before the amendment took effect. Public attitudes were changing, and Tin Pan Alley had finally begun to catch up. The chorus addresses husbands directly:

She's good enough to love you and adore you,
She's good enough to bear your troubles for you;
And if your tears were falling today,
Nobody else would kiss them away.
She's good enough to warm your heart with kisses

When you are lonesome and blue,
She's good enough to be your baby's mother
And she's good enough to vote with you!
> (Herman Paley and Alfred Bryan, "She's Good Enough to
> Be Your Baby's Mother and She's Good Enough to Vote with You," 1916)

In the 1910s, as the country moved closer to giving women the vote, the number of suffrage songs diminished as the general public increasingly gave its attention to the War in Europe, especially after the sinking of the *Lusitania* in May 1915. From 1916 to 1918, several suffrage lyrics alluded to the First World War, yet the images of battle, war, and the struggle for peace, all linked to suffrage, had been part of the movement's songs for at least half a century. Now, though, they stood out more vividly (though not more often) as Congress moved closer to declaring war while suffrage promised a return to a revised domestic tranquility:

When sister Helen casts her ballot
Goodnight war and welcome peace,
Bid farewell to your big airship,
Graceful stork our homes will seize,
When sister Helen casts her ballot.
> (Peter J. Bast and John Kirk, "When Helen Casts Her Ballot," 1916)

Once women won the right to vote, they moved on to other causes. They were very much out of fashion in the silly 1920s and struggled along with everyone else during the Depression and the First World War. Only with the affluence of the 1960s and beyond did the cause of women—now called feminism—reemerge. It had put its racist elements behind it, although racism itself lived on in America and its songs.

# 11

# Racist Songs and African Americans

*[Note: Many of the songs in this chapter use offensive language. ML]*

A racist may carry the flag, but racism is the antithesis of patriotism. So are minstrel shows and "coon songs," yet a distinctively American strain runs through them. In their way, they help to define their subjects (however erroneously) and influence American attitudes despite everything repulsive about them. Little about race in America is ever simple or lacking in irony.

Nobody can say when the first white performer donned blackface, although Black performers were forced to wear it in vaudeville as late as the first decades of the twentieth century. The refusal to wear it by the songwriters and vaudeville performers Eubie Blake and Noble Sissle in the 1910s was the first significant sign that blackface was nearing its end, although it took a long time for it to disappear.

A white performer named George Washington Dixon may have been the first to "black up." He appeared in New York City in 1827 to sing two early "Negro songs," in which he claimed:

Some Niggers they have but one coat,
But you see I've got two;
I wears a jacket all the week,
And Sunday my long tail blue.

(George Washington Dixon?, "Long Tail Blue," 1827)

Of all the early blackface performers, though, Thomas Dartmouth Rice is the most important. We know about him mainly because his onstage antics were so popular and influential. He blacked up in the late 1820s to create a character he called Jim Crow. He wore ragged clothing and accompanied his song, "Jump

Jim Crow," with a dance that he claimed to have learned from a disabled Black man who had energetic but unusual ways of moving.

Because he grew up in an integrated Northern neighborhood, Rice had close contact with Black people but then added exaggerated humor to the "Jim Crow" character to transform him into what became a stereotypical buffoon:

> Oh I'm a roarer on de fiddle, and down in old Virginny,
> They say I play de skyentific like Massa Paganinni.
> Weel about and turn about and do jis so,
> Eb'ry time I weel about and jump Jim Crow.
> (Thomas Dartmouth Rice, "Jump Jim Crow," 1828)

The result was the first popular blackface minstrel character. Dale Cockrell writes, "There was no effort here at an accurate representation of black Americans or of their music; the intent was comic ridicule, and audiences in the lower-class theaters of New York's Bowery district loved it."[1] Rice's performance as a stereotypical Black man soon led to the formation of the Virginia Minstrels, the first professional minstrel company.[2] From the beginning, two decades before the Civil War, minstrel shows entertained white audiences by having other white people exaggerate how Black people supposedly spoke and behaved. The effect was a strange mix of mockery, condescension, and sentimentality.

Songs about race from the nineteenth century were less motivated by hatred than by disdain and perhaps fear, but also by the deep, persistent racism of the time and the popularity of minstrel and then "coon songs." They remained popular from the 1840s through the early twentieth century. Although minstrel songs reflected contemporary racial attitudes, minstrelsy's mournful, sentimental ballads were especially affecting. In the midst of a minstrel line's hullabaloo, suddenly someone would sing a gentle, often tearful song.

At times, the complexity of emotion that sentimental ballads give to Black people is surprising, despite the assumption that slaves and former slaves were simple and irresponsible, and incapable of the so-called finer feelings. The songs humanize people otherwise seen as chattel or inferiors. Most often, whites wrote these songs.

"Darling Nelly Gray," written by Benjamin Hanby in 1856, is a sentimental antislavery ballad that is also sympathetic to the young Black man who speaks in the lyric. He bemoans his separation from the woman he loves. She has been sold to a slave owner in Georgia, down the river, where the treatment of Black people was harsher, a common form of punishment (and suffering) in these songs. Hanby's language is stronger and more direct than "Miss Lucy Neale":

> One night I went to see her, but "She's gone!" the neighbors say.
> The white man bound her with his chain;
> They have taken her to Georgia for to war her life away,
> As she toils in the cotton and the cane.
>
> (Benjamin Hanby, "Darling Nelly Gray," 1856)

It remains only for Nelly to die and for her loving young man to follow soon "as the angels clear the way."

These sentimental ballads use the trappings of melodrama to create sympathy for Black characters before Emancipation. Nothing matters more than love, especially love denied. Separated Black lovers wither away and die rather than try to escape to the North. The urgency in these songs is romantic rather than the implied protest and need for freedom so important in spirituals. However, they borrow from the spirituals' traditional imagery of the River Jordan ("Jordan Is a Hard Road to Trabbel") and the more modern imagery of the railroad ("De Gospel Train"). Leaving behind the suffering of this life is a common theme in these minstrel songs, regardless of the slave's age and circumstance:

> Den lay down de shubble and de hoe
> Hang up de fiddle and de bow:
> No more work for poor Old Ned
> He's gone where the good Niggas go.
>
> (Stephen Foster, "Old Uncle Ned," 1848)

In a stunning but not uncommon melodramatic twist, Ned's master "take it mighty bad, / De tears run down like de rain." A slave attests to a slave owner's decency before an audience of white onlookers.

No one wrote greater sentimental ballads for minstrel shows than Stephen Foster, although he traveled to the South only once—when he and his wife rode a steamboat down the Mississippi to New Orleans on their honeymoon. His use of Alabama, Kentucky, Florida's Suwannee River, and any number of "old plantations" was an act of the imagination. Foster, along with most of the others who wrote minstrel songs, had never been to a plantation, but from their lack of experience, they created a mass view of Black people as "uncivilized, inane, emotional, crude, overly sexual, but also 'naturally' musical and athletic."[3]

In an interview with Terry Gross, Ken Emerson, Foster's most recent biographer, remarked "that Southern nostalgia was, in part, invented by a Yankee who spent almost no time in the South, long before the South was even something to be nostalgic about." He describes "the American pop song," beginning with "Foster," as "deeply, even proudly, inauthentic"[4] in its borrowings and adaptations from European and African American music—drawing on everything from the polka, waltz, and march to ragtime, jazz, and the blues. Eventually, songwriters merged these various elements into a popular music hybrid that was, by its very nature, American. Yet during the decades of minstrelsy's popularity, the overt—and acceptable—racism of the songs is appalling, even when the songs view the characters sympathetically.

Foster's first minstrel song, "Oh! Susannah," from 1848, is far from being a sentimental ballad, but it borrows from the themes and viewpoints commonly found in the ballads written for minstrel shows. Although much of the song is comic nonsense ("The sun so hot I froze to death") and Foster wrote it a dozen years before the Civil War, it portrays an apparently free Black man who travels alone from Alabama to Louisiana to find his true love, Susannah. With a melodramatic touch, the narrator's hope for success fills him with joy, but if he fails, "Dis darkie'l surely die." Perhaps because it's largely a comic song, it holds out hope rather than enduring separation.

Typically, Foster used the exaggerated Black dialect that characterized minstrel and "coon songs" into the twentieth century. Although he used the word *n----r* infrequently, his most shocking example comes in the rarely sung second verse of "Oh! Susannah's":

I jumped aboard de telegraph,
And trabbled down de riber,
De lectric fluid magnified,
And killed five hundred nigger.

(Stephen Foster, "Oh! Susannah," 1848)

Much more typical are the sentimental ballads that Foster wrote for minstrel shows, including two of America's most beloved songs: "My Old Kentucky Home" and "Old Folks at Home." When Foster wrote "My Old Kentucky Home" for Christy's Minstrels, he found inspiration in Harriet Beecher Stowe's abolitionist novel, *Uncle Tom's Cabin*. He originally called the song, "Poor Uncle Tom, Good Night." Yet it doesn't sound as if a slave is singing it. It has the elevated formality of a sentimental ballad; it observes the satisfactions of slavery, but it gives no voice to the slaves:

> The sun shines bright in the old Kentucky home,
> 'Tis summer, the darkies are gay,
> The corn top's ripe and the meadow's in the bloom
> While the birds make music all the day.
> The young folks roll on the little cabin floor,
> All merry, all happy and bright.
>
> (Stephen Foster, "My Old Kentucky Home" 1852)

Foster introduces a darker note in the next lines with language that hints briefly at the speech of a slave: "By 'n by Hard Times comes a knocking at the door, / Then my old Kentucky Home, good night." Yet even here, the song never moves closer than observation, although it remains sympathetic. When the "darkies have to part," is it time to separate until tomorrow, or is it the sale of a slave to a new owner or an understated reference to escape? Except for the sudden shift in tone, the song remains ambiguous:

> The day goes by like a shadow o'er the heart,
> With sorrow where all was delight:
> The time has come when the darkies have to part,
> Then my old Kentucky Home, good night!

Emily Bingham reports that as a child growing up in Kentucky, she sang it under "the misguided belief that it portrayed defeated Confederate soldiers" struggling to return home after their defeat in the Civil War. She later learned that it was "first and foremost a song about slavery. . . . A song about slavery became a treasured anthem" for whites.[5] The song, like so much from minstrel shows, was a prime example of grotesque cultural appropriation that accompanied the Industrial Revolution and the rise of Jim Crow. It served as an alternative to the upheavals of a new age as railroads spread far and wide, steam engines proliferated, and the value of craft diminished. Filth and disease undermined the social compact. Large-scale migrations within the country also weakened the sense of belonging, as did the arrival of millions of foreigners who redefined what it meant to be an American as they claimed some of the land for themselves.

Those who were already well-settled may have embraced many of the changes at the same time that cultural anxiety helped to shape social and cultural attitudes. Whites who took advantage of loosening class barriers and the opportunities available in growing cities also longed for a more tranquil, more predictable time. Among the most persuasive songs of the time are those that contemplate the return to an idyllic past—the small town or farm, the family, and the beloved who patiently waits. Yet the most powerful of these songs speaks not for white people, but for Black. They depict Black people's desires to return to a familiar world, rooted in the "carefree" life of slavery, overseen by compassionate owners. They also long to return to what they knew. Often, Black people spoke for themselves in these songs, where "the sun shines bright on *my* old Kentucky home" (emphasis added).

The same lyrics confirmed what white people believed or at least felt to be so. They reassured through distortion and contradiction. Bingham writes that the result is "a toxic illusion of contented bondage"[6] in which Black people are a willing participant as "the head must bow and the back will have to bend, / Wherever the darky may go." The song, its genteel language set to the melodic strains of the Sentimental Ballad, is both cultural appropriation and cultural deception, as white performers in blackface tell white audience members what they want to believe. It includes the graces of slavery with the inherent subservience and inferiority of Black people, now made safe and carefree for all time, at least within the confines of a song. What started as a view of a slave's lowly cabin had become, by the early twentieth century, "a spacious plantation house." Ignoring the lyrics' reference to a cabin and to an understanding that "By 'n by hard times will / Come a-knockin' at the door," the song became a song about family, home, and better days gone by—a song about white life in the South. The shift occurred despite the evidence within the lyric.[7]

A little over a decade ago, some African American members of the Yale Glee Club refused to sing the song. Ironically, its inspiration was an important abolitionist novel, and Frederick Douglass described it as a song that "awakens sympathies for the slave, in which anti-slavery principles take root, grow and flourish."[8] Perhaps as a nineteenth-century man, he was used to the exaggerated dialect in song lyrics but saw past it to the way in which the lyric humanizes Black people. Despite their heavy burdens, they respond emotionally as anyone would, from gaiety and happiness to "sorrow, where all was delight."

In "Old Folks at Home," written a year earlier, Foster had relied heavily on stereotypical Black pronunciation to let a freed or escaped slave speak for himself. He still longs for the old plantation and "de old folks at home." He remembers how happy he was playing with his brother and being with his mother; when he was young, he failed to realize how precious they were. Now he wants to return to live out his days, but he never turns desire into action. His failure to act suggests that the song is the memory of an escaped slave:

> All round de little farm I wandered
> When I was young;
> Den many happy days I squandered,
> Many de songs I sung.
> When I was playing wid my brudder,
> Happy was I,
> Oh! take me to my kind old mudder,
> Dere let me live and die.
>
> (Stephen Foster, "Old Folks at Home," 1851)

Because the white performers in a minstrel line appeared as African Americans, their songs often let the characters speak for themselves despite the racist elements. One of the most important of them is rarely performed anymore, but it's as important to the history of minstrel songs as those of Stephen Foster. Henry Clay Work was a significant American writer of songs even though few still recognize his name. He wrote "Marching Through Georgia," "The Ship That Never Returned," "Crossing the Grand Sierras," and a song that I and many other children learned in elementary school, "My Grandfather's Clock."

Work's father believed in abolition, and the family home in Middletown, Connecticut, was a stop on the Underground Railroad. Work was an abolitionist, too. In 1862, he wrote "Kingdom Coming," using an exaggerated dialect that might reflect what he thought was typical Southern Black speech. Black people at the time embraced the song, and Black troops were said to have sung it as they marched into Richmond during the final days of the war.[9] Ironically, all-Black minstrel companies after Emancipation adopted the song to celebrate their freedom as they performed in front of white audiences. Race and irony go together: the African American performers were Black people portraying white people portraying Black people by wearing blackface.

Although we find the song's use of dialect offensive, Work was following the song standards of the day and, at the same time, was committed to abolition. I suspect that he would not have seen anything contradictory or demeaning in what he was doing. Also known as "The Year of Jubilo," the song portrays slaves who celebrate their new freedom as Union troops approach. They lock their overseer in the cellar and drink their owner's wine and cider. The song is serious, but it also has a sense of humor:

> De massa run? ha, ha!
> De darkey stay? Ha, ha
> It mus' be now de Kingdom comin',
> An' de year ob Jubilo!
>
> (Henry Clay Work, "Kingdom Coming," 1862)

In that same year, Work wrote one of the most affecting of these songs, an abolition song in which an old man named Joe speaks for himself as he nears the end of his life. Now in his nineties, Uncle Joe has survived long enough to be free at last. Work views him sympathetically as he sings in response to the Emancipation Proclamation:

> Blessed days, I lib to see dem,
> Hail, Columby!
> I hab drawn a breff of freedom—
> Now let me die.
> Ninety years I bore de burden,
> Den he heard my cry;
> Standin' on de banks ob Jurdan—
> Now let me die.
>
> (Henry Clay Work, "Uncle Joe's 'Hail Columbia,'" 1862)

The old man gives thanks to the Lord because he links the freeing of the slaves and the preservation of the Union to divine providence:

> O! dis Union can't be broken,
> Dar's no use to try;
> No such ting de Lord has spoken—
> Now let me die.

Many of the lyrics to these songs suggest a major change that will help to reshape popular music early in the twentieth century. Some songs about Black people use diction more suitable to a sentimental ballad. That's especially true when an observer tells the story of a slave, as in Hanby's "Darling Nelly Gray": "Oh! my darling Nelly Gray, they have taken you away, / And I'll never see my darling any more." When Black people speak for themselves, the songwriters fall back on dialect, though sometimes with restraint. In "Old Folks at Home," Foster changes the spelling and pronunciation of only a few words but also uses the sentimental ballad's more formal diction in the same verse:

> One little hut among de bushes,
> One dat I love,
> Still sadly to my mem'ry rushes,
> No matter where I rove.
>
> (Stephen Foster, "Old Folks at Home," 1851)

"Kingdom Coming" is one of the most extreme examples of stereotypical dialect: "Say, darkies, hab you seen de massa, / Wid de muffstash on his face?" What we're seeing in the dialect, despite its repugnance, is the beginning of what would come to be called the conversational lyric, one of the defining elements of the Great American Songbook. Despite its distortions and exaggerations, the stereotypical dialect feels rooted in the speech of ordinary people.

In their portrayal of African Americans, minstrel shows traded on a fictionalized version of authenticity: an entertainment that told white audiences what Black people were supposedly like. This was especially true after the Civil War, when newly liberated slaves were free to move among the general population in greater numbers. It was far from being an agenda, but African Americans had long been invisible, mysterious, or repugnant to many of their fellow countrymen.

Lynn Abbott and Doug Seroff write, "Blackface characters were meant to be 'authentic' representations of African Americans instead of a carnivalesque mask." In the face of widespread industrialization and the movement of people from farms to cities, performers in blackface were seen to reflect a widespread longing to return to agrarian life. Post-Emancipation African Americans, even when they were white people in disguise, evoked simpler rural days of safety, security, and slavery. As a result, many minstrel songs portray the longing of ex-slaves to return to the plantation. It was a stable, predictable world, a happier time and a haven from the unpredictability, anonymity, and violence of city life.[10]

# 12

# "I'll Be Down to Get You in a Taxi, Honey"

Ernest Hogan was an African American minstrel performer and the first Black individual to produce and star in a Broadway show. He also wrote the first important "coon song," "All Coons Look Alike to Me," in 1895. A variation on both minstrel songs and ragtime, the "coon song" relied heavily on syncopation, although it soon followed the movement of African Americans to Northern cities. It placed its characters at rent parties, in saloons and barbershops, or on street corners. It also dressed them up to sashay down the avenue or attend a cotillion on a Saturday night.

In the foreground of the sheet music cover to "All Coons Look Alike to Me," four African American men preen for the same African American woman. They dress in what they think is finery. Diamonds are everywhere. With their outlandish clothes and oversized bright-red lips, they are grotesque figures whose attempts to impress both the woman and, by implication, white Americans are ludicrous.

The song is about a barber whose "honey gal" ditches him for another, more prominent "coon barber." Although he was good to Lucy Jane and gave her "presents by the score," he ends up as a Jonah Man, a perennial loser, who tries to become rich to win her back. She will have none of it:

All coons look alike to me,
I've got another beau, you see,
And he's just as good to me as you, nig! ever tried to be,
He spends his money free,
I know we can't agree,
So I don't like you no how,
All coons look alike to me.

(Ernest Hogan, "All Coons Look Alike to Me," 1895)

Richard Crawford writes that Lucy Jane's "sneering dismissal mocks the very idea of love, except perhaps as a ploy to corral a partner for display in public and sex in private." He further suggests that "an outlook like this, no matter how thickly layered with irony, allowed sheet-music buyers to glimpse a realm of male-female relations beyond the limits that Tin Pan Alley had explored."[1] Only African Americans could be presented in that way. Actually, Tin Pan Alley was just getting underway in the 1890s and would soon embrace "coon songs." Before long, romance and implied sex would become its stock in trade.

"Coon songs" like Hogan's and those who came after him had a harder urban edge than the minstrel songs that preceded and overlapped them. Violence was often part of the new mix, just as it was increasingly part of life in all ethnic neighborhoods with their atrocious living conditions—the crowded tenements, the filth, the poverty.

On the sheet music cover of Theodore Metz's "Do Your Honey Do," a Black man in work clothes reaches into his pocket as he watches a finely dressed couple walk away from him. That simple act is ominous. The betrayed lover is the character who speaks. "When you feel in your bones dat gal you love, / Is another nigger's beau," you turn to murder: "And I done him, cause I loved her. / I carved him long, I carved him deep" (Theodore Metz, "Do Your Honey Do," 1897).

The popularity of the "coon song" reflected the country's strong tide of racism and fear, in both the North and the South. Once Reconstruction came to an end in the 1870s and African Americans began to move North, "coon songs" flooded the nation. From the beginning, some of these songs emphasized Black people's "natural rhythm" and their gift for music and dancing. They climaxed, but didn't stop, thirty years later with "Alexander's Ragtime Band." Because "coon songs" were also "ragtime songs," their content contributed to white America's acceptance of ragtime and other forms of African American music. It made something appealing (and essentially American) from something ugly and degrading. Nearly all "coon songs" were ragtime songs, but not all ragtime songs were "coon songs."

The quintessential "coon song" character, even when his name doesn't appear in a lyric, is the city-dwelling "Zip Coon," whose garish clothes and dandified behavior are supposed to conceal his threatening manner. His dress is supposed to impress his white betters.[2] He and his lady might also win a prize at a Saturday night dance as the "hottest dress'd couple in the hall."[3] He is still as lazy and foolish as he was in minstrel songs, but now he is also a dishonest, sexually aggressive drunk, who gambles and hustles and probably has a razor up his sleeve. He also flouts common morality by living with a woman not his wife.

> Last night I did go to a big Crap game,
> How dem coons did gamble wuz a sin and shame . . .
> I'm gambling for my Sadie,
> Cause she's my lady,
> I'm a hustling coon, . . . dat's just what I am.
>
> (Nathan Bivins, "Gimme Ma Money," 1898)

Jim Crow was often depicted in rags, but Zip Coon turned out in what he considered to be finery. Between them, "they represented (and defined) the stereotypes between which most black Americans at the time lived their lives."[4]

"Coon songs" drew a dehumanizing and demoralizing portrait set to the irresistible syncopation of ragtime. "Zip Coon" fed the basest assumptions about race to city-dwelling white people as African Americans moved into nearby neighborhoods. As they sought social acceptance, Zip Coon's behavior and dress made him a figure of mockery and danger.

Because a number of the most prominent performers who blacked up were Jewish, you begin to notice the cultural links and antagonisms between them. Like Black people, Jews were also seeking freedom, not from slavery but from centuries of oppression. Despite the customs and attire that Americans found odd, they still had the advantage of being white. Jewish songwriters in early Tin Pan Alley escaped being alien by writing "coon songs." Their success made African American music into something distinctively American.

Ironically, blacking up gave such Jewish performers as Al Jolson and Eddie Cantor a sense of freedom and belonging. Concealing their Jewish identities freed them to leave the old ways behind and become American: antic, insinuating, prosperous, and sexual. They used performance as a way to make themselves over. White people singing "coon songs" mocked Black people; Jews singing "coon songs" in blackface also mocked Black people. The political scientist Michael Rogin writes, "Blackface becomes the instrument that transfers identities from immigrant Jew to American."[5]

In "coon songs," as in minstrel songs before them, most of the writers and singers were white, although now the songs came more often from Tin Pan Alley. Ragtime had swept the country by the late 1890s. Lynn Abbott and Doug Seroff describe one of its effects:

> Ragtime released a pent-up reservoir of modernism in African American culture, providing the antidote to "Ethiopian minstrelsy," which had stifled the development of race entertainment for most of the nineteenth century. Just as the century drew to a close, the lid blew off, unleashing a torrent of creativity that swept thousands of black writers, performers, musicians, and entrepreneurs into the professional ranks.[6]

The Harlem Renaissance was only two decades away.

It was as if other assumptions about African Americans had somehow come true—the belief that they possessed an innate sense of rhythm that white people could only try to imitate. The so-called primitive feel for the music persisted in "coon songs" right to the end. A lot of these songs also derived at least indirectly from the great success of Irving Berlin's "Alexander's Ragtime Band." It wasn't the first song about Black music or the first that encouraged Black people to go out dancing, but it did influence a number of songs over the following years. In the same year as Berlin's super hit, another stereotypical song describes lazy Ephraham Jones, who never moves unless he has to—until he hears a band: "Other times he's doggone lazy, / But it seems the music sets him crazy, / And the folks all call him Brass Band Ephraham Jones" (G. W. Meyer and Joe Goodman, "Brass Band Ephraham Jones," 1911).

As the major European powers rearmed for what would become the First World War, American isolationism dominated at home. An awareness of what was happening in Europe also led to a patriotic surge that made its way into songs. In this one, a white observer watches a military parade but finds himself drawn mainly to the band:

> Oh! Lordy, that band!
> For there is something about it that is grand,
> And altho' I never felt this way before,

I want to do a two-step right to war,
When I hear that colored ragtime regiment band.
> (Melville Morris and A. Seymour Brown, "That Ragtime Regiment Band," 1913)

Shelton Brooks, the African American songwriter, also wrote the most important of these songs after "Alexander's Ragtime Band." Late in his life, Berlin said that the secret of his song's success was "the idea of inviting every receptive auditor" to join "the happy ruction." He replaced the traditionally formal invitation to dance with a call—"Come on and hear!"—to join the revelry.[7] A half dozen years later, Brooks wrote "The Darktown Strutters' Ball," in which he replaced Berlin's bugle call with something less urgent and more confident, something smoother—"I'll be down to get you in a taxi, honey"—that leads to an evening of joyful dancing:

Goin' to dance out all my shoes:
When they play the "Jelly Roll Blues"
Tomorrow night, at the Darktown Strutters' Ball.
> (Shelton Brooks, "The Darktown Strutters' Ball, 1917)

During those years, Chicago held an annual ball in which prostitutes wore elegant gowns, and their pimps arrived in white tie, spats, and top hats. The police looked the other way as long as nobody caused trouble. When Brooks was in his eighties, he told an interviewer how he turned a story he had heard into a song: "Now I heard about this working man.... He gets an invitation to an affair to be given by the local pimps.... All a mistake and he never should have been asked."[8]

That same spirit infused an even later "coon song," although it set the band in a stereotypical "jungle town," where the monkey plays the saxophone, the bear the trombone, and "the lion bangs the drum." Everyone from "the elephants, the camels, and the kangaroos, / Harmonizing with the cats and cockatoos, / In jungle land, in the Jazzbo Jungle Band" (Carlton Whidden, "That Jazzbo Jungle Band," 1918). The use of animals in songs like this suggests the minimal civilization of African Americans.

Two years after "The Darktown Strutters' Ball," white songwriters Benny Davis, Ernie Erdman, and Sid Erdman began a song with a waiting taxi to take a couple to the dance. The lyrics use no dialect; only one reference makes it a "coon song": "We've got to show some class, that's all, / At the High Brown Babies' Ball" (Benny Davis, Ernie Erdman, and Sid Erdman, "At the High Brown Babies' Ball," 1919). Similarly, this song has only a single reference, a name, that makes it a "coon song": "Ephraham, the Leader man, who led the band last Fall, / He plays the music at the Devil's Ball" (Irving Berlin, "At the Devil's Ball," 1913).

Some songs about dancing were "coon songs," some not, but they were everywhere. Ragtime and jazz, and the way the Castles danced to them, were shaping our popular music and loosening the rigidities of Victorian America. They added grace to syncopation to make it acceptable to white audiences. They also removed at least some of the sexual charge of Black dancing. Soon, songs about going to balls to dance became more and more fanciful as songwriters searched for new ways to keep the craze for dancing alive. In 1913, Jean Schwartz and William Jerome announced, "Springtime gave a flower garden ball." The results were charming and amusing:

> The Tulip and the stately Goldenrod
> Saw Morning Glories peeping over the wall
> The Tiger Lilies in disguise
> They fluttered 'round the Butterflies,
> While dancing at the Flower Garden Ball.
> (Jean Schwartz and William Jerome, "At the Flower Garden Ball," 1913)

Then, in the year of Prohibition and women's suffrage, Tom Delaney and Sidney Easton linked a song about dancing to Prohibition and jazz: "When the jazz band struck up, You'd be surprised, / Ev'rybody in the hall was google eyed" (Tom Delaney and Sidney Easton, "At the New Jump Steady Ball," 1920).

Despite the end of "coon songs" after the First World War, white perceptions of African Americans persisted. They changed rather than disappeared. During the 1920s and 1930s, when the Harlem Renaissance flourished and affluent white urbanites discovered psychoanalysis, they raced uptown nightly to see Black stars at the Cotton Club and Connie's Inn, or they went to Broadway to watch high-powered all-Black revues. Sophisticated white people who thought themselves in the know considered African Americans to be authentic creatures of the id. Their civilized behavior was seen as recent and only skin-deep.

Ironically, African American songwriters also wrote minstrel and "coon songs," even though Black audiences generally detested them. They were what the much larger white market wanted and provided employment for both ex-slaves and freeborn African Americans in show business. As Tin Pan Alley took form just before the turn of the twentieth century, Black songwriters lacked the same access to music publishers as their white counterparts. Tom the Tattler, a columnist in the African American newspaper *The Freeman*, wrote, "The colored man writes the 'coon' song, the colored singer sings the 'coon' song, the colored race is compelled to stand for the belittling and ignominy of the 'coon' song, but the money from the 'coon' song flows with ceaseless activity into the white man's pockets."[9]

The most important of the early African American songwriters was James A. Bland, who wrote minstrel songs before the turn of the century. Alec Wilder called him the songwriter who "broke down the barriers to white music publishers' offices."[10] Accurate, but inadequate. From the 1880s on, African American songwriters played an increasingly important role in American music through ragtime, jazz, and the blues, and eventually in Tin Pan Alley and even on Broadway, but it took them another half century to gain full access to publishers and the market.

Ironically, Bland, whose songs used a thick Southern dialect, was born free in Flushing, New York, in 1854 and was a graduate of Howard University. He never experienced slavery. Like the white songwriter Stephen Foster, he learned about the sentiments and points of view in his songs by listening to other minstrel songs. By the mid-1870s, he was touring in all-Black minstrel shows in the United States and England.

African Americans formed their own minstrel companies after the Civil War because white companies wouldn't hire them. They followed all of minstrelsy's conventions: Mr. Interlocutor, the End Men, and the line of men in blackface. James A. Bland was the exception. He appeared onstage as a solo act to sing the songs he'd written as he accompanied himself on the banjo. He did not black up.

His important songs are better than most, but they still fit the accepted outlook of minstrelsy. One of those songs encouraged white audiences to accept slavery as something that treated Black people kindly. It provides a gently uplifting look at what was both degrading and cruel. "Carry Me Back to Old Virginny" relies on dialect to depict someone who was once a slave but still yearns to return to the fields where "the cotton and corn and taters grow." Although he "labored so hard for old Massa," it will always be the place "where this old darkey's heart am longed to go." If he can find a way to return, "Virginny" will also be the place where he will "live till I wither and decay." A Southern sentimental ballad reflects something demeaning to Black people but reassuring to whites (James A. Bland, "Carry Me Back to Ol' Virginny," c1878).

"Massa and Missis" have already died, but they will meet soon "on that bright and golden shore," where they and their former slave will "be happy and free from all sorrow." Bland's character has endured slavery but keeps a mostly sunny disposition as he remembers the plantation, "Massa," and "Missus." He goes so far as to link the three of them in their escape from earthly sorrow, as if they had endured equally. It's an unsettling conclusion. Bland wrote the song within the conventions of minstrelsy and with an awareness of what white audiences wanted to hear.

Among Bland's best-known songs are "De Golden Wedding," "Golden Slippers," and "Hand Me Down My Walking Cane," but the only one as well-known as "Carry Me Back to Old Virginny" is "In the Evening by the Moonlight." It remains known because others have altered its lyrics and eliminated its racist dialect to make it acceptable as attitudes changed. Yet, at the same time, it underscored white people's assumptions about the inferiority of Black people, just in a more polite way. Using the language of minstrel songs, Bland sets it at the end of the slaves' (or sharecroppers') long workday. After a simple dinner of hoecake, they gather to entertain themselves:

> In de ebening by de moonlight, you could hear us darkies singing
> In de ebening by de moonlight, you could hear de banjo ringing,
> How de old folks would enjoy it,
> They would sit all night and listen,
> As we sang in de ebening by de moonlight.
> (James A. Bland, "In the Evening by the Moonlight," 1879)

The song is an accurate portrayal of one aspect of slavery life. As Nikki Giovanni writes, "They were tired but they did not go to bed. Instead, they brought whatever they had—a pot for a drum, they could make a flute out of wood; a comb for a mouth harp—they brought what they had, and they made music."[11]

When the all-white Edison Quartet recorded the song in 1905, the word *darkey* remained, but the dialect had disappeared. Their version sounds like something between a barbershop quartet and a stately hymn. On the other hand, when the African American singer Nina Simone recorded it in 1960, she sang:

> In the evening by the moonlight
> You could hear banjos ringing,
> You could hear them by the moonlight
> You could hear my folks all singing.

Her version removes the dialect and any overt indication of race but gives the song the measured force of a spiritual. The second time through, she ups the tempo so it feels more like a gospel song. It's a remarkable example of reinventing and reclaiming.

The First World War produced a large number of patriotic songs. The most surprising of them are also "coon songs." Despite discrimination, African Americans joined the military in large numbers to fight for the United States. They assumed that their bravery in the trenches would lead to better conditions and greater acceptance at home. They were wrong. Things got worse before they got better, but African Americans' response to increasingly violent discrimination helped to fuel the Harlem Renaissance of the 1920s and 1930s.[12]

A number of songs portrayed African American soldiers both stereotypically and admiringly at the same time. They rarely drop the stereotypes that make us cringe but were common then. When white children reject a child "because his skin was brown," he runs home to his mother, who comforts him, "Come and lay your kinky head on Mammy's shoulder, / Don't you cry you're Mammy's little choc'late soldier." Years later, that same mother, now elderly, watches with pride as her son marches off to fight: "He is really Mammy's choc'late soldier, and his gun is not a toy" (Archie Gottler and Sidney D. Mitchell, "Mammy's Choc'late Soldier," 1918).

What's most striking about some of these songs is their attitude toward African American soldiers. They depict them as they do white soldiers: patriotic, even heroic, and prepared to leave their loved ones to risk their lives to do their duty. Eventually, the lyric focuses on Dinah Lee as she watches her Alexander march away:

> Goodbye Alexander,
> Goodbye honey boy
> Dressed up in that uniform, you fills my heart with joy.
> 
> (Henry Creamer and Turner Layton, "Good bye Alexander, Good bye Honey-Boy," 1918)

That same attitude defines another song that never escapes stereotypes. It admires "Old black Joe" and condescends to him at the same time. A white man comes upon an aged Black man in uniform, ready to leave for France. The sheet music cover depicts him as a "coon" with a rumpled uniform and white hair sticking out beneath his cap, especially compared to the meticulous white officer standing nearby. Joe is rightly proud of his service, which included fighting in the Civil War. The white man asks why he's going at his age:

> He said, "My Uncle Sammy's callin',
> And for him I'll live or die . . .
> I'll give the whole world liberty
> Just like Lincoln did for me,
> Then they'll be doggone proud in Dixie
> Of their Old Black Joe."
> 
> (Harry Carroll, "They'll Be Mighty Proud in Dixie of Their Old Black Joe," 1918)

It may be a "coon song" for a character who truly believes his pipe dream about Dixie, but the need for volunteers to fight the war shifts its point of view. The song portrays a "coon" as a patriot.

# 13

# Come On and Hear!

*[Note: Many of the songs in this chapter use offensive language. ML]*

Men in uniform during the Second World War had served with others of every possible background except African Americans, whose units were segregated. Yet antisemitism and racial violence persisted in the years after the war ended. To fight discrimination, Hollywood made movies about antisemitism (*Gentleman's Agreement*, 1947) and racial tension (*Home of the Brave* and *Pinky*, both 1949). The truth was direr than the movies suggested. After serving in the South Pacific, Corporal Lewis W. Matthews sailed home in May 1946. He spent most of the thirty-day trip belowdecks in a separate area for Black troops. He had also served in an all-Black unit. He was one of 1.2 million African Americans in the military, but the army, like the rest of the nation, was still segregated. At home, Matthews and his fellow Black countrymen found the same discrimination and violence they had faced before the war.[1]

According to history professor Charissa Threat, "At the heart of it was a kind of nervousness and fear that many whites had that returning Black veterans would upset the racial status quo."[2] Many African Americans who served had been trained as mechanics, carpenters, or electricians, but employment counselors refused to recommend them for skilled and semiskilled jobs. Matthews used the G.I. Bill to learn how to make denture molds. When he finally landed a job, he was allowed to do nothing but mix plaster. Eventually, he studied business administration at New York University and sold life insurance, but he was denied a government loan when he wanted to open his own office. He said, "I know Black veterans who couldn't get loans and had real problems."[3] President Harry S. Truman eventually desegregated the military in 1948.

Racist attitudes persist throughout the culture in different forms of expression, sometimes assertively, sometimes almost hidden. Despite continuing discrimination against African Americans, racist language had become increasingly less acceptable in polite Northern society after the turn of the century, but it refused to disappear, even in Code-bound Hollywood movies and Broadway musicals. Racist language, including the word *n----r*, appeared occasionally in talkies in the 1930s and even the 1940s. I have a fragment of memory of watching an old Western movie on TV before I started my homework one day and being aware that the cowboy hero called the grown Black stable hand, "Boy."

The chorus for the hit song "Chattanooga Choo Choo," introduced by the Glenn Miller Orchestra in the 1941 movie *Sun Valley Serenade*, uses it too. It begins: "Pardon me, boy, / Is that the Chattanooga Choo Choo?" (Harry Warren and Mack Gordon, "Chattanooga Choo Choo," *Sun Valley Serenade*, 1941). As far as I know, the Motion Picture Production Code did not require changes in that sort of language for a very long time. In fact, it took several decades to ban the use of *n----r* and then only begrudgingly.[4]

In her great 1918 novel, *My Antonia*, Willa Cather describes a Black pianist, Blind d'Arnault, who comes to the small prairie town of Black Hawk, Nebraska. His playing is unpolished but infectious; soon, dancing sweeps the town, and the servant girls begin to stray—from their responsibilities and toward young men. Could Cather have been thinking of ragtime?

> As piano-playing, it was perhaps abominable, but as music it was something real, vitalized by a sense of rhythm that was stronger than his other physical senses. . . . It was as if all the agreeable sensations possible to creatures of flesh and blood were heaped up on those black and white keys, and he were gloating over them and trickling them through his yellow fingers.[5]

It remains essential to face the racist attitudes so prevalent and acceptable in the past while also understanding that at least some songwriters were alert to the plight of Black people but were also men and women of their own time—among them Irving Berlin, Oscar Hammerstein II, and E. Y. Harburg. They saw themselves as politically liberal patriots. Like all lives, theirs were complicated and sometimes contradictory. As Barack Obama put it, the idea of America "has never been easy."[6]

Many major songwriters from the Great American Songbook had well-earned reputations for supporting the rights of African American citizens, but the reality is more complex. Irving Berlin meant it when he said, "A good song is one that sells." Not because he needed the money, but because he believed in the judgments of what he called the mob. He was our most democratic songwriter. At the same time, he held certain beliefs about the history of American popular music. As attitudes changed, his remained firm.

Berlin came to see opera and minstrelsy not as high culture and low, but as "two pillars holding up the artifice of his vision" of what American popular music could look like.[7] Throughout his career, he kept a photograph of Stephen Foster on his office wall. It's important to remember that when Berlin wrote his first song in 1907, minstrelsy was still part of American show business, although vaudeville was quickly replacing it.

Because ragtime was so popular, the pros in Tin Pan Alley soon borrowed its distinguishing characteristic: the syncopation that made it so easy to dance to. The resulting "ragtime songs" were not rags at all, but highly syncopated 32-bar popular songs. Many of them were also "coon songs" because of the way they depicted African Americans. They qualified as love songs because they described the couples who danced to the one-step and the two-step. Into this musical melee stepped young Irving Berlin, eager to make a buck by writing songs.

Between 1907 and 1914, he wrote about thirty songs with Black characters.[8] Most of them rely on predictable stereotypes and themes, including exaggerated dialect, sexual innuendo, and a longing to return to an idealized rural South.[9] He later requested that performers no longer sing them. In later songs, he toned down the stereotypes, the epithets, and the accent, but he also believed that minstrelsy was "a fundamentally American theatrical style"[10] long after it had become unfashionable and even taboo. Between 1914, when he wrote his first complete Broadway score, and the end of the Second World War, he included a minstrel number or something suggestive of minstrelsy in all his shows.[11]

Berlin recognized minstrelsy as a form of theater accessible to all Americans during its eighty years of popularity. Many others have seen it as a reflection of white supremacy and the oppression of African Americans. Jeffrey Magee argues that Berlin's understanding of entertainment, formed early in the twentieth century, blinded him to the ugly side of minstrelsy: "It shaped Berlin's notion of a kind of ideal American 'common man,' for whom all his work was designed."[12] His contribution, Jeffrey Melnick wrote, "was to distill the sights and sounds of minstrelsy into a usable modern musical grammar."[13]

A Jewish immigrant who arrived with his family at the age of five from a village in Russia, Berlin thought of himself as a patriot; he was grateful for what America had given him. In addition to "God Bless America," he wrote fifteen musicals, two of which—*Yip Yip Yaphank*, during the First World War, and *This Is the Army*, during the Second World War—raised money to provide assistance to the families of those lost in combat. For *This Is the Army*, he wrote "Song of Freedom" to link his work to the nation he loved. Rather than writing a hymn or a march, he turned to swing time, the dominant beat of the day: "I'm singing a song of freedom / To all people wherever they may be" (Irving Berlin, "Song of Freedom," *Holiday Inn*, 1942).

After *This Is the Army* closed its limited run on Broadway in September 1942, Berlin spent most of the war years traveling with the company to military bases in Europe and the Pacific, sometimes close to the front lines. He felt a bond with the young men in the cast. Each night, he would don his First World War uniform (it still fit him in his mid-fifties) to gripe like anyone who's ever served in the military, except Berlin did it in song. He stood alone at center stage, tapping out the time with his right foot, singing in his small, reedy voice. Mockery of authority is an ingrained American virtue, and Berlin celebrates it in comic terms: "Someday I'm going to murder the bugler, / Someday they're going to find him dead" (Irving Berlin, "Oh! How I Hate to Get Up in the Morning," *Yip Yip Yaphank*, *This Is the Army*, 1918, 1942).

For *This Is the Army*, Berlin also wrote a number for Black singers and tap dancers. With the Harlem Renaissance still fresh in people's minds, he wrote "What the Well-Dressed Man in Harlem Will Wear." It was the time of zoot suits, but now the well-dressed Harlemite arrives in an army uniform. The song celebrates the patriotism of African Americans and praises their contributions to the war effort. The number is jazzy and appealing, but it also includes stereotypical wide-eyed grins, along with a man (in the all-male cast) dressed as a woman to mock the Harlem style of the day. The staging is athletic and rapid-fire as a dozen African American tap dancers turn the song into a showstopper (Irving Berlin, "What the Well-Dressed Man in Harlem Will Wear," *Yip Yip Yaphank, This Is the Army,* 1918, 1942).

Berlin originally wrote "Mandy" for *Yip Yip Yaphank* (1918) but cut it before opening night. He revived it as part of his score for the *Ziegfeld Follies of 1919* and, more than twenty years later, for *This Is the Army,* where he used it as part of a minstrel medley with Stephen Foster's "Old Folks at Home." In the 1940s, audiences still found such minstrel numbers palatable.[14] The singers in the all-male cast appear in military uniforms, but the dancers in the cast dress as minstrel performers complete with blackface and are soon joined by "women," also in blackface and dressed in "Jemimah" costumes. Although the song hearkens back to nineteenth-century minstrelsy, the cast sings without resorting to dialect, and the lyrics are charmingly old-fashioned. Despite its appeal, the number's staging and costuming are offensive eighty years later, even though the lyrics are innocent:

> Mandy, there's a minister handy
> And it sure would be dandy
> If we'd let him make a fee.
>
> (Irving Berlin, "Mandy," *Yip Yip Yaphank,* 1918)

Aside from the cringe-worthy stereotypes in both lyrics and performances, many of the songs that trace back to minstrel shows are appealing. That's where the dilemma lies. What shall we do with such songs as Foster's "Old Folks at Home" and "Oh! Susanna"? Just how much history are we willing to do without, no matter how much it embarrasses and offends people, and how much explaining it requires?

Berlin began to write songs in earnest after his first song, "Marie from Sunny Italy" (1907), earned him thirty-five cents in royalties. He soon figured out that if he could set catchy words to an equally catchy tune, he might be able to earn as much as $25 a week. After sleeping in flophouses and alleys for far too long, he must have found the possibility of an escape from poverty thrilling. The songs themselves had nothing to do with him personally; they were strictly what the market would bear. He was borrowing from what he heard in the streets and dance halls, and the tough Chinatown bar where he worked as a singing waiter. The customers at Mike Salter's Pelham Bay Café knew him for the bawdy parodies of hit songs that he wrote and performed. Salter was a Jew with a dark complexion, so the neighborhood customers called him "Nigger Mike." Such was the blunt humor of the day.

The ironies abound throughout Berlin's longtime affection for minstrel shows as an essential American form. For the first fifteen years of his career, he wrote mainly ragtime songs, "coon songs," and ethnic songs, along with an occasional ballad. Implied sex was more important than romance in these early songs; ragtime's effect on "spoony coons" was unmistakable: "I'm goin' crazy that rag's a daisy / I just can't make my feelings behave" (Ted Snyder and Irving Berlin, "Wild Cherries Rag," 1909).

Like many songwriters of the day, Berlin often combined ragtime's syncopation with a "coon song" lyric in a single number, as in "Alexander and His Clarinet." "Alexander" was a commonly used name in "coon songs," designed to mock the pretentious names that African Americans supposedly gave their children. Alexander Adams woos Miss Eliza Johnson with his clarinet, which brings "out music that no one has brought out yet." They quarreled last Sunday, though, and she's not ready to forgive, even though she still loves him and "I love your clarinet." The lyric obviously uses the clarinet as a sexual joke. Many "coon songs" emphasized the supposed sexual prowess of African Americans as well as what was considered their instinctive musical abilities. The image of the clarinet provides both (Ted Snyder and Irving Berlin, "Alexander and His Clarinet," 1910).

Most of these syncopated numbers were funny or easy to dance to; they were likable and entertaining, and that's what sold the sheet music. Yet Berlin's "coon songs" were more restrained and less offensive than most. That was especially true of the landmark "Alexander's Ragtime Band." Aside from the bandleader's implicitly comic name, only a few references give away its identity: the use of "ma" for "my," and the line, "That's just the bestest band what am, honey lamb" (Irving Berlin, "Alexander's Ragtime Band," 1911).

Berlin first wrote the song as an instrumental and then added words after his mentor, George M. Cohan, urged him to do so. At a Friar's Roast where

Berlin first performed it, Cohan introduced him as "the Jew boy" who "writes a song with a good lyric, a lyric that rhymes, good music, music you don't have to dress up to listen to. But it is good music."[15]

Right from the start, the repeated martial call, "Come on and hear," grabs your attention before you learn that an African American man is trying to sweet-talk his "honey lamb" into going to a dance with him—the dance where the "ragged meter man" leads the "bestest band what am." They can even play the "Swanee River" in ragtime.

Large numbers of Americans knew the song, sang it, and danced to it. It was one of those moments when nearly everybody was in on the game—before radio and television, and long before the internet—but we pulled it off. Sheet music, vaudeville, society orchestras in hotel ballrooms, and early recordings all helped. The most successful songs encapsulated what Americans felt and then returned it to them in a form and performance style they found irresistible. Singable music and memorable words created a moment that was as insignificant as going to a dance on a Saturday night. The song felt important, though, because it re-created in different ways the pulse we had come to expect from our best patriotic anthems, but with a lot of syncopation and a touch of sex thrown in. It was more casual and less serious, obviously, but the emotional connection—a different kind of emotional connection—was there as well. In its way, even a lighthearted song like "Alexander's Ragtime Band" told a nation full of turkey trotters that America and its people were up-to-date and in on the pleasures the country had to offer. They were shaking their shoulders in the pursuit of happiness.

With his all-American hit, a Jewish immigrant songwriter had helped to complete the "translation" of African American syncopation into "American." It was the musical modernity of Tin Pan Alley, and it "came directly from the African American tradition." It was "the progenitor of a field and forest full of 'animal dances,'"[16] known for their unrestrained sexiness, especially compared to the waltz.

"Alexander's Ragtime Band" simply refused to disappear. A great star of the day, Emma Carus, introduced it in vaudeville[17] shortly before Arthur Collins and Byron G. Harlin's recording became the number-one hit of 1911. The blues singer Bessie Smith had a hit recording of it in 1927, as did the Boswell Sisters in 1934. In 1938, Alice Faye sang it in a successful movie entitled *Alexander's Ragtime Band*, and by 1951, it had had at least a dozen hit covers.[18]

What was going on musically beneath the veneer of Victorian society in America was astounding. At a time of increasingly proper middle-class behavior designed to parallel the rigid norms of the Gilded Age, disreputable saloons encouraged the mixing of the races, especially when the prostitutes were white and their male partners Black. At worst, they danced together in newly named places called *dives*. The word came into use during the nineteenth century's last years because, to find these places, you had to go down a flight of stairs and then often down a long, dark hall until you came to a dimly lit room with a bar along one wall, a few musicians tucked into a corner playing wild music, and a waxed floor for the sexually charged dancing.

The author Dale Cockrell writes, "The music they fashioned—exhilarating rhythms, a brass sound, the thumping bass, and sinuous melodies—came out of an improvised, oral tradition, a music-of-the-air that was not published or written down."[19] As the dancing became more boisterous, the prostitutes and even the men might start shedding clothes and grinding their hips together. A lot of these places also had cribs nearby, so the women could take their partners to finish what they'd started on the dance floor. Respectable people began to attend to watch the goings-on. Some found the decadence reprehensible; others found it seductive.

Not all dives allowed the mixing of the races. Those that did soon became known as "Black and Tans," places that "welcomed patrons both black and white, that enabled music enjoyed by both races, and that encouraged the sharing of bodies, both through dance and through sex."[20]

In Black and Tans, dancing to ragtime found its first home. Ragtime had grown up in saloons and whorehouses in and around St. Louis before it spread quickly across the country. Its ragged melodies required a different way of moving that often led to a casting off of restraints. It wasn't respectable, but it was irresistible. Through much of the nineteenth century, minstrel songs, along with sentimental and parlor ballads, shaped America's taste, but dives were also flourishing, especially in New York City. Every attempt by the forces of reform to shut them down led to closings, but the owners simply moved to another block and reopened. This jubilant sinning seems to have had a life of its own. George P. Hammond of Parkhurst City Vigilance League was not the only moralist to connect immorality and ragtime.[21]

Berlin had worked in one of these joints as a young man, though it was a step or two up from the most sordid places. The Pelham Bay Café, down on Pell Street in the heart of Chinatown, had a tough male clientele with some rooms with Chinese whores up a flight of stairs. Berlin had left home at thirteen to ease the financial burden on his family and, by the age of eighteen, had a steady job as a singing waiter at the café. His salacious parodies of the songs of the day made him popular with the customers and would eventually lead to his providing the lyrics for his first song, "Marie from Sunny Italy."[22] This parody isn't by Berlin, but it's typical of what was going on. The lyrics to "Chinatown, My Chinatown"—"Hearts that knew no other land / Drifting to and fro"—became "Where you can get a hump / For fifty cents a throw."[23]

In 1911, the same year as "Alexander's Ragtime Band," Berlin asked a fellow songwriter named George Botsford about his appealing but unsuccessful "Grizzly Bear Rag." Berlin offered to provide a set of lyrics for it. Botsford agreed, and the song became one of Berlin's major early hits. The heat and syncopation of ragtime gave it a sexual drive, especially compared to the elegant melodies of sentimental ballads. Berlin softened its hard sexual edges with indirection and humor so they became both recognizable and acceptable: "Snuggle up to your baby, / Sway me every way" (George Botsford, Irving Berlin, "Doing the Grizzly Bear," 1912).

A story, perhaps apocryphal, says that soon after the song appeared, a reformist group in Boston sued to have it suppressed. At one point, the reformers' lawyer asked that it be performed to demonstrate its impropriety. Almost immediately, the members of the jury began to sing along. The judge threw the case out of court.

What remains, though, is the need to try to explain the phenomenal popularity of "Alexander's Ragtime Band." As the historian Mark Sullivan explained, with "Alexander's Ragtime Band," Berlin "lifted ragtime from the depths of sordid dives to the apotheosis of fashionable vogue."[24] Ragtime appeared to be on its way out after more than fifteen years of popularity. "Alexander's Ragtime Band" revitalized it for another decade, even though it was a march rather than a rag and had barely a trace of syncopation. But its punchy tempo and simple, repetitive lyrics made it easy to sing and remember: "Oh, ma honey, / Oh, ma honey?" It struck a chord with the public. It sold a million copies of sheet music in 1911 and then, to prove that was no fluke, sold another million in 1912. And then the Castles latched on to it.

In 1912, broke and stranded in Paris, Vernon and Irene Castle landed a job dancing in a not especially chic nightclub called the Café de Paris. They soon became the talk of Paris when they rose from their table each night at midnight to wait for a single spotlight to pick them out. They bowed to one another and then began to dance. The song each night was "Alexander's Ragtime Band," whose popularity had spread to England and France, even though its muscular tune, eager lyric, and overriding confidence made it distinctively American. It reveled in its own modernity, and Americans couldn't wait to welcome the Castles back home. People mobbed the Manhattan pier when they arrived.

Despite Berlin's restraint and the changes in racial attitudes over twenty-five years, his most shocking blackface number was part of the score for the 1942 movie *Holiday Inn*, in which Bing Crosby runs an inn that opens only on holidays. The rest of the time, his character lazes about contentedly. In addition to "White Christmas," "You're Easy to Dance With" (for costar Fred Astaire), "Be Careful, It's My Heart," and "Easter Parade," the score includes the offensive "Abraham." For Lincoln's birthday, still celebrated separately in 1942, Berlin wrote it to praise the president who came to see that ending slavery was as important as preserving the Union and politicked successfully for the passage of the Thirteenth Amendment abolishing slavery.

Crosby sings "Abraham" without dialect, although he often did turn to it briefly for comic effect on his recordings and radio show. However, he appears in blackface in the demeaning costume of a Black preacher, complete with muttonchops. The orchestra plays in blackface, and costar Marjorie Reynolds appears in the second half of the number dressed as Topsy from *Uncle Tom's Cabin*. Meanwhile, in the kitchen, a Black maid played by Louise Beavers sings to her children, "Who was it set the darkey free? / Abraham! Abraham!" (Irving Berlin, "Abraham," *Holiday Inn*, 1942).

In the 1920s through the 1940s, Northerners pointed the finger at Jim Crow laws in the South, often without recognizing Jim Crow practices all around them—the force of custom rather than law. In 1933, though, despite his early "coon songs," Berlin championed Ethel Waters, the first African American singer to cross over and, in the process, pave the way for such performers as Lena Horne and Nat King Cole. Waters began her singing career as a blues singer, but in the late 1920s and early 1930s, she modified her style and repertoire to appeal more broadly to white audiences.

Berlin traveled uptown to Harlem to hear the song that Waters had recently introduced in *The Cotton Club Parade of 1933*, Harold Arlen and Ted Koehler's "Stormy Weather." Berlin, the insomniac songwriter, rarely went nightclub hopping. He preferred to work through the night before going to sleep in the early hours of the morning. After hearing Waters's performance, he went backstage to hire her for *As Thousands Cheer*, the new musical revue that he and the playwright Moss Hart were writing. It marked the first time an African American woman starred in a Broadway musical.

Once she agreed, Berlin wrote three songs for her: "Harlem on My Mind," a portrayal of Josephine Baker, the star of the *Folies Bergere*, who misses Harlem despite her luxurious life in Paris; the comic "Heat Wave," about a young woman who "started a heat wave / By making her seat wave"; and "Supper Time," one of our two great songs about lynching. The striking contrast between the first two songs, both set in New York City, reflects the way they embody two sides of African American—and thus American—music. "Heat Wave" is raucous good fun. Suggestive and sexy, it features a grinning Ethel Waters topped by a turban, who lets us know that she, also known as the heat wave that blew into town last week, began on Martinique. As a result, "The can-can she dances will make you fry, / The can-can is really the reason why." Rather than reporting, the narrator in the lyric is actually singing a third-person story about herself:

> Her anatomy
> Made the mercury
> Jump to ninety-three.
>
> (Irving Berlin, "Heat Wave," *As Thousands Cheer*, 1933)

Berlin wrote "Harlem on My Mind" for Waters with Josephine Baker in mind. Baker appeared in chorus lines in Harlem clubs and Broadway musicals before sailing to France in 1925 at the age of nineteen. Her erotic dancing in Parisian clubs soon made her a success and earned her several nicknames, including "Black Pearl" and "Black Venus." She danced almost in the nude, especially in her iconic performance of "Dance Sauvage," in which she wore nothing but a string of artificial bananas and a rope of pearls. She worked for French military intelligence during the Second World War and returned to the United States for an appearance that got panned and led to her renouncing her American citizenship. She returned a final time in 1951 for a nightclub appearance in Miami. She got raves but returned to France after a successful national tour.

The chic, bluesy lament portrays her melancholy in a song that has her missing her homeland. The song is fictional; Baker had no desire to return to a segregated America. Berlin's lyric lets her speak for herself. Although she has jewelry, a chateau, and a million francs, and dines on this particular night with a marquis, she feels unattached despite her success. She whispers, "*Mon cheri*," but in her heart, she sings, "Hi-de-ho," an allusion to the African American bandleader and singer, Cab Calloway, who led the house band at the Cotton Club in Harlem and was known for his use of boisterous nonsense syllables. She misses America and Harlem, and she blames herself: "I've become so darned refined." She knows that she'll return to her elegant Parisian apartment, "the high-falutin' flat that Lady Mendel designed," but she still has "Harlem on my mind" (Irving Berlin, "Harlem on My Mind," *As Thousands Cheer*, 1933).

As unlikely as its Broadway setting is, "Supper Time" is America's first great song about lynching, written six years before Abel Meeropol's "Strange Fruit." It deserves to be as well known. Waters, born in Chester, Pennsylvania, and raised in poverty, toured in vaudeville and worked in carnivals. She also sang the blues, billing herself as Sweet Mama Stringbean because she was skinny and stood five-foot-ten.

On the advice of an older Black piano player, she adapted her style to appeal to white audiences as well. She was the first major singer to cross over and helped to open the door for such singers as Lena Horne and Nat King Cole. During the Harlem Renaissance of the 1920s and 1930s, she starred at the Cotton Club and appeared in all-Black Broadway revues. She later starred in movies, took on serious roles on Broadway, and went on to become the first African American woman to star in a TV series (*Beulah*, 1950–2).

The singer and band leader Cab Calloway was supposed to introduce the song at the Cotton Club, but he rejected the club's contract for 1933. The song went to Waters instead. Berlin wanted to hear her sing it. As soon as he had, he went backstage to offer her a major part in *As Thousands Cheer*, a new Broadway revue that he and playwright Moss Hart were writing. It opened in 1933 and marked the first time an African American woman starred in a Broadway musical.

A fast-paced satiric revue that made fun of prominent people from Mahatma Gandhi to Herbert Hoover, the show began each scene with a newspaper headline: "Heat Wave Hits New York" led to the comic "Heat Wave" ("She started the heat wave / By letting her seat wave") and "Unknown Negro Lynched by Angry Mob" led to "Supper Time."

Although such popular performers as Marilyn Miller, Helen Broderick, and Clifton Webb appeared in *As Thousands Cheer*, Waters was clearly the star attraction. Shortly before opening night, the rest of the cast—all white—told Berlin that they would not take their bows with a Black performer. He told them that he understood and would never make them do anything they didn't feel that they could do. He explained that there would be no bows. That ended the protest. Everyone bowed together, including Ethel Waters.

# 14

# "The Sweetest Taste of Freedom for My Soul"

*Show Boat* is one of the most revolutionary musicals in the history of the American theater, also one of the greatest.[1] Yet almost from the beginning, it and its creators, composer Jerome Kern and librettist-lyricist Oscar Hammerstein II, have faced charges of racism. Every important revival rekindles the debate about its treatment of interracial marriage, its portrayal of Black workers, and its use of *n----r*.

The show opens with people gathering at a pier to await the arrival of the Cotton Blossom, a show boat that works the towns and cities along the Mississippi. In the original 1927 production, an all-Black chorus sings the musical's first lines: "Niggers all work on de Mississippi, / Niggers all work while de white folks play" (Jerome Kern and Oscar Hammerstein II, "Cotton Blossom," *Show Boat*, 1927). These are Black stevedores singing among themselves. The year is 1887, ten years after the failure of Reconstruction.

In 1998, the conductor and musical theater historian John McGlinn oversaw a three-CD studio recording of *Show Boat* that used the original language. He explained: "'Nigger' is a hateful word but it's there for shock value, to stun an audience and make them think about what conditions were like for African Americans in those days."[2] Black cast members in numerous revivals were at first uneasy about singing the word and later resisted it. They wanted to alter what they saw as racist elements in the book and lyrics. Revivals have responded to performers' protests and changing social attitudes. Over the years, a few major productions on Broadway and elsewhere have used "niggers," but most have replaced it with "darkeys," "colored folks," "Negroes," and even the pablum of "Here we all . . ."

This last substitution is much too weak to reflect Kern and Hammerstein's understanding of the racial tensions within the show. They wanted to underscore them in the opening scene. It's important to remember that Hammerstein was an especially important figure in the development of the integrated musical that merged theme, plot, score, and character into a single work. His collaborators, Kern and, later, Richard Rodgers, played significant roles, but neither matched the importance of Hammerstein.

*Show Boat* departs from the familiar, not only in the opening lines but also throughout the largely sung first scene. The curtain rises, not on a chorus line of peppy tap dancers, but, for the first time, on two choruses, one Black, the other white, onstage at the same time, singing in thematic counterpoint. The Black stevedores await the show boat's arrival so they can load the bales of cotton aboard, in anticipation of the lyrics to "Ol' Man River": "Tote dat barge / Lift dat bale" (Jerome Kern, Oscar Hammerstein II, "Ol' Man River," *Show Boat*, 1927). At the same time, the fashionable young white people who have come to see the show boat arrive, flirt with one another in song, and look forward to attending the performance that night.

The Black workers are grounded in the privations of everyday life, while the whites are free to play. The two groups stand in sharp contrast—men doing hard labor and ladies and gentlemen with leisure time to spare. To make the point dramatically, the choruses sing different lyrics, "Loadin' up boats wid de bales of cotton, / Gittin' no rest till de Judgment Day" versus "Thrills and laughter, / Concert after, / Everybody's sure to go!" In the show's first words, Hammerstein creates the gulf between Black people and white.

Racial implications emerge in a more personal way in the roles of the African American cook Queenie and the African American stevedore Joe, and their place in the show-boat hierarchy. Cap'n Andy and the others treat them well, even affectionately and with respect, but the two African Americans know their place. It's how they keep it.

At the same time, Kern and Hammerstein created in Queenie and Joe the first three-dimensional Black characters in a Broadway musical and view them sympathetically instead of condescendingly. Queenie and Joe have no formal education and speak in a stereotypical Southern Black dialect, and Joe admits that he's lazy in a song added to the 1936 film version (Jerome Kern and Oscar Hammerstein II, "Ah Still Suits Me," *Show Boat*, 1936). He and Queenie are also observant and insightful. In "Ol' Man River," Kern and Hammerstein borrowed from the language of spirituals to give Joe a song that expresses the suffering and suppressed rage of African Americans after centuries of discrimination and violence against them: "You an' me, we sweat an' strain / Body all aching an' wracked wid pain." His only escape is across "de river Jordan" on "de judgment day."

Just as important is the tragic story of Julie, the mixed-race entertainer who passes for a white woman and is married to Steve, a white man. *Show Boat* was also the first American musical to focus on interracial marriage. When Steve punches the show boat's engineer, who's been making passes at Julie, the engineer swears revenge and exposes her secret to the police. Marriage between the races was illegal at the time. Julie and Steve flee, but their marriage eventually falls apart. She ends up as an alcoholic trying to make a living singing in nightclubs.

Early in the play, Cap'n Andy's daughter, the innocent Magnolia, falls for a wayfaring riverboat gambler, Gaylord Ravenal. In the great torch song, "Can't Help Lovin' Dat Man," Julie tries to caution the younger woman about falling in love too quickly (Jerome Kern and Oscar Hammerstein II, "Can't Help Lovin' Dat Man," *Show Boat*, 1927). Once you fall, she explains, you'll love that man until you die. The song foreshadows Julie's tragedy as well as Magnolia's (Ravenal eventually leaves their marriage). Joe enters to say that "Can't Help Lovin'" is his "favorite" song. He and Queenie then sing a more up-tempo version in which they pledge their fidelity to one another. Queenie finds Julie's version "beautiful," but she's also struck by what she hears. She asks Julie how she knows that song because, "I didn't never hear nobody but colored folks sing that song." The song and the scene early in act 1 combine to advance *Show Boat*'s exploration of race—daring in its time, especially in a musical.

Partway through the song in the 1936 movie version, Magnolia begins to dance the shuffle. She has obviously learned it by watching Black people on the show boat and along the river. Julie also knows how to do it. In the 1994 Broadway revival, Magnolia ventures a few steps until Queenie and Julie step forward to teach her how to do it. Times had changed, but the African American shuffle is an essential part of the scene. The director of the later version solved the problem without undermining Kern and Hammerstein's work. Hammerstein was liberal politically and optimistic in outlook, but also a man of his time. Context and history continue to matter.

Are these elements of the show part of the racial obtuseness of the 1920s, when violent suppression of Black people in the South and their exclusion in the North were common, or do they reflect Kern and Hammerstein's determination to try to say something true about Black lives in America within the often-frivolous context of a Broadway musical? I side with those who believe that the two men worked from a generosity of spirit that came to offend people for what they called its paternalism as Black consciousness arose and social attitudes changed. It's important to keep reviving *Show Boat* as a major work of the American theater to allow audiences in different times to see and judge for themselves. It's too important a work to distort or ignore.

E. Y. Harburg was the most politically engaged of any of his songwriting contemporaries. A democratic socialist who was never a Communist, he was nevertheless blacklisted during the McCarthy era. More than any other lyricist, "he championed racial and gender equality and union politics." He was raised in terrible poverty on the Lower East Side, so he understood it firsthand. He learned from reading W. S. Gilbert and George Bernard Shaw that "humor is an act of courage and dissent."[3] Of course, George S. Kauffman said, "Satire is what closes on Saturday night."[4] E. Y. Harburg defied the odds.

In addition to such protest songs as "Brother, Can You Spare a Dime?" Harburg wrote three shows between 1944 and 1951 built around his political beliefs while also entertaining their audiences—usually: *Bloomer Girl* (1944), *Finian's Rainbow* (1947), and *Flahooley* (1951). *Flahooley* was the only one of the three not to address matters of race and women's rights and the only one to flop; it ran for forty performances. Apparently, the complexity of the plot's mix of social activism and whimsy didn't work this time around. Harburg and Saidy weighted their book with too many issues, including the rise of Senator Joseph McCarthy and Harburg's own blacklisting. All of them were important, but a single musical could carry only so much political heft despite the fantasy. A genie and a raft of singing puppets were insufficient to save it from closing only weeks after it opened.

*Bloomer Girl*, the earliest of these shows, is, in Mark Robinson's words, "adventurous and courageous"[5] to raise domestic issues in the middle of the Second World War. Set in the North shortly before the Civil War, it tackles the issue of women's rights by focusing on Amelia Bloomer, the nineteenth-century activist who favored women's suffrage and invented pants for women to free them from the burdensome hoop skirts of the time. They let women walk as men did and encouraged their independence.

The main character, though, is "Aunt Dolly's" niece, Evelina, a proper but rambunctious young woman who believes in women's rights and is also an abolitionist. She drives her father, a manufacturer of skirt hoops, to distraction. She describes her grandmother, who contentedly sewed, scrubbed, and raised her children, but "the thing that wore the britches / Was boss." She had "no voice in gov'ment / And bondage was her state." After describing the situation, Evelina draws her own conclusion:

> It was good enough for Grandma . . .
> But it ain't good enough for us.
>
> (Harold Arlen and E. Y. Harburg, "It Was Good Enough for Grandma," *Bloomer Girl*, 1944)

The characters also include Pompey, a slave owned by Evalina's love interest, Jefferson Lightfoot Calhoun. To test his conviction, she asks him to free Pompey before she agrees to marry him. Eventually, he agrees. Earlier in the play, the still-enslaved Pompey, played by Dooley Wilson, sings about his need for freedom. He describes the river, the eagle, the possum, ivy, a "bird in the tree," and a bumblebee, each free to follow its own nature. He concludes, powerfully: "We gotta be free / The eagle and me" (Harold Arlen and E. Y. Harburg, "The Eagle and Me," *Bloomer Girl*, 1944).

In 1985, the songwriter Roger Miller and the librettist William Hauptman adapted Mark Twain's *The Adventures of Huckleberry Finn* into a musical they called *Big River*. When the slave Jim (identified as "Nigger Jim" in Twain's novel) escapes from his owner, he and Huck ride a raft toward the Ohio River together. It is Jim's route to freedom. He celebrates with the spiritual-like, "Free at Last," which also echoes the rhythms of gospel music as well as such previous Broadway songs as "The Eagle and Me":

> To be like eagles when
> They ride upon the wind
> And taste the sweetest taste of freedom for my soul.
>
> (Roger Miller, "Free at Last," *Big River*, 1984)

In 1947, Harburg and composer Burton Lane collaborated on *Finian's Rainbow*, Harburg's most important Broadway show. Consistent with his strong political convictions, he was ultimately an idealist who was drawn to fancy and fantasy, and for whom the rainbow was an especially potent image. He demonstrated his mastery of the image in songs as diverse as "Over the Rainbow," "I've Got a Rainbow Working for Me," and, for *Finian's Rainbow*, "Look to the Rainbow."

The book, also written by Harburg with Fred Saidy, takes place in the fictional state of Missitucky. Its mix of satire and romance combines union struggles against landowners, a fantasy concerning an Irishman (Finian) who steals gold from the leprechauns and flees to America to hide it, and deep Southern bigotry. It also features two love stories, one serious and one comic, typical of the musicals of the day. Overall, though, it's one of Harburg's most directly political works. Its major innovation lies in its use of an integrated chorus line in which Black and white people danced together for the first time.

The setting is a small town called Rainbow Valley, where Black farmers and most white sharecrop together. As a result, in purely practical terms, the show offered jobs to a large number of Black performers. The local senator, Billboard Rawkins, borrows his name from the notorious racist from Mississippi, Theodore G. Bilbo, who served in the U.S. Senate from 1935 to 1947.

Because Finian and his daughter, Sharon, are living with Black sharecroppers, Rawkins tells them that they are breaking the law and must leave. Outraged by the bigotry, Sharon says, "I wish you were black!" Because she happens to be standing right over the leprechaun's gold her father has buried, her wish comes true. When the sheriff sees this unfamiliar Black man, he chases him off. The irony was effective in 1947, and it remains a powerful idea. At the same time, it's also hard, more than seventy years later, to accept the idea that becoming Black is Rawkins's punishment.

Seeing the white actor playing Rawkins in blackface has discouraged some theaters from reviving the show. Perhaps they missed the pointed mockery in what Harburg and Saidy had written. In the early 1990s, Beverly Sills, then general director of the New York City Opera, sent a copy of the script to David Dinkins, an African American who was then the mayor of New York City. He had his staff read it. The revival never went forward.

Gabriel Barre, who directed a revival at the Goodspeed Opera House in Connecticut in 1997, observed at the time, "I was impressed with the political satire of the piece and how it was so beautifully tied to the romance."[6] Deena Rosenberg, the founding chair of the musical theater graduate program at New York University's Tisch School of the Arts, added, "It comes back to the producers and their projected fears about the audience. And most of the time they're wrong."[7]

Many of the songs in this chapter are dishearteningly racist. The steps forward that I've described in the last part of this chapter may be small and inadequate from our absolutist perspective many years later, but they were largely applauded at the time. No matter what else they may be, Tin Pan Alley songs and Broadway musicals are commercial undertakings that seek to entertain. Harburg learned that lesson early. Satire and a political point of view in a musical score needed to go down smoothly. He made his point clearly, but he remembered not to rattle the cage too hard at any one moment. Better to find a way to make a point for a large audience than being blunt for a dozen and a half people who already agree with you. He embedded his point of view in his often-clever lyrics.

This is neither an apology nor a whitewash but, I hope, a recognition of what these songwriters accomplished within the boundaries of their world. Some songwriters were guilty of unadulterated racism; others were oblivious. But we also need to take note of the composers and lyricists who, in their time and place, tried to do what they could and nothing less. They were out to make a buck, but many of them were, in their own less-than-perfect ways, inching us toward "a more perfect Union."

# 15

# "They're All Good American Names"

*[Note: By "ethnic songs," I do not mean the songs that so many new arrivals brought from their homelands, but the American songs that portrayed them. Many of these songs use language that we now find offensive, but they were acceptable in their own time. At the risk of sounding pompous, my purpose is to try to explain the past, not erase it. ML]*

Their mother had sent Jacob Goldenthal and his older brother to live in a Jewish orphanage in Jerusalem because pogroms had erupted near their village, and she wanted them to be safe. The man who would become my wife's great-uncle told us this story when he was in his eighties, still as feisty as ever, although he stood only five feet, two inches.

When he was a teenager, he set out on his own to find his mother, who had since emigrated to New York. He somehow made his way to Le Havre or Marseille and sailed to New York in steerage. The ship docked in Lower Manhattan, and he rode the ferry to Ellis Island. He walked into the busy main building, climbed up on his suitcase, and called out as loudly as he could, "Is anyone here for Jacob Goldenthal?" No one answered. He passed through the processing and was soon back on the ferry to Lower Manhattan, where he would acquire the more American name of Charlie.

People would gather to watch the greenhorns (often shortened to "greenies") arrive. It was a form of spectator sport. You got to mock the newcomers, but the Tammany boys showed up to help them get settled in exchange for their vote. Uncle Charlie remembered, "I was in awe. I looked around at all the people laughing and pointing. I saw this woman. There was something about her, so I walked over. It was my mother."

I don't know if it was coincidence, fate, or dumb luck. I also don't know if Jacob Goldenthal embellished the story or left things out. It doesn't matter. His story fits with our idealized view of what the Melting Pot was. It wasn't easy or quick, but it worked well enough often enough to lift it to the level of myth. It meant the promise of America for those who arrived, as well as those who were born here. The immigrants came by choice; they chose America because it offered a better life. Despite the exclusion, discrimination, and violence, they stuck it out. They did not flag in their devotion to the nation. The Irish were the first to come in large numbers, detesting the English but embracing America despite the discrimination they faced. Many of their songs combined the melancholy of leaving with the jubilation of finding a new home:

> My father is old and my mother's quite feeble,
> To leave their own country, it would grieve their heart sore.
> But what matter to me, where my bones may lie buried
> If in peace and contentment I can spend my life.
> The green fields of Amerikay, they daily are calling,
> It's there I'll find an end to my misery and strife.
>         (Douglas Buchanan, "Green Fields of Amerikay," date unknown)

As recently as 2021, the United States "has by far a higher number of immigrants (about forty-six million) . . . than any other country."[1] By the first decades of the twentieth century, the changes for Irish immigrants were visible. They were no longer the greenhorns but had woven themselves into the fabric of American life. They were everywhere. A song by a couple of Jewish songwriters—Tin Pan Alley pros—celebrated their successes as streetcar drivers and policemen, but also boxers and movie stars, judges and diplomats. As the lyric crows, "Even the money here is green":

> From way out 'Frisco to New York, they walk and talk just like in Cork,
> You'd think that you were home in Ireland.
>         (Abner Silver and Alex Gerber, "There's a Typical Tipperary Over Here," 1920)

The gates for many closed in the 1920s, but for a half century the millions came. In the process, they developed a deep love for their chosen country and redirected our sense of what it meant to be an American. More and more, we would have to adjust to those different from ourselves. Patriotism, inclusive by definition, was becoming more inclusive in fact. That doesn't mean the new brew went down easily.

What the Declaration of Independence affirmed about natural rights, the Constitution confirmed in its formation of a republican government and the extension of rights to every American. An Enlightenment document promised liberty, but the Bill of Rights gestured toward the Romantic Revolution of the nineteenth century. It saw a new nation with a republican government committed to individual freedom and perhaps the most revolutionary (and most often trivialized) idea of all—the pursuit of happiness. We've abused those rights, but they remain bedrock. Simply because America was here, it provided an escape from oppression, a chance to earn a decent living, and an opportunity to live free. It continues to this day in weakened form, especially in recent years. The immigrants embodied the promise of America—even though they took their lumps everywhere, including in our popular songs.

It's folly to conflate the actor with the role, the novelist with the character, or the songwriter with the sentiment in a song. It may happen from time to time, but that part about the songwriter would have to wait until the 1960s and after when songwriters and audiences alike came to value what they called authenticity. Yet something unusual was going on in many of the ethnic songs that were popular from the late nineteenth century into the early 1920s—some sort of unlikely link between songwriters and performers on one hand and songs on the other—nothing as obvious as autobiography or confession, but some kind of mirroring, a shifting, indirect, yet revealing parallel between the lives and the songs.

What happened was rooted in the effects of the Melting Pot, even though Tin Pan Alley songwriters wrote many of their songs by formula. Beneath the reassuring story of becoming American as told by those who succeeded, imagine the self-consciousness and anger that so many of the songwriters must have felt. Many were immigrants or the children of immigrants, men and women who recognized their own worth and ability but who found themselves excluded until they could force their way in, not only on their merits, but also after extensive reinvention.

The songs they wrote used stereotypes and exaggerated dialects to portray the Irish, the Italians, the Jews, the Chinese, and every other ethnic group that came to America in large numbers beginning in the decades after the Civil War. The setting of stereotypes and clichés to the syncopated beat of ragtime was the sound of greenhorns coming to terms with America and America grudgingly making room. It could take as much as a generation or more. Jia Lynn Yang, a national editor at the *New York Times* and the child of Taiwanese immigrants, observed in an interview, "We as a nation are always tussling over who gets to count as an American."[2]

Purposely or not, ethnic songs—usually comic songs depicting the assumed characteristics of an ethnic group—suggested to newcomers that they needed to adapt to their new country. Their behavior, dress, and accents were funny or foolish, and it was time to change. Come to the cities of the New World, the songs said, and give up the ways of the foreigner.

The songwriters created a body of songs that portrays the struggles of immigrants to become American in the years before 1920. The songs mix insult and condescension on one hand, with empathy and encouragement on the other. They encourage assimilation by giving the newcomers a broad picture of what America is all about, and at the same time, they mock anything foreign. Those not portrayed in these songs enjoyed what we find offensive—the rough racist humor of the day. Yet these songs held up a view of the nation to which immigrants might aspire as they also reflected America's changing sense of itself.

By 1916, the Melting Pot had been at work for more than thirty years. That year, Dave Stamper and Gene Buck wrote a love song with the unlikely title, "The Melting Pot." A young man praises the woman he loves because she's become American. He links her appeal to qualities she's taken from different immigrant groups. It's a song about the Melting Pot disguised as a love song:

> She has the Russian spirit
> And she has the German smile
> Like a Belgian she is true,
> Roguish Irish eyes of blue,
> And from France she gets her style
> She has the English manner and teeth of Turkish pearl

She's a mixture of all
This wonderful doll
My beautiful Ziegfeld girl.

(Dave Stamper and Gene Buck, "The Melting Pot," 1916)

A group of University of Chicago sociologists concluded from their studies of immigrants that those who came to a new and not always welcoming country went through three distinct stages—contact, accommodation, and assimilation. The most important of these academics, Robert Park, asserted that even assimilation did not mean the elimination of ethnic identity, but what he called a "superficial uniformity" that concealed persistent differences between old-timers and newcomers. Yet he and his colleagues were most impressed by how rapidly immigrant groups adopted the forms and style of American life.[3] Bayes had assimilated quickly and well, helped by the open-minded world of show business and the liberating life of an entertainer.

The same was true of many Irish and Jewish performers and songwriters who came from immigrant families. Though it was easier for the Irish because they spoke the same language as native-born Americans, they, too, suffered discrimination, largely because they were Roman Catholic, were villagers who were now dwelling in cities, and had endured centuries of invasion and occupation by the English.

Unlike many in the first wave of Italian immigrants, who worked as day laborers to earn some money and then returned home,[4] the Irish dreamed of returning to Ireland as many of their songs attest, but they stayed put. Until they discovered a local colleen who attracted them, they longed in song for the beloved they had left behind. The songs resemble the sentimental ballads of the day; they are deeply romantic, but with a feeling of loneliness and loss beneath:

The ocean's blue waters wash by the shore
Of that dear land of shamrock, where thou dost abide,
Waiting the day when I'll call thee my bride!
God bless you, darling, I know you are true.
True to the boy, who would die now for you.

(E. S. Maeble and J. R. Thomas, "Eileen Allanna," 1876)

Unlike the Irish, the Jews had nowhere to go back to. Ultimately, the immigrant songwriters—mainly Irish and then Jewish—were outsiders who sought to make their way by describing America to the Americans. Although Jews dominated Tin Pan Alley and vaudeville after the Irish, this was more than simply having a newer group of immigrants replace an older one—the typical pattern of the Melting Pot. Instead, show business became one of the Jews' defining occupations in America. Many Irishmen built the railroads and manned the police forces and later gravitated with great success to politics, but Jewish performers made America laugh and cry from stage and then screen. The songs they made famous came from Jews as well—the composers and lyricists of Broadway and Tin Pan Alley.

In the great struggle between the synagogue and the street down on the Lower East Side, the poor *shul* had never had a chance. Jewish youngsters used the vaudeville houses and nickelodeons to escape into freedom, self-expression, sexuality, and prosperity. In the early years of the twentieth century, if you managed to get yourself on a vaudeville bill, "People asked not who are you but what can you do? It was a roughneck sort of egalitarianism, with little concern for those who might go under, but at least it gave the people a chance to show their gifts."[5] It was also the Progressive Era, a time of great social change in America: both the emergence of great wealth in the hands of a few men and the muckrakers who worked to expose them. Jeremy Rosen takes note of the long-forgotten "composers and performers who turned Jewish-dialect ditties into Progressive Era pop hits."[6] In this protean world, Irving Berlin published his first song and changed his name from Israel Baline to Irving Berlin.

Young Mr. Berlin, aged nineteen, soon began to write songs for Fania Borach, Israel Iskowitz, and Asa Yoelson, whom the rest of America came to know as Fanny Brice, Eddie Cantor, and Al Jolson. As perennial outsiders, such early Jewish songwriters as L. Wolfe Gilbert, Jean Schwartz, and Gus Kahn cultivated a chameleon's gift for assimilation and a keen sense of how to strike a recognizably American pose in a song lyric and sell it to a broad American public. Gilbert, born in Odessa, wrote "Waitin' for the Robert E. Lee" even though he had never been to Alabama and did not know that the state had no levees; Schwartz, born in Budapest, wrote "The Hat My Father Wore Upon St. Patrick's Day"; and Kahn, originally from Coblentz, wrote "Carolina in the

Morning" along with a long list of standards from "Ain't We Got Fun" to "Yes Sir, That's My Baby."

They wrote every kind of song and mocked every kind of lingo, including their own. It was a mad dash from escape to safety: "Jewish comics and singers would develop into the fiercest imitators of them all, as if their mockery were hiding a certain hysteria, an obsession to succeed at any cost."[7] This included not only the singers but also the composers and lyricists who gave them their songs.

Composer Jean Schwartz and lyricist William Jerome formed one of the important songwriting teams in Tin Pan Alley in the first decade of the twentieth century. Schwartz was a Hungarian Jew who arrived in New York at the age of thirteen, and Jerome was an American-born son of Irish immigrants. His full name was William Jerome Flannery, but when he saw that Jews were becoming increasingly prominent in Tin Pan Alley, he began to use his middle name. To his ear, "Jerome" sounded vaguely Jewish.

Two of their songs especially underscored the importance of the Melting Pot and their commitment to what it promised. They also understood that ethnic songs were likely to sell. In 1911, they wrote, "They're All Good American Names," although they limited themselves to the Irish and the Jews. The lyric devotes the second verse and chorus to baseball, played largely then by Irish athletes, and the third to merchants, many of whom were Jewish:

> There's not a game like baseball, it's the best of all our games . . .
> Jennings and McCann, Doyle and Callahan,
> Hanlon, Scanlon, Kirk and Donlan,
> Devlin, Keeler, Walsh, and Conlan,
> Joe McGinnity, Shea, and Finnerty,
> Farrell, Carroll, Darrell and McAmes,
> Connie Mack and John McGraw, all together shout Hurrah!
> They're all good American names!
> I love to stroll along Broadway and gaze at ev'ry sign;
> The Yankee Doodle notion store is run by Rosenstein . . .
> Abraham and Stine, Oppenheim and Kline,
> Rosenberger and Levinsky, Harris, Cohen and Rosinsky,
> Hammerstein and Guest, Stern and Rosenguest,
> Simon, Hyman, Wyman, men of brains,

> Levy, Wilsky, Berg, and Falk are the men who run New York!
> They're all good American names!
>     (Jean Schwartz and William Jerome, "They're All Good American Names," 1911)

A year later, Schwartz and Jerome wrote "If It Wasn't for the Irish and Jews," in which a traveler to Europe returns to the United States. He reflects on what the country might have become without the arrival of immigrants: "We'd surely have a Kingdom there'd be no democracy / If it wasn't for the Irish and the Jews." The lyric explores the two groups' different contributions, but eventually brings them together as part of the "more perfect union" envisioned by the Founders and reaffirmed in the vision—if not always the everyday reality—of the Melting Pot, captured in popular songs. A song designed to sell copies to Irish and Jewish citizens managed to find the heart of American patriotism, even though it dwelt in stereotypes and played fast and loose with some of the facts:

> What would this great Yankee nation really really ever do
> If it wasn't for a Levy, a Monahan or Donohue?
> Where would we get our policemen?
> Why Uncle Sam would have the Blues
> Without the Pats and Isadores
> There'd be no big department stores
> If it wasn't for the Irish and the Jews.
>     (Jean Schwartz and William Jerome, "If It Wasn't for the Irish and the Jews," 1912)

In *The Jazz Singer*, the first talkie to succeed commercially, Al Jolson plays Jack Robin, a younger version of himself. Robin is an ambitious singer who uses the democratic world of show business to transform himself from an immigrant kid on the Lower East Side to a star of vaudeville and then Broadway. It was the American story played out in front of enthusiastic audiences within the movie and many more in movie houses around the country. Everybody recognized the rough outlines of the story because it had happened for so many in America's recent past.

To hear Jolson sing "Sonny Boy" or "My Mammy" on Broadway or in an early talkie is to recall the most lugubrious sentimental ballads of the previous century, but to hear "Toot, Toot, Tootsie!" or "California, Here I

Come," with Jolson singing off the beat and using retards as he stamps his feet and claps his hands, is to hear how American Asa Yoelson (and Jack Robin) had become, and how jazz-influenced our songs had also become by the end of the 1920s.

In Tony Kushner's play, *Angels in America*, a rabbi presides over the funeral of an old Jewish woman who had come to America years earlier:

> The ones who crossed the ocean, who brought with us to America the villages of Russia and Lithuania. . . . You can never make that crossing that she made, for such Great Crossings in this world do not any more exist. But every day of your lives, the miles of the voyage between that place and this one you cross. Every day. You understand me? In you that journey is.[8]

The Melting Pot required two voyages, the first across the Atlantic, the second from Ellis Island to the real America. To complete the second, Irving Berlin had to make the psychic leap away from Israel Baline, E. Y. Harburg from Isidore Hochberg, and George Gershwin from Jacob Gershvin. What they achieved resembles in its own way what the playwright Christopher Fry wrote about comedy years later: "It is an escape, not from truth but from despair."[9]

You also couldn't be too finicky. Those who made the leap were driven but shrewd. They had smarts, but they also had nerve. The only rules they played by were Tin Pan Alley's, and dumb luck put them in the right place at the right time. They were waiting for something, anything, to come along. When it did, they pounced. It turned out to be ragtime—not the elegant piano music of Scott Joplin, Joseph F. Lamb, or James Scott, but "coon songs" and then ragtime tunes for the Dance Craze in the years leading up to the First World War. Charles Hamm observed, "Even after having been recast by Tin Pan Alley songwriters, syncopated dance music represented a new, brash dynamic sensibility that Americans found refreshing and exciting."[10]

Once the styles changed, Irving Berlin and the others would adapt again to keep the hits coming. Instead of conviction, they wrote with a headlong sense of survival. They knew they were on their own with no place to flee. Survival is usually about the present; these songwriters made it about the future and never looked back.

What immigrants at a vaudeville show saw, even when their own group was not represented in the sketches or songs, "were characterizations, often comic and grotesque, of people whose original homes and homelands lay far beyond the boundaries of the city, not just to survive, but to make it in an environment that was at once alien and mesmerizing, grim, dirty, and, at the same time, glittering with promise."[11] During the early years, when syncopation and ethnic jokes were all the rage, songwriters picked each other's brains, scavenged among yesterday's sheet music, and haunted the streets trying to hear something they could make over into something new. Before commercial radio and widespread recordings, a lot of songwriters also worked as song pluggers. Thumping on the ivories backstage in vaudeville houses and Broadway theaters, they heard everything that was new and up-to-date.

During the ragtime years, when ethnic songs were twisting everybody's tongue, men who might have become peddlers of trinkets and tablecloths became instead "peddlers" of songs. They drew them from the sounds in the streets and aimed them back, recast just enough, at those same streets. They set Yiddish aside and mastered not only English, but also New York City's fractured dialects, from "mick" to "wop."

When Al Jolson and Eddie Cantor were singing syncopated songs while they hid behind greasepaint, songwriters, many of them Jewish, were proffering Black music for a white audience that suddenly couldn't get enough of it. Rachel Rubin and Jeffrey Melnick write, "Nationalizing black cultural material was one of the major triumphs of Tin Pan Alley songwriting and marketing."[12] It was there for the taking, and they had to have known that Blacks were in no position to do anything about it.[13]

The result, according to Theodore Vincent, is that whites in the music business diminished the public's awareness of many Black writers and performers and took control of Black music.[14] Eventually, white songwriters started their own publishing houses because that's where the money and control were, but first, under contract to other publishers, they cranked out the songs—vulgar, funny, irreverent, romantic, sometimes downright racist. Why did they do it? Speculation abounds in writings about American music because nobody knows for sure, but there is always this: when somebody once asked Ira Gershwin why songwriters write so many sad songs, he borrowed his answer verbatim from Willie Sutton. Somebody had once asked Sutton why he robbed banks: "'Cos that's where the money is."

By the 1920s, the danger for Jewish songwriters had diminished. They had begun their careers writing whatever sold. But the market and the styles changed after the First World War. The new decade was frenetic, caught up in a streak of youthful madness, but it also cared about love, both romantic and sexy, and nobody wanted to sing about "dagos" and "kikes" anymore. Everybody but Jolson had already dropped the blackface, except for occasional minstrel numbers in movies and musicals that lasted as late as the 1940s.

In the mid-1920s, Irving Berlin posed for a photograph that was more revealing than any publicity shot is meant to be.[15] He sits smack in the middle of the frame, looking straight into the camera, surrounded by eight sexy blonde chorus girls, eight *shiksas*. He wears a dark suit and tie and a white shirt; his hair is well groomed, and his nails are manicured. The prettiest of the girls has taken his arm as if they are together. It doesn't faze him. He was thirty-seven at the time of the photograph. He had already written such songs as "Alexander's Ragtime Band," "All Alone," and "Always," and had started a company to publish his own songs. He had also built his own theater, the Music Box, to house the annual Broadway revues he wrote.

Although he grew up in poverty, he had been wealthy and famous for more than a decade. Now he looked the part of a prosperous businessman in his mid-thirties, entirely at ease even though he was obviously posing. Then you notice his mouth. He appears to be just about to smile, with a trace of whimsy at the corners of his lips. It's as if he's saying to himself, "How do you like the little Jewboy now?" Irving Berlin had nothing to prove to anyone but spent a lifetime acting as if he did. Jerome Charyn wrote, "He would feel poor until the day he died."[16]

More than other songwriters, Berlin saw the comic implications in the severe familial conflicts between the old ways—what his family would have called *Yiddishkeit*—and assimilation. As the melting pot recast foreigners as Americans, conflicts deepened between new and old values, between, for instance, the repressive sexual attitudes of the ghetto and the relative freedom of America. Shattered families became commonplace on the Lower East Side or Little Italy when Jewish and Italian husbands came here to earn money to pay for their families to join them and breathed freedom's heady air in the bargain.

Other families fractured when husbands who had been scholars or skilled workers in Europe found they could not earn a living in America. As millions of greenhorns learned the ropes in the great ports of entry—New York, Boston, Philadelphia, Baltimore, and Galveston—it was also a time of terrible social wrenching.

When love songs from these years tackled something controversial, they often relied on humor to soften the blow; laughter made it easier for audiences to accept the message and buy the sheet music. The use of comedy in ethnic songs implicitly encouraged immigrants who were willing to adapt and eager to act. The songs were especially interested in the young, and even more so in young women. Even though these women were still constrained by their European backgrounds, as characters in songs they could behave with irrepressible daring. They became American by taking on the world, not by going to school or becoming nurses or teachers—something they might have done in real life—but by dancing the night away to ragtime or running off to perform in vaudeville.

The men in these songs were usually more restrained and less imaginative than the women because they possessed greater authority and independence; they had more to lose. Song after song discovered comedy in the tense relationship between an adventurous young woman and a conventional young man, helped along by the way in which people at the time found foreign accents funny. The songs' most immediate comedy lay in the lyricists' attempts to transcribe the accents of foreigners; fractured English became a part of the conversational lyric at the same time that George M. Cohan was snapping off his own slangy self-introduction, "I'm a Yankee Doodle Dandy, / A Yankee Doodle do-or-die" (George M. Cohan, "Yankee Doodle Boy," *Little Johnny Jones*, 1904). Their use of language was an exaggerated and often mocking version of the way foreigners actually attacked English.

Take a look at the comic implications in the terrible upheaval that adaptation and then assimilation required. That's what Irving Berlin did. He was an immigrant with a profound need to assimilate. His father had been a cantor in Russia, yet in America, he worked at ill-paying jobs before he died soon after his son turned thirteen. Young Berlin, still known as Izzy Baline, took to the streets. He must have felt his father's failure, yet he eventually expressed it in the form of a Tin Pan Alley ethnic song. It was what he had learned how to write.

Eight years after leaving home, Berlin suggested to a fellow songwriter, the New England WASP Edgar Leslie, that they turn assimilation topsy-turvy in a song they called "Sadie Salome (Go Home)" (Edgar Leslie and Irving Berlin, "Sadie Salome [Go Home]," 1909). The idea was Berlin's; it figures. Ostensibly, it was one of many comic songs written to exploit the popular furor over Richard Strauss's controversial opera, *Salome*, with its scandalous Dance of the Seven Veils.[17] It also—and more significantly—offered an example of successful assimilation by a young Jewish immigrant—and a woman, at that! That's what was daring about it. Years later, Berlin said that he and Leslie wrote it to see if they could get away with it.[18]

Did Berlin realize that he was writing a masked, inverted version of his own life? Sadie is the grown-up immigrant girl who dances in vaudeville to get away from the Lower East Side, just as Berlin had danced outside saloons to pick up a few pennies for the cost of a flophouse bed, and eventually tried to make a go of it in vaudeville.

Imagine how thrilling and terrifying that first performance must have been for Sadie. After growing up in a sexually repressed Orthodox Jewish ghetto, she shows off her body and writhes and wriggles for a theater full of ogling men. It is an act of *chutzpah* that earns her the censure of Mose, her boyfriend, but frees her from her past. The song is not about what will happen to her, because it has already happened. Sadie is more modern—and thus more American—than the more respectable Mose. As Ian Whitcomb puts it, Berlin and Leslie had replaced the stereotype of the "money-grubbing . . . old creeper"[19] with an innocent who is scandalized by Sadie's dance:

> Oy, Oy, Oy, Oy,
> Where is your clothes?
> You better go and get your dresses,
> Everyone's got them opera glasses.
> Oy! such a sad disgrace
> No one looks in your face;
> Sadie Salome, go home.

Sadie is the heroine and Mose the butt of the joke in a song that rewards a young woman for throwing off restraint along with her clothes, and mocks her boyfriend for his comic shame. Berlin and Leslie may very well have written the song to have some fun and make some money, but the result was a comic lesson in the courage to assimilate. The twenty-two-year-old songwriter gave a new name to his autobiographical doppelgänger. Who knows what last name Sadie was born with, but for now, at least, she has become Sadie Salome just as he had become Irving Berlin.

The Broadway and vaudeville star Nora Bayes and her second husband, song lyricist and vaudevillian Jack Norworth, interpolated several songs into the score of the 1910 Broadway musical *The Jolly Bachelors*. "Young America," the most important of them, affirms Tin Pan Alley's embrace of the values and goals—and the mythology—of the Melting Pot. The woman within the song "dropped into" a public school where the children of different immigrant backgrounds surprise her with their desire to become American. One at a time, Irish Mickey O'Donohue, Jewish Ikie Cohen, and German Gretchen Stein sing patriotic songs. They sing with heavy accents and sometimes mangle the words, but their purpose is laudable and anticipates a future of great promise:

> Their daddies may be English,
> Irish, German, French or Dutch,
> But if the kids are born in Yankee-land,
> The rest don't count for much.
> We'll put them in our Melting Pot,
> Teach them the Golden Rule,
> Then we'll hatch our future president
> In any public school.
> (Jack Norworth and Nora Bayes, "Young America," *The Jolly Bachelors*, 1910)

Although it never mentions love, the lyric provides an emotional and cultural setting for many of the ethnic love songs that encourage immigrants to assimilate. It then praises the ways they adapt to America. They are to learn the language and then get jobs, shed their names and even their past, and ultimately find true love in their new land. When immigrants appeared in the love songs of the early twentieth century, they wore the songs' gentle mockery just beneath the romance: "Ach my what a German when she kissed her Herman, / It stayed on my cheek for a week" (Ted Snyder and Irving Berlin, "Oh, How That German Could Love!" 1910).

Ethnic songs were usually comic, even when they were about love; they depicted ethnic groups by resorting to the most common stereotypes because that's where the laughs were. In ethnic songs, anyway, becoming American and falling in love often seemed to go hand in hand, even if the people in the songs were often treated with condescension. Yet, despite the crude insults, the immigrants had songs that used a combination of mockery and encouragement to guide them along the often-thorny way.

# 16

# "There She Lies, the Great Melting Pot—Listen!"

The idea of a free and prosperous future, embodied in the metaphor and myth of the Melting Pot, stood as the fulfillment of the American dream for millions of newcomers who changed the fabric of American life. Immigrants from Central and Eastern Europe crossed the Atlantic, and from China the Pacific, because things were terrible where they came from. It was an act of hope. The America they imagined was a golden land to which they could escape and make themselves new. The American ideal of self-transformation is as old as Crevecoeur's *Letters from an American Farmer*; as capable of irony as the character of Meyer Wolfsheim in *The Great Gatsby*; and as recent as the latest batch of immigrants, with such guideposts along the way as Abraham Cahan's *The Rise of David Levinsky*, Willa Cather's *My Antonia*, Jerre Mangione's *Mount Allegro*—and the songs of Tin Pan Alley.

The America the immigrants dreamed of was startlingly different from the one they discovered. Yet even though it turned out to be a place of poverty, disease, and exclusion, it was also rich in possibility, if not for them, then certainly for their children. For those who arrived as escapees from oppression, the freedom to remake oneself was both liberating and terrifying as they set out to create a "more perfect union" for themselves. Eventually, they or their children would begin their own "pursuit of happiness."

David Quixano, the lead character in Israel Zangwill's 1908 play, *The Melting Pot*, is a Jewish immigrant who holds on to his belief in America despite the betrayals and antisemitism he encounters. When he finally succeeds as a composer, he speaks as the sun sets over the Statue of Liberty:

> Look, it is the fires of God round His Crucible. There she lies, the great Melting-Pot—listen! Can't you hear the roaring and the bubbling? There gapes her mouth—the harbour where a thousand mammoth feeders come from the ends of the world to pour in their human freight. Ah, what a stirring and seething! Celt and Latin, Slav and Teuton, Greek and Syrian—black and yellow—Jew and Gentile—Yes, East and West, and North and South, the palm and the pine, the pole and the equator, the crescent and the cross—how the great Alchemist melts and fuses them with his purging flame! Here shall they all unite to build the Republic of Man and the Kingdom of God . . . where all races and nations come to labour and look forward![1]

Charles Hamm suggests that Quixano and Berlin, who had written his first song only a year earlier, took similar paths to success in America.[2] For David, the sight of a thousand Jewish children saluting the American flag is "the roaring of the fires of God"; he is ecstatic at the thought that they will grow up to be Americans. The feelings that Zangwill ascribed to David and, by extension, the children, are the same ones that Irving Berlin came to feel. He expressed them in "God Bless America," which he first wrote in 1918 but did not publish until 1938, and in his musical setting for Emma Lazarus's poem, "The New Colossus." Lazarus wrote the poem in November 1883 to help raise money for the Statue of Liberty. The poem was eventually memorialized in a plaque at the base of the Statue: "Give me your tired, your poor, / Your huddled masses yearning to breathe free," and set to music by Berlin for the finale of his 1949 Broadway show, *Miss Liberty*.[3]

The dozens of ragtime songs that Berlin wrote in the decade before 1918 were immediate responses to what he saw and heard, presented in ways that fit the formulas of Tin Pan Alley. Many of them were ethnic songs, but they also suggested something essential about Berlin's exuberant embrace of life in America as he came of age:

> What did you do, America?
> They're after you, America
> You got excited and you started something
> Nations jumping all around
> You've got a lot to answer for

They lay the blame right at your door
The world is ragtime crazy from shore to shore.
       (Irving Berlin, "That International Rag," 1913)

Then, two years later, he followed with a song called "Everything in America Is Ragtime." He knew what he was doing, that without ragtime he would still be shlepping schooners of beer at the Pelham Bay Café. The songs were often self-referential; ragtime's most important subject was itself, regardless of who did the writing. In 1900, Gene Jefferson and Robert S. Roberts wrote "I'm Certainly Living a Ragtime Life"; Donald Grainard and Nora Bayes wrote a ragtime song about writing a ragtime song, "Ragging the Songs Mother Used to Sing"; and Cliff Hess, Alfred Bryan, and Edgar Leslie explained that America would win the First World War hands down "When Alexander Takes His Ragtime Band to France."

Because ragtime and ragtime songs led to a wide variety of new dances from the Turkey Trot to the Grizzly Bear—all of them variations on the one-step and the two-step—Tin Pan Alley churned out dozens of songs about whoever showed up to dance. In 1915, a year after the First World War began in Europe, Berlin wrote "While the Band Played an American Rag," in which someone dreams that "the warring nations were at a ball." Ragtime and patriotism interweave:

They started drinking to each other, like brothers,
They drank a toast to each other's flag
The Russian Czar said to the Kaiser,
"Let's drink some Budweiser."
Then he shook his hand while a German band
Played an American, made in America, an American Rag.
    (Irving Berlin, "While the Band Played an American Rag," 1915)

Three years later, once the United States was in the war, three collaborators borrowed from Berlin's "Alexander's Ragtime Band" to write a comic patriotic song:

Those ragtime tunes will put the Germans in a trance;
They'll throw their guns away, Hip-hoo-ray!
And start right in to dance.
They'll get so excited they'll come over the top,
Two-step back to Berlin with a skip and a hop;

Old Hindenberg will know he has no chance,
When Alexander takes his ragtime band to France.
> (Alfred Bryan, Cliff Hess, and Edgar Leslie, "When Alexander
> Takes His Ragtime Band to France," 1918)

The pliancy of ragtime songs was little short of remarkable. Songwriters wrote syncopated thirty-two bar melodies and then added whatever words they thought would work. As is often the case in ragtime songs, they're also "coon songs," no matter how mild. They might be love songs, of course, but also songs about ragtime itself and the new ways you danced to it:

Hug up close to your baby,
Throw your shoulders t'ward the ceiling,
Lawdy, Lawdy, what a feelin'.
> (George Bottsford and Irving Berlin,
> "[The Dance of the] Grizzly Bear," 1910)

Songs about ethnic groups were an important part of the great expansion of the popular music business in the years before the First World War. As prosperity and the population increased, the music publishers' and songwriters' influence over popular taste exploded. It began with ragtime and "coon songs" just a few years before ethnic songs reached their height of popularity. The syncopated tunes and the use of demeaning stereotypes and exaggerated dialect in "coon songs" helped to define the approach in songs about immigrant groups as well. Only with the waves of immigration that began in the mid-nineteenth century and the emerging ideal of the Melting Pot did ethnic songs and their themes become important. But the truth, as always, was darker than the dream or symbol.

Immigration in the late nineteenth and early twentieth centuries threw America into a patriotic tizzy. This wasn't what the Federalist Papers had promised a century earlier: "Providence has been pleased to give this one connected country to one united people—a people descended from the same ancestors speaking the same language, professing the same religion, attached to the same principles of government, similar in their manners and customs."[4] Who was an American to include and who was not?

Before the 1840s, most white Americans were of English, Scottish, Scandinavian, or German stock. Then, in response to the great potato famines of 1845 and thereafter, the Irish began to fill the new tenement neighborhoods in the cities along the Eastern seaboard. As if that weren't enough for those whose families had preceded them by as much as two centuries, the Italians, Jews, and miscellaneous poor of Eastern and Southern Europe followed in their footsteps. They were non-Anglo-Saxon, non-Protestant, non-English-speaking, and the welcome was often less than warm. The poet Thomas Bailey Aldrich wrote in 1895:

> Wide open and unguarded stand our gates.
> And through them presses a wild motley throng...
> These bringing with them unknown gods and rites,—
> Those, tiger passions, here to stretch their claws.
> In street and alley what strange tongues are loud,
> Accents of menace alien to our air.[5]

The novelist Henry James added in 1907, "There is no claim to brotherhood with aliens in the first grossness of their alienism."[6]

Despite Aldrich and James's vitriol, not all responses were limited to language. The nativist response took various forms of exclusion and discrimination, sometimes violent. The response of Tin Pan Alley was more benign. It was sometimes insulting, sometimes condescending, even offensive, but it also eased disapproval with humor, especially since many of the songwriters belonged to the same ethnic groups that their songs mocked.

Between 1870 and 1900, twelve million immigrants came to the United States; another fifteen million arrived between 1900 and 1915. "The peopling of America," writes Thomas Sowell,

> is one of the great dramas in all of human history.... Today, more people of Irish ancestry live in the United States than in Ireland, more Jews than in Israel, more Black people than in most African countries. More people of Polish ancestry settled in Detroit than in most of the leading cities of Poland, and more than twice as many people of Italian ancestry were in New York as in Venice.[7]

Since most of these new Americans arrived within a single half century, it would have been surprising only if they had not figured in our popular music.

Many came to find work that paid well, but many others sought escape from political or religious persecution, or they wanted to live in a country that promised personal freedom. The desire of many immigrants to assimilate changed them when they got here, but it also changed what it meant to be an American. In the long run, the immigrant waves created greater tolerance of diversity than before, loosened class barriers, broadened educational opportunities, and certainly enriched the language.

A half century earlier, the Irish had been the first large immigrant group driven to America by adversity. During the great potato famines of the mid-nineteenth century, they came in vast but unwelcome numbers, mainly to Boston and New York. In the windows of rooming houses, the signs read, "No Irish Need Apply," but in the song that takes the sign for its title, the Irishman gets his revenge and claims his place:

> I couldn't stand it longer: so, a hoult of him I took,
> And I gave him such a welting as he'd get at Donnybrook.
> He hollered: Millia murther! and to get away did try,
> And swore he'd never write again: No Irish need apply.
> Sure, I've heard that in America it always is the plan
> That an Irishman is just as good as any other man;
> A home and hospitality they never will deny
> The stranger here or ever way: No Irish need apply.
>
> (John F. Poole, "No Irish Need Apply," 1862)

As the Irish established themselves in America, songwriters produced large numbers of songs about them. Comic songs eventually gave way to love ballads. Typical of their time, these ballads lack the romantic ardor and intensity we came to expect from love songs in the 1930s and 1940s. The attitudes and the behavior they describe are sentimental portraits of the lives of Irish working girls with names like Sweet Rosie O'Grady, Peg o' My Heart, and Mamie Rorke. The most famous one is so widely known that many might think it's an urban folksong. In fact, it's a product of Tin Pan Alley. In the lyric, a man remembers his growing up on "The Sidewalks of New York":

> East side, West side,
> All around the town,
> The tots sang "ring a rosie,"

> "London Bridge is falling down";
> Boys and girls together,
> Me and Mamie Rorke,
> Tripped the light fantastic,
> On the sidewalks of New York.
> (Charles B. Lawlor and James W. Blake, "The Sidewalks of New York," 1894)

Large numbers of immigrants remained in the big cities where they first landed and clustered together in tight neighborhoods that got denser rather than larger, especially in New York. As other Americans began to move west in large numbers, these immigrants tried to survive in tightly packed tenements in filthy urban neighborhoods. From the Irish in Hell's Kitchen to the Jews on the Lower East Side to Little Italy to Chinatown to the Germans in Yorkville, much of Manhattan was a borough of ethnic enclaves. By the 1890s, though, Tin Pan Alley was writing songs that treated the Irish with affection. The most popular song of the day about New York City was also a nostalgic remembrance of a working-class Irish neighborhood. The narrator's affection for the place is palpable, as he remembers the "merry group" of young people who gathered to "sing and waltz" on evenings in the summer after work. Even someone like "pretty Nellie Shannon," who was so good at attracting the boys but who didn't know how to dance, "first picked up the waltz step" on "the sidewalks of New York."

The lyric is a series of quick impressions and lasting memories set against a chorus in which the speaker and Mamie Rorke, the girl he courts, "tripped the light fantastic." The song opens with an iconic reference to the East Side and the West, followed by mentions of Casey's "old brown wooden stoop," children's sidewalk games of "Ring-a-rosie" and "London Bridge is falling down," and Tony, whose hand organ provides the music for dancing. These are urban references confirmed as Tin Pan Alley fare by the hint of a love story as "me and Mamie Rorke" dance away the evening. It is also an idealized America, enriched by the blessings of the Melting Pot, where the Irish, the Italian organ grinder, and the German baker Jakey Kraus live in perfect harmony.

The Irish eventually established themselves in large part through politics, but long before Honey Fitz and the Kennedys up in Boston, the stereotype of the Irishman entered American life—physically strong but not very bright;

an imaginative liar with a gift of gab; a hard drinker, a brawler, and a weepy sentimentalist. Like all stereotypes, the Irishman was a figure of sometimes-cruel mockery; he was, in the words of William Brooks, "the moronic butt of America's broadly racist humor."[8] Though he was the butt of the joke in vaudeville, as well as in plays and musicals, the stage was also one of the places where the stereotype began to break down.

Edward "Ned" Harrigan, who worked as a playwright, lyricist, and actor in New York from the 1870s to the 1890s, was one of the first songwriters to push back against the insulting portrait of the Irish. His lyrics kept the blarney and the brogue, but he invested his characters with common humanity and viewed them with humor and understanding. As Harrigan's biographer, Richard Moody, wrote, "No playwright had ever explored New York's low life so lovingly."[9] This was a new America in the making. It was not for the faint of heart, but it was the real democratic deal—in song if not always in fact. In addition to the Irish, Harrigan also portrayed the Germans, Italians, and African Americans, whose neighborhoods abutted the Irish in Lower Manhattan. His outlook was affectionate and satirical as he "jumbled" them together in the same tenement alley. They got along better in his plays than they did in real life as he laid out in theatrical terms a view of America as a Melting Pot that thrived on disagreement, competition, and more than an occasional free-for-all to create a comic, commonsense version of "we the people."

> It's Ireland and Italy, Jerusalem and Germany,
> Oh, Chinamen and nagers, and a paradise for cats,
> All jumbled up together in the snow or rainy weather,
> They represent the tenants in McNally's row of flats.
> (Dave Braham and Ed. Harrigan, "McNally's Row of Flats," *The McSorley's*, 1882)

Harrigan began his writing career by turning out broad farcical sketches for variety theaters. Eventually, he turned to writing full-length melodramas, but they flopped until he brought back the farce. By 1877, "farce sprinkled with melodrama was the new game. Death, near death, abduction, and unjust incarceration alternated with the farcical misadventures"[10] of his broadly drawn ethnic characters. Harrigan's plays were especially popular with lower- and middle-class audiences, many of them immigrants, who relished seeing themselves depicted in ways that were both comic and sympathetic.

As the Irish adapted to life in America, and especially New York, they still kept their stereotypes on the stage. Yet, Harrigan also had a keen eye for how they changed over time. He understood "the sad side of tenement living, but he chose to write about the holiday time, when the clouds lifted, games replaced work and worry, and Irish, Germans, and Negroes discovered a sunny and funny side to their animosities."[11]

Beneath the extravagant nonsense of his farces, he recognized the primary importance of family and neighborhood. They were always central to his work, but he also recognized that one of the changes was the growing value of culture and education. Yet even here, the hyperbole lends his lyric a touch of teasing. In addition to all the languages she knows, a young woman named Mary Ann masters the popular dances of the day, from the "Mazourka" to the "Polka" or Quadrille. She is also a teacher: "She has charge of all the children / You never find a fool, / For Mary Ann gives all the proper steer." The hyperbole is primarily an expression of his affection; after all, she's *his* Mary Ann:

> She's a darling, she's a daisy,
> She's a dumpling, she's a lamb.
> You should hear her play on the pi-an-a,
> Such an education has my Mary Ann.
>     (David Braham and Ed. Harrigan, "Such an Education Has My Mary Ann," 1878)

Once Harrigan started to write full-length plays, his most important works were a series of seven farces that helped to shape the early American musical. Known as the "Mulligan Guard plays" after their main character, Dan Mulligan, they dominated the New York stage from 1879 until the turn of the century.

In the years after the Civil War, pseudo-military guards grew up in large and small cities across the country. They wore lavish uniforms and paraded down the streets and avenues mainly on weekends. Their drills usually ended with a bout of beer drinking in a local saloon. Immigrant groups formed most of them because the city's official militia wouldn't admit them. New York had more than a hundred of these "Guards" at the time. They were the perfect target for Harrigan's affectionately satiric farces.

The Mulligan Guard's only real competition came from the all-Black Skidmore Guard, which appeared in all seven of the Guard plays. They were as proud and cocky in their way as the Mulligans were in theirs:

> Talk about your Mulligan Guard,
> Dese darkies can't be beat,
> We march to time, we cut a shine,
> Just watch dese darkies' feet.
>
> (David Braham and Ed. Harrigan, "The Skidmore Guard,"
> *Mulligan Guard's Ball*, 1879)

Yet they always lose in the end. Ultimately, they are foils for the Mulligans. They resemble the Mulligans, but Harrigan doesn't develop individual Black characters as fully as their Irish counterparts. Both groups bicker endlessly, but one man associated with the Skidmores, Simpson Primrose, a Zip Coon–like barber who owns a razor, brings the threat of violence to the banter.

Toward the end of *The Mulligan Guard Ball*, the Skidmores, playing for a dance on the floor above, suddenly crash through the ceiling and land in the Irish bar below. As Richard Moody describes it, "The pile-up of arms and legs, smothered in plaster and entwined with the chandelier, created an astonishing spectacle."[12]

The Irishman remained a sunny stereotype, but for the first time, Harrigan individualized him, made him sympathetic, and allowed him to win in the end through luck, quick thinking, and decency despite the farcical melees that Harrigan's audiences loved. Moody wrote, "He reported what he saw and heard, truthfully, with a warm heart, without bitterness or malice, and always with his mirror fixed on the lighter side."[13]

Harrigan was George M. Cohan's hero. Thirty years after Harrigan altered the stereotype, Cohan took it a step further when he created the character he played again and again with great success—a strutting cock-of-the-walk Irishman who wore his Americanism on his sleeve and owned the streets of New York. For the first twenty years of the twentieth century, Cohan owned his audiences as well. In 1908, he decided to honor his idol. Ned Harrigan was old and infirm by then, but Cohan got him to the theater for the opening night of his new show, *Fifty Miles from Boston*. For the act 1 finale, James C. Marlowe as Tim Harrigan marched front and center, took the spotlight, and sang the score's big hit to the man who had inspired it. Its words weren't about Ned Harrigan, but they were Cohan's tribute to him:

H - A - double R - I - G - A - N spells Harrigan,
Proud of all the Irish blood that's in me;
Divil a man can say a word agin me.
H - A - double R - I - G - A - N, you see,
Is a name that a shame never has been connected with,
Harrigan, That's me!

      (George M. Cohan, "Harrigan," *Fifty Miles from Boston,"* 1907)

# 17

# His Immigration Rose

As the new immigrants adapted to America and began to seek out entertainment in English, they joined the largely working-class audiences in neighborhood vaudeville houses. Those in the seats and on the stage had something in common. Robert Snyder observes:

> Vaudeville was created largely by people from immigrant and working-class backgrounds who supplied both its talent and its audiences.
>
> Together, they . . . helped fashion new ethnic identities formed more from American popular culture than from old world ways; they gave big-city popular culture much of its buoyant, egalitarian style; and they challenged and subverted the genteel Victorianism of middle-class, native-born Americans. . . . Vaudeville's creative roots lay largely in a world of tenements, immigrants, and street-corner wise guys.[1]

As Minnie Marx, mother of Groucho, Harpo et al., put it, "Where else can people who don't know anything make so much money?"[2]

Vaudeville was the show-business face of the Melting Pot as well as Tin Pan Alley's primary promoter of songs. It gave songwriters, music publishers, and song pluggers their best hope of turning a new tune into a hit. As soon as the ink dried on the sheet music, the pluggers were off to the backstage dressing rooms of vaudevillians all over New York City and beyond. Whether it was big-time vaudeville or small, two-a-day or six-, performers spread the songs across the country like no one else. At the same time, booking agents chose acts because they suited an individual theater's location. They "paid close attention to local audiences but knit them into a modern mass constituency. . . . The genius of such shows lay in their ability to speak to a complex and infinitely varied audience."[3] For the immigrants in the big cities, the sketches and songs provided "an initiation of hazing and caricature that assured the Swedes, the Germans, the Irish, and then the Jews that to be noticed, even through the cruel lens of parody, meant to be accepted."[4]

For audiences of Russians and Rumanians, Swedes and Greeks, vaudeville was "an arena for communication between otherwise separate people. There they encountered strangers and novelties and tried on new ways of thinking, feeling, and behaving."[5] A night of vaudeville was a way to begin to feel American. After a while, even the greenhorns started getting the jokes. In the big cities, where most of the immigrants lived, it is no wonder that ethnic songs thrived. Their stereotypes were immediately recognizable to the various ethnic groups and to everyone else as well. William H. A. Williams observes that "stereotypes, especially in ethnically diverse America, were . . . powerful forces in our popular culture."[6]

The Irish were the first large group to come, five million of them by 1920, but by the time they arrived, their stereotype was set in the popular mind: "a club in one fist, a jug in the other, and a necklace of stale mackerel round its neck."[7] Ironically, the grasping, hand-wringing, hook-nosed Jew was a figure not only of antisemitic diatribes, but also of Yiddish theater. The Jews in the vaudeville audience knew what to make of him. That doesn't mean that the immigrants in the audience in a vaudeville house liked the stereotypes of their own kind, although they probably enjoyed laughing at everybody else's. Imagine what it would take for a Jew to laugh at a song like "When Mose with His Nose Leads the Band" (Theodore Morse, Bert Fitzgibbon, and Jack Drislane, "When Mose with His Nose Leads the Band," 1906) or an Italian at a line like "They're the wops with the mops who manicure the boulevards" (Clarence Gaskill and Al Dubin, "Tony Spagoni's Cabaret," 1917). But Jews understood the figure of the shrewd Jew, Germans the oafish German, Italians the Italian barber who cared only about food, and the less-common but predictably coquettish Frenchwoman and seductive Spaniard. Audiences also grasped the point of many of the songs that portrayed them, at least unconsciously: in America, you are supposed to look to the future.

These were people who looked for a new place to put down roots, but America's amorphous, always changing culture made the task difficult. The stereotypes of ethnic songs made ethnic differences "unimportant by being made ridiculous. They were the differences that made no difference, provided they were eventually shed."[8] In Ballard MacDonald's lyric for "Rose of Washington Square," even the minimally talented Rose, a Jewish girl who poses for "girlie" magazines but never finds true love, can trace her way from "up in the Bronx . . . down to Washington Square / And Bohemian Honky Tonks." Now she boasts ironically, "And that's how I first got my start / Now my life is devoted to art." She may be a joke, but she's a strictly American joke (James F. Hanley and Ballard MacDonald, "Rose of Washington Square," 1920).

The tensions between various groups were real and could turn violent. Ethnic neighborhoods were often crammed next to one another, and the people competed for the same low-paying jobs. Since most came from rural villages, they were also xenophobic and territorial. Heaven help the young Italian man who wandered mistakenly into an Irish neighborhood, or vice versa, and neither had any use for the "sheenies" down on the Lower East Side. They must have laughed uproariously at the demeaning portraits of the others that they saw on the stage and heard in the songs.

Yet, at the very least, the vaudeville theater and its ethnic songs were neutral ground: every group got raked over the coals, but nobody got raped or murdered. Vaudeville provided "an easy truce"[9] that gave all immigrants an opportunity to absorb the same lessons. Beginning in 1906, "A Bintel Brief" in the Yiddish-language newspaper, *The Jewish Daily Forward*, gave its readers advice for coping with the hard realities of life on the Lower East Side. Meanwhile, ethnic songs encouraged immigrants of every group to rise above their circumstances to find their way in America. Probably unintentionally, the songs became exemplars.

The Italians took their place in American popular songs somewhat differently from the Irish. The Irish had the advantage of knowing English and speaking it in a particularly musical way, and they made a name for themselves in variety, vaudeville, and Tin Pan Alley before the turn of the century. With the exception of Enrico Caruso, the Italians played only a small role in show business between 1900 and 1920, until a generation of Italian crooners followed in the footsteps of Frank Sinatra in the years after the Second World War. Among the movers and shakers of Broadway, Hollywood, and Tin Pan Alley, whether as studio heads, theater or movie producers, songwriters, or music publishers, there were few Italians.

Early ethnic songs about Italian Americans relied largely on their accents and stereotypically broad behavior. They were considered loud and funny. Typical comic songs about them feature a recent immigrant talking about American life, a common laborer whose understanding is a good deal less fractured than his speech. That is the source of the joke. He may make a mess of English, but he wants to do the right thing; he wants to become American, and he has found a way to do it. In "Teddy Da Roose," a 1910 novelty song that makes fun of the Italian immigrant's heavy accent, the Irish American lyricist Ed Moran praises him for admiring Theodore Roosevelt even though he can't pronounce his name. Despite his strange way of speaking and the mockery it opens him to, a newcomer has begun to become an American:

> Hey! Walyo, you know a da greatest-a man in this country of all-a-da rest? . . .
> You know it-a who?
> Teddy da Roose!
>
> (Fred Helf and Ed Moran, "Teddy Da Roose," 1910)

Even love was less important than freedom in many ethnic songs, and the promise of a traditional marriage lost its appeal for a lot of the Kates and Sadies whom the songs portrayed. The stage became for them what it had already become for such real-life stars as Fanny Brice and Sophie Tucker. It let them choose freedom (sexual and otherwise) and independence over conformity and fidelity, and more often than not, the song lyrics seemed to approve. In real life, no one was more daring than brassy vaudevillian Eva Tanguay, who belted out such songs as "It's All Been Done Before but Not the Way I Do It" and "I Don't Care." But *within* song lyrics, no one was more daring than Rosie Riccoola, whose sexy writhing and wriggling took form as nonsense syllables that managed to combine a parody of an Italian accent with ragtime, the hula, and sex:

> Rosie Riccoola, she lay ona da ground,
> Rosie Riccoola make-a mournfula sound,
> Tella Joe da ice-a man to come around,
> and lift three hundred pound.

> Next time I'm goin' to do the hoola maboo.
> I'll do it on da beach at waikiki too.
> Then when I fall, I falla softa dat's all,
> Like they do in Honolu.
>
> (Arthur Lange and Andrew B. Sterling, "When Rosie Roccoola Do Da Hoola Ma Boola [She's a Hit in Little Italy]," 1917)

What's unusual is that, instead of being ostracized in her repressed neighborhood, this very modern Italian girl is so delectable that she becomes "a hit in little Italy."

For an immigrant woman in songs, just as in show business, becoming American often involved sex—perhaps marriage, perhaps becoming the mistress of a wealthy man. But songs often used sex approvingly to demonstrate that a young immigrant woman had embraced life in New York and America in the early twentieth century. With a job and a sugar daddy, she was one face of the New Woman, ready to take on the world. In "Becky Joined a Musical Show" from 1912, Irving Berlin took the story of an emancipated young Jewish woman even further than he and Edgar Leslie had in "Sadie Salome, Go Home" only a few years earlier. Encouraged to go into show business, Becky shows "off her figure in the very front row" until "all the boys are calling her a 'Yiddisha chicken.'" No boyfriend comes to berate her, though, and she soon finds herself wearing a sealskin coat and arriving at the theater in an automobile, all on twenty dollars a week. Her success as a chorine and as a sexually available young woman affects her family as well, though not in traditional ways: "All of Miss Rebecca's relatives want to go with a musical show" (Irving Berlin, "Becky Went with a Musical Show," 1912).

Assimilation was apparently catching, and songs never seemed to run out of jokes about it. They either mocked or encouraged the greenhorns, and some did both at the same time. Lyricist Alex Gerber told the tale of a young woman named Becky Bifkowitz, who prepared herself for a show business career by washing dishes, doing laundry, and taking cold showers. The frigid bathwater, for example, taught her how to shake and shimmy. Now this "Yiddish baby" is in an "Oriental show" where she removes "all of her veils" in a performance that bills her as "Princess Oy-vay-is-meer" (Abner Silver and Alex Gerber, "Becky from Babylon," 1920). Becky may be a figure of fun, but as usual, she is a woman who has achieved not only notoriety but also independence as she moves from Babylon, Long Island, to Manhattan, from drudgery to freedom, though not without paying the price of a lost heritage and a discarded past.

Songwriters of every background wrote ethnic songs for forty years, from the 1880s into the 1920s, because they sold. David Jasen writes, "Waves of new immigrants led to heightened interest in Italian, German, Jewish, and Irish characters, in both comic and sentimental portrayals. . . . It is not surprising that Tin Pan Alley catered to this interest."[10] Hardly a songwriter passed up a chance to write about the Irish, Jews, Italians, and Chinese primarily, but also the Germans, Japanese, Swedes, and, in one song, "The Argentines, the Portuguese and the Greeks." Perhaps these songs were so popular because their use of mockery implied the cultural superiority of those who had come earlier and for whom living in America was effortless.

One of the best examples is a silly novelty song written by Frank Silver and Irving Cohn that portrays a Greek immigrant who owns a fruit and vegetable store. In response to a question, he explains, "Yes! we have no bananas; we have no bananas today" (Frank Silver and Irving Cohn, "Yes, We Have No Bananas," 1923). For the rest of the song's nine choruses, the proprietor insists that yes, he has no bananas, but boasts about everything he carries, from eggs to cucumbers to "bologny," but he makes everything sound terrible ("We just killed a pony, / So try our bologny"). Silver explained that every day he passed a fruit stand whose Greek owner began every sentence with "Yes." "The jingle of his idiom haunted me and my friend Cohn. Finally, I wrote this verse and Cohn fitted it with a tune."[11] It uses a few mispronounced words for comic effect but has no trace of a Greek accent.

Seven years later, Irving Berlin tried his hand at something he called "Yes! We Have No Bananas Variations" for Al Jolson to sing in blackface in a movie called *Mammy*. Jolson plays the leading man in a traveling minstrel show in this parody of opera.

Ethnic songs seemed to assume that people who were different were either dangerous or, more likely in Tin Pan Alley, ridiculous. Over time, the point of view changed. In "The Argentines, the Portuguese, and the Greeks," the lyric starts by praising groups who came earlier "to help this country grow," and then tracks the progress of those who have recently arrived.[12] They begin by selling newspapers, shining shoes, and giving shaves. Now, though, they collect the rent each week and drive a Mercedes or a Rolls-Royce. They struggle with the language, but when it's time to sing "My Country, 'Tis of Thee," they're the only ones who know the words. Despite the reluctance to accept them, they have become Americans (Arthur M. Swanstrom and Carey Morgan, "The Argentines, the Portuguese, and the Greeks," 1920). The attitude within the song changes rapidly from fear to jealousy to respect, although the envy never entirely disappears. The story of American immigrants combines a contradictory mix of open ports and borders with nativist exclusion and discrimination.

In a song like "Sadie Salome, Go Home," the writers of Tin Pan Alley ethnic songs did not usually draw on personal experience. They produced formulaic lyrics derived from other songs, as well as from stereotypes and from the casually racist humor of the day. Everybody wrote about everybody. The songs reflected what the audiences (and the songwriters) saw onstage night after night: "whites in blackface, blacks in blackface, Jews mimicking Italians, Italians impersonating the Irish, the Irish performing as Chinese, New Englanders pretending to be Southern 'rubes.'"[13]

In the same year that Irving Berlin wrote "Sadie Salome, Go Home," he also wrote the Italian dialect song "Dorando"; an Irish number, "I Wish That You Was My Gal, Molly"; and a song that the Dutch comic Burt Lahr made into a hit in burlesque, "Oh, How That German Could Cook." Berlin wasn't the only one. Jewish lyricist M. K. Jerome wrote "My Irish Rosie" in 1907, Halsey K. Mohr and Edgar Leslie wrote "The Police Won't Let Mariuch-a Dance (Unless She Move Da Feet)" in the same year, and Fred Fischer and Joseph McCarthy wrote "That Little German Band" in 1913.

In 1922, Anne Nichols's enormously popular Broadway comedy, *Abie's Irish Rose*, celebrated the Melting Pot by telling the story of a Jewish boy and an Irish-Catholic girl who marry despite their parents' objections.[14] Abie and Rose were a generation removed from the immigrants and were well on their way to becoming American. Yet for two decades before Nichols's play, songwriters of every background had been telling similar stories. In a switch on Nichols's plot, lyricist Edgar Leslie has Patrick J. O'Brien pursuing Sadie Katzenstein in "Love Me to a Yiddisha Melody." They soon marry, and Patrick becomes a policeman who returns home one day to find his Sadie alone with Captain Ikey Rosenthal. The tale has a happy ending as Sadie sings to her Patrick:

> Don't lose your mind 'bout Rosenthal,
> He came to bring your pay, that's all.
> Oh! you Kiddisha!
> Love me to a Yiddisha Melody.
>
> (Joe Young and Edgar Leslie, "Love Me to a Yiddisha Melody," 1911)

Often, though, the controversial arrangements did not work. Poor Cohn marries Kate O'Hare, only to find that her favorite food is "cold pig's feet," and her brother calls him a "kike." He addresses his plaint to those who think he must be happy because he has a wife:

> Maybe our little baby Will have a name like Benjamin O'Hooligan or A'bram Levy Mulligan, She's not my kind, But I don't mind there's worse than her. But they're hard to find. Maybe you think I'm happy.
>
> (L. Wolfe Gilbert, "Maybe You Think I'm Happy," 1911)

In reality, marrying your own kind was more important than finding happiness with somebody different, but both points of view were common in songs. The contradiction did not matter because audiences appreciated both. The songs accommodated the various ethnic groups' opposition to intermarriage, but they also encouraged members of ethnic groups to look beyond their own neighborhoods for romance. In the context of a song lyric, it was the most important way to affirm their new American identity:

> I got da mucha trouba Marianina fly da coop,
> One night she go
> To burlesque show,
> De Irisha comeeda take Marianina with da troup,
> She pack da grip, she make da skip,
> I buya me a ticket in da gall'ry high I sit,
> Da turn de lights, she wear green tights,
> She sing da Irish songa, she no sing of Sunny It,
> To her I write, like dis one night,

> Marianina won't you come back home,
> And cook spaghetti for Antone?
>
> (James Brockman, "Marianna," 1907)

Despite Antonio's pleas, Marianina says "nineteen and four," an oblique form of the common slang brush-off, 23-Skidoo.

Throughout these songs, lyricists relied heavily on stereotypes for nearly every character, both sympathetic and otherwise. In "Beckie, Stay in Your Own Backyard," for instance, a "Talyaner wop" pursues "Beckie, my daughter," as a father urges his daughter to marry one of her own kind. The positive Jewish stereotype of strong family ties plays off against the father's use of the darkest Italian stereotypes to frighten her back into the fold. The father who lovingly reassures her

> Beckie, don't hurry,
> See how I worry,
> Your happiness is my wish;

is the same father who tries to terrify her:

> Look how I'm looking, dear,
> Italian cooking, dear,
> Aint like our gefilta fish.
> Beckie, dear, spare my life,
> Italians speak with a knife.
> The "Black Hands" will steal you away.
>
> (Norman and Young, "Beckie, Stay in Your Own Backyard," 1910)

Unlike Beckie, whose father cautions her to stay close to home, the outspoken Rose in James F. Hanley and Grant Clarke's "Second Hand Rose" is more venturesome in what she says and where she goes (James F. Hanley and Grant Clarke, "Second Hand Rose," *Ziegfeld Follies of 1921*, 1921). Of all the comic ethnic heroines portrayed by the great clown Fanny Brice, Rose is the most complex. Yet Brice first introduced the song in the *Ziegfeld Follies of 1921*, when interest in ethnic humor was in decline. It was also a theater song in the upscale *Follies*, even though most ethnic songs had been Tin Pan Alley fare designed to turn a quick buck through some combination of rough street humor and maudlin sentimentality. Brice sang "Second Hand Rose," just as she had sung "Good Bye, Becky Cohen" in her first *Follies* in 1910, and continued to sing such Yiddish dialect songs as "I Was a Floradora Baby" and "Oi, How I Hate That Fellow Nathan" until she gave up the theater for the movies in the 1930s, and began to portray the demonically mischievous Baby Snooks on the screen and then on the radio.

Many of Brice's most successful theater songs touched on love and marriage, but none came anywhere close to sweet romance. They preferred a comic outlook, especially since Brice resorted to dialect in nearly all of them. Even "Cooking Breakfast for the One I Love" sounds as if she cooks breakfast after she and her man have engaged in a night of lovemaking. Only when she sings the second chorus in a comic Yiddish accent does Brice spring the punch line—they're married (Henry Tobias and Billy Rose, "Cooking Breakfast for the One I Love," 1930).

From her earliest days in show business, Brice knew how to win an audience's sympathy through pathos and by exploiting her own weakness or folly; it was the source of her comedy and her mastery over an audience. As a child riding the trolley to Coney Island, she had learned to drop a handkerchief filled with rocks out the window and cry that she had lost her fare. The other passengers would soon help out the tearful child, and she and her brother Lew would have more money to spend on rides and hot dogs. Some years later, when she was working as a package wrapper in a department store, she told her coworkers that her father was blind and her family was starving. "I had them all crying," she said, "and I loved it."[15]

Brice was one of the few women Ziegfeld hired who wasn't gorgeous. She was a skinny kid with a big mouth, a bigger nose, and scrawny legs. But her mind was sharp, her eyes were expressive, and her clowning was antic. Her vulnerability, combined with her remarkable gift for mimicry, made her one of Ziegfeld's greatest stars. When she mocked what other people were doing seriously, she was funny rather than cruel. As Madame Du Barry, she'd enter in a gorgeous gown, wave her elaborate fan, and say in a rich Yiddish accent, "I'm a bad voman. But I'm in dem' good company."

She once explained, "You must set up your audience for the laugh. So you go along and everything is fine, like any other act, and then—boom! You give it to them. Like there is a beautiful painting of a woman and you paint a moustache on her." What made Brice a great comic was her ability to combine mockery and pathos. "On stage," Stanley Green writes,

> she was prone to the most outlandish outbursts and facial expressions as she distorted her remarkably mobile features into a variety of comic grimaces. With little apparent motivation other than an irresistible urge to cut up, she would cross her eyes, puff out her cheeks, slap her forehead, buckle her knees, and collapse her long, slim body. Even when she wasn't milking a laugh, there was always something ludicrous about her wide, half-moon smile that gave her the appearance of a canary-swallowing cat.[16]

"Second Hand Rose" was the kind of song Brice had sung throughout her career: a comic treatment of Jewish urban life in New York City, except in this case, Grant Clarke's lyric took her more deeply into the character. The song builds from a single, immediately recognizable joke: Rose is a working-class Jewish girl from the Lower East Side who has never had anything that wasn't a hand-me-down, from her pajamas to the "piano in the parlor." Even her fiancé, Jake, "had the nerve to tell me / He's been married before." As she strolls through the Ritz one day—and it is fair to wonder why she was there—a woman gets her goat when she nudges her friend, nods in Rose's direction, and observes, "Oh! look, there goes my old fur coat."

The joke in the song is straightforward, but Rose is also a character of surprising emotional complexity. She confronts the world with a knowing eye and a skeptical demeanor; nothing gets past her, and she expects nothing to be easy. Aside from being funny, beneath her resilient resignation, a defining mix of anger and resentment simmers. Her healthy skepticism only partially protects her from the hurts she encounters. She emerges as a rueful survivor with a sense of humor. We can laugh at her, but it is important not to disregard her. In Clarke and Hanley's writing and Brice's performance, a stereotype takes on dignity and individual identity. The Melting Pot is working.

While all these comic shenanigans were going on, Tin Pan Alley also produced large numbers of conventional ethnic love songs that praised beautiful young women, usually Irish. Songs praising the loved one are probably as old as song itself. Their titles often name the object of love and devotion and build a lyric of praise from the repetition of her name.

When it comes to Tin Pan Alley's ethnic songs, more of them are Irish than anything else, but songwriters touched nearly every base, from what audiences expected all the way to "the Valley of the Nile" (about "a sweet Egyptian maid") and "Borneo, where southern breezes blow" (about a maid who marries King Bonga Boo). Yet no name appeared in songs more often than Rose—from "Georgia Rose," "Mexicali Rose," and "My Wild Irish Rose" to "Rose of the Rio Grande," "My Little Persian Rose," and "Honeysuckle Rose."

Occasionally, the beloved remained behind in Ireland or Italy, or more exotically in Egypt as a young man calls out to her from his caravan somewhere in the desert. Even so, the songs are virtually interchangeable. The young woman is sweet, beautiful, and usually innocent, and her suitor praises her eyes and lips, and he longs to be married (at least to hold her in his arms). But in most of them, nothing else happens. It's simply a matter of rearranging the formulaic references for the color of hair and eyes, and the varied geography of their dreams, from

> Where the dreamy Nile is flowing,
> She's waiting there for me;
> 
> (Dave Radford and Richard A. Whiting, "In the Valley of the Nile," 1915)

to the more-familiar

> Her lips are red and sweet, and when she smila,
> I feela for one kiss, I walk a mila. . . .
> 
> (George Lyons and Bob Yosco, "Margarita," 1912)

All those songs about so many different kinds of people, yet having "Rose" in all the titles suggests the natural, nonideological populism of so much popular music. It spoke to listeners in terms of their own lives by attributing familiar emotions to unfamiliar people and by relating their common experiences in equally common imagery. In 1923, Jimmy McHugh, Eugene West, and Irwin Dash wrote what amounted to an *envoi* for ethnic songs. "Immigration Rose" is a sentimental little song that offers a moment of heartbreak before it affirms, one last time, Tin Pan Alley's view of the Melting Pot ideal. Arriving in steerage with no one to meet her, "little immigration Rose" fears that she will be deported. She begins to cry when suddenly someone calls out, "Rosie, here am I":

> He holds her close
> To his heart for he knows
> In this land that he chose
> Will bloom his Immigration Rose.
>
> (Jimmy McHugh, Eugene West, and Irwin Dash,<br>"Immigration Rose," 1923)

# 18

# Feasting on the Stereotypes

*[Note: Many of the songs in this chapter use offensive language. ML]*

Even though Jewish, Irish, and Italian families in America treated their daughters differently, all three groups imposed strict bans on anything resembling premarital sex. That certainly applied to the Irish, even though a majority of the women who came from Ireland were young and single and arrived on their own. They were less focused on marriage than on finding good jobs and supporting themselves. No wonder they had a reputation for being saucy and independent.

Vaudeville and Tin Pan Alley had long feasted on the stereotypes of the Irish, but the bitter insults had eased by the coming of the new century, especially as Irishwomen emerged as the object of affectionate attention in many songs. America had a new stereotype, a much gentler one, of feisty colleens named Molly, Peg, Kate, and Kitty, with their bright eyes, warm laughter, and loving hearts. In love songs, anyway, young American men found them irresistible.

There were many more songs about the Irish than any other ethnic group because they had been here longer and had moved so far along the road to acceptance. Many of them were also fair and blue-eyed, long the standard of beauty in America. Most of these songs defined themselves by a lighthearted approach to love and romance, as if they were a reaction against the formality of the sentimental ballads that preceded them. The melodies sometimes sound vaguely Irish, and you can hear a bit of the brogue in the conversational lyrics:

> When Irish eyes are happy
> All the world seems bright and gay
> And when Irish eyes are smiling
> Sure they steal your heart away.
>
> (Ernest Ball, Chauncey Olcott, and George Graff Jr., "When Irish Eyes Are Smiling," 1912)

From "Sweet Rosie O'Grady" in 1896 to "The Daughter of Rosie O'Grady" in 1918, love songs praised Irish girls even though their Irishness was often irrelevant except to suggest that they were pretty and sweet, with the flashing eyes and lilting laughter that made them distinctive. Yet like depictions of American girls without a trace of the Irish in them, they were often as passive as their beaus were eager. In what may be the most famous of these songs, "When Irish Eyes Are Smiling," the chorus consists almost entirely of references to the young woman's eyes and her laughter. Though a young man begins broadly—"In the lilt of Irish laughter / You can hear the angels sing"—he soon becomes more intense as he moves from the general—"When Irish hearts are happy, / All the world seems bright and gay"—to something more personal, but the song never gets past observing: "And when Irish eyes are smiling, / Sure, they steal your heart away."

The song's narrator is obviously talking about himself; the stolen heart is his. What is more interesting about the song is the way its two verses never mention marriage but rather urge the lovely young girl with a tear in her eye to smile instead of cry, and take full advantage of the passing years of her youth, preferably with him. In contrast to all those songs that anticipate spending a lifetime together, "When Irish Eyes Are Smiling" prefers the immediate satisfactions of *carpe diem*. Yet he asks for nothing more than a smile:

> For the springtime of life
> Is the sweetest of all
> There is ne'er a real care or regret;
> And while springtime is ours
> Throughout all of youth's hours,
> Let us smile each chance we get.

American songs transformed these girls into conventional, somewhat old-fashioned objects of love. This is not the nineteenth century, though. They are irresistible rather than perfect, flirtatious rather than demure, loved rather than idealized, and young men of the early twentieth century were less likely to put them on a pedestal than to find their own "hearts in a whirl," complete with sexual implications as they eagerly awaited marriage. Yet the girls are much more likely to receive than give compliments—or anything else.

Among the songs that give the girl an Irish name even though the song itself has nothing to do with being Irish, Albert Von Tilzer and Jack Norworth's "Take Me Out to the Ballgame" is probably the most famous. It revels in the outspoken spunk of a young Irishwoman but also demonstrates that Tin Pan Alley had absorbed her traits so fully that she could actually represent all American women. The colleens had become typical rather than stereotypical.

In this case, nothing recognizably Irish about the song or the girl appears in the lyric. Regardless of her name, this young woman has lived in America long enough to be recognized as an American. The song's very first line announces that "Katie Casey was baseball mad." How can you be more American than that! When her beau invites her to see a musical show, she declines but adds, "Take me out to the ballgame / Take me out with the crowd." Her charmingly outspoken manner appears more directly in the rarely sung second verse:

> Katie Casey saw all the games,
> Knew the players by their first names;
> Told the umpire he was wrong,
> All along good and strong.
> When the score was just two to two,
> Katie Casey knew what to do,
> Just to cheer up the boys she knew,
> She made the gang sing this song. . . .
> 
> (Albert Von Tilzer and Jack Norworth, "Take Me Out to the Ballgame," 1907)

Dozens, perhaps hundreds, of songs about someone named Molly might never mention the word "Irish" or dwell in stereotypes, but her name is the giveaway. She is charming, lovely, and desirable—"You looked so swell, I couldn't help but wonder, / If a gal like you would ever fall for me?" (Ted Snyder and Irving Berlin, "I Wish That You Was My Gal, Molly," 1909)—so much so that being Irish matters less than her individual appeal. With her freshness and beauty, Irish Molly has become the all-American girl.

There are also songs in which feistier Irishwomen speak out, especially Madeline Mooney, who falls for Willie Fitzgibbons in one verse of "Waltz Me Around Again, Willie," and Willie De Vere in the next. One is a ribbon seller who is exhausted by the end of the day, and the other a dry goods cashier who never gets any exercise. Madeline will have none of it. As soon as the music starts, "She's up like a silly and grab tired Willie, / Steer him to the floor and she'd say":

> Waltz me around again, Willie, around, around, around;
> The music is dreamy, it's peaches and creamy,
> Oh! don't let my feet touch the ground.
> I feel like a ship on an ocean of joy,
> I just want to holler out loud, "Ship Ahoy!"
> Oh! waltz me around again, Willie, around, around, around.
> (Ren Shields and Will D. Cobb, "Waltz Me Around Again, Willie," 1906)

Like the women in songs about other ethnic groups as well, Madeline's assertiveness and ebullience make her more modern than her beau, but they also give the song a sense of humor. A songwriter might view an assertive woman as admirable but also understand that the broad public would see her as threatening if she were not amusing.

Another group of songs, closer to reality, acknowledged Irish girls as independent working women in a series of genially humorous love songs. In "Kitty, the Telephone Girl," a young man named Tommy discovers that an attractive young woman rides the tram to the city every day to her job as a telephone operator. Before long, he calls her up to hear her voice and to tell her:

> Kitty, Kitty, isn't it a pity
> That you're wasting so much time,
> With your lips to close to the telephone
> When they might be close to mine.
> (Harry Gifford, Huntley Trevor, Tom Nellor, and Alf J. Lawrence, "Kitty, the Telephone Girl," 1912)

All that remains is a predictable pun on "ring" and his intention to marry her so they can "both ring on for life." Even though young Irishwomen prized their independence and married later than women from other backgrounds, marriage remained the goal in popular songs. Their audience was not Irish, but a broad swath of the American public.

Jerome Kern and Paul's West's "Katy Was a Business Girl" from 1906–1907 is a more cynical song, both in its use of comedy and its attitude toward love and marriage. It starts with a young Irishwoman who has the confidence to work as "a cashier in a men's café." Calling her "a business girl," though, refers to something more than having a job, especially since she's not very good at it. She "always managed to get tangled making change," but even though she had a devoted beau, "she sacked him for a chap of sixty-two." Kitty never mentions marriage, but all the regulars are horrified by her calculating nature:

> Chaps could hardly eat their lunch,
> The thing was so absurd,
> Katy wouldn't look at Jack
> Or seem to hear a word.
> The café rang with gossip,
> Which Katy must have heard
> But then she was a business girl.
>
> (Jerome Kern and Paul West, "Katy Was a Business Girl," *Fascinating Flora*, 1906–1907)

Unlike the Irish, fewer Italian girls in America held down jobs; they tended to stay close to home and rarely ventured out without supervision. They and their families came largely from villages in Southern Italy, where they worked the poor soil and struggled against poverty. When they came to America, at first they held to the old ways. Unlike "Sadie Salome," young women, especially of the immigrant generation, did what was expected of them:

> Italian girl no dance Salome,
> Italian girl she stay-a home,
> When she get-a lonely
> She's-a send-a for her Tony.
>
> (George W. Meyer and Joe Goodwin, "Italian Girl," 1911)

Yet some found work eventually because their families needed the money. Unlike the Irish, though, they rarely worked in shops or offices, or as domestics. Because Southern Italian families rigorously protected their young women from even the appearance of sexual impropriety, they set up sweatshops at home, although eventually, the daughters began to work outside the house. As with all the immigrant groups, their exposure to different groups of people and broader experiences encouraged them to give up their traditional roles.[1]

Because Italian girls were so retiring, ethnic songs might have done nothing more than praise them for their flashing eyes and gleaming black hair. Before long, though, the girls from the first native-born generation began to move out of Little Italy, change their names, and marry non-Italian men.[2]

The combination of reluctance to change and its necessity influenced songs about Italian women. Even though lyricists wrote many fewer songs about the Italians than the Irish, a surprising number of them were daring. They seemed to take particular pleasure in having the Italian girls kick up their heels. One even tells a story similar to "Sadie Salome, Go Home," as Mariutch performs a hoochy-kooch dance on Coney Island to the consternation and embarrassment of her boyfriend:

> Mariutch she make-a de hootch a ma kootch down at Coney Isle,
> Make me smile, she go like-a this, like-a that, like-a this,
> She make-a such-a dance and never move-a de feet that's a funny style;
> Some one yelled like-a that, "Hey look out! you'll break-a your back."
> (Harry von Tilzer and Andrew B. Sterling, "[Mariutch Make-a the Hootch-A-Ma-Kooch] Down at Coney Isle," 1907)

In the same spirit, Edgar Leslie and Halsey K. Mohr's "The Police Won't Let Mariuch-a Dance (Unless She Move-Da-Feet)" is one of many songs in which an immigrant girl gets in trouble by dancing—in the wrong place, with the wrong man, or to the wrong kind of music. All too often, she dances to ragtime or does the shimmy, a sure sign of trouble. As Mariuch's long-suffering boyfriend reveals, her dancing is both sexual and funny:

> The police won't let Mariutch-a dance unless she move da feet,
> She'll have to go like dis, no more she'll go like dat,
> The captain he no like dat hooch-ma-kooch,
> He tell Mariutch, "Hurry up, skidooch,"
> The police won't let her dance unless she move da feet.
> (Edgar Leslie and Halsey K. Mohr, "The Police Won't Let Mariuch-a Dance [Unless She Move-Da-Feet]," 1907)

Jewish girls had substantially more freedom than their Italian counterparts; their families urged them to take classes and attend lectures with other young people and eventually to join their fellow workers in left-wing labor organizations. But the seriousness of their interest in self-improvement and social reform rarely dampened their desire for fun; America was having its effect on them. Gail Collins quotes an unmarried Jewish girl who begged to learn to dance, "I wanted a new thing," she remembered years later, "happiness."[3] In Irving Berlin's "That Kazzatsky Dance," Abie's darling turns the popular Russian folk dance, also done by Jews, into ragtime. It so excites her that "it makes me lose my sense." She tosses away sexual restraint and nearly falls for an Irishman:

> Come and get handy its dandy, dandy
> Kiss me kid, I'm candy.
> Oi that Kazzatsky dance,
> I'm going in a trance, I love my ham and cabbage kid,
> But Oi, that Yiddisher, That Yiddisher,
> Oi that Kazzatsky dance.
>
> (Irving Berlin, "That Kazzatsky Dance," 1910)

Jewish women became assimilated as rapidly as other ethnic groups, but Tin Pan Alley produced very few songs that idealized them. There were no passive, perfectly beautiful Jewish women comparable to sweet Rosie O'Grady. It is hard to know exactly why. Even though Jews were more generally accepted in the large cities, where most of them lived, antisemitism remained strong across the country. Songwriters, including Jewish songwriters, were hardly shy about using Jewish stereotypes in comic songs or in depicting Jewish girls as sexually aware. Perhaps, though, they felt less at ease writing love songs about beautiful Rachel and enchanting Sophie rather than Katie and Maria. It's almost as if writing jokes about a sexy ragtime-dancing Sadie was easier to pull off than something serious. It is not clear if this choice reflected their own insecurities as outsiders or their practical sense that the broad population would resist these songs.

Other than the lack of idealizing in songs about Jewish women, Jews were treated pretty much the same as the other ethnic groups. In songs where someone woos them, though, young Jewish women succumb before marriage more often than Italian or Irish girls—not often, but more often. When "Esther from Hester Street" and her beau turn down the lights:

> On such fine trips we go,
> We are both content;
> We simply close our eyes,
> Travel to Paradise,
> It don't cost a cent.
>
> (Melville Gideon and Edgar Selden, "My Little Yiddisha Queen," 1909)

In a more troubling song, especially since Orthodox Jewish custom required that anyone marrying outside the faith shall be presumed dead, Sadie Cohn comes to America from Poland, where she

> met an Irisher one day,
> He made love to Sadie right away;
> Oh, what a change in her
> There's something strange in her . . .
> Though she dresses up in Irish styles,
> You can tell she's Jewish when she smiles . . .
> And even with her Jewish face she's a credit to the Jewish race.
> There's a little bit of Irish in Sadie Cohn.
>
> (Jack Stern and Alfred Bryan, "There's a Little Bit of Irish in Sadie Cohn," 1916)

Sadie and the "Irisher" marry and have a child within a year. Despite the strictures for observant Jews, the song's ending is a satisfactory resolution and the source of a good laugh for its outcome and also for its bawdy pun, perhaps because "Irish" had come to equal "American" in the popular songs of the time, and the song's outlook was American rather than Jewish: "She married Pat O'Flaherty and lost her nationality. / There's a little bit of Irish in Sadie Cohn." In the end, the song encourages assimilation through its use of a dirty joke.

Despite their differences, the young Irish, Italian, and Jewish women had experiences and attitudes in common as they struggled to break away from the confines of custom and pursue American lives. Gail Collins quotes a woman who wanted to return to Italy to "show everyone that a poor peasant girl could learn to hold her head high and stand up for her rights. 'They wouldn't dare hurt me now I come from America,' she said. 'Me, that's why I love America. That's what I learned in America: not to be afraid.'"[4]

One of the more controversial and entertaining ethnic songs confronts the Americanizing of a young immigrant with directness and good humor, although she happens to be Jewish rather than Italian. At an Orthodox Jewish wedding, where men and women traditionally dance in separate circles, Sadie not only breaks the social taboo fearlessly, but she does it to that seductive new music, ragtime, with all its sexy shoulder-shaking and hip-wiggling. She may speak with an accent, but she has begun to pick up the slang of the day. It may be mildly racist, but she also recognizes that ragtime is African American music that is becoming acceptable everywhere in America. Yiddle, whom she calls her "chocolate baby" even though he's a white man, is no more than a bit of stereotypical sexual teasing. Yiddle's music exerts a mesmerizingly erotic hold over her:

> Get busy, I'm dizzy,
> I'm feeling two years young,
> Mine chocolate baby, if you'll maybe
> Play for Sadie, some more ragtime,
> Yiddle don't you stop, if you do I'll drop,
> For I just can't make my eyes shut up,
> Yiddle on your fiddle, play some ragtime.
>
> (Irving Berlin, "Yiddle, on Your Fiddle, Play Some Ragtime," 1909)

Sadie even drops a quarter in Yiddle's hat to persuade him to play. That sort of confidence also appears in a large number of songs in which young immigrant women assimilate enough to want to fall in love with men they find in America, not the men their parents would have chosen.

# 19

# More Than Fifteen Million Immigrants

*[Note: Many of the songs in this chapter use offensive language. ML]*

Although popular songs usually relied on common emotions and recognizable characters, they also took a fancy to the exotic from time to time—the dashing sheik, the provocative hula dancer, the seductive Latin lover. But the alien Chinese were different from anyone else; to Americans, they were odd in dress and language and opaque in manner. They were the embodiment of the "other," even in love songs. Of the Chinese girl he loves, this troubled American sings:

> She don't understand my talkin',
> I don't understand her walkin' . . .
> Though my love's as deep as oceans,
> We can only talk in motions,
> O Oh, O Oh, O Oh.
> 
> (Andy Lewis and Aaron S. Hoffman, "Pinky Panky Poo," 1902)

Some of the first Chinese immigrants were well-received on the West Coast because they were successful merchants and skilled workers. However, their apparent implacability and their singsong English became targets as American attitudes hardened when newly arrived unskilled laborers began to compete for jobs by working for very low pay. Eventually, they became one of the main groups to build the transcontinental railroad, the Chinese from the West and the Irish from the East.

The deepening animosity led to the Naturalization Act of 1870, which limited immigration to "white persons and persons of African descent." For the first time, Congress limited free immigration into the United States, particularly by Asians. Fifteen years later, the harsh feelings remained, especially in San Francisco. W. S. Mullaly, a well-known minstrel performer, and John E.

Donnelly wrote a locally popular song that was also the first important ethnic song about the Chinese. More than a century later, its vitriol remains striking:

> For a crying disgrace is this abominable race,
> The Chinese, the Chinese, you know.
> 
> (W. S. Mullaly and John E. Donnelly, "The Chinese, the Chinese, You Know," 1885)

By the time Tin Pan Alley discovered the Chinese after the turn of the century, Chinatowns had sprung up in large cities around the country. Instead of writing flagrant attacks, though, songwriters preferred Tin Pan Alley's formulas. They wrote love songs about the Chinese that used a familiar combination of mockery and sentiment. But even in Tin Pan Alley, songs about the Chinese were different. The people in the songs spoke a version of pidgin, an odd singsong dialect that was clearly foreign and thus implicitly foolish, though it was also simplified enough to be immediately understandable.

Even those with "pigtails flying here and there" and "almond eyes of brown" (Jean Schwartz and William Jerome, "Chinatown, My Chinatown," 1906), Chinese maidens paralleled the Irish and Italians in other ethnic songs. But only rarely did songs about European ethnic groups convey much of a sense of place. Their songs were set in a generic urban America and were about learning new ways and finding someone to marry. But no matter how often Chinese men and women fell in love in songs, their exoticism was an essential part of their depiction, and that included the song's setting.

While the occasional Irish or Italian song was about a girl back in Ireland or Italy, many of the gentlest ethnic songs about the Chinese depicted lovers who remained in China, where "in a little rickshaw built for two, / We'll go on a China honeymoon" (Egbert Van Alstyne and Gus Kahn, "My Dreamy China Lady," 1916). Whether describing a girl in nearby Chinatown or far-off China, these songs conjured up places that did not feel like Fifth Avenue or Main Street.

Sweethearts who remained in China were lovely but passive; they are, in Krystyn R. Moon's words, "pieces of porcelain or playthings for lovers." They inhabit "a pre-industrial world untouched by modern life."[1] Even when they come to America, many will resist its enticements. The lyric to "Chen, My

China Girl" affirms that "Oriental maidens that never yet have bobbed their hair / Never will in our country." Frequently, the beloved remains in China when her young man leaves, only to sing about her or to her from America. In a place "where the poppies grow . . . 'neath the lantern's glow," a young man meets a maiden and wins her hand but now must sail away. "My love is true," he writes each day, "I yearn for you" (Jack E. Slattery, "Chen, My China Lady," 1913).

Even here, though, ethnic songs about the Chinese sometimes encourage assimilation in comic terms. A young man named Allee Fo Chong has moved from Hong Kong to New York's Chinatown where "he loved his rag the same as you." In the midst of the mania for ragtime songs and the accompanying Dance Craze, he plans to return to Hong Kong to

> teachee his China girl how to dance
> Like in a trance.
> Teachee peachee Melican song
> All day long,
> To his China girl in old Hong Kong.
> 
> (Harold Weeks, "Chong [He Come from Hong Kong]," 1919)

As he sails off, he announces that when he returns to America, he will bring his bride with him because she will know how to dance to ragtime and thus be ready to become an American.

The next song takes on the subject of interracial marriage in a more daring way: a marriage in the United States between a white man and an Asian woman. A number of these songs drew their inspiration in a general way from the success of John B. Hymer's 1918 play, *East Is West*. The plot tells the story of a Chinese woman named Ming Toy, whose father sells her to a slave trader, but who is rescued after a series of plot machinations. She ends up in the United States in love with Billy Benson, the American who rescued her. Despite the melodramatic plot, the story is similar to *Abie's Irish Rose*, Anne Nichols's hit Broadway play from 1922.

In ways that were reassuring to audiences of popular theater, both plays explored questions of identity in America—religious, cultural, and racial. The character of Ming Toy was so popular that she appeared in a number of songs, including one that appropriated the play's title. In the song "East Is West," "a Melican lad with a Melican smile" steals the heart of "little Ming Toy," but first, he must rescue her from the evil Chinese man who wants her "to be his little shimmy Chinee tiny bride." The American boy carries her off to the United States where "the cynical world shook a sorrowful head," as he asserts that:

> East is West and West is East,
> Come with me to the marriage feast
> West is East and East is West,
> I'll marry little girlie, the one I love the best.
> Mute little beauty, cute Chinee,
> The love boat girl is the girl for me
> Sing song, sing song, say Hoptoy,
> All the same to Chinee boy
> Lo San Gee and I know best,
> That Love's not bound by East or West.
> (Hassard Short and Silvio Hein, "East Is West," 1919)

Despite Ming Toy's devotion and compliance, and the song's heavy reliance on dialect, such an interracial marriage might have been acceptable only within the idealized world of popular love songs. That she comes to America with a "Melican lad" suggests that she will successfully learn to be an American. The song also comes near the end of Tin Pan Alley's eagerness to write ethnic songs. Most of them came before 1916, but this one is from 1919, on the cusp of the Roaring Twenties. Race makes the adaptation to America more difficult than ethnicity, but not impossible, at least not in songs. Once again, the Melting Pot is doing its work.

Not surprisingly, courtship and marriage were the most common subjects in ethnic love songs, though their tone was often comic, especially when people from different groups had an affair or actually married. Despite the bugaboo of racial intermarriage in a country that had long feared it,[2] the popularity of Giacomo Puccini's *Madama Butterfly*, with its story of the tragic love between an American sailor and a Japanese geisha, made songs about American men and Asian women possible, even acceptable.

Unlike this rural, Eden-like China, far off and always alluring, Chinatown, close at hand yet exotic, was an insinuatingly mysterious place: smoky, slow-paced, and dreamy, yet strangely seductive. Its foreignness, especially after nightfall, makes it a respite of sorts from the frenetic world beyond its limits, even though its streets are filled with busy stores and bustling streets.

Many of the young men who long for a beloved left behind in China work in shops and laundries. One song portrays a "little China man" who toils late into the night, "all the linen polishing until it's clean and bright." People passing by wonder why he sings and is never lonely "mid the foreign throng"; it is because he thinks about his "Hong Kong baby" and wonders when she will come to be his bride. Though the song is formulaic, Paul West's lyric nicely contrasts the busy urban setting and the young man's laborious work with the dream of a still-unrealized perfect future (John W. Bratton and Paul West, "My Little Hong Kong Baby," 1902).

The suggestion and even the outright use of opium-induced dreams are also frequent in songs set in Chinatown, from "Pipe dreams banish ev'ry care" in "Chinatown, My Chinatown," to "Dreamy, dreamy Chinatown" and "Queer Oriental mysteries" in "All Aboard for Chinatown" (Winthrop Brookhouse and Frank Davis, "All Aboard for Chinatown," 1916):

Down where dreamy dreamers dream sweet dreams,
In that land of gladness,
Picking little poppies there among the hoppies,
There's no tomorrow, sorrow, grief and care.
(Jean Schwartz and William Jerome, "In Blinky, Winky, Chinky, Chinatown," 1915)

None of these songs is more explicit than "Pipe Dream Blues," in which an aging Chinese man cannot forget the beloved he left behind in Hong Kong many years earlier. Opium dreams bring her back to him and make him believe that "back in China he is young again":

See old Di Dong puff and blow those thick blue rings,
Can't you guess he dreams of distant lands,
Sweetest face in Hong Kong town his dream pipe brings,
How he loved her now he understands,
Drifting on he sinks to slumber deep,
Sighs and mumbles over in his sleep.
(Spencer Williams, Marguerite Kendall, and J. Russel Robinson, "Pipe Dream Blues," 1918)

Some songs also suggest a demimonde that may be irresistible but is also potentially dangerous. After spending a night in an opium den, white people wander Chinatown's streets near dawn and hear a "squeaky, sneaky," obviously alien cry that lures them to a lantern-lit, underground place of oriental mysteries (Egbert Van Alstyne, Raymond Egan, and Gus Kahn, "China Dreams," 1917). This kind of song rarely culminates in disaster but trades instead in mysterious and sometimes ominous ambiguity.

One of the strangest of them, "Ching-a-Ling," also involves racial intermarriage. The song dates back to 1907 and may have been acceptable to audiences that long ago only because it was subtitled "an African-Chinese Oddity" and involved having "a cautious coon" play the role of the American. Songs that portrayed love affairs and intermarriage between whites and Chinese were occasional, while those between whites and Polynesians were more or less routine.

Tin Pan Alley knew that it could cross some ethnic barriers. It could push against some limits, but it also knew which ones not to try. Instead of having Ching-a-Ling, the Chinese girl, become American, the Black man becomes Chinese. Krystyn Moon makes the point that an African American character named Ephraim *Brown* "is only a blackface version of a Chinese man.... Most of these songs conform to white perceptions."[3]

The lyric is an unbroken line of offensive stereotypes. He is "a love sick clown," and his beloved "a little Chinee gal from Tokio," as if the Chinese and Japanese are interchangeable—not the only song that lumps together several Asian nationalities. When her father insists on the marriage, he calls his future son-in-law "black face Chinee velly swell." The Black suitor then proposes by looking ahead to a future together—common fare in a popular song, but given a racist twist that is downright bizarre:

In a Chinese bungalow
I will let my pigtail grow.
Wedding bells will then ring tingaling
Name the pickaninny Wingaling,
Won't you be my Chingalingaling?
(Theodore F. Morse and Edward Madden, "Ching-a-Ling: An African Oddity," 1907)

When songwriters first began the unlikely task of mixing African Americans and Chinese in their songs, they were most likely to give a Chinese subject or title to a rag or a ragtime song.[4] One of the first to use Chinese references in ragtime titles was W. C. Powell's "Ragtime Laundry" in 1901, followed by such works as "The Chinatown Rag" in 1910 and "Chop Suey Rag" in 1915. At least one blues song written nearly thirty-five years later has a chorus sung by a man with a Chinese dialect (Fred D. Moore and Oscar Gardner, "Chinese Blues," 1949).

Contemporary comparisons of the two groups saw the Chinese as quintessential foreigners, while Black people, despite everything else, were Americans. With full recognition of their treatment from the time they first arrived as slaves, they had been here longer, they had American surnames, and a broad public had begun to embrace their music. Krystyn R. Moon writes with telling irony that Black people managed to be both American and racially inferior at the same time.[5]

It was only a matter of time until both groups began to appear as stereotypes in the same songs. In "I Don't Care If I Ever Wake Up" from 1899, a Black man admits that he likes opium because it lets him live out his fantasies (Paul J. Knox, "I Don't Care If I Never Wake Up," 1899).

By 1925, Tin Pan Alley's ethnic songs felt dated, but in a final fling between 1919 and 1923, Broadway paraded feisty Irish heroines before audiences in a series of successful musical comedies known as Cinderella shows. Rarely innovative, nearly all of them followed the boy-meets-girl, boy-loses-girl, boy-gets-girl formula made so popular by George M. Cohan fifteen years earlier. That helps to explain why it took audiences only five years to tire of them.

Of the 120 musicals that opened on Broadway between 1921 and 1924, 58 were, to one degree or another, Cinderella shows.[6] Their heroines were working class and almost always Irish. Like so many young Irishwomen, they usually worked as shop girls or secretaries, but because they appeared in musical comedies, they won the men of their dreams—usually millionaires at the pinnacle of society. Just as any man could become president, so the American myth went, any woman could marry a loving millionaire. John Bush Jones comments that Cinderella shows reflected the increasing number of workingwomen after the First World War. Before the war, musical heroines rejected aristocracy and wealth for a poor but honest American boy. Not in the Twenties, though, when "our Cinderella heroines almost always go for the gold as well as the guy," and, in the process, suggest to more recently arrived immigrants that they, too, can make it in America.[7]

If anything, the young women are a new breed of American Cinderellas, sweet and loving, but also self-made and assertive. No cleaning somebody's fireplace for them. They achieve happiness in the form of true love and great wealth, not through the intervention of a fairy godmother, but because America's class distinctions are flexible and fuzzy, and because these women have moxie. For every dowager ordering her servants to keep the doors barred, thousands of immigrant girls stood ready to push their way in without forsaking charm or humor in the process.

*Irene*, the first and most important of these shows, opened in 1919. In act 1, the heroine sings Harry Tierney and Joseph McCarthy's "Alice Blue Gown" to demonstrate her charm and appeal (Harry Tierney and Joseph McCarthy, "Alice Blue Gown," *Irene*, 1919). The song, like the show, is a nostalgic transition between an orderly prewar world and the headlong 1920s to follow. Its title alludes to the shade of blue that was the favorite of young Alice Roosevelt when her father, Theodore, was president.

Despite Irene O'Dare's admission in the song that she once had a gown, "it was almost new," she emerges as self-aware and self-confident, a modern young woman who admits that "in every shop window I primped, passing by" (Harry Tierney and Joseph McCarthy, "Alice Blue Gown," *Irene*, 1919). She is urban rather than urbane, and down-to-earth and decent as a product of her working-class background—not unlike the Pegs and Mollys of earlier Tin Pan Alley songs. She's hardworking, but she's no charwoman. She works as a shop girl, but she's a lot sharper than her place in society suggests. By the end of the play, Irene has found her heart's desire in a world that, at least for her and her beloved, is more democratic than it was when the curtain rose.

The show's appeal came partly from its timing. The nation endured a deep recession following the end of the First World War. Violence by and against immigrants, especially those active in unions, had led many Americans to long for the good old days. But it was also a swan song for an irretrievable past. One year later, Francis Marion wrote a popular silent movie called *The Flapper*, and such a character appeared on Broadway for the first time the following year in Rachel Crothers's play, *Nice People*.

Unlike the happy-go-lucky flappers who were about to inherit the earth for a few years, Irene is a shop girl who meets Donald Marshall, her husband-to-be, when she runs an errand to his family's Long Island mansion. Confronted by Donald's wealth and social position, she discovers a world beyond anything she has ever dreamed. Though the heroines were almost always Irish, the heroes almost never were. They were not only rich; they were Protestant. Irene, who is proudly and sentimentally Irish, reflects the rising opportunities for the children of immigrants in her song, "The World Must Be Bigger Than an Avenue," but nowhere in the original score does anything resemble a stereotypical ethnic song.

Before Irene and Donald can marry, though, both families must overcome their prejudice against the mingling of social classes, but that is a matter of class rather than ethnicity. Mrs. O'Dare's distrust of the rich reflects the narrowness and suspicion of many ethnic groups, as well as a greater democratization of American life after the First World War, especially with the coming of the flapper, the spread of free public education, and the rise of affluence until the Great Depression interceded.

Higher taxation and the coming of Prohibition also contributed to America's sense that the nation and its values were in flux. Gerald Bordman writes, "World War I had . . . brought about perceptible cracks in society's former impregnability . . . minorities began to weave themselves into the national fabric."[8]

The happy endings that Cinderella shows provided for heroines who were ordinary people gave audiences a reassuringly optimistic lift a year after the war ended. It was a brightening after the dangers of combat overseas and the high inflation, increased taxes, and shortages of food and coal at home that had contributed to a repressive climate of narrowed civil rights and free speech, and discrimination against citizens of German descent.

After *Irene* came other hit Cinderella shows, usually with the heroines' names in the title: *Mary, Sally,*[9] *Little Nellie Kelly*, and *Mary Jane McKane*, all of them with Irish heroines. *Plain Jane*, in which a tenement waif marries a factory owner's son, was the last of them. It opened in 1924, only five years after *Irene*. The craze did not last long, but the shows' admiration for spunky working girls who rise socially through love and marriage, their mixing of the classes with the arrival of boisterous Irish families in Park Avenue mansions, and their bouncy melodic scores made them an essential part of the spirit of the new decade.

Nineteen twenty-four was also the year of the Immigration Quota Law. As anti-immigration sentiment reasserted itself to oppose the values of the Melting Pot (and especially the large numbers of Roman Catholics and Jews who were its particular beneficiaries), and as corporations learned from the First World War that they could function effectively without large numbers of new unskilled immigrants, the law lowered the number of newcomers dramatically, especially from Asia and Eastern and Southern Europe.

Between 1900 and 1915, more than fifteen million immigrants had reached the United States. In 1924, nearly 707,000 arrived, over 56,000 from Italy alone. One year later, following the law's enactment, 294,000 immigrants arrived, only 6,200 of them from Italy.[10]

At the same time, large numbers of immigrants had been in America long enough to achieve a certain level of accommodation and assimilation. Discrimination persisted, but the Irish had been here for nearly a century, and, after a generation or two, even the Italians and Jews had come to seem less alien to many of the Anglo-Saxon Protestants who preceded them. Tastes in humor also changed as America gave itself over to the youthful excesses of the Jazz Age and the silliness of college humor. Flappers and college boys found "dumb blondes" much funnier than those lumbering greenhorns who had butchered the language. Like "coon songs" before them, ethnic songs had finally run their course, but they had left generations of loyal new Americans in their wake.

# 20

# The Urge to Roam

The urge to roam lies deep in our history and in what it means to be an American. It dates back to the Pilgrims and then to the early settlers who struck out beyond the safety of the Massachusetts Bay Colony or pushed into the freer climes of Rhode Island, where Roger Williams and Anne Hutchinson found a home for their unorthodox beliefs. From the time European settlement began in earnest until well into the twentieth century, we wandered and settled, and then some of us moved on from there. This story started with the United States, the new nation, expanded until it was continental in size and scope, and then focused on one individual. Setting out and returning, one by one, became two of the great themes of American song.

The wanderlust might take form as extreme individualism, a restlessness of the spirit that had us always on the move, always setting out, chasing the setting sun. You were on your own, so it came with a deep loneliness as well. You were out there on the prairie and its endless black nights after days of walking where the terrain never changed. We celebrated the idea of movement. We did, after all, settle a continent and build a nation despite the many degradations we imposed on Native people. We feared and despised the tribes until the end of the Indian Wars in the later decades of the nineteenth century. Despite the many cruelties along the way, we never quite gave up the urge to turn our faces West to wherever it would take us. We would endure the isolation and deep loneliness to be free.

A sense of place is everywhere in our songs, from isolated farms to jam-packed cities. Airplanes that hop from coast to coast in a few hours may dull our awareness of the nation's vastness and variety, yet its open spaces and tall buildings can still stretch the imagination. From a car or train, we pass through deserts, prairies, and rolling hills; over mountains; and along great rivers, just as in elevators we rise high while urban life skitters below. We've grown so used to the towering buildings that we don't notice the clever metaphor. They truly do scrape the sky. America's topography is constantly changing. It feels as if everyone is always on the go, never more so than on Broadway.

Broadway is an essential American place, yet we've defined it less through description than by its electricity and the people who inhabit it. At a time when America was changing from a rural to an urban nation, New York City became the place millions of us wanted to be, especially if they were young. Broadway embodied what the rest of America thought New York was. Sometimes it even embodied America itself. In 1917, when the Doughboys sailed to France, "Good-Bye, Broadway, Hello France" described their spirit: "Goodbye, Broadway, hello France, / We're ten million strong" (Billy Baskette, C. Francis Reisner, and Benny Davis, "Good-Bye Broadway, Hello France," *The Passing Show of 1917*, 1917). Not from the United States to France, but from Broadway. Everybody got it. We were somehow an incomplete nation without it. As much as endless prairies, urban drive came to define us.

Other cities may have streets with the same name, and many small cities and towns find definition on Main Street, but the true Broadway cuts from the East Side to the West, from Bowling Green at Manhattan's southern tip, up through the Bronx and Westchester County for thirty-three miles. But the Broadway of song, the Broadway that nearly every American knows, is located in Midtown Manhattan. That's the Broadway that used to give off the city's vibe. It never slowed; it never shut down.

The Broadway vibe that I remember is gone now, but there used to be a particular excitement in walking to the theater after dark: the whirl of people, the flashing marquee lights, the chattering crowds gathered under those same marquees before the doors opened, the buzz of anticipation. You might grab a bite at one of the many subterranean restaurants in the West 40s between Broadway and Eighth Avenue, or you might wait to grab a cab to the Russian Tea Room for dinner after the final curtain—before it became a tourist joint. The songs about Broadway reflected what you felt yourself a part of, and the rest of the country got it as well. The out-of-towners couldn't wait "to mingle with the old-time throng" on their way to a Broadway hit.

Broadway's frenzied melodies possess us: "Broadway rhythm! / It's got me! / Everybody dance!" (Ralph Rainger and Leo Robin, "Broadway Rhythm," *Broadway Melody of 1936*, 1936). The "street of a million lights" takes your breath away: "Gotta dance! Gotta dance!" Those dreaming of stardom arrive with a combination of anxiety and eagerness. They come and go and the world keeps spinning, but Broadway stays the same. It ignores sorrow and failure. The lights flicker each night, and "Broadway always wears a smile" (Ralph Rainger and Leo Robin, "Broadway Melody," *The Broadway Melody*, 1929). Despite the flux as hits and flops come and go, Broadway also has a conservative streak. Back in the 1920s and 1930s, and even into the 1940s and 1950s, we wanted it just as it was. We were sold on the place. Cole Porter wrote, "But please, please, I beg on my knees, / Don't monkey with old Broadway" (Cole Porter, "Please Don't Monkey with Broadway," *Broadway Melody of 1940*, 1940).

Some of these songs focus on the unknowns who long for stardom. Someone still young and eager seeks a spot in a chorus; she calls herself a Broadway Baby. She refuses to give up. She studies singing and dancing, waiting for her break: "Walking off my tired feet, / Pounding Forty-Second Street / To be in a show" (Stephen Sondheim, "Broadway Babies," *Follies*, 1971). At the other end, onetime performers live in a retirement hotel on New York's Upper West Side, but they remember what it was like and long to reclaim the spotlight:

> So let me hear the cymbals crash
> And let me hear the trumpets play,
> And let me hear that I'm a smash.
> (John Kander and Fred Ebb, "Broadway, My Street," *70, Girls, 70*, 1971)

In the Broadway adaptation of the movie *Forty-Second Street*, the producer added other songs by Harry Warren and Al Dubin, including "Lullaby of Broadway." Toward the end of the second act, the ingenue announces that she's quitting the show just before opening night to return to Allentown, Pennsylvania. Her hard-boiled producer can't believe it. He sets out to change her mind: "Think of musical comedy, the most glorious words in the English language.... Think of Broadway, dammit!" And then he begins to sing: "Come on along and listen to / The lullaby of Broadway."

"Lullaby of Broadway" matters more than any of the other songs about Broadway. First featured in a larger-than-life production number in *Gold Diggers of 1935*, it captures the glitter and glamour, the cynicism and sordidness, of Broadway after dark (Harry Warren and Al Dubin, "Lullaby of Broadway," *Gold Diggers of 1935*, 1935). The number tells a story of people driven to find pleasure, and of a sudden death and the coming of dawn, played out against massed tap dancers on a set of huge, abstract forms. It feels dehumanizing, yet it never stops. The number starts at 6:30 a.m. with alarm clocks, coffee, and people getting dressed, and advances to an evening of gowns, tuxedos, and champagne. Then the massed dancing begins. The sound of the tapping is the sound of Broadway given a sexual charge. And then a young woman plunges to her death. The women scream, but Broadway goes on. The "daffydils who work at Angelo's and Maxie's" take to their beds before it starts again tomorrow.

The American musical theater took recognizable form in the early years of the twentieth century. Many people were leaving the farms and small towns of the Midwest and South for large Northern cities, where they encountered millions of immigrants from Eastern and Southern Europe. As Broadway began to pulsate, the muckrakers stood to one side, the elite of the Gilded Age to the other. America's cities exploded in size, and New York became America's emotional capital. It was where everybody wanted to be. Those who arrived got an apartment, found work, learned the ropes, and became New Yorkers. Songs about Broadway paralleled the shift, both geographical and cultural, never more so than by 1950, with arguably the greatest of all New York musicals, Frank Loesser's *Guys and Dolls*.

Based mainly on two stories by the largely forgotten short story writer and newspaperman Damon Runyon, and with a vibrant urban score by Frank Loesser, *Guys and Dolls* tells two parallel love stories about four Broadway types. The comic story, which is more important, concerns Nathan Detroit, a lovable no-account who runs craps games and handicaps the horses, and Miss Adelaide, a "chantoosie," who develops a cold after waiting for fourteen years for Nathan to marry her ("Adelaide's Lament"). On their way to Niagara Falls, they keep getting off at Saratoga for the races. The more serious story is also the more unlikely, between Sky Masterson, a high-stakes gambler and smooth operator, and Miss Sarah Brown, a Salvation Army stalwart who falls in love with him while she's trying to reform him.

In other words, *Guys and Dolls* reflects the ways in which New York became the urban capital of America, in attitude if not in fact. It is a fairy tale devoted to a batch of irresistible lowlifes. It and *Gypsy* (Jule Styne and Stephen Sondheim, 1959), ostensibly a backstage story about a driven stage mother and her children, are quintessentially New York and America in one. They thrive on the drive to succeed, to fall in love and settle down, to work a deal and get yourself through troubles that keep recurring, and to discover unfamiliar people.

Skye and Sarah sing Loesser's romantic ballads, but everything about all four characters smacks of Broadway. Detroit and his cronies—Harry the Horse, Benny Southstreet, and Nicely-Nicely Johnson—are trying to find a place to hold their floating craps game, but the cops are on the lookout rather than on the take. Observing the ups and downs of the two lovers, several Broadway types discuss what it's like. The New York places in the lyrics are all located in the shadow of Broadway:

> What's playing at the Roxy?
> I'll tell you what's playing at the Roxy . . .
> What's in the *Daily News*?
> I'll tell you what's in the *Daily News*.
> 
> (Frank Loesser, "Guys and Dolls," *Guys and Dolls*, 1950)

"Sue Me," perhaps the most important Broadway song in the score, never mentions Broadway. When *Guys and Dolls* opened, five years after the end of the Second World War, Americans were feeling optimistic again. Minority groups (except for African Americans) had faced postwar discrimination, but even they were beginning to prosper, and thanks to the growing popularity of the Borscht Belt and appearances by new Jewish comedians on early TV, Yiddish words, expressions (often in translation), and rhythms began to sprinkle American English. Jewish songwriters for Broadway—especially Jerry Herman, and Jerry Bock and Sheldon Harnick—were confident enough to take on Jewish material directly in Herman's *Milk and Honey* and, most significantly, Bock and Harnick's *Fiddler on the Roof*. *Guys and Dolls* preceded them by a decade or more. No one was overtly Jewish, but how could Nathan Detroit be anything else? In the ironic love song, "Sue Me," Adelaide has finally had enough. Nathan pleads with her not to leave him in a lyric that is pure Yiddish patois.

Sam Levene, who originated the part of Nathan, was the son of a rabbi. He was fluent in Yiddish and masterful in adapting its rhythms to English. In his portrayal of Nathan Detroit, Jews came home to America. Loesser, a New York wise guy with a hot temper, who had the city and its language in his DNA, wrote the song with Levene in mind:

> I'm just a no-goodnik;
> Alright, already,
> It's true, so nu?
>
> (Frank Loesser, "Sue Me," *Guys and Dolls*, 1950)

America got it. With theater parties from Long Island and New Jersey, and tourists from the Midwest, all arriving at the 46th Street Theater, and after a run of 1,200 performances, *Guys and Dolls* had become an all-American musical.

More than mere setting, place plays an essential role in defining the outlook in songs, including those about roaming or returning. Many of them interweave the two. In song after song, wanderers weary of the road or city dwellers weary of the noise and light long to return to the home where they began.

The sense of place may appear as a particular state or town, farm or hilltop: an allusion or a set of images whose purpose is to shape mood and point of view, or evoke a moment or memory. It may be real or fantastical. Written only four months before the First World War armistice, "The Land of Beginning Again" anticipates such songs as "Over the Rainbow" in 1939, and "When You Wish Upon a Star" in 1940. It gleams with a kind of optimism born from exhaustion that Jay Gatsby might have understood (George W. Meyer and Grant Clarke, "In the Land of Beginning Again," 1918).

> There's a land of beginning again
> Where skies are always blue.

> Though we've made mistakes, that's true,
> Let's forget the past and start life anew.

Puritans from East Anglia came to build a Wilderness Zion in a new land. A century and a half later, their offspring helped to build a new, largely free nation and occupy a continent. For three centuries, we raised our eyes to the West. It was a place to dream of and settle. Beginning at least as early as Daniel Boone's forays into what became Kentucky, we set out to roam. We sought elbow room and wealth, individual freedom but also the building of farms and then towns. If roaming was the goal in itself, eventually we returned home, often from the city to the small town we came from. Just as often, we made a new home.

That said, the land of beginning again is a hard place to pin down. It doesn't appear on Abel Buell's first map of America in 1784 or Google Maps' latest satellite shot, even though songs often link it to a specific place. Is it a home left behind, returned to, or reimagined? Is it a new beginning where you follow the setting sun until you stop to put down roots? Or do you keep wandering, hoping you'll never run out of space? What the early Western settlers found at the rim of the Pacific created opportunity but also marked the diminishing of a dream. As more and more people arrived, the West would begin to close. We covered over the dream with the grittier task of building a nation. The songs of home can sometimes embrace the nation, a state, a city or town, a single house, or the person who lives there.

Setting out and moving on are part of our myth of ourselves. They date back to the Pilgrims, who ventured West from Europe to escape persecution (although they persecuted others who came after them) and include Daniel Boone's foray west in 1775; legendary Paul Bunyan's turn to logging in Minnesota and the North woods; and the exploits of Pathfinder, one of several names for Natty Bumppo, a man most at home in the wilderness in James Fenimore Cooper's five *Leatherstocking Tales*. Mythic America also finds expression in a line like Woody Guthrie's "I'd like to settle down but I'm forced to ramble all o' my time" and Willie Nelson's great signature song, "On the Road Again." True stories, novels, tall tales, and songs interweave in the shaping of the nation and the identity of its people.

Our first stories of arrival required crossing an ocean to discover a new world and create a new self. Rather than transplanted British men and women, they came to see themselves as Americans in less than a century. They became independent, sometimes prickly so. In England, the New World became a place to scorn as mere wilderness or to dream on—or even as a common metaphor used in uncommon ways. In John Donne's seventeenth-century erotic love poem, "To His Mistress Going to Bed," a lover cries out as his mistress removes her final garment: "O my America! my new-found-land."[1]

Once we discovered the great stretches of wilderness that extended to the West, we realized that we had a continent to explore and settle. Heading out seemed to offer an opportunity for what has become the old American trick of self-making. We made our own destinations by choosing to stop and stay put, perhaps because the elbow room looked endless. Or did others eventually wander for the sake of wandering? As Johnny Mercer's lyric puts it, "There's a voice in the lonesome wind / That keeps whispering, 'Roam!'" (Harold Arlen and Johnny Mercer, "Anyplace I Hang My Hat Is Home," *St. Louis Woman*, 1946).

The answer to all those questions is, in one form or another, "Yes." The questions and the many answers, some contradictory, gave a distinctive flavor to our history and songs. You can't get away with only one of them. It takes many truths to encompass America, some of them contradictory. As Sherwood Anderson wrote in *Winesburg, Ohio*:

> There was the truth of virginity and the truth of passion, the truth of wealth and of poverty, of thrift and profligacy, of carelessness and abandon . . .
> And then the people came along. Each as he appeared snatched up one of the truths and some who were quite strong snatched up a dozen of them. . . . [T]he moment one of the people took one of the truths to himself, called it his truth, and tried to live his life by it, he became a grotesque and the truth he embraced became a falsehood.[2]

At the end of *Winesburg*, the main character flees the town, just as Huck Finn "lights out for the territory," and Dean Moriarty leaves New York to land, more often than not, in San Francisco.

Each person is fleeing or seeking in their own way. This urge to move on is distinctively American, although today it often involves little more than flying to a condo in Florida. Nowadays, many Americans set out to put their feet up and flip on the air-conditioning. Yet the urge to roam persists. From the start, our novels and histories overflowed with the idea. We retraced trails or made our own, followed rivers and pushed through mountain passes, and eventually rode the railroads. The idea appears as a need to head west along with an equally deep need to remake oneself. It is as much a matter of self-awareness and seizing the day as it is of journeying and geography. Roving is the American itch.

At one time or another, nearly everybody everywhere leaves and arrives; it has been part of our defining myth since the birth of the nation. Even the indigenous people came from somewhere else. Yet, ultimately, another set of wanderers became occupiers and conquerors. The wanderlust has long been a national birthright, a signpost for what we call America. In its totality, it combines seeking the new with escape, returning to the past or discarding it—as if you could. As John Updike wrote in "Shillington," a poem to celebrate his hometown's centennial: "We have one home, the first, and leave that one. / The having and leaving go on together."[3] Yet we imposed that assumption on Native peoples, cruelly and without understanding or sympathy. The Native Genocide remains, with slavery, the great stain on the building of a nation devoted to both liberty and freedom.

Since the victors get to tell the stories, we also have the histories that began with Francis Parkman's *The Oregon Trail* and others that took decades to explore the land and its waters in the *American Trails* and *Rivers of America* series, along with Van Wyck Brooks's *Makers and Finders*, a record of the lives and the inner and outer journeys of nineteenth-century American writers played out against the history of their times. Thoreau and Emily Dickinson rarely left Concord, but Walt Whitman, originally from Long Island and then Brooklyn, sounded his "barbaric yawp over the roofs of the world."[4] The writer and broadcaster Bill Moyers's friend and Jungian analyst Steven Hermann once explained to him that the "barbaric yawp . . . rests at the core of the American soul." It is, he said,

> a primal cry from the depths of the American Soul for the emergence of a spiritual human being in whom the aims of liberty and equality have been

fully realized and in whom the opposites of love and violence, friendship and war, have been unified at a higher political field of order than anything we have formerly seen in America.[5]

That yawp also took form in a hundred different songs that people on the move made up and sang as they walked along, usually heading west. As Jack Larkin wrote, those "who traveled to the West came to see a new country in the making, sometimes to better understand what the future looked like, but more often to be a successful part of that future."[6]

In "The Gift Outright," Robert Frost looks back from the twentieth century to a land "vaguely realizing westward, / But still unstoried, artless, unenhanced, / Such as she was, such as she would become."[7] The tough frontier towns were hardly unifying and elevating, but moving west to open lands and, later, east and north to overflowing cities at least gave us a chance. We lived up to the opportunities scattershot. We discovered and rediscovered what the nation was supposed to stand for, but we also disregarded it, sometimes brutally.

It makes sense that "America the Beautiful" celebrates the American people and their land from a high point in the West, and that Paul Simon, on an imaginary cross-country bus ride more than half a century later, wonders where his America has gone. He ends up looking out the bus window at the cars driving east—on the New Jersey Turnpike headed for Manhattan. He wonders about the drivers and the nation we have in common. We exploited the land, loved the country, and eventually came to fear that we might lose it. We tell the story revealingly in our songs, one lyric at a time.

During the second half of the nineteenth century, large numbers of people on the move changed the nation. Americans, many of them young and single, left the farms and small towns of the Midwest and South for cities, and still larger numbers arrived from Europe to start farms in the Midwest but mainly to settle in the great immigration ports, especially New York. They and those who continued to push west embodied the three transforming American migrations of their century: the movement West, the arrival of immigrants mainly from Central and Eastern Europe, and the leaving of small towns for great cities. The great confluence of those from the Midwest and South and those from Ireland and then Eastern and Southern Europe provided much of the impetus that transformed New York into a throbbing cosmopolitan city.

Technology was also part of the story. In 1880, the city's first streetlamps illuminated a stretch of Broadway from 14th to 26th Streets. New York's first skyscraper, the twenty-story Tower Building on Lower Broadway, opened in 1889, followed in 1904 by the iconic Flatiron Building located at the triangle where Broadway and Fifth Avenue cross at 24th Street. The first subways began to operate in Manhattan in that same year. I have a fanciful but not frivolous democratic image of recent arrivals from Alabama and Indiana, Sicily and Galicia, watching together in wonder on Lower Broadway as somebody switched on the lights for the first time. The mix of progress and diversity appears to me as part of the American stew. With all the many hundreds of songs about New York, none captures the pulsating pace of the city and its frenetic rhythm better than Irving Berlin's "Manhattan Madness" (Irving Berlin, "Manhattan Madness," *Face the Music*, 1931). Harry Warren and Al Dubin's "Forty-Second Street" and "Lullaby of Broadway" do it; so in a different way does Cole Porter's "I Happen To Like New York"—"the sight and sound and even the stink of it" (1930). But Berlin's song is less interested in buildings and streets than in the feel of those places and their hold over the narrator, who tells his story. America is quickly becoming a nation of city dwellers. The lyrics are inseparable from the melody's staccato beat and constricted lines; they feed off each other. The person sees and understands everything that makes the city what it is: "Buildings go up with wrecking crews waiting / To tear them down again." It isn't easy to be a New Yorker; the city feels "restless," "packed," and "gyrating." Somebody feels "like a fly upon a steeple / Watching seven million people / Do a rhythm." The city races by too fast to keep up; even at night, "in my bed I tumble / But never sleep, / For I hear the rumble."

# 21

# Thousands of Miles from Home

Through the decades, the urge to settle the continent continued—although the idea of the West had changed dramatically by the early twentieth century. Pulp novels and Western movies kept alive a fantastical place where every man wore a six-gun and the hero was a wanderer who found identity in a strict moral code of his own. These mythical solitary riders brought justice and honor to small towns scattered across the prairie. The West soon became an essential part of the story that Americans told about themselves. We had crossed an ocean, and now we could cross a continent to make it our own. Deprivations and cruelties describe a lot of what actually happened, but we would not be stopped. The opportunities were too hard to resist; we would do whatever it took. It turned out that the pot of gold at the end of the continental rainbow was actually a river where a few searchers found real gold, but most of the rest of us never stopped searching—for wealth, independence, and the opportunity to start over. Americans, especially in the nineteenth and early twentieth centuries, were busily remaking themselves.

By the time the century turned, we had reached the Western sea and had begun to drive cattle back East, farm the open land, and build towns and cities. The West retains its romance to this day as people continue to move to California and Arizona. Yet, by the early decades of the last century, it had begun to diminish from a dream to a place. In the 1976 movie *The Shootist*, set in Carson City, Nevada, in 1901, the West is moving past its raw pioneer days. The town has a bank and a church to go along with its saloon and unpaved Main Street, and the new automobiles backfire and frighten the horses. J. B. Books (John Wayne in his final role), an aging gunfighter dying of cancer, explains his code to a youngster (Ron Howard) not far from his coming of age, "I won't be wronged. I won't be insulted. I won't be laid a-hand on. I don't do these things to other people, and I require the same from them." The gunfighter was a largely fictitious character made larger, even indispensable, by pulp fiction and movies, but the Old West, in which he rode into town for a shoot-out on a dusty street outside a saloon, was dying out, too. The movies' sets and costumes had some of the feeling of what it had looked like, but the rest was chimera.

Meanwhile, year in and year out, we reenacted the explorations of Hernando de Soto, Henry Hudson, John Cabot, and more. Meriwether Lewis and William Clark largely invented the American West by walking through its unnamed prairies, over its unnamed mountains, and along its unnamed rivers—unnamed, at least, in English. They joined fact to dream without diminishing the dream. Sometimes borrowing from the indigenous settlers, they left new American names behind for others to use and returned East to tell the tale, more riveting over two centuries ago than any fiction. Mountain men and trappers followed; then came the ranchers who kept the prairie open for grazing, followed by the despised homesteaders who established farms and put up fences in cattle country. Wagon trains stretched across the prairie, all headed in the same direction, the settlers protected by the US Army, which eventually turned its might to the mass destruction of the Western tribes.

These three largely concurrent journeys—to cities, from Europe, and to the West—became essential parts of America's story, but the idea of seeking out the uninhabited open spaces of the West and then settling them was the oldest and most insistent of all. The dream changed, but we never gave up on it. We nourished ourselves on movies and songs because they gave us simplified, idealized versions of the American story. Even if you stayed put in New Jersey or Massachusetts, the idea of the West was an elemental part of what you intuited about the meaning and destiny of our common history. Only when the West began to close did the nation begin to exercise its imperial muscle. The frontier had reached the sea.

There were many reasons for redefining the West, not only as a place to live free and independent but also to test your grit, raise a family, and prosper. Sometimes the most idealized and symbolic is also the most practical. As the embattled labor organizers used to say in the early twentieth century, people need bread and roses too.

What gives so many of our songs what I think of as a patriotic edge is not their rousing melodies or inspiring lyrics, but their attitude. If, despite everything else, America remains in part an idea, then many of its varied parts are ideas, too. They are real places you can map—from New York City to the Mississippi, and from Pikes Peak in the Colorado Rockies to Basin Street in New Orleans' Tenderloin—but they also fire the American imagination. Sometimes you hear parts of the map in a song, even in one that's restless and dissatisfied:

> I've been wanderin' early and late
> From New York City to the Golden Gate
> And it looks like I'm never gonna cease my wanderin'.
> 
> (Songwriter unknown, "Wanderin'," turn of the twentieth century)

Or maybe from Tin Pan Alley. Not long after the Second World War ended, a driver with a tankful of gas follows Route 66 "through Saint Looey / Joplin, Missouri," and then on to Oklahoma City, Flagstaff, and Winona before reaching his goal: "Won't you get hip to this timely tip / When you make that California trip." He invites us to get our "kicks on Route 66" (Bobby Troup, "[Get Your Kicks On] Route 66," 1946). The trip is effortless and joyful. In fact, Bobby Troup, a jazz pianist, wrote it on just such a trip. He and his wife drove from Pennsylvania to California so he could try to establish himself as a songwriter in Hollywood. He wrote the song by consulting maps as they drove west on Route 66 and then finished it in Los Angeles.

By 1850, the United States stretched to the Pacific Ocean and from Canada to Mexico. Though it remained largely unexplored and unsettled, it was a continental nation growing in population and confidence. Such rapid expansion made the nation and its people eager, aggressive, and sometimes violent. The Wisconsin Territory had opened in 1836 to push what Congress called "the permanent Indian frontier" farther west.[1] In "The Wisconsin Emigrant," a farming couple somewhere in the East considers a move west:

> Since times are so hard, I've thought, my true heart
> Of leaving my oxen, my plough, and my cart
> And away to Wisconsin, a journey we'd go
> To double our fortune as other folks do.
> 
> (Songwriter unknown, "The Wisconsin Emigrant," date unknown)

He's eager to go, but his wife reminds him that it will take years for him to clear the land and they will be "surrounded by Indians who murder by night." She convinces him to stay put:

> I love my dear children, although they are small
> But you, my dear wife, are more precious than all
> We'll stay on the farm, and suffer no loss
> For the stone that keeps rolling will gather no moss.

The farmer is unusual because most people who consider moving on in stories and songs do exactly that. Pete Seeger used to sing a Pacific Northwest folk song called "The Old Settler's Song." My wife and I were in the audience one night when he taught it to everyone and had us sing it with him. Despite its regional references, its narrative uses one man's reasons for pulling up stakes to tell a capsule history of Western settlement. He acts spontaneously, but he's no fool; it's an appealing combination in a song that looks at him with humor but also takes him seriously. The man begins by prospecting for gold in 1849, but like so many others, he fails to find his fortune and turns instead to farming. We were a very messy people who abused the land that we praised: "So rolling my grub in my blanket / I left all my tools on the ground" (Songwriter unknown, "The Old Settler's Song: Acres of Clams," date unknown).

He reaches Puget Sound in the middle of a midwinter fog only to discover that the timber is as "thick as hair on the back of a dog." He has made it to the Pacific with nothing to show for it. He weeps in frustration, but he doesn't give up. He stakes a claim and starts to chop down trees. He chops for two years, "but I never got down to the soil." His poverty forces him to stay until he realizes that enough time has passed for him to have become an old settler. For the first time, he sees that nothing could force him away. Instead, he contemplates what remains of his life: "I think of my pleasant condition / Surrounded by acres of clams."

Songs trace the trek. John A. Lomax, the great collector of folk songs, first recorded the next two early in the twentieth century.[2] He rediscovered the sound of our history. It starts with the hunters, trappers, and mountain men—the wanderers who have no home. They keep moving on, regardless of the weather:

> Hurrah for the great white way—
> Hurrah for the dog and the sledge!
> As we snow-shoe along,
> We give them a song,
> With a snap of the whip and an urgent "mush on,"—
> Hurrah for the great white way! Hurrah!
> (Songwriter unknown, "The Song of the 'Metis' Trapper," date unknown)

The end of the Mexican-American War added over a million square miles to the United States, including California. Only a few days before the signing of the treaty, James Marshall found gold on the American River in the Sacramento Valley. Thousands of people back East and down South pulled up stakes to race west to pan for gold. No more settling for farming. They began with great optimism, confident that they would return home once they "panned out their pile." They were ready to make themselves over with gold in their pockets. In fact, the trip was grueling, and only a few of the forty-niners hit it big:

> They swam the wide rivers and crossed the tall peaks,
> And camped on the prairie for weeks upon weeks,
> Starvation and cholera, hard work and slaughter—
> They reached California 'spite of hell and high water.
> (John A. Stone, "Sweet Betsy from Pike," before 1858)

When a group of Massachusetts men seeking their fortunes set off for the gold fields, the singer and songwriter Jesse Hutchinson bade them farewell and wished them good fortune in a new song he called "Ho! For California!" The lyric lets the men speak for themselves. More than expressing confidence in their success, acknowledging the privations to come, and "the love of those we left behind," Hutchinson's lyric strikes a patriotic note that borders on triumphalism as it also affirms abolition. As the men "journey afar to the promised land," they affirm what Hutchinson believed:

> Oh the land we'll save for the bold and brave
> Have determined there never shall breathe a slave
> Let foes recoil, for the sons of toil
> Shall make California God's Free Soil.
> (Jesse Hutchinson, "Ho! For California!" 1849)

The trip West took people to California, Oregon, and Washington state, but earlier they had pushed as far west as Ohio in the first decades of the republic. There was a time when what became Ohio was the Northwest Territory, and settlers were eager to make their way beyond the Alleghenies to build a cabin and eventually a town in the Ohio River Valley. They wandered, not to explore, but to domesticate. The speaker in this song urges them on:

> Come all ye brisk young fellows who have a mind to roam
> All in some foreign country, a long way from home.
> All in some foreign country, along with me to go
> And we'll settle on the banks of the lovely Ohio
> We'll settle on the banks of the lovely Ohio.
>
> (Songwriter unknown, "The Lovely Ohio," before 1842)

It was as if they were taking their lead from what Ralph Waldo Emerson allegedly said, "Europe extends to the Alleghenies; America lies beyond."[3]

As the nation and its people continued to move West, variations on the same song included hunting buffalo, growing sugarcane, catching fish, and fighting the "wild Indians," but even in these later versions the setting remained "the lovely Ohio," and the patriotic drive to make a continental nation—to move, settle, and conquer—did not abate.

One of America's best-loved songs sounds as if it's part of the Western movement. It began as a poem written by an Indiana physician named Brewster M. Higley VI after he moved to Kansas in 1873 to live in a small cabin along West Beaver Creek. He celebrated his new home in a poem, "My Western Home." It never mentions "home on the range," but it does praise the home "where seldom is heard a discouraging word / And the sky is not clouded all day." Daniel E. Kelly, Higley's friend and a musician, set the poem to music. Some years later, a lawyer who was investigating the origins of the song for a copyright lawsuit wrote that a song called "Home on the Range" was "well known to and generally sung by cowboys and other people traveling through that section of the country in stage coaches prior to 1890." In other words, the song traveled West along with the people.

Words and music first appeared together in print in 1904 under the name of "Arizona Home" by William Goodman. A number of other people claimed to have written it until a judge declared it in the public domain. In 1904, on a trip to collect songs of the West, Lomax learned it from an African American bartender in San Antonio. He called it "A Home on the Range" and said he'd heard it on cattle drives in the 1880s. The early country singer Vernon Dalhart cut the first recording in 1927.[4]

Whether it's a song about homesteading in Kansas or punching cattle on the open range, its deep delight in the American land springs from its sense of place and specific imagery.

> Oh, I love these wild flowers in this dear land of ours
> The curlew I love to hear scream
> And I love the white rocks and the antelope flocks
> That graze on the mountaintops green.
> 
> (Daniel E. Kelly and Brewster M. Higley VI, "A Home on the Range," 1873)

The cowboy plays a major role in the story of the West; songs about him and his life abound. They face up to his hard life, but they also romanticize it. There's nothing else he'd rather do despite the struggles. He was a man of the late nineteenth and early twentieth centuries who lived a life of self-reliance in the outdoors. He settled into a life of constrained, but long-term meandering, serving the ranch owner who employed him and driving the cattle to market. He owned little more than his horse and saddle and the clothes on his back. He joined the other buckaroos who wrangled the herds for a thousand miles from Texas, say, along the Chisholm Trail to Abilene, Kansas, but he was ultimately a lone iconic figure, turned out in a ten-gallon hat, bandanna, and chaps, with a weathered face and no home to return to. He earned a dollar a day and, before and after a cattle drive, slept in a bunkhouse on the ranch that paid his wages. John Lomax wrote that "he has always been on the skirmish line of civilization."[5]

Lomax also wrote that

> most cowboys . . . were bold young spirits who emigrated to the West for the same reason that their ancestors had come across the sea. They loved roving; they loved freedom; they were pioneers by instinct; an impulse and an opportunity turned their faces away from the East, put the tang for roaming in their veins, and then ever, ever westward.[6]

It seems fitting that at least one-third of the cowboys in the nineteenth and early twentieth centuries were Black men.

The cowboy was also a romantic embodiment of American individualism, especially before the 1890s, when the open range began to close. The work was grueling and dangerous, but he did things his own way: "If you don't understand him, an' he don't die young / He'll probably just ride away" (Ed Bruce and Patsy Bruce, "Mammas Don't Let Your Babies Grow Up to Be Cowboys," 1975). Many of the songs about him do not appear until after his heyday. They trade in loss:

> The cowboy may roam from his homeland
> Way out on the great divide,
> But in his heart he will still be a cowboy
> And long for his pony to ride.
>
> (Gene Autry, "Dear Old Western Skies," 1935)

The cowboy's outlook in songs will grow more melancholy as the years pass. He will soon learn that he is obsolete except as a figure of myth, yet he faces the future clear-eyed. First, though, he reaches his height in Rodgers and Hammerstein's *Oklahoma!*, written during the Second World War. Both composer and lyricist knew they were writing a new kind of show. Rather than relying on a high-spirited opening number to engage the audience and lift their spirits, they set the tone for what follows by beginning with a song from offstage, somewhere in the distance. A cowboy named Curly sings, "There's a bright golden haze on the meadow" (Richard Rodgers and Oscar Hammerstein, "Oh, What a Beautiful Mornin'," *Oklahoma!*, 1943). It is a song of optimism and delight in the new day.

> Oh, what a beautiful day!
> I got a beautiful feelin'
> Ev'rythin's goin' my way.

From Curly's first words, we learn that beneath his bravado lives a gentle, even loving spirit. He drinks in the delights of the new day in a new kind of beginning for a new kind of show. In retrospect, he also completes the story of the idealized cowboy in song. Standing at the back of the house with Rodgers on opening night, choreographer Agnes DeMille remembered that the song "produced a sigh from the entire house that I don't think I've ever heard in a theater; it was as though people hadn't seen their homeland."[7]

Conflict soon emerges in the dispute between Curly and Aunt Eller's hired man, Jud Fry, over who will take the innocent young Laurey to the box social. Laurey finds Jud frightening, but she is also drawn to him in an awakening of her sexuality, while she and Curly constantly bicker as a way to deflect their true feelings. He tries to entice her to choose him by promising to rent a surrey to take them to the social. The song shimmers with the relish he takes in describing it to her and his anticipation of the evening, especially when they are returning home late at night:

> Whoa! You team, and just keep a-creepin at a slow clip-clop;
> Don't you hurry with the surrey with the fringe on the top.
> (Richard Rodgers and Oscar Hammerstein, "The Surrey with the Fringe on Top," *Oklahoma!*, 1943)

The dream is the first indication of Curly's love for Laurey even though she doesn't recognize it. It also suggests his eventual domestication. In the end, after he has won Laurey, Curly will give up the cowboy's life to farm.

In songs about the West, a zest for living mixes with a deep elegiac strain. Many of the songs are laments that feel personal; they focus on a single cowboy and his recognition of his own approaching death. They range from folk songs invented by the cowboys themselves to Tin Pan Alley and movie songs from the 1930s and 1940s, when Western movies were so popular. In an anonymous song from the nineteenth century, a dying cowboy pleads not to be buried "on the lone prairie / Where the coyote howls and the wind blows free" (Songwriter unknown, "The Dying Cowboy," c1910). As late as 1933, another song lets a dying cowboy speak for himself in metaphors of the cowboy's life as he anticipates what's to come. He joins his death to the end of the mythic West he cherishes:

> I'm heading for the last roundup
> To the far away ranch of the Boss in the sky.
> (Billy Hill, "The Last Round Up," 1933)

The elegiac tone of these songs marks the end of an American figure who would be sculpted and painted by Frederick Remington and portrayed in hundreds of movies by such stars as John Wayne, Gary Cooper, James Stewart, and Randolph Scott. He embodied an essential part of the nation's dream of itself and its hunger for the West. By now, though, concrete covers the trails:

> This is the last cowboy song
> The end of a hundred-year waltz . . .
> Another piece of America's lost.
> (Ron Peterson and Ed Bruce, "The Last Cowboy Song," 1980)

# 22

# Hard Travelin'

A lot of the songs about roaming and roving come from folk and country music. Most of them have a strong connection to rural life and the broad, open spaces beyond the small towns. They usually mention cities only to demonstrate how much of the country the wanderers cover. Yet during the Depression, when these songs were dark but especially resonant, broken men prowled the streets in places such as New York and Chicago. They were out of work with no place to go, nothing to do but beg or line up at the nearest soup kitchen. They appear in songs like "Brother, Can You Spare a Dime?" and "Remember My Forgotten Man," or a movie like *I Was a Fugitive from a Chain Gang* from 1932. The men in the songs and the movie return home from combat in the First World War to work hard and follow the rules, but their lives unravel after the Crash.

The most obvious place to start is with Woody Guthrie. His most important songs about being on the road come mainly from the Dust Bowl Ballads, written during the Great Depression. Guthrie hailed from Oklahoma originally and felt a particular bond with the Okies who lost their farms and homes to the dust and the banks and tried to find a new start in California. Guthrie's lyrics reflect his left-wing populism and the deep kinship he felt for ordinary working people.

A song like "Goin' Down the Road Feeling Bad" ranges from bitter protest to a determination to find something better. The character in the song is married with three children and is out of work; he pushes ahead because he has nothing to go back to. He never flinches from his troubles. He calls himself "a dust bowl refugee," who longs to find a place where "the dust storms never blow" and "the water tastes like wine."

Unlike the hopeless urban songs, Guthrie's lyric combines bitter experience with a dream of something better. At the end of every verse, the song's title aligns with the angry determination to fight back: "An' I ain't gonna be treated this a-way." Despite everything, he has not given up (Woody Guthrie, "Blowin' Down the Road," 1940).

Less angry and with a touch of humor, "So Long, It's Been Good to Know Yuh" describes the world the Dust Bowl refugee is about to lose because "the dusty old dust is a-getting' my home, / And I got to be drifting along" (Woody Guthrie, "So Long, It's Been Good to Know Yuh," 1935). Like the dust, the people drift away in search of something, a dream perhaps but first shelter and a job. The parting expressed in the title is straightforward but underplayed in the face of all that's happened as the dust "blocked out the traffic an' blocked out the sun." The narrator and the other men sit together for an hour without saying a word before they bid one another goodbye and head for the road. All the while, sweethearts hug and kiss in the dark, but in the end, "they sighed and cried" and parted.

The dust gets to everyone.

In country music, anyway, the theme of wandering finds its deepest roots in the songs of Jimmie Rodgers in the late 1920s and early 1930s. He portrayed hoboes—mostly men who had no home and no companions except one another—who worked when they were broke or needed a meal, and who traveled from place to place in boxcars until the railroad bulls hunted them down. The work they did from town to town helped to build America's infrastructure, including the railroads they hitched rides on. In the last decade of the nineteenth century, according to the folk singer and folk music historian Matthew Sabatella, about sixty thousand hoboes were riding the rails without paying fares.[1] By 1911, a professor named Layal Shafee estimated that there were, amazingly, seven hundred thousand hoboes in the country.[2] During the Great Depression, their numbers increased significantly, perhaps as high as two million. In 1933, the worst year of the Depression, approximately eleven million people were homeless and out of work. Many of the men took to the railroads to try to find work in other towns.

For the Library of Congress Archive, Woody Guthrie explained his song, "Hard Travelin'": "This is a song about the hard traveling of the working people, not the moonstruck mystic traveling of the professional vacationists"[3] (Woody

Guthrie, "Hard Travelin'," 1930s?). The hobo narrator recounts the hard work he's done as he rides "them fast rattlers" to wherever they take him. It's not working he minds, but what work takes out of him. "Hard-rock minin'," for instance, where he leans on a pressure drill, "hammer flyin', air-hose suckin', six foot of mud and I shore been a muckin'." He has harvested wheat, stacked hay, and dumped "red-hot slag in a steel mill." Now he walks Route 66 with a "heavy load and a worried mind, lookin' for a woman that's hard to find." The song captures the flavor and the sweat of the hobo's life without glamour or sentimentality.

No one questions Guthrie's importance, especially during the Depression. Yet the critic Dave Marsh argues that "it was Rodgers—far more than Woody Guthrie—who was the true voice of the Depression."[4] Although he died at only thirty-five, he wandered and rode the rails across much of the country before his early death. Born in Meridian, Mississippi, in 1897, he was working for the railroad by the time he was in his mid-teens. Rail workers and hoboes taught him to play the guitar. He claimed that he learned to yodel "after he caught a troupe of Swiss emissaries doing a demonstration at a church."[5] By 1927, he was beginning to write and record his own songs.

Although his songwriting lasted for less than a decade, he wrote on a wide variety of themes. The music critic and historian Tom Piazza writes: "He sang of rural nostalgia, cabins in the pines, Mother and Daddy waiting (or no longer waiting) at home, freight trains, mean brakemen, rough barrooms, policemen, jail cells, long nights away from home, springtime again, and work in the fields."[6] Piazza rightly sees in Rodgers's work "the endless American dynamic: Strain at the leash, transform yourself into something unrecognizable, burn off the old, claim every possibility for yourself—contain, as Whitman suggested—multitudes."[7]

Yet the songs of wandering are at the heart of Rodgers's work for all the reasons Piazza gives but also perhaps as an indirect response to his declining health. A white Southerner, he sang the blues with conviction.[8] Whether or not each song of wandering is a blues, their subject matter and Rodgers's often-forlorn yodel linked them to the Black Mississippi Delta music that captured both melancholy and defiance.

Songs about wandering rely on a number of themes that range from anticipation and excitement to disappointment, loneliness, and exhaustion.

Eventually, some of these songs forsake the road to return home. Those that only dream about returning are the most melancholy of all. Although Rodgers wrote a wide range of songs, his hobo songs beginning before the Crash are an essential part of the themes of wandering in American music.

A combination of the blues, the sound of a train whistle, and Rodgers's strategically placed yodels adds to the emotionalism of a number of these songs, none more so than "Train Whistle Blues" (Jimmy Rodgers, "Train Whistle Blues," 1929). It is one of his first songs about wandering, a traditional blues that begins with a yodel to evoke the whistle of a train and suggest the character's sadness. The lyric starts with a truism that quickly turns into personal testimony. It's as if it's an introductory chapter. When a woman feels blue, the song's character asserts, she cries, "but when a man gets the blues he grabs a train and rides." From that point until the end, Rodgers's narrator sings about his own life. He projects his emotions onto "that lonesome railroad train" and wishes that he was going home again. It's been a while since he grabbed a train and rode.

As he watches the train approach, he gets "the blues so bad till the whole round world look blue." Broke and stuck, he laments, "I ain't got a dime, I don't know what to do." He's weary, and he wants to leave but can't find a job. The song provides no respite and no hope, as in so many songs of wandering about the hobo's life, especially during the Great Depression.

Yodeling punctuates a number of Rodgers's songs about the need to return. Someone alone and lonely is longing for home and a loved one (Jimmie Rodgers, "Down the Old Road to Home," 1932). Although he'd give all he has if he could only rediscover "that old hill headed that way," he can't return. Although the lyric doesn't explain why, it's easy enough to fill in the likely reasons. He ends with "a troubled mind and a heart full of pain." At the end of each of the song's three choruses, the lyric repeats its loneliest lines, preceded by a yodel that calls attention to what's to follow, especially its hopelessness: "For I'm lonesome and blue for some place to roam / And I wish it could be down the old road to home." The yodel is an expression of keening despair.

None of Rodgers's songs is more desperate than "Waitin' for a Train" (Jimmie Rodgers, "Waitin' for a Train," 1928). During the Depression, it felt like a rural version of "Brother, Can You Spare a Dime?" Like many of Rodgers's hobo songs, its lyric is a set of associations that express the life of a hobo. He tries to talk a brakeman into letting him ride, but he hasn't got even a penny: "Get off get off you railroad bum he slammed the boxcar door." If he wants to make his way home, the hobo will have to do it on foot. Coming right after this climax, Rodgers's yodel intensifies the emotion. It suggests the sound of the train whistle and evokes the wail of the blues. The hobo bemoans his life as the song concludes without much hope:

> I'm on my way from Frisco I'm going back to Dixie Land
> Though my pocketbook is empty and my heart is full of pain
> I'm a thousand miles away from home just waiting for a train.

Some of Rodgers's lyrics describe the hobo's approaching death. In "Hobo's Meditation," a man lying in a boxcar wonders, "What will become of the hobo / Whenever that time comes to die?" (Jimmie Rodgers, "The Hobo's Meditation," 1932). It's the kind of blunt question a man without means, home, or even hope might ask as the years pass without relief. He wonders about heaven in the hope of finding a better life there. His vision of the afterlife is an extension of what he's endured in this life. It starts in fearfulness—"Will there be any tough cops and brakemen?"—but soon makes room for hope. Everything takes form as a question to suggest the hobo's lingering uncertainty: "Will they have respect for the hobo / In the land that lies hidden up there?"

That sympathetic attitude toward hoboes runs through all of Rodgers's songs of wandering; the saddest songs of all are laments for the struggles and loneliness of the life. Perhaps his writing about a hobo's death reflects his awareness of his tuberculosis and his sympathetic understanding of what's to come. "Hobo Bill's Last Ride" describes a hobo's last night. He lies in a boxcar without warmth or light, only wind, cold, and rain. The chorus consists of only two words, "Hobo Bill," drawn out into a yodel of sorts to underscore the song's sadness and its setting on a train. Yet when Bill hears "a whistle blowing in a dreamy kind of way / The hobo seemed contented for he smiled there where he lay." By morning, Hobo Bill is dead, "just a weary railroad bum who died out in the cold" (Jimmie Rodgers, "Hobo Bill's Last Ride," 1929).

Dissatisfaction underscores a lot of these songs, but others accept the pleasures of the road despite its demands—on foot along a highway or riding in a freight car on its way to whatever town comes next. For the characters in these songs, rambling is in their blood. Unlike the hoboes who hit the road out of necessity, for them, its lure is irresistible. The lyrics may start with "an old train rollin' down the line" or hearing "a lonesome whistle blow."

In his song from 1977, the country songwriter and singer Merle Haggard wrote about a "ramblin' fever" that gives his narrator no choice. "Rambling" is the perfect word—covering ground without a destination in mind, moving on for its own sake. He drifts: "My hat don't hang on the same nail too long." It suggests the urgency of what he knows about himself. He imagines times when "I'd like to bed down on a sofa / And let some pretty lady rub my back," but "I want to die along the highway and rot away like some old high-line pole, / Rest this ramblin' fever in my soul" (Merle Haggard, "Ramblin' Fever," 1977). In both songs, the narrators know that life on the road is something they will never escape.

Dream or no dream, in the long run, life wears you down. In "Weary from Wandering," someone has been on the road for "ten thousand nights and a million beers." He confesses to a friend that being on the road is wearying; it isn't fun anymore (Bob McDill, "Tired of the Road, Joe," 1977). Here, too, the wanderer faces the passing of the years and the simple truth about things that don't work, "the way you had 'em planned / One day you just turn around / And it's slipped right through your hand."

The country singer and songwriter Roger Miller takes a different tack. His irrepressible humor and elliptical brevity lend one of his best-known songs, "King of the Road," an unusual way of looking at the hobo's life. Life's no easier than it is in other hobo songs, but there's no melancholy or despair in it. The hobo takes life as it comes and never loses his sense of humor:

> Ah, but two hours of pushin' broom
> Buys an eight by twelve four-bit room.
> I'm a man of means by no means, king of the road.
>
> (Roger Miller, "King of the Road," 1964)

Another song, among the most famous of all hobo songs, relies on fantasy instead. It's so successful and it's been around for so long that most listeners don't recognize it as the dream of a hobo. Nobody knows who wrote it, but Harry McClintock first recorded it in 1928. He claimed that he'd written it in 1898, when he was sixteen and living on the streets. His original version includes some of the song's bawdiest verses:

> I've hiked and hiked till my feet are sore
> And I'll be damned if I hike any more
> To be buggered sore like a hobo's whore
> In the Big Rock Candy Mountains.
> (Harry McClintock?, "Big Rock Candy Mountain," 1898?)

The folk singer Burl Ives's cleaned-up version became popular with children when he first recorded it in the late 1930s. Eventually, singers such as Pete Seeger, the country singer Mel Tillis, the popular crooner Bing Crosby, and dozens of other performers also recorded it.

The hobo's life remains what it is, but in this song, he prefers to dream, especially with a sense of humor that relies on hyperbole and nonsense. He continues his wandering, but this time he's "headed for a land that's far away / Beside the crystal fountains." There are "cigarette trees," "lemonade springs," and "the little streams of alcohol / Come trickling down the rocks." It also includes the dangers of the hobo's life, here made safe through humor:

> In the Big Rock Candy Mountains
> The jails are made of tin
> And you can walk right out again
> As soon as you are in.

# 23

# Wandering and Returning

Too many love songs from Tin Pan Alley feel detached from the everyday world. Their allusions to "paradise" and "forever" separate them from ordinary day-by-day life. A boy and a girl and the preciousness of their feelings, and that's sufficient to carry us through thirty-two bars. But an equal number of songs, no less devoted to love, are rooted, at least emotionally, in a specific place inseparable from the lovers and their feelings for one another.

In the folk and country songs about wandering and returning, love usually appears in passing as something that can't tie a character down or something that he seeks but never finds. Roving is at the heart of things. It is an individual search for America, one man or woman's "pursuit of happiness." In Tin Pan Alley, though, love is the motivation. Between the late nineteenth century and the early 1920s, "returning" became one of popular music's essential themes.

Many Tin Pan Alley songs have a purpose that supersedes wandering for its own sake. Music publishers aimed them specifically at the new arrivals in New York City during the first three decades of the twentieth century, when large numbers of young men and women from small towns resettled in New York. They found places to live, got jobs, and made friends. They became city dwellers. Yet I know of only a few songs that celebrate leaving the small towns for New York. For the most part, country folk arrived unaccompanied by music, but when songs do compare life back home to what they've found in the city, they crow with pleasure.

In what must be the jolliest of these songs, a farmer comes to the city, where he takes in the sights, but he spends most of his nights going to the theater, staying up late in cabarets and clubs, and meeting stylish young women. Eventually, his wife back on the farm begs him to come home. He tells her he's staying and invites her to join him:

I love the cows and chickens,
But this is the life,
This is the life!
I love to raise the dickens
While I'm cabareting,
Where the band is playing! . . .
No more picking berries,
Me for cocktail cherries! . . .
This is the life for mine!

(Irving Berlin, "This Is the Life," 1914)

Most—but not all—of those who left for the city made their way successfully. Enough struggled and failed for their plight to become the subject of a major American novel, Theodore Dreiser's *Sister Carrie*, as well as a dozen tearful, sentimental ballads. Most of them are cautionary tales for young women that tell of virtue compromised. Those who went before them have learned that shame keeps them from returning home. In "In the Heart of the City That Has No Heart," the best-known of these songs, a young woman leaves her "old home" because she longs "for the sights and bright city lights" (Joseph M. Daly and Thomas S. Allen, "In the Heart of the City That Has No Heart," 1913). When she arrives, she begins to mingle with strangers, but "nobody said, 'You are being misled,' / For what did the stranger care?" In the city, everything is temporary and transactional: "In the heart of the city that has no heart, / That's where they meet, and that's where they part."

In a song written by Paul Dresser, a major songwriter from the time, a young man who has established himself in the city sees an old schoolmate from their "village far away" (Paul Dresser, "Just Tell Them That You Saw Me," 1895). When he calls her name, she shrinks from him. He tries to reassure her, telling her that he's still her friend. He also notes that her cheeks are pale and her face is thin. He offers to take a message to her family when he visits the following week. Her reply calls up a forlorn memory of happy family life:

Just tell them that you saw me,
She said, they'll know the rest,
Just tell them I was looking well you know,
Just whisper if you get a chance to mother dear, and say,
I love her as I did long, long ago.

Even those who adapted to city living were homesick. Mainly, though, the Alley turned out song after song in which young men ached to return to the farms and hometowns they had left. They longed to regain what they had lost.

Irving Berlin's "Settle Down in a One-Horse Town" expresses the feelings of a young man who is living in the city but longs to return to marry his hometown sweetheart (Irving Berlin, "Settle Down in a One-Horse Town," *Watch Your Step*, 1914).

The lyric feels as if he's writing her a letter in which he envisions marrying her before they settle in the one-horse town that is their version of paradise:

> And from the time the rooster calls
> I'll wear my overalls
> And you'll wear a simple gingham gown.
> So if you're strong for a shower of rice,
> We could make a paradise
> Out of a one-horse town.

Berlin wrote this and "This Is the Life" about the excitement of life in the city in the same year. Ultimately, in the body of their work, songwriters are honest brokers who give their characters their own say.

The songs of returning often speak of a specific state or town. The people the narrators miss are there. The references might be brief, but they serve to ground the song's emotionalism in the memories and hopes of ordinary people. They assume that you can go home again. Remembrance and anticipation are inseparable through details of place. A young man away from home remembers a girl who waits for him. The lyric begins in memory:

> I know a plain old-fashioned farmhouse
> Down a pretty little lane,
> Where yellow daisies make a pathway
> To the fields of golden grain.
>
> (Richard A. Whiting and Dave Radford, "Where the Black-Eyed Susans Grow," 1916)

In that farmhouse, a girl waits for him. Like the black-eyed Susans that grow around the family's farm, the daughter's name is also Susan. In the mind of the young man who loves her, she, the flower, and the place weave together as one. From that point on, with great confidence, he turns anticipation into action:

> I'm going back to a shack
> Where the Black-eyed Susan's grow,
> I love 'em so,
> They're all around on the ground
> Where I found the one I know
> So long ago . . .
> I'll bring out the ring for the finger of my sweet,
> She's mighty sweet.

Although the idea of returning is essential to these songs and dozens more like them, they are love songs first and foremost. The narrators are almost always men. Their return is often to a town, a house or farm, and a loving mother, but most importantly to a girl who lives next door or down a nearby country lane. Sometimes the imminence of the return is exciting enough. They're part of the dream in such songs as Irving Berlin's "When the Midnight Choo-Choo Leaves for Alabam'" and "I Want to Go Back to Michigan (Down on the Farm)"; Albert Von Tilzer, Charles McCarron, and Charles S. Albert's "Down Where the Swanee River Flows"; and Walter Donaldson and Gus Kahn's "Carolina in the Morning."

These songs are either dreams of the future, or they're set at the moment of departure. The character in each of them anticipates what will happen when he returns to the life he used to know. The lyric gives immediacy to his envisioning, especially when he announces that he's leaving today. In one of the best-known of these songs, a young man about to leave the city feels as if he's ready to leap down the stairs and race to the station. He can hardly wait until midnight. The melody and lyrics are lively and energetic. The young man has packed his things and given the landlord the key. When he finally gets on board, he erupts with glee when he sees the conductor:

> I'll grab him by the collar
> And I'll holler,
> "Alabam'! Alabam'!"
>
> (Irving Berlin, "When the Midnight Choo-Choo
> Leaves for Alabam'," 1912)

Two years later, Berlin wrote a dreamier song about returning, this time to Michigan. It is no less committed, but it feels almost like a reverie that never quite turns dream into reality: "That's why I wish again, / That I was in Michigan, / Down on the farm" (Irving Berlin, "I Want to Go Back to Michigan [Down on the Farm]," 1914). Perhaps that's because many of the new city dwellers might have felt homesick, but they also stayed where they were. The city was about the future.

The lyric's detailed sense of place lends immediacy to the young man's longing to return to the farm where he was born and raised. He longs to "fish again, / In the river that flows beside the fields of waving grain." The images deepen his loneliness for now but also hold out hope. The bouncy melody fails to conceal the lyric's underlying sadness despite the clever touch of wordplay. All he can do is wish:

> I miss the rooster, The one that useter
> Wake me up at four A.M.
> I think your city's very pretty, nevertheless—
> I want to be there,
> I want to see there
> A certain someone full of charm;
> That's why I wish again,
> That I was in Michigan,
> Down on the farm.

Roving isn't always sad. The character in this song has no regrets, no second thoughts (Richard A. Whiting, Haven Gillespie, and Seymour Simons, "Breezing Along with the Breeze," 1926). His home is "wherever I may be." He knows that no one misses him and no one wonders where he is, but he's happy to be on his own. The song is jubilant, nearly ecstatic: "The sky is the only roof I have over my head, / And when I'm weary, Mother Nature makes me a bed." He may be alone, but he never feels lonely. He meanders without a destination in mind: "I'm just goin' along as I please, / Breezing along with the breeze."

Walter Donaldson and Gus Kahn's "Carolina in the Morning" is one of the best of these songs (Walter Donaldson and Gus Kahn, "Carolina in the Morning," *Passing Show of 1922*, 1922). Like many others, it lets a young man speak for himself. He misses his home in Carolina and a particular girl who lives there; place and name are identical. But Kahn's lyric underplays the thought of leaving the city. The refrain begins and ends with the same brief lines: "Nothing could be finer / Than to be in Carolina / In the morning." He seems to mean not the overnight train ride, but the delight of waking early for one who never left. It's a slight but useful indirection.

The rest of the refrain has such a youthful, airy feel, such delight in what the young man imagines, and so detailed a sense of place that it creates a sense of immediacy. It's as if everything is happening now rather than in his imagination. The narrator could be basking in contentment; truly, nothing *could* be finer than what he envisions. He might be saying it to her about something they have done before and will continue to do, perhaps as soon as tomorrow "at dawning." Or more likely, "could" suggests a dream of the future. The lyricist Gus Kahn's use of the present tense and his playful language add to the feeling and also soften the sadness of separation. It's actually a song of anticipation, even though it feels as if he's already there.

The lines, "No one could be sweeter / Than my sweetie when I meet her / In the morning," lead to an early morning stroll together shaped by a combination of close observation and wordplay:

> Strolling with my girlie
> Where the due is pearly early
> In the morning.
> Butterflies all flutter up
> And kiss each little buttercup
> At dawning.

For Tin Pan Alley, the free and easy life continued into the Great Depression. The title song from the 1933 movie, *Hallelujah, I'm a Bum*, celebrates living from hand to mouth on the road. A hobo lives in Hooverville and gets from place to place on foot or in boxcars. The railroad bulls could roust you out and take a few swings with a billy club, but it was all in all a life romanticized by songs and movies in the early 1930s. Among the best of the movies are *Sullivan's Travels* and *It Happened One Night*, both about prosperous people who wind up on the road having to fend for themselves.

The hobo in this song spends most of his time avoiding work, but the weather's good, he says, and "the coffee tastes like wine" (Richard Rodgers and Lorenz Hart, "Hallelujah, I'm a Bum," *Hallelujah, I'm a Bum*, 1933). Unlike the character of Al in "Brother, Can You Spare a Dime?" his home is wherever he finds himself:

> The moon's your chandelier;
> Your ceiling is the sky,
> Way up high.

Traveling wherever his feet take him, he sings about how joyful he feels: "Hallelujah, I'm a bum again."

We sing about mountains and open fields with affection, but nothing seems to reach us in the way that rivers do. Because we can linger on their banks and watch them flow by, they encourage us to imagine a faraway place, somewhere we can't see but yearn for. We can walk along beside them and not feel quite so alone. We romanticize them because of what they seem to promise—escape, challenge, discovery, independence, sustenance. Who knows where they lead? That's what we want to find out, so we put up with the loneliness that comes with the seeking. Many of the characters in river songs are solitary wanderers. It's a theme that never completely disappears from our songs—country, folk, or mainstream pop. It's part of what makes them American even when the river is a product of the imagination:

> Henry Mancini and Johnny Mercer's "Moon River" is one of our greatest songs about wanderlust. Written for the movie, *Breakfast at Tiffany's*, it propelled Mancini's career and revived Mercer's, which had almost been destroyed by the coming of rock and roll. (Henry Mancini and Johnny Mercer, "Moon River," *Breakfast at Tiffany's*, 1961)

It is a graceful, misty, but compelling song in which a young man is drawn to setting out, the river his only companion. Mercer was raised in genteel poverty in Savannah, but he was drawn to the music and singing in the African American churches near his home. From that, he developed a deep affection for jazz and left home to sing and eventually write in the large cities where jazz flourished. Years later, he drew on those memories, however indirectly, to write a lyric about setting out from the familiar into the alluring unknown.

Mercer finds his defining image in a river that draws the narrator forward but also waits around the bend, a combination of reassurance and mystery. The title suggests a dream confirmed by a search for "the same rainbow's end" and an initially mysterious reference to a "huckleberry friend." The reference echoes Huck Finn but also alludes to a boyhood friend of Mercer's. They used to pick huckleberries together, but now the narrator leaves him behind although he remains in his memory. The friend accompanies him, but only in his imagination. Departing without his friend adds to an undercurrent of breaking away and loneliness, but the river and the friend are always there, one real and one rooted in memory:

> We're after the same
> Rainbow's end
> Waitin' 'round the bend
> My Huckleberry friend
> Moon River, and me.

Each will have to do it on his own. The young man and the river drift together, the river always slightly ahead of him—"Waitin' 'round the bend." The writer Robert Wright calls it "a love song to wanderlust" but also speculates that it might be "a romantic song in which the romantic partner is the idea of romance."[1] No suggestion could be more persuasive about the songs of the Great American Songbook.

The song is elusively autobiographical. Its languid pace implies a setting in the South. At the same time, the character can't wait to see the rest of the world. The words are refractions of Mercer's growing up in the Deep South. He kept his ties to his family but left for New York and Hollywood, lured by the jazz he'd come to love. Although all this may be part of what grounds the song's emotion in memory, Mercer has transformed it into something that stands on its own, apart from the facts of his life. The song is a masterful remaking of self into art.

# 24

# Longing for My Homeland

Wandering initially meant pushing through the thick grasses of the prairie or following where the next river led. We crossed "the wide Missouri" and sailed the great highway of the Mississippi. Beyond them lay the West, but first the grasslands and mountains that stretched nearly to the Pacific. Yet the Mississippi remains the great symbolic American river, vast and inexorable. Before and after the railroads left it in their dust, it never stopped "rolling along," an image of whatever America you chose it to be. It was something to leave behind when you set out for somewhere or anywhere; it was also the way back home.

As in so many of these songs, place plays an essential role. A solitary wanderer roams "always alone and blue, so blue." He finds his only happiness in a memory of the songs of the mockingbirds. Although he's alone, he speaks to the one he loves: "Longing for my homeland, muddy water shore / Miss the Mississippi and you" (Jimmie Rodgers, "Miss the Mississippi and You," 1932). We never learn why he doesn't return, but to say that this is a song from the Great Depression may be explanation enough.

Although the Mississippi flows and bends from Northern Minnesota to the Gulf of Mexico, the image that recurs as much as any other is the mud. It's a reference to the river and a sign of returning and home. In another Rodgers song written three years earlier, the narrator is ready to return after wandering mainly back and forth along the river. Now, though, he's packing his grip because "I'm just like a seagull that's left the sea / Oh, your muddy waters, they keep on calling me" (Jimmie Rodgers, "Mississippi River Blues," 1929).

During the first act of *Big River*, a musical adaptation of *The Adventures of Huckleberry Finn* from 1985, Huck and the escaped slave, Jim, have teamed up but are still being pursued. Huck rouses Jim: "They're after us—we ain't got a minute to lose." They leap upon their raft and pole out into the Mississippi to catch the current as Jim begins to sing. He fears for his freedom and his life, but willingly trusts himself to the vast river that he needs, but that lies beyond his understanding. He will risk everything to be free.

> Look out for me, oh muddy water
> Your mysteries are deep and wide . . .
> And I need to climb upon your back and ride.
> (Roger Miller, "Muddy Water," Big River, 1985)

No matter how far someone roams, there seems to be no escape. You can never shake the river. Jim needs it to find his way home, but other narrators in songs remain bound to it, shaping their lives and identities around its mysteries regardless of where they are. One who never leaves, but spends his years riding a steamboat down the Mississippi and then back up, comes to understand how inscrutable it is and how uncaring it can be in the face of human trouble:

> Ol' Man River, that Ol' Man River,
> He must know somethin', but don't say nothin',
> He just keeps rollin', he keeps on rollin' along.
> (Jerome Kern and Oscar Hammerstein, "Ol' Man River," Show Boat, 1927)

Some songs offer hope instead of resignation. Instead of feeling sorrow, the character here calls the river his friend (R. S. Adams and J. Greer, "River's Taking Care of Me," 1933). He never names it; it could be a river invented by the song's lyricist, but at the end of the journey, the traveler expresses only gratitude. "I love the river," he says. "That river's takin' care of me!" He doesn't claim to understand it: it seems to be reciprocal acceptance in a place of safety, thanks to the river:

> He never stops to ask the reason I'm here,
> Just fills my empty bowl . . .
> I guess that river has a soul!

Another man with a menial job, no money, and an abusive boss quits on impulse to escape "the man" by hitching a ride on a riverboat named Proud Mary (John Fogerty, "Proud Mary," 1968). The people who work onboard treat him with kindness and generosity; they are "happy to give" even though they don't have much themselves. The river and those who live along it sustain him. He finds a home of sorts as he urges the riverboat on in a driving melody: "Big wheel, keep on turning, / Proud Mary, keep on burning."

Few American places evoke memories and dreams more widely and deeply than the Mississippi River because they are inseparable from its size, variety, and grandeur. You know about it intuitively, even if you've never seen it. I was an adult the first time I crossed over it; I couldn't stop looking at it, taking in its breadth and watching it disappear in a haze to the north and south. From this side of the Canadian border to New Orleans, it used to carry barges poled by rivermen. Then came the paddle wheelers until the railroads built their tracks to parallel its banks. The railroad was one of the great transformative technologies of the nineteenth century, and a romantic image that somehow combines the vastness of the nation with our understanding of it as something closer to home—a way to leave or return.

Americans have hundreds of railroad songs to sing. Nearly everybody knows "I've Been Working on the Railroad" and "Casey Jones," but other songs make the locomotive, whistle, and rails into essential American images of our determination to be out in the open and free.

Not every train song is famous, but many of them raise essential American themes, none more so than "Crossing the Grand Sierras." On May 10, 1869, Leland Stanford drove a ceremonial gold spike to complete the Transcontinental Railroad. Later that same year, Henry Clay Work's triumphalist song celebrated the journey west to the Pacific as "The hissing breath of the iron steed . . . springs at the touch of the engineer" (Henry Clay Work, "Crossing the Grand Sierras," 1869). The lyric traces the course west of the "Lightning Palace Train." It praises the technological achievement as the train thunders "o'er trestl'd deeps, / Through tunel'd steeps," but it also praises the varied land from deep canyons to snow-covered mountains. It never stops until it views "the Golden Gated main."

But this is more than a thrilling train ride and a tribute to American ingenuity and invention. Lincoln had believed in the railroad. In the midst of the Civil War, he signed the Pacific Railway Act, which began a ten-year project to complete a railroad to the Pacific Ocean. Seven years later, at Promontory Point, Utah, a lofty goal became an everyday reality.

The early trains from the East lined up in Council Bluffs in Western Iowa. Passengers boarded the Pacific Railroad and stepped off in San Francisco. The journey from New York to Iowa to California took about four days. Those who made the trip helped to translate Lincoln's dream of the Union into practical reality. The song's stirring lines echo Daniel Webster in the U.S. Senate on January 26, 1830: "Liberty and union, now and forever, one and inseparable":[1]

> We sing a wond'rous story,
> No nation sang before!
> A Continental Chorus,
> That echoes either shore.

The train keeps moving. Motion serves as a balm. As a lonesome wanderer sings, "Miles from where I am to the only one for me," he finds solace as the smoke billows and the whistle wails (Lionel Alton Delmore and Rabon Delmore, "Blue Railroad Train," 1933?). The lyric ranges from nostalgia to the joys of rambling. He rides the rails like a hobo on the train he calls "a good old pal to me."

Just as spirituals rode a train to the Promised Land, more recent songs made common cause with the blues. It had something to do with a melancholy cry across vast distances. When love comes to an end, the speeding train gives you the escape you crave (John D. Loudermilk, "Blue Train [Of the Heartbreak Line]," 1962). It's a blue train, though, as the character links a man's loneliness to the "click-clack of the wheels." Riding the rails eases his despondency: "Conductor, go and tell the man to shovel on the coal— / It doesn't seem half as bad as long as I can roll."

The folk singer and songwriter Steve Goodman understood that when he wrote about a railroad train, it was more than mere locomotion over distances. He made a river and a train—the natural and the man-made—embody a nation. Both keep passing places, not to leave them behind, but to gather them as part of the nation. Goodman did it by giving the train a voice of its own. The song begins with a jubilant, driving melody that never flags, and a lyric that opens with information: "There are fifteen cars and fifteen restless riders

/ Three conductors and twenty-five sacks of mail." It doesn't soft-soap what the train passes: "And freight yards full of old black men / And the graveyards of rusted automobiles." And then something wondrous happens. Although the narrator appears and reappears throughout the song, the train—City of New Orleans—begins to speak. It offers a welcome and introduces itself. It encapsulates the nation:

> Singing' "Good morning, America, how are ya?"
> Saying "Don't ya know me? I'm your native son."
> (Steve Goodman, "City of New Orleans," 1970)

From there, it describes some of its passengers—old men playing cards in the club car, for instance, and mothers rocking their sleeping babies. The song pulsates to the rhythm of the rails, but it also has something darkly nostalgic about it, as if the narrator sees and understands the Pullman porters and the engineers, who sing as "They ride their father's magic carpet made of steel." But is it a magic carpet for them, as things lost and left over pile up along the way? This is a song about loss and the ravages of time disguised as something that pushes through the night to its destination:

> And all the towns and people
> They seem to fade into a bad dream . . .
> This train's got the disappearing railroad blues.

No matter how bleak the landscape may be, though, the narrator continues to hear the confidence in the voice of the train once again, for better or worse: "Don't ya know me? I'm your native son."

Goodman's train follows the Mississippi to New Orleans. It is forever setting out and covering ground. Yet the train is also the way home, regardless of when it was written. In 1915, for his first Broadway show, Irving Berlin wrote the jubilant lines:

> When the rhythm of the engine seems to say,
> We're getting nearer to it. We're getting nearer to it,
> When you're homeward bound.
> (Irving Berlin, "Homeward Bound," *Watch Your Step*, 1915)

Forty-five years later, Paul Simon, unable to return, dreams of what he wants but cannot yet have. Unlike Berlin, who is caught up in the joy of movement, Simon is similar to Goodman in his ability to see what surrounds him, but with a melancholy point of view:

> The movies and factories
> And every stranger's face I see,
> Reminds me that I long to be
> Homeward bound.
> (Paul Simon and Art Garfunkel, "Homeward Bound," 1966)

Wanderers in song return home. Whether they are homesick, worn out from years on the road, tired from a day of work, happily anticipating their arrival, or remembering what they had, home appears most often in songs as the place they want to go without having to deserve it. The reality of home doesn't always live up to what we expect or remember, but that's a different matter. Bruce Springsteen's "My Hometown" from 1985 is a lament for a dying town where a boy grew up and still lives (Bruce Springsteen, "My Hometown," 1985).

Springsteen's lyric describes what has happened to his hometown. The song is close to autobiography as the songwriter, then in his mid-thirties, remembers what Freehold, New Jersey, was like when he was growing up, especially his father's pride in living there. His father would drive him around the town in his "big old Buick" with the son on his lap, and say, "Son, take a good look around, / This is your hometown."

Over the years, though, the town endured racial conflict, vacant stores, and rising unemployment. Now a married man with a child, he and his wife talk about getting out and moving South. Before they go, though, the father relives his memory of father and son in the old Buick. He's thirty-five and has his own son:

> Last night, I sat him up behind a wheel and said,
> "Son, take a good look around.
> This is your hometown."

Springsteen has said that in some of his songs, his protest appears in the verses and his patriotism in the choruses. "My Hometown" fits that pattern. In a 2021 podcast with President Barack Obama, Springsteen, seventy-one at the time, said that he still "marvels at the universality and patriotism that comes through when concert crowds roar out its line, 'This is your hometown.'"[2] He added, "I always get a sense that they know the town they're talking about isn't Freehold. It's not Washington. It's not Seattle. It's the whole thing—it's all of America."[3]

In 1932, Harry Woods and Gus Kahn offered a different take on a similar town. Someone still away from home looks forward to wandering back. Is the town still as he describes it, or has he idealized it in his imagination? There's nothing distinctive about the place. It's "old and sort of tumble down," but it means a lot to the people who live there. Things may be tough, but they haven't given up on it or one another:

> It's just a little street where old friends meet
> And greet you in the same old way.
>
> (Harry Woods and Gus Kahn, "A Little Street Where Old Friends Meet," 1932)

In the 1937 Hollywood musical *High, Wide, and Handsome*, Sally Watterson (Irene Dunne) sings "The Folks Who Live on the Hill" to Peter Cortlandt (Randolph Scott), the man she's just married (Jerome Kern and Oscar Hammerstein, "The Folks Who Live on the Hill," *High, Wide, and Handsome*, 1937). Jerome Kern and Oscar Hammerstein envisioned it as a counterpoint to the boisterous wedding reception still underway. Peter takes Sally off to show her the spot where he plans to build a house for them. His excitement is contagious. The couple sits together in a lovely, intimate moment as she describes the future she envisions for them.

The song is a tribute to the interplay of change and permanence. They will have children and add onto the house to give themselves the extra room they need, but always the home remains: the building itself but also the sense of place it evokes to shape and ground the married life they've lived:

> We'll sit and look at the same old view . . .
> And we'll be pleased to be called
> The folks who live on the hill.

In John Denver's "Back Home Again," a truck driver who's been on the road for ten days anticipates "a fire softly burning, supper's on the stove / It's the light in your eyes that makes him warm." Sometimes this old farm feels like a long-lost friend: "Yes, an', hey, it's good to be back home again" (John Denver, "Back Home Again," 1974).

Like "Back Home Again," some songs celebrate the arrival or the home itself and the welcome it offers. The man and his wife talk about their day, but ultimately Denver has written a love song. When the man lies down, he can "feel your fingers feather soft upon me / The kisses that I live for, the love that lights my way." Songs of return feel limitless in their relevance to the lives of Americans, happy and sad, eager and desperate, year in and year out.

It's hard to find a more optimistic writer than Oscar Hammerstein II or a more optimistic Broadway musical than his and Richard Rodgers's landmark show, *Oklahoma!* Written in the middle of the Second World War, it is larger than life in its openhearted joy in the land and its people, and in its joining of romance and patriotism. It is also nostalgic in its affection for a past America in which audiences in 1943 could discern the symbolic rural America they were fighting for. Like Irving Berlin, Hammerstein could project emotion in the simplest of lyrics, although, also like Berlin, he was capable of wit and irony. The show's simple plot turns on Laurey's decision to go to a church social with the sweet-tempered cowboy, Curly, or the menacing hired man, Jud Fry. In other words, a story about two young lovers who eventually discover their futures together becomes an expression of an idealized American identity so many longed to affirm.

Yet within the plot, everything is in flux: the coming of statehood to the Oklahoma territory, the lingering conflicts between farmers and cowmen, the earthy comic love story between Ado Annie and Will Parker, and the outsiders—the dangerous Fry and the comic but amoral Ali Hakim—who threaten to destroy Laurey and Curly's nascent romance. Hakim is the peddler who sells Fry the device that will maim and perhaps kill Curly.

Once the conflict between Jud and Curly boils over and Jud dies in the ensuing fight, Laurey and Curly can truly begin their married life and start a home. Only then can everyone turn their attention to the larger matter of statehood for Oklahoma. The newlyweds "couldn't pick a better time to start in life" because they'll "soon be livin' in a brand-new state!" (Richard Rodgers and

Oscar Hammerstein II, "Oklahoma!" *Oklahoma!*, 1943). The title song brings together the show's different strands; love, marriage, place, and time become one. At first, the people sing excitedly to one another about what living in a new state will mean. It will give them "Barley, / Carrots and pertaters." The chorus builds from sustenance to pleasure and then delight: "Plen'y of heart and plen'y of hope." In a spacious new place defined by plenty and love, the newlyweds will build their home as the Myth of the Garden reaches fulfillment.

At this point, the song changes from bits of conversation between friends and neighbors to a performance number, an anthem to American optimism that happens to be set in Oklahoma in a time of new beginnings, and a fading away, at least for a moment, of differences. The cast turns to face the audience to sing the final chorus. It is a rousing democratic moment that traces back to the opening number of the second act, "The Farmer and the Cowman," in which Aunt Eller sings, "I don't say I'm no better than anybody else, / But I'll be damned if I ain't just as good" (Richard Rodgers and Oscar Hammerstein II, "The Farmer and the Cowman," *Oklahoma!*, 1943). It is also the fulfillment of what Curly had sung with such innocent optimism as the curtain first rose: "I've got a wonderful feelin' / Ev'rything's goin' my way."

It is also the moment when the lyric links people to place. This is the place "where the wind comes sweepin' down the plain," but it's also the place where a hawk circles above while "my honey lamb and I / Sit alone and talk." Laurey and Curly, deeply in love, will find their happiness in this bounteous place. In the end, the anthem completes Robert Frost's observation that "The land was ours before we were the land's."[4] That has changed now: "We know we belong to the land / And the land we belong to is grand." In *Oklahoma!* and its songs, in the midst of a worldwide war, America continued to reinvent itself. A Broadway musical told us what we needed to hear about ourselves.

# Epilogue

America historically has found ways to renew itself. There have been huge failures along the way: the Civil War and Reconstruction, most grievously, and the irreconcilable differences in the aftermath of the 2020 and 2024 elections, and the January 6 insurrection. It's hard to know where that goes because it's still playing out. If our democratic values and our long-shared sense of American identity survive, we will probably emerge changed, bearing new scars, and embracing what we agree is at the heart of the nation. I refuse not to believe in the nation's capacity for reinvention. We use popular songs to label where we are, remind us where we've been, and lay out where we want to go. No guarantees, but always the sense of a nation and people in flux, yet still very much here.

The Empire State Building and the Grand Coulee Dam stand as icons of American invention, both built during the Great Depression, but both representing the "can-do" attitude that Americans claim for themselves. As part of it, we settled the frontier and eventually rode the trains back East and North to build great cities. It's the American tension embodied in the compromises in the Constitution and lived out in innumerable ways through the nation's people for nearly two hundred and fifty years. Many of us would not have known it, and many of us would have denied it, but we were searchers—and we counted out the steps with our songs.

We are a people who march to different drummers, but we sing the same songs. As I wrote at the start, we find in our songs a national past, family histories, personal memories, today and tomorrow, and home. Our songs are about us in ways that mirror what we feel, know, and believe. They affirm our commitment to the nation at one end and to self at the other.

Praising and condemning, and then departing, wandering, returning, and settling down appear throughout these songs. The idea has been to make one's way or, in desperate times, to survive by finding companionship, work, and boxcars to get you to the next town as, most often, you long to be back home. Love never declines in importance. Home is where we've been headed from the start: to discover and build a nation and then find a home, old or new, "where the deer and the antelope play" or in a high-rise apartment building, complete with a penthouse, where we find, to our amusement and amazement, "hinges on chimneys for clouds to pass by." Whether we return or build anew, it remains "good to touch the green, green grass of home" (Claude Putnam Jr., "Green, Green Grass of Home," 1965). "The house I live in" is America and its people.

Crossing an ocean, following a river, riding the rails, turning the earth, walking the streets, climbing in an elevator, building a house, praising and protesting. They are an essential part of the songs that mirror who we are, who we've been, and who we may yet become. Singing the anthems and the hymns, the songs of work and play and always love: all these are inherent in the crafting of the nation. In these songs and so many others like them, amid open prairies and crowded streets, we rediscover our America.

# Notes

## Introduction

1. Dan Rather and Elliot Kirschner, *What Unites Us: Reflections on Patriotism* (Chapel Hill, NC: Algonquin Books of Chapel Hill, 2017), 15.
2. Steven B. Smith, *Reclaiming Patriotism in an Age of Extremes* (New Haven, CT: Yale University Press, 2021), 4–5.
3. Quoted in Michael S. Rosenwald, "John Wilmerding, Who Helped Give American Art an Identity, Dies at 86," *New York Times*, June 14, 2024, https://www.nytimes.com/2024/06/14/arts/john-wilmerding-dead.html.
4. Washington Irving, *Complete Tales of Washington Irving*, ed. Charles Neider (Garden City, NY: Doubleday, c1975), 1.
5. Washington Irving, *A Tour of the Prairies*, 1835, cited in Davis, 81.
6. Davis, 106.
7. Davis, 83–84.
8. Smith, *Reclaiming Patriotism in an Age of Extremes*, 5.
9. Smith, *Reclaiming Patriotism in an Age of Extremes*, 15.
10. Sarah J. Purcell, *Sealed with Blood: War, Sacrifice, and Memory in Revolutionary America* (Philadelphia, PA: University of Pennsylvania Press, 2002), 6.
11. Laura Lohman, *Hail Columbia! American Music and Politics in the Early Nation* (New York: Oxford University Press, c2020), 3.
12. S. J. Woolf, "Sergeant Berlin Re-Enlists," *New York Times*, May 17, 1942.
13. David Lehman in Robert Philipson's documentary film, *Body and Soul: An American Bridge*, 2017, https://therokuchannel.roku.com/watch/73a96e96828651259f3bd73603b1a447.
14. Jeff Melnick in *Body and Soul*.
15. Harold Meyerson and Ernie Harburg, *Who Put the Rainbow in* The Wizard of Oz? *Yip Harburg, Lyricist* (Ann Arbor, MI: University of Michigan Press, c1993), no page.
16. Gerald Leinwand, *Patriotism in America* (New York: Franklin Watts, c1997), 12.
17. Stephen Holden, "Pop View: Irving Berlin's American Landscape," *The New York Times*, May 10, 1987, https://www.nytimes.com/1987/05/10/arts/pop-view-irving-berlin-s-american-landscape.html?.?mc=aud_dev&ad-keywords=auddevgate&gclid=CjwKCAjw7--KBhAMEiwAxfpkWHG1ETrrhKB6cVLBctys5iFbNZ9rvxqCRlXm5IwDO3QNMQwO8J_sdhoCTuYQAvD_BwE&gclsrc=aw.ds.

18 William H. A. Williams, *'Twas Only an Irishman's Dream: The Image of Ireland and the Irish in American Popular Song Lyrics, 1880–1920* (Urbana and Chicago, IL: University of Illinois Press, 1996), 7.
19 Josh Kun in *Body and Soul*, videodisc.
20 David M. Rubenstein, *The American Experiment: Dialogues on a Dream* (New York: Simon and Schuster, c2017), 273.
21 Rubenstein, *The American Experiment*, 284.
22 John Edward Hasse, "A Track That Danced into Music History," *Washington Post*, February 4, 2022 (Typescript sent to me by Hasse, no pagination).
23 Quoted in Hasse, "A Track That Danced into Music History."
24 Rose Rosengard Subotnik, "Shoddy Equipment for Living? Deconstructing the Tin Pan Alley Song," in *Musicological Identities: Essays in Honor of Susan McClary*, eds. Steven Baur, Raymond Knapp, and Jacqueline Warwick (Burlington, VT: Ashgate Publishing Company, c2008), 216.
25 Subotnik, "Shoddy Equipment for Living?," 217.
26 See Michael Lasser, *City Songs and American Life, 1900–1950* (Rochester, NY: University of Rochester Press, 2019).
27 Ellen Harper, "Voices of the People: On Folk Music as a Living Art Form," *Literary Hub*, January 27, 2021, https://lithub.com/voices-of-the-people-on-folk-music-as-a-living-art-form/.
28 Rather and Kirschner, *What Unites Us*, 11–12.
29 Catherine T. Hodges, "America a 'Stew Pot,' Not a 'Melting Pot,'" *Philanthropy Journal*, August 16, 2005, https://pj.news.chass.ncsu.edu/2005/08/16/94200/.
30 Quoted in *Songfacts*, https://www.songfacts.com/facts/irving-berlin/alexanders-ragtime-band/1000.

# Chapter 1

1 Rick Atkinson, *The British Are Coming: The War for America: Lexington to Princeton, 1775–1777* (New York: Henry Holt and Company, c2019), 532.
2 David Hackett Fischer, *Washington's Crossing*, cited in Atkinson, *The British Are Coming*, 410.
3 Virginia L. Arbury, "Washington's Farewell Address and the Form of the American Regime," in *Patriot Sage: George Washington and the American Political Tradition*, eds. Gary L. Gregg II and Matthew Spalding (Wilmington, DE: ISI Books, 1999), 204–6.
4 J. Hector St. John Crevecoeur, *Letters from an American Farmer* (Garden City, NY: Doubleday & Company, n.d.), 49.
5 Peter Ackroyd, *Foundation: The History of England from Its Earliest Beginnings to the Tudors* (New York: Thomas Dunne Books, c2011), 446.

6 Anon., "An Interview with Eleanor J. Harvey," *American Battlefield Trust*, July 31, 2020, https://www.battlefields.org/learn/articles/civil-war-and-american-art.

7 Henry Nash Smith, *Virgin Land: The American West as Symbol and Myth* (Cambridge, MA: Harvard University Press, 1950), 123–24.

8 Simran Khurana, "The History of 'My Country, Right or Wrong!'" *Thoughtco*, March 23, 2018, https://www.thoughtco.com/my-country-right-or-wrong-2831839.

9 Christopher Wilson, "Where's the Debate on Francis Scott Key's Slave-Holding Legacy?," *Smithsonian*, July 1, 2016, https://www.smithsonianmag.com/smithsonian-institution/wheres-debate-francis-scott-keys-slave-holding-legacy-180959550/.

10 James Weldon Johnson, "Lift Every Voice and Sing," *Poetry Foundation*, September 6, 2020, https://www.poetryfoundation.org/poems/46549/lift-every-voice-and-sing.

11 Henry David Thoreau, *Walden* (New York: Thomas Y. Crowell & Company, 1910), 109.

12 Ace Collins, *Songs Sung Red, White, and Blue: The Stories Behind America's Best-Loved Patriotic Songs* (New York: HarperResource, 2003), 98–105.

13 Although few Americans recognize the melody or can sing the words, "Hail, Columbia" remains the vice president's official anthem.

14 The quotation appears in many books and websites. "Top Ten Civil War Songs," *Imaginative Conservative*, October 27, 2020, https://theimaginativeconservative.org/2016/09/top-ten-american-civil-war-songs-stephen-klugewicz.html.

15 "Battle Cry of Freedom: 'If We'd Had Your Songs,'" *The Hardtacks: Folk Music of the Antebellum & Civil War Eras*, November 12, 2015, https://civilwarfolkmusic.com/2014/11/12/1865-battle-cry-of-freedom-if-wed-had-your-songs/.

16 George Kimball, "Origins of the John Brown Song," *New England Magazine*, 373–4.

17 Julia Ward Howe, *Reminiscences: 1819–1899* (New York: Houghton Mifflin, 1899), 275.

18 Dominic Tierney, "'The Battle Hymn of the Republic': America's Song of Itself," *Atlantic*, October 28, 2020, https://www.theatlantic.com/entertainment/archive/2010/11/the-battle-hymn-of-the-republic-americas-song-of-itself/66070/.

19 Irwin Silber, *Songs of the Civil War* (New York: Dover Books, c1960), 92.

20 "Civil War Music: The Battle Cry of Freedom," *American Battlefield Trust*, October 28, 2020, https://www.battlefields.org/learn/primary-sources/civil-war-music-battle-cry-freedom.

21 Henry Stone, "Memoranda on the Civil War: A Song in Camp," *Century Illustrated*.

22 Collins, *Songs Sung Red, White, and Blue*, 52.

23 Christian L. McWhirter, "Birth of the Battle Cry," *The New York Times*, July 27, 2012.

24 Collins, *Songs Sung Red, White, and Blue*, 17.

25 Tim Yeager, "America the Beautiful a Call to Struggle," *People's World*, September 17, 2004, https://www.peoplesworld.org/article/america-the-beautiful-a-call-to-struggle/.

26 Jeffrey Melnick, "Tin Pan Alley and the Black-Jewish Nation," in *American Popular Music: New Approaches to the Twentieth Century*, eds. Rachel Rubin and Melnick (Amherst, MA: University of Massachusetts Press, c2001), 31.

27  Isaac Goldberg, *George Gershwin: A Study in American Music* (New York: Simon and Schuster, 1931), 275.

## Chapter 2

1  Philip Furia, *Irving Berlin: A Life in Song* (New York: Schirmer, 1998), 58.
2  See Edward Jablonski, *Irving Berlin: Troubadour* (New York: Henry Holt, 1999), 56.
3  Segal, 6.
4  John McCabe, *George M. Cohan: The Man Who Owned Broadway* (New York: Da Capo Press, 1973), 72–75.
5  John Edward Hasse, "Patriotism, Optimism and Energy in Overdrive," *Wall Street Journal*, July 1, 2022, https://www.wsj.com/articles/john-philip-sousa-the-stars-and-stripes-forever-the-marine-band-sousaphone-john-twomey-eubie-blake-massed-bands-of-the-soviet-army-11656710675?st=8pu0w62vgxyycob&reflink=desktopwebshare_permalink.
6  In the first act of *Show Boat* (Jerome Kern and Oscar Hammerstein II, 1927), the mixed-race Julie sings, "Can't Help Lovin' Dat Man" to the innocent Magnolia. The African American cook, Queenie, asks Julie how she knows that song because, "I didn't never hear nobody but colored folks sing that song."
7  Michael Lasser, *City Songs and American Life, 1900–1950* (Rochester, NY: University of Rochester Press, c2019), 58.
8  Similarly, in 1942, Glenn Miller and His Orchestra recorded F. W. Meacham's popular march from 1885, "American Patrol," in swing time.
9  Rimler, 174.
10  Ira Gershwin, *Lyrics on Several Occasions* (London: Omnibus Press, c1959), 187–88.
11  For a much fuller explanation of the songs of the Second World War, see Lasser, *City Songs and American Life, 1900–1950*.
12  Max Wilk, *They're Playing Our Song; from Jerome Kern to Stephen Sondheim—The Stories Behind the Words and Music of Two Generations* (New York: Atheneum, 1973), 172.
13  Rob Nixon, "Gold Diggers of 1933," *TCM*, http://www.tcm.com/tcmdb/title/3463/Gold-Diggers-of-1933/articles.html.

## Chapter 3

1  Kimberly Gelbwesser, "'To Be an American': How Irving Berlin Assimilated Jewishness and Blackness in His Early Songs," Unpublished Doctoral Dissertation, University of Cincinnati, 2011, 1–2.
2  Charles Hamm, *Irving Berlin: Songs from the Melting Pot: The Formative Years, 1907–1914* (New York: Oxford University Press, 1997), xxi.

3   Lawrence Bergreen, *As Thousands Cheer: The Life of Irving Berlin* (New York: Viking, 1990), 69.
4   Mark Twain, *The Adventures of Huckleberry Finn (Tom Sawyer's Comrade)* (New York and London: Harper & Brothers, 1884), 405.
5   Dale Cockrell, *Ev'rybody's Doin' It: Sex, Music, and Dance in New York, 1840–1917* (New York: W.W. Norton & Company, 2019), 197.
6   George Gershwin, "Jazz Is the Voice of the American People," *Theatre Magazine* (June 1926), 528, in *The George Gershwin Reader*, eds. Robert Wyatt and John Andrew Johnson (New York: Oxford University Press, 2004), 90–94.
7   E. E. Cummings, *Viva* (New York: Liveright, 1931), xx.

## Chapter 4

1   Philip Furia and Michael Lasser, *America's Songs: The Stories Behind the Songs of Broadway, Hollywood, and Tin Pan Alley* (New York: Routledge, 2006), 17–18.

## Chapter 5

1   Woody Guthrie, *Roll On, Columbia: The Columbia River Songbook* (No city, no publisher, 1942), no pagination. Also found in "Woody Guthrie's Biography," *Woody Guthrie*, September 29, 2020, https://www.woodyguthrie.org/biography/biography6.htm.
2   Will Kaufman, "The Misguided Attacks on Woody Guthrie," *Conversation*, August 20, 2019, https://theconversation.com/the-misguided-attacks-on-this-land-is-your-land-121169.
3   Buffy Saint-Marie, "The Power of Protest," *American Indian: Magazine of the Smithsonian's National Museum of the American Indian,* Spring 2013, v14, nr1, https://www.americanindianmagazine.org/story/power-protest-songs.
4   Furia and Lasser, *America's Songs*, 150–51.
5   Mary Ellin Barrett, *Irving Berlin: A Daughter's Memoir* (New York: Simon & Schuster, 1994), 173.
6   Furia and Lasser, *America's Songs*, 151.
7   Marilyn Berger, "Irving Berlin, Nation's Songwriter, Dies," *New York Times*, September 23, 1989, https://www.nytimes.com/1989/09/23/obituaries/irving-berlin-nation-s-songwriter-dies.htm.
8   William H. A. Williams, *'Twas Only an Irishman's Dream: The Image of Ireland and the Irish in American Popular Song Lyrics, 1880–1920* (Urbana and Chicago, IL: University of Illinois Press, 1996), 7.
9   Marc Eliot, *Paul Simon: A Life* (New York: John Wiley and Sons, 2010), 95.

10  Tom Moon, "Paul Simon Discusses Political References in Songs," *Paul Simon*, https://www.paulsimon.com/news/paul-simon-discusses-political-references-songs/.
11  Waylon Jennings with Lenny Kaye, *Waylon: An Autobiography* (New York: Warner Books, 1996), 293.
12  Jennings, *Waylon*, 293.
13  Quoted in Steve Inskeep with Daoud Tyler-Ameen, "What Does 'Born in the U.S.A.' Really Mean?," *NPR*, March 26, 2019, https://www.npr.org/2019/03/26/706566556/bruce-springsteen-born-in-the-usa-american-anthem.
14  Quoted in Inskeep, "What Does 'Born in the U.S.A.' Really Mean?"
15  Marc Dolan, "How Ronald Reagan Changed Bruce Springsteen's Politics," *Politico Magazine*, June 4, 2014, https://www.politico.com/magazine/story/2014/06/bruce-springsteen-ronald-reagan-107448.
16  Jon Pareles, "His Kind of Heroes," *New York Times*, July 14, 2002, http://candysroom.freeservers.com/bruceweb63.html.
17  Quoted in Inskeep, "What Does 'Born in the U.S.A.' Really Mean?"
18  Bruce Springsteen, *Born to Run* (New York: Simon & Schuster, c2016), 314.
19  Jim Cullen, *Born in the U.S.A.: Bruce Springsteen and the American Tradition* (New York: HarperCollins Publishers, 1997), 77.

# Chapter 6

1  Quoted in Robin Wright, "Is America a Myth?" *New Yorker*, September 8, 2020, https://www.newyorker.com/news/our-columnists/is-america-a-myth?utm_source=nl&utm_brand=tny&utm_mailing=TNY_DavidsonSorkin_09102020&utm_campaign=aud-dev&utm_medium=email&bxid=5eeb982d2e59087b007e4869&user_id=61442626&hasha=cd8d22f26cc60ee8d32b2c51d0aa01ad&hashb=52c631f112ee59a2f21859885d9c3b476dc4762c&hashc=7790a7094ab8b921668c4b20b67833c4b2b0d88ba12ce4b2d20bcf2af4ac3ab3&esrc=subscribe-page&utm_term=TNY_DavidsonSorkin.
2  Wright, "Is America a Myth?"
3  King made the remark in his Baccalaureate sermon as part of Wesleyan University's commencement in the spring of 1964. See https://quoteinvestigator.com/2012/11/15/arc-of-universe/#:~:text=In%201964%20King%20delivered%20the%20Baccalaureate%20sermon%20at,said%20in%20closing%2C%20%E2%80%9Cbut%20it%20bends%20toward%20justice.%E2%80%9D.
4  Quoted in "Acoustic Guitar: Coolness Acoustified," *The Sound of Fighting Dogs*, March 31, 2016, https://thesoundoffightingdogs.wordpress.com/tag/morrissey/.
5  Ronald D. Cohen and Dave Samuelson, liner notes for *Songs for Political Action* (Bear Family Records, 1996), 78.

6  Kim Ruehl, "Folk Song History of 'We Shall Not Be Moved,'" *liveaboutdotcom*, February 13, 2020, https://www.liveabout.com/we-shall-not-be-moved-traditional-1322516.

7  Kaitlyn Greenidge, "Black Spirituals as Poetry and Resistance," *New York Times Style Magazine*, March 5, 2021, https://www.nytimes.com/2021/03/05/t-magazine/black-spirituals-poetry-resistance.html?action=click&module=Top%20Stories&pgtype=Homepage.

8  Alan Howard, *The Don McLean Story: Killing Us Softly with His Songs*, 2007, https://lulu.com.

9  Nikki Giovanni, *On My Journey Now: Looking at African American History Through the Spirituals* (Cambridge, MA: Candlewick Press, 2007), 2.

10  James H. Cone, *The Spirituals and the Blues: An Interpretation* (New York: The Seabury Press, c1972), 5.

11  W. E. B. Du Bois, *The Souls of Black Folk* (Oxford: Oxford University Press, c2007), 175.

12  Alain Locke, ed., "The Negro Spirituals," in *The New Negro* (New York: Touchstone, c1925, c1992), 199.

13  Frederick Douglass, *My Bondage and My Freedom* (New York and Auburn, NY: Miller, Orton, & Mulligan, 1855), 98.

14  Sarah H. Bradford, *Scenes in the Life of Harriet Tubman* (Auburn, NY: W.J. Moses, Printer, 1869), 26.

15  Douglass, *My Bondage and My Freedom*, 278.

16  Douglass, *My Bondage and My Freedom*, 99.

17  Bradford, *Scenes in the Life of Harriet Tubman*, 19.

18  Bradford, *Scenes in the Life of Harriet Tubman*, 2.

19  Giovanni, *On My Journey Now*, 18.

20  Patricia Hill Collins, *Black Feminist Thought: Knowledge, Consciousness, and the Politics of Empowerment* (New York: Routledge, 2009), 50.

21  Paul Du Noyer, *The Illustrated Encyclopedia of Music* (London: Flame Tree Publishing, 2003), 95–96.

22  Tilford Brooks, *America's Black Musical Heritage* (Upper Saddle River, NJ: Prentice-Hall, 1984), 20.

23  Kip Lornell, *Deep River of Song: Minstrelsy, Work Songs, and Blues*, CD Liner Notes (Rounder Select, 2000).

24  Norm Cohen, *Long Steel Rail: The Railroad in American Folklore* (Urbana and Chicago, IL: University of Illinois Press, 1981), 535.

25  Cone, *The Spirituals and the Blues*, 111.

26  Quoted in Russell Ames, *The Story of American Folk Song* (New York: Grosset and Dunlap, 1955), 262.

27. Quoted in Cone, *The Spirituals and the Blues*, 112.
28. Sterling A. Brown, Arthur P. Davis, and Ulysses Lee, eds., *The Negro Caravan: Writings by American Negroes* (New York: The Citadel Press, 1941), 426.
29. Jim White, "'Rich Man's War'—Blues Protest Music," *Community Voices*, PostGazette.com, October 23, 2008, http://communityvoices.post-gazette.com/arts-entertainment-living/blue-notes/item/21755-rich-man-s-war-blues-protest-music.
30. Quoted in Tony Russell, *Blacks, Whites and the Blues* (New York: Stein and Day, 1970), 77.
31. LeRoi Jones, *Blues People: Negro Music in White America* (New York: William Morrow, 1963), 142.
32. Quoted in Paul Oliver, *The Blues Tradition* (New York: Oak Publications, 1970), 47.
33. Jones, *Blues People*, 87–88.
34. David Hajdu, "A Song That Changed Music Forever," *New York Times*, August 8, 2020, https://www.nytimes.com/2020/08/08/opinion/sunday/crazy-blues-mamie-smith.html.
35. Pete Wendling, untitled article, *Ethnomusicology* (Champaign and Urbana, IL: University of Illinois Press), 343–45.
36. Wendling, *Ethnomusicology*, 343–45.
37. Roger Kimmel Smith, "In 1920 Mamie Smith's 'Crazy Blues' Paved the Way for Black Music," Sycopatedtimes.com.
38. Hajdu, "A Song That Changed Music Forever."
39. Hajdu, "A Song That Changed Music Forever."

# Chapter 7

1. Timothy J. Gilfoyle, *City of Eros: New York City, Prostitution, and the Commercialization of Sex, 1790–1920* (New York: W.W. Norton & Company, 1992), 203.
2. Dale Cockrell, *Ev'rybody's Doin' It: Sex, Music, and Dance in New York, 1840–1917* (New York: W.W. Norton & Company, c2019), 190.
3. Duke Ellington, *Music Is My Mistress* (New York: Da Capo Press, 1976), 90. Quoted in *The Product of Our Souls: Ragtime, Race, and the Birth of the Manhattan Musical Marketplace* (Chapel Hill, NC: University of North Carolina Press, c2015), 19.
4. Ron Kaplow, *Listening for America: Inside the Great American Songbook from Gershwin to Sondheim* (New York and London: Liveright Publishing Co., c2019), 5.
5. Kaplow, *Listening for America*, 5.
6. Saidiya V. Hartman, *Scenes of Subjection: Terror, Slavery, and Self-Making in Nineteenth-Century America* (New York: Oxford University Press, 1997), 27.
7. James Kaplan, *Irving Berlin: New York Genius* (New Haven, CT and London: Yale University Press, c2019), 96.
8. Cockrell, *Ev'rybody's Doin' It*, 125.

9 "Creole Show—Breaking Stereotypes," *Kreol*, February 11, 2016, https://kreolmagazine.com/culture/history-and-culture/creole-show-breaking-stereotypes/#.X7aH2xNKg3k.
10 Marvin McAllister, *Whiting Up: Whiteface Minstrels and Stage Europeans in African American Performance* (Chapel Hill, NC: University of North Carolina Press, 2011), 74.
11 David Gilbert, *The Product of Our Souls: Ragtime, Race and the Birth of the Manhattan Market Place* (Chapel Hill, NC: University of North Carolina Press, c2015), 19.
12 Gilbert, *The Product of Our Souls*, 41.
13 Quoted in Cockrell, *Ev'rybody's Doin' It*, 124.
14 Quoted in Eric J. Sundquist, *To Wake the Nations: Race in the Making of American Literature* (London and Cambridge, MA: Belknap Press of Harvard University, 1993), 106.
15 Thomas L. Morgan, "Will Marion Cook," *Jass Roots*, November 11, 2020, http://jassroots.com/wcook.html.
16 Gerald Bordman, *Musical Theatre: A Chronicle* (New York: Oxford University Press, 1978), 190.
17 "Biographies: Will Marion Cook (1869–1944)," Performing Arts Reading Room, Library of Congress, November 11, 2020, https://www.loc.gov/item/ihas.200038839/.
18 Morgan, "Will Marion Cook," http://jassroots.com/wcook.html.
19 Krystyn R. Moon, David Krasner, and Thomas L. Riis, "Forgotten Manuscripts: *A Trip to Coontown*," *African American Review* 44, no. 1 (2011): 7.
20 Thomas L. Riis, foreword, *The Songs of Cole and the Johnson Brothers* (New York: Edward B. Marks Music Company, 2015), i.
21 Riis, *The Songs of Cole and the Johnson Brothers*, iv.
22 Riis, *The Songs of Cole and the Johnson Brothers*, 28.
23 James Weldon Johnson, *Along This Way* (New York: Viking, 1933), 155–56.

# Chapter 8

1 Maurice Peress, *Dvorak to Duke Ellington: A Conductor Explores African American Music and Its African American Roots* (New York: Oxford University Press, 2008), 64.
2 See Robert Kimball and William Bolcom, *Reminiscing with Sissle and Blake* (New York: Viking, 1973), 79–80.
3 Gilbert, *The Product of Our Souls*, 1.
4 Cited in Reid Badger, *A Life in Ragtime: A Biography of James Reese Europe* (New York: Oxford University Press, 1995), xxx.
5 Douglas Gilbert, *Lost Chords: The Diverting Story of American Popular Songs* (Garden City, NY: Doubleday, Doran and Co., 1942), 347.
6 Badger, *A Life in Ragtime*, 89.
7 Gilbert, *The Product of Our Souls*, 13.

8   Gilbert, *The Product of Our Souls*, 14.
9   John Strausbaugh, *Victory City: A History of New York and New Yorkers During World War II* (New York and Boston: Twelve, 2018), 120.
10  Badger, *A Life in Ragtime*, 167.
11  Badger, *A Life in Ragtime*, 195.
12  Gunther Schuller, *Early Jazz: Its Roots and Early Development* (New York: Oxford University Press, 1968), 249.
13  Peress, *Dvorak to Duke Ellington*, 64.
14  Badger, *A Life in Ragtime*, 97.
15  Gilbert, *The Product of Our Souls*, 5.
16  Gilbert, *The Product of Our Souls*, 60.
17  *New York Globe and Commercial*, October 27, 1905, Robinson Locke Collection, Billy Rose Theater Collection, Library for the Performing Arts, New York Public Library.
18  Camille Forbes, *Introducing Bert Williams: Burnt Cork, Broadway, and the Story of America's First Black Star* (New York: Basic Books, c2008), 93.
19  Forbes, *Introducing Bert Williams*, 94.
20  Lester Walton, "Bert Williams, Philosopher," *New York Age*, December 29, 1917, 6.
21  Johnson, *Along This Way: The Autobiography of James Weldon Johnson*, 171.
22  Forbes, *Introducing Bert Williams*, 200.
23  Forbes, *Introducing Bert Williams*, 36–37.
24  Eddie Cantor, *As I Remember Them* (New York: Duell, Sloan, and Pearce, 1963), 50.
25  Quoted in Forbes, *Introducing Bert Williams*, 298.
26  Dorothy Berry, "When Black Celebrities Wore Blackface," *JSTOR Daily*, August 12, 2020, https://daily.jstor.org/when-black-celebrities-wore-blackface/?utm_term=Read%20More&utm_campaign=jstordaily_08132020&utm_content=email&utm_source=Act-On+Software&utm_medium=email.
27  James Weldon Johnson, "The Dilemma of the Negro Author," in *The Essential Writings of James Weldon Johnson*, ed. Rudolph P. Byrd (New York: Random House, 1990), x.
28  Quoted in Furia and Lasser, *America's Songs*, 67–68.
29  Furia and Lasser, *America's Songs*, 68.
30  Quoted in Aida Amoako, "Strange Fruit: The Most Shocking Song of All Time," *BBC Culture*, April 17, 2019, https://www.bbc.com/culture/article/20190415-strange-fruit-the-most-shocking-song-of-all-time.
31  Michael Lasser, *America's Songs II: From the 1890s to the Post-War Years:* (New York, Routledge, c2014), 166–67.
32  Lasser, *America's Songs II*, 167.
33  Furia and Lasser, *America's Songs*, 167.

34  Billie Holiday with William Dufty, *Lady Sings the Blues* (New York: Harlem Moon, 1956), 94.
35  Furia and Lasser, *America's Songs*, 107.
36  Ethel Waters with Charles Samuels, *His Eye Is on the Sparrow* (New York: Da Capo Press, 1992), 222.

# Chapter 9

1  Miriam Reed, *Hurrah for Woman Suffrage! Songs of the Woman Suffrage Movement 1848–1928* (Los Angeles, CA: Miriam Reed Productions, 1995), 14.
2  Reed, *Hurrah for Woman Suffrage!*, 14–15.
3  Irwin Silber, Liner notes for Elizabeth Knight, *Songs of the Suffragettes*, Folkways Records FH 5281, c1958.
4  See Bonnie S. Anderson, *Joyous Greeting: The First International Women's Movement* (New York: Oxford University Press, 2000).
5  *Modern History Source Book: Seneca Falls: The Declaration of Sentiments, 1848* (November 1998), https://sourcebooks.fordham.edu/mod/senecafalls.asp.
6  Sally Gregory McMillen, *Seneca Falls and the Origins of the Women's Rights Movement* (New York: Oxford University Press, 2008), 21.
7  Judith Wellman, *The Road to Seneca Falls: Elizabeth Cady Stanton and the First Women's Rights Convention* (Champaign and Urbana, IL: University of Illinois Press, 2004), 192.
8  "Human Equality, Song Lyrics," *Protest Songs*, December 13, 2020, http://www.protestsonglyrics.net/Women_Feminism_Songs/Human-Equality.phtml.
9  Nellie Bly, Interview with Susan B. Anthony, *New York World*, February 2, 1896, quoted in "Songs of Women's Suffrage," Library of Congress, December 13, 2020, https://www.loc.gov/item/ihas.200197395/.
10  Rosalyn Terborg-Penn, *African American Women in the Struggle for the Vote, 1850–1920* (Bloomington, IN: Indiana University Press, 1998), 108.
11  "Woman Suffrage Parade," *Library of Congress*, December 10, 2020, https://www.loc.gov/resource/rbcmil.scrp7006502/?st=text.
12  Mary Wollstonecraft, "A Vindication of the Rights of Women," quoted in Megan O'Grady, "Why Are There So Few Monuments That Successfully Depict Women?," *New York Times*, February 18, 2021, https://www.nytimes.com/2021/02/18/t-magazine/female-monuments-women.html?action=click&algo=random_desk_filter&block=editors_picks_recirc&fellback=false&imp_id=805041072&impression_id=65de2c50-7b63-11eb-be13-29f7bdd80024&index=0&pgtype=Article&region=ccolumn&req_id=544932797&surface=home-featured&variant=0_random_desk_filter&action=click&module=editorContent&pgtype=Article&region=CompanionColumn&contentCollection=Trending.

## Chapter 10

1. Except for a passing reference in Gerald Bordman, *American Musical Theatre: A Chronicle* (New York: Oxford University Press, 1978), 288, no other source that I could find, including the Internet Broadway Database, lists *A Broadway Honeymoon*. The only other reference, complete with sheet music cover and lyrics, is in Danny O. Crew, *Suffragist Sheet Music* (Jefferson, NC: McFarland & Company, c2002), 264–65.

## Chapter 11

1. Dale Cockrell, *Everybody's Doin' It: Sex, Music, and Dance in New York, 1840–1917* (New York: W.W. Norton & Company, c2019), 14.
2. "Jump Jim Crow," in University of South Florida exhibition, *History of Minstrels from "Jump Jim Crow" to "The Jazz Singer,"* August 15, 2020, https://exhibits.lib.usf.edu/exhibits/show/minstrelsy/jimcrow-to-jolson/plantation-nostalgia.
3. Bingham, 16.
4. Terry Gross's interview with Ken Emerson, April 16, 2020, https://www.npr.org/transcripts/126035325.
5. Bingham, xvi.
6. Bingham, xvi.
7. Bingham, 65.
8. Douglass, *My Bondage and My Freedom*, 278.
9. "Kingdom Coming," "Songs of the Civil War," August 18, 2020, https://www.civilwarpoetry.org/union/songs/jubilo-exp.html.
10. Lynn Abbott and Doug Seroff, *Ragged but Right: Black Traveling Shows, "Coon Songs," and the Dark Pathway to Blues and Jazz* (Jackson, MS: University Press of Mississippi, 2007), xxx.

## Chapter 12

1. Richard Crawford, *America's Musical Life* (New York: W.W. Norton, 2005), 487.
2. "Ragtime and the 'Coon Song,'" *History of Minstrels from "Jump Jim Crow" to "The Jazz Singer,"* https://exhibits.lib.usf.edu/exhibits/show/minstrelsy/jimcrow-to-jolson/ragtime-and-the-coon-song.
3. W. K. McNeil, "Syncopated Slander: The 'Coon Song,' 1890–1900," *Keystone Folklore Quarterly* 17, no. 1 (Summer 1972): 69.
4. Cockrell, *Ev'rybody's Doin' It*, 15.
5. Michael Rogin, *Blackface, White Noise: Jewish Immigrants in the Hollywood Melting Pot* (Berkeley, CA: University of California Press, 1996), 32–33.
6. Abbott and Seroff, *Ragged But Right*, 3.

7 Quoted in Michael Lasser, *America's Songs II: Songs from the 1890s to the Post-War Years* (New York: Routledge, c2014), 63.
8 Lasser, *America's Songs II*, 63–64.
9 "Tom the Tattler," *The Freeman, an Illustrated Colored Newspaper*, August 24, 1901, 6. "Ragtime and the 'Coon Song.'"
10 Alec Wilder, *American Popular Song: The Great Innovators, 1900–1950* (New York: Oxford University Press, c1972), 6.
11 Giovanni, *On My Journey Now*, 22.
12 Sarah Delany and A. Elizabeth Delany, with Amy Hill Hearth, "Harlem Town," in *The Harlem Reader: A Celebration of New York's Most Famous Neighborhood, from the Renaissance Years to the Twenty-First Century*, ed. Herb Boyd (New York: Three Rivers Press, 2003), 12.

# Chapter 13

1 Alexis Clark, "Returning from War, Returning to Racism," *New York Times*, July 30, 2020, https://www.nytimes.com/2020/07/30/magazine/black-soldiers-wwii-racism.html.
2 Quoted in Clark, "Returning from War, Returning to Racism," https://www.nytimes.com/2020/07/30/magazine/black-soldiers-wwii-racism.html.
3 Clark, "Returning from War, Returning to Racism," https://www.nytimes.com/2020/07/30/magazine/black-soldiers-wwii-racism.html.
4 Matthew Wills, "White Hollywood's Romance with the N-Word," *JSTOR Daily*, February 7, 2020, https://daily.jstor.org/white-hollywoods-romance-with-the-n-word/.
5 Willa Cather, *My Antonia* (New York: Everyman's Press, 1996), 142.
6 Barack Obama, "Remarks by the President and First Lady at a Reception for Governor Ted Strickland," *The White House*, October 17, 2010, https://obamawhitehouse.archives.gov/the-press-office/2010/10/17/remarks-president-and-first-lady-a-reception-governor-ted-strickland.
7 Jeffrey Magee, *Irving Berlin's American Musical Theater* (New York: Oxford University Press, c2012), 13.
8 Charles Hamm, *Irving Berlin Songs from the Melting Pot: The Formative Years, 1907–1914* (New York: Oxford University Press, 1997), 68.
9 Jeffrey Melnick, *A Right to Sing the Blues: Jews, African Americans, and American Popular Song* (Cambridge, MA: Harvard University Press, 1999), 45.
10 Magee, *Irving Berlin's American Musical Theater*, 26–28.
11 Magee, *Irving Berlin's American Musical Theater*, 28.
12 Magee, *Irving Berlin's American Musical Theater*, 26–28.

13 Melnick, *A Right to Sing the Blues*, 45.
14 Tim Brooks, *The Blackface Minstrel Show in Mass Media: 20th Century Performances on Radio, Records, Film, and Television* (Jefferson, NC: McFarland, 2019), 170–71.
15 Quoted in Edward Jablonski, *Irving Berlin: American Troubadour* (New York: Henry Holt, c1999), 65.
16 Cockrell, *Ev'rybody's Doin' It*, 127.
17 Edward Jablonski, "'Alexander' and Irving," in *The Irving Berlin Reader. Readers on American Musicians*, ed. Benjamin Sears (New York: Oxford University Press, 2012), 34.
18 Frank S. Nugent, "The Roxy Plays Host to 'Alexander's Ragtime Band,' a Twentieth Century Tribute to Irving Berlin," *New York Times*, August 6, 1938, 7.
19 Cockrell, *Ev'rybody's Doin' It*, 40.
20 Cockrell, *Ev'rybody's Doin' It*, 104.
21 See Cockrell, *Ev'rybody's Doin' It*, 123.
22 Bergreen, *As Thousands Cheer*, 21, 27–28.
23 Cockrell, *Ev'rybody's Doin' It*, 182.
24 Quoted in Eve Golden, *Vernon and Irene Castle's Ragtime Revolution* (Lexington, KY: University Press of Kentucky, 2007), 54.

# Chapter 14

1 For a full study of *Show Boat* and its racial implications, see Todd Becker, *Show Boat: Performing Race in an American Musical* (New York: Oxford University Press, 2015).
2 Stephen Holden, "'Show Boat' Makes New Waves," *New York Times*, September 25, 1988, https://www.nytimes.com/1988/09/25/theater/show-boat-makes-new-waves.html.
3 Robert Mackey, "BBC Won't Ban 'Ding Dong! The Witch Is Dead,' Adopted as Anti-Thatcher Anthem," "The Lede" (blog), *New York Times*, April 12, 2013.
4 Robert Mankoff, "One and a Half Cheers for Satire," *New Yorker*, December 13, 2013, https://www.newyorker.com/cartoons/bob-mankoff/one-and-a-half-cheers-for-satire#:~:text=The%20playwright%20George%20S.,hundred%20and%20forty%2Done%20performances.
5 Mark Robinson, "Remembering Bloomer Girl," *Mark Robinson Writes*, September 2, 2020, http://www.markrobinsonwrites.com/the-music-that-makes-me-dance/2018/12/16/remembering-bloomer-girl.
6 Quoted in Frank Rizzo, "Goodspeed Boldly Tackles 'Finian's Rainbow,' Despite Racism Theme That Has Made the Play a Hot Potato," *Hartford Courant*, April 18, 1997, https://www.courant.com/news/connecticut/hc-xpm-1997-04-18-9704180037-story.html.

7  Rizzo, "Goodspeed Boldly Tackles 'Finian's Rainbow,' Despite Racism Theme That Has Made the Play a Hot Potato."

# Chapter 15

1  Jia Lynn Yang, in David M. Rubenstein, *The American Experiment: Dialogues on a Dream* (New York: Simon and Schuster, c2021), 356.
2  Rubenstein, *The American Experiment*, 356.
3  Stephen Steinberg, *The Ethnic Myth: Race, Ethnicity, and Class in America* (New York: Atheneum, 1981), 48.
4  Thomas Sowell, *Ethnic America: A History* (New York: Basic Books, 1981), 144–45.
5  Irving Howe, *World of Our Fathers: The Journey of the East European Jews to America and the Life They Found and Made* (New York: Harcourt Brace Jovanovich, c1976), 557.
6  Jeremy Rosen, "Cohen Owes Me Ninety-Seven Dollars," in *The Song Is Not the Same: Jews and American Popular Music*, edited by Josh Kun, Bruce Zuckerman, and Lisa Ansell (West Lafayette, IN: Purdue University Press, c2011), 11.
7  Charyn, 123.
8  Quoted in Jack Vertiel, *The Secret Life of the American Musical: How Broadway Shows Are Built* (New York: Farrar, Straus and Giroux, 2016), 243.
9  Quoted in Gale, 416.
10  Hamm, *Irving Berlin*, xxi.
11  Williams, *'Twas Only an Irishman's Dream*, 127.
12  Rachel Rubin and Jeffrey Melnick, eds., *American Popular Music: New Approaches to the Twentieth Century* (Amherst, MA: University of Massachusetts Press, c2001), 5.
13  For a controversial but much more fully developed argument about the appropriation of Black music by Jewish songwriters, see Jeffrey Melnick, *A Right to Sing the Blues: African Americans, Jews, and American Popular Song* (Cambridge, MA: Harvard University Press, 1999).
14  See David Sanjek, "They Work Hard for Their Music," in *American Popular Music: New Approaches to the Twentieth Century*, eds. Rachel Rubin and Jeffrey Melnick (Amherst, MA: University of Massachusetts Press, c2001), 10–17.
15  The photograph, credited to the Frank Driggs Collection, appears on the back of the dust jacket for Irving Berlin, *The Complete Lyrics of Irving Berlin*, Robert Kimball and Linda Emmet, eds. (New York: Alfred A. Knopf, 2001).
16  Charyn, 122.
17  Among the many Salome songs were Harry Von Tilzer and Vincent Bryan's "When Miss Patricia Salome Did Her Funny Little Oo-La-Pa-Lome" (1907), Gus Edwards and Will D. Cobb's "My Sunburned Salome" (1908), Ben M. Jerome and Edward

Madden's "The Dusky Salome" (1908), and Dorothy Russell and William J. McKenna's "If You Can't Do That Salome Dance, You'll Never Make a Hit with Me" (1908).
18 Whitcomb, *Irving Berlin and Ragtime America* (New York: Limelight Editions, 1988), 28.
19 Whitcomb, *Irving Berlin and Ragtime America*, 37.

## Chapter 16

1 Israel Zangwell, *The Melting-Pot* (New York: The Macmillan Company, 1914), 85.
2 Hamm, *Irving Berlin*, v–viii.
3 "Emma Lazarus," *Statue of Liberty National Monument New York*, https://www.nps.gov/stli/learn/historyculture/emma-lazarus.htm#:~:text=In%20turn%2C%20Lazarus%2C%20inspired%20by,%22%20on%20November%202%2C%201883.
4 John Jay, "Federalist No. 2." See also Erik Amfitheatrof, *The Children of Columbus: An Informal History of the Italians in the New World* (Boston, MA: Little, Brown and Company, 1973), 102.
5 Thomas Bailey Aldrich, "Unguarded Gates," in *An American Anthology, 1787–1900*, vol. 1, ed. Edmund Clarence Stedman (Cambridge, MA: Riverside Press, 1900), 380.
6 Henry James, *The American Scene* (London: Chapman & Hall, 1907), 121.
7 Sowell, *Ethnic America*, 3.
8 William Brooks, *The Hand That Holds the Bread* (New York: New World Records, 1978), 19.
9 Richard Moody, *Ned Harrigan: From Corlear's Hook to Herald Square* (Chicago, IL: Nelson-Hall, c1980), 5.
10 Moody, *Ned Harrigan*, 78.
11 Moody, *Ned Harrigan*, 111.
12 Moody, *Ned Harrigan*, 87.
13 Moody, *Ned Harrigan*, 109.

## Chapter 17

1 Robert W. Snyder, *The Voice of the City: Vaudeville and Popular Culture in New York* (New York: Oxford University Press, 1998), 28.
2 Quoted in Snyder, *The Voice of the City*, 118.
3 Snyder, *The Voice of the City*, xv.
4 Howe, *World of Our Fathers*, 402.
5 Snyder, *The Voice of the City*, xv.
6 Williams, *'Twas Only an Irishman's Dream*, 157.
7 Williams, *'Twas Only an Irishman's Dream*, 2.

8   Williams, *'Twas Only an Irishman's Dream*, 128–29.
9   Armond Fields and L. Marc Fields, *From the Bowery to Broadway: Lew Fields and the Roots of American Popular Theatre* (New York: Oxford University Press, 1993), 49–50. For a fuller discussion, see Hamm, 30–50.
10  David Jasen, *Tin Pan Alley: The Composers, the Songs, the Performers, and Their Times* (New York: D.I. Fine, 1988), 129.
11  Quoted in Mark Steyn, "Yes! We Have No Bananas," *The Mark Steyn Club*, April 5, 2020, https://www.steynonline.com/10190/yes-we-have-no-bananas.
12  Kostis Kourelis, "The Argentines, the Portuguese, and the Greeks," *Objects-Building-Situations: Musings on Architecture and Archaeology*, May 11, 2011, http://kourelis.blogspot.com/2011/05/argentine-portuguese-and-greeks-1923.html.
13  "Vaudeville! A Dazzling Display of Heterogeneous Splendor!," August 27, 2008, http://xroads.virginia.edu/~MA02/easton/vaudeville/vaudeville.html.
14  Anne Nichols, *Abie's Irish Rose* (New York: Samuel French, 1922). The play opened on May 23, 1922, and closed on October 1, 1927, with a run of 2,327 performances. It ran for so long and its success was so widely known that Lorenz Hart included a reference to it in his lyric to "Manhattan" in 1925:

> Our future babies we'll take to Abie's Irish Rose
> I hope they'll live to see it close.

15  Herbert G. Goldman, *Fanny Brice: The Original Funny Girl* (New York: Oxford University Press, 1992), 14–16.
16  Stanley Green, *The Great Clowns of Broadway* (New York: Oxford University Press, 1984), 3.

## Chapter 18

1   Sowell, *Ethnic America*, 112–13.
2   J. Philip di Franco, *The Italian Americans* (New York: Chelsea House Publishers, 1988), 59.
3   Collins, *Black Feminist Thought*, 271–78.
4   Collins, *Black Feminist Thought*, 271–78.

## Chapter 19

1   Krystyn R. Moon, *Yellowface: Creating the Chinese in American Popular Music and Performance, 1850s–1920s* (New Brunswick, NJ: Rutgers University Press: 2005), 123–24.
2   The most powerfully ironic literary view of miscegenation, Mark Twain's *The Tragedy of Pudd'nhead Wilson* (1894) was disguised as a murder mystery. It is Twain's darkest

novel. In it, he wrote, "October 12, the Discovery. It was wonderful to find America, but it would have been more wonderful to miss it."

3 Moon, *Yellowface*, 132–33.
4 Moon, *Yellowface*, 132–34.
5 Moon, *Yellowface*, 130–31.
6 Gerald Bordman, *American Musical Comedy* (New York: Oxford University Press, 1982), 107.
7 John Bush Jones, *Our Musicals, Ourselves* (Waltham, MA: Brandeis University Press, 2003), 58.
8 Bordman, *American Musical Comedy*, 106–9.
9 To take full advantage of the fad, there was even a musical titled *Sally, Irene and Mary* in 1922. It was a hit, too.
10 Immigration Act of 1924, http://www.digitalhistory.uh.edu/database/article_display.cfm?HHID=446 and August 21, 2020, http://www.u-s-history.com/pages/h1398.html.

## Chapter 20

1 John Donne, "To His Mistress Going to Bed," in *The Complete Poems of John Donne*, ed. Robin Robbins (New York: Routledge, 2014), 328.
2 Sherwood Anderson, *Winesburg, Ohio* (New York: Penguin Books, 1995), 4.
3 John Updike, "Shillington," in *Collected Poems, 1953–1993* (New York, Knopf, 1993), 15.
4 Walt Whitman, "Song of Myself," in *Leaves of Grass* (Boston, MA: Small, Maynard & Company, 1904), 78.
5 Quoted from a letter from Steven Hermann to Bill Moyers in Moyers, "On Howling in Mill Valley and Walt Whitman's 'Barbaric Yawp,'" *Moyers on Democracy*, April 20, 2020, https://billmoyers.com/story/on-howling-in-mill-valley-and-walt-whitmans-barbaric-yawp/.
6 Jack Larkin, *Where We Lived: Discovering the Places We Once Called Home: The American Home from 1775–1840* (Newtown, CT: Taunton Press, c2006), 226.
7 Robert Frost, "The Gift Outright," in *The Poetry of Robert Frost*, edited by Edward Connery Lathem (New York: Macmillan, 1979), 348.

## Chapter 21

1 Matthew Sabatella, "The Story of the United States in Twelve Songs," *Ballad of America*, January 11, 2011, https://balladofamerica.org/downloads/The%20Story%20of%20the%20United%20States%20in%2012%20Songs.pdf.
2 See John A. Lomax, collector, *Cowboy Songs and Other Frontier Ballads*, Intro. by Barrett Wendell (New York: Sturgis & Walton Company, 1910).

3 This unverified statement, allegedly from 1841, appears often in online discussions of Emerson. I took it from Bartleby.com, March 30, 2021, https://www.bartleby.com/73/557.html.
4 Matthew Sabatella, "Home on the Range: About the Song," *Ballad of America*, https://balladofamerica.org/home-on-the-range/#song-history, and David Ewen, *All the Years of American Popular Music* (Englewood Cliffs, NJ: Prentice-Hall, 1977), 96–97.
5 Lomax, *Cowboy Songs and Other Frontier Ballads*, xxi.
6 Lomax, *Cowboy Songs and Other Frontier Ballads*, xxi–xxii.
7 Agnes DeMille, quoted in Purdum, 91.

## Chapter 22

1 Matthew Sabatella, "Wanderin': About the Song," *Ballad of America*, March 8, 2021, https://balladofamerica.org/wanderin/.
2 Layal Shafee, "What Tramps Cost Nation," *Washington Post*, June 18, 1911, D2.
3 Woody Guthrie in the Library of Congress Archive, quoted in "Hard Travelin'," *Genius*, March 19, 2021, https://genius.com/Woody-guthrie-hard-traveling-lyrics.
4 Dave Marsh, *The New Rolling Stone Record Guide* (New York: Random House, 1983), 429.
5 Amanda Petrusich, "The Magnificent Cross-Cultural Recordings of Kenya's Kipsigis Tribe," *New Yorker*, February 16, 2017, https://www.newyorker.com/culture/cultural-comment/the-magnificent-cross-cultural-recordings-of-kenyas-kipsigis-tribe.
6 Tom Piazza, *Devil Sent the Rain: Music and Writing in Desperate America* (New York: Harper Perennial, c2011), 6.
7 Piazza, *Devil Sent the Rain*, 7.
8 Piazza asserts that he was the first to do so, 8.

## Chapter 23

1 Robert Wright, "Andy Williams's Moon River—Decoded and Vindicated at Last," *Atlantic*, September 27, 2012, accessed January 6, 2016, https://www.theatlantic.com/entertainment/archive/2012/09/andy-williamss-moon-river-decoded-and-vindicated-at-last/262933/.

## Chapter 24

1 Daniel Webster, "Liberty and Union, Now and Forever, One and Inseparable," *USA Patriotism*, March 10, 2021, https://www.usapatriotism.org/speeches/dwebster1.htm.

2   Ben Sisario, "Barack Obama and Bruce Springsteen: The Latest Podcast Duo," *New York Times*, February 25, 2021, https://www.nytimes.com/2021/02/22/arts/obama-springsteen-podcast-spotify.html.
3   Sisario, https://www.nytimes.com/2021/02/22/arts/obama-springsteen-podcast-spotify.html.
4   Frost, "The Gift Outright," 348.

# Index

Abbott, Lynn 157, 161
Abenaki tribe 68
*Abie's Irish Rose* (Nichols) 220, 238
abolitionism 27, 29–30, 154
"Abraham" 177
Abt, Franz 35
*Abyssinia* 119–20
Adams, John 61
Ade, George 143
Adkinson, William P. 134
Afghanistan War 28
African Americans 5, 22, 51–2
　authenticity of music of 115
　on Broadway 105–7
　citizenship of 7–8
　"coon songs" written by 163–4
　Foster, S., portraying 153–5
　in Manhattan 100–1
　music of 86–7
　patriotism of 112, 171–2
　racism against 40–1, 102
　songwriters 7–8, 33–4, 103–5, 163–4, 197–8
　stereotypes of 102, 109, 152–5, 166
　white Americans mingling with 101–2
　in World War I 166–7
　in World War II 168
Ager, Milton 62
"Ah! May the Red Rose Live Alway" 34
"Ah Still Suits Me" 182
"Ain't Dat Scan'lous" 110
"Ain't Misbehavin'" 122
"Ain't We Got Fun" 194
Albert, Charles S. 277
Aldrich, Thomas Bailey 207
"Alexander and His Clarinet" 173
*Alexander's Ragtime Band* 175
"Alexander's Ragtime Band" 9, 15, 75, 159, 162, 174–7, 198

"Alice Blue Gown" 243
"All Aboard for Chinatown" 240
"All Alone" 198
"All Coons Look Alike to Me" 158–9
Allen, G. N. 89
Allen, Lewis. *See* Meeropol, Abel
"All Goin' Out and Nothin' Comin' In" 117
the Almanac Singers 84
"Alone at a Drive-in Movie" 7
Alter, Lewis B. 51
"Always" 198
"America" 21, 76, 78
"America, I Love You" 56
American colonies 16–17
American dream 203
American-Mexican War 31
"American Pie" 85–6
American Revolution 4–5, 23
"American Tune" 76
"America the Beautiful" 31–3, 55, 83, 255
Anderson, Sherwood 253
*Angels in America* 196
Anthony, Susan B. 129
anti-Semitism 168
Aquash, Anna Mae 69
Arbury, Virginia L. 16
Arlen, Harold 9, 53, 122, 178, 185
Armstrong, Louis 103
"As Far as I Can Tell" 142
Asian Americans. *See* Chinese Americans
assimilation 192, 198–9, 218
*As Thousands Cheer* 123, 125, 180
"At the High Brown Babies' Ball" 163
automobiles 6
Autry, Gene 264
Ayer, Nat D. 144

"Back Home Again"   288–9
Baez, Joan   95
Baker, Josephine   178
Balch, M. E.   136
Baline, Israel   196
Ball, Ernest   227
ballads   25
    parlor   35
"Bandana Days"   121
Baraka, Amiri   95
Barre, Gabriel   187
Bast, Peter J.   147
Bates, Katherine Lee   31–3, 47
"Battle Cry of Freedom"   29
Battle for the Alamo   31
"The Battle Hymn of the Republic"   9, 26, 28, 139
Battle of Saratoga   37
Battle of Yorktown   23
Bayes, Nora   201
"Beautiful Dreamer"   18
"Be Careful, It's My Heart"   74, 177
"Beckie, Stay in Your Own Backyard"   222
"Becky from Babylon"   218
"Becky Joined a Musical Show"   218
Beiderbecke, Bix   102
Benet   15
Berkely, Busby   45
Berlin, Irving   8, 15, 36, 52, 101, 169
    identity of   199–200
    on minstrel shows   170–1
    patriotism of   69–72
    political convictions of   72
    on popular songs   5
    ragtime popularized by   176–7
    as songwriter   47–8, 56–7, 73–5, 123–5, 170, 172–3, 196, 198, 204–5, 220, 276, 286–7
    Waters and   178–9
Bernstein, Leonard   78
Bierstadt, Albert   3
the Big Bopper   85–6
"The Biggest Thing That Man Has Ever Done"   65, 76
*Big River*   282–3
Bill of Rights, American   190

Bingham, Emily   152–3
"Bird in a Gilded Cage"   19
Bishop, Henry   11
Bivins, Nathan   160
"Black, Brown and White"   100
"Black and Blue"   122–3
Black and Tans   175–6
blackface   5, 155, 186–7
    history of   148–9
    Jewish Americans performing in   160–1
Blake, Eubie   51, 114, 121
Blake, James W.   209
Bland, James A.   164–5
Blane, Ralph   75–6
Blinken, Anthony   71
Block, Martin   10
Blondell, Joan   45
Bloomer, Amelia   128
*Bloomer Girl*   184
"The Bloomer's Complaint"   129
"Blue Railroad Train"   285
the blues   12–3, 269–70
    history of   51–2
    as protest music   99
    spirituals and   94
    talking blues   99
"Blues in the Night"   53
Bly, Nellie   129
Bonneville Power Administration   65
Boone, Daniel   252
Borach, Fania. *See* Brice, Fanny
Bordman, Gerald   106–7, 244
"Born in the U.S.A."   45, 79–81
Botsford, George   176, 206
Bouchillon, Christopher Allen   99
"The Bourgeois Blues"   94–5
Bradford, Perry   97
Bradford, Sarah H.   89
Braham, David   212
Bratton, John W.   240
*Breakfast at Tiffany's* (film)   280–1
Brennan, J. Keirn   11
Brice, Fanny   183, 222–4
Broadway (theater district)   6, 12, 102, 104–5, 242–3, 256
    African Americans on   105–7

American identity and   247–8
*A Broadway Honeymoon*   144
"Broadway Melody"   248
Brock, Jerry   250
Brockman, James   222
Broderick, Helen   180
Brookhouse, Winthrop   240
Brooks, Shelton   162
Brooks, Tilford   93
Broonzy, Big Bill   100
"Brother, Can You Spare a Dime?"   44, 184, 267, 280
brotherhood   33
Brown, Dee   69
Brown, John   26, 28
Brown, Lew   57
Brown, William Wells   92
Bryan, Alfred   206, 234
Bryan, Vincent   143, 144
Buck, Gene   191, 192
Buell, Abel   252
Bunyan, Paul   252
Burleigh, Harry   112
Burnett, Carol   119
Burns, Robert   128
*Bury My Heart at Wounded Knee* (Brown, D.)   69
"Bury My Heart at Wounded Knee"   68–9
"By the Light of the Silvery Moon"   142

cabaret   49–50
Cabot, John   258
Caesar, Irving   41
Café Society   124
Cagney, James   36–7
"California, Here I Come"   195–6
*Call Me Madam*   72
*Call Me Mister*   63, 64
Calloway, Cab   179
Calvinism   47–8
Camel Walk   49
"Can't Help Lovin' Dat Man"   183
Cantor, Eddie   118, 160, 193, 197
"Carolina in the Morning"   193–4, 277–9
Carpenter, Matthew Hale   20–1
Carroll, Earl   143
Carroll, Harry   167

"Carry Me Back to Old Virginny"   165
Carter Family   67
Carus, Emma   144, 145, 174
Casey, Warren   7
"Casey Jones"   284
Cash, Johnny   119
Castle, Irene   112
Castle, Vernon   112–3
"Castle Half and Half"   114
"The Castle House Trot"   114
"The Castle Walk"   114
Cather, Willa   169
Chamberlain, Neville   70
Charles, Ray   33
Charyn, Jerome   198
*Chasing Rainbows*   62
"Chattanooga Choo-Choo"   169
Chicago   32
"China Dreams"   241
"The Chinatown Rag"   242
"The Chinese, The Chinese, You Know"   237
Chinese Americans   239–40
  ethnic songs about   237
  stereotypes of   241–2
"Ching-a-Ling"   241
Chitty, Cathy   76
"Chong (He Come from Hong Kong)"   238
"Chop Suey Rag"   242
Christmas   74–5
Cinderella shows   242–5
citizenship   133–4
  of African Americans   7–8
"City of New Orleans"   286
civic religion   5
Civil Rights Movement   22, 71, 84–5
Civil War, American   18, 24–6, 40, 129–30, 191, 291
  songs of   30–1
"Clarinet Marmalade"   115
Clark, William   258
Clarke, Grant   58, 222, 224
Clef Club   112–3
Clef Club Orchestra   113–4
Clementi, Muzio   23
Clooney, Rosemary   10

*Clorindy, or the Origin of the Cakewalk*   105–7
Cobb, Will D.   142, 230
Cockrell, Dale   149, 175
Cohan, George M.   46, 101, 173–4, 199, 212–3, 242
   career of   36–7
   patriotism of   38
   as songwriter   55–6
Cohn, Irving   219
Colbert, Claudette   60
Cold War   100
Cole, Bob   104, 107–11
Cole, Nat King   10, 178, 179
Cole, Thomas   3
Coleridge-Taylor, Samuel   113
Collins, Arthur   174–5
Collins, Gail   234–5
Colorado College   31
Columbia (record label)   124
"Columbia, the Gem of the Ocean"   24, 38
"Columbia's Daughters"   132
"Come with Thy Sweet Voice Again"   34
Commodore (record label)   124
common good   3
Communists   69, 100
Como, Perry   119
concentration camps, Nazi   71
Cone, James H.   86–7
Confederate army   24, 39–40
*Connie's Hot Chocolates*   122
Connie's Inn   10, 163
Cook, Will Marion   104–7, 119
"Cooking Breakfast for the One I Love"   223
"coon songs"   40–1, 102, 106, 109–10, 142, 151, 161. *See also* minstrel shows
   African Americans writing   163–4
   popularity of   159–60
   in ragtime   206
   Weldon Johnson on   109
Cooper, Gary   266
Cooper, James Fenimore   252
Cotton Blossom   181
Cotton Club   10, 122, 163

*The Cotton Club Parade of 1933*   178
country music   268–9
Coward, Noel   125
Cox, Ida   98
Crawford, Richard   159
"Crazy Blues"   41, 97–8, 121
Creamer, Henry   167
Crevecouer, Michel Guillaume Jean de. *See* St. John, John Hector
Crosby, Bing   119, 177, 274
"Crossing the Grand Sierras"   154
Crothers, Rachel   244
Crouse, Russel   72
cultural appropriation   152–3
Cummings, E. E.   54

Dabney, Ford   114
"(The Dance of the) Grizzly Bear"   206
dances: ragtime and   49
   Tin Pan Alley and   49
darkness, in song   2
"Darktown Is Out Tonight"   106
"The Darktown Strutters' Ball"   162
"Darling Nelly Gray"   149–50
Dash, Irwin   225–6
"Dat Gal of Mine"   107
"The Daughter of Rosie O'Grady"   228
Davis, Benny   162–3
Davis, Frank   240
*A Day at the Races* (film)   5
"Dear Old Western Skies"   264
De Chesney, A.   142
"Deck the Halls"   74
Declaration of Independence, American   127, 190
Declaration of Sentiments   127–8
"Defense of Fort McHenry" (Key)   21
"De Golden Wedding"   165
Delaney, Tom   163
Delmore, Lionel Alton   285
Delmore, Rabon   285
DeMille, Agnes   264–5
*Democracy in America* (de Tocqueville)   16
Denver, John   288–9
desegregation   113
   of military   168–9

DeSylva, B. G.   41
DiMaggio, Joe   7
Dinkins, David   187
dives   175
Dixon, George Washington   148
Doctorow, E. L.   45–6
"Do It Again"   41
Donaldson, Walter   277–9
Donne, John   253
Donnelly, John E.   236–7
"Don't Get Around Much Anymore"   73
"Don't Let the Women Vote"   140
Douglass, Frederick   88–90, 127, 154
"Down Where the Swanee River Flows"   277
"Do Your Honey Do"   159–60
"Dream On, Little Soldier Boy"   57
Dreiser, Theodore   275
Dresser, Paul   275
Dubin, Al   44, 215, 248, 256
Du Bois, W. E. B.   87
Dunbar, Paul Laurence   105
Duncan, Laura   124
Dunn, Julia Mills   134
Dust Bowl   67, 267
    ballads   99
Dylan, Bob   95

Earl, Mary   58
*Early Jazz* (Schuller)   114
"Easter Parade"   125, 177
"East Is West"   239
Easton, Sidney   163
Ebb, Fred   248
Edison Quartet   166
Edwards, Gus   142
Egan, Raymond B.   59, 241
Eighteenth Amendment, U.S. Constitution   139
Eisenhower, Dwight   73
"Eliza Jane"   129
Ellington, Duke   12, 101
Emancipation, from slavery   86–7, 92–3, 155, 157
Emerson, Ken   151
Emerson, Luther   28–9
Emerson, Ralph Waldo   262

"Empty Bed Blues"   52
Erdman, Eddie   162–3
Erdman, Ernie   162–3
"Esther from Hetser Street"   234
ethnic songs   141–2, 197, 202, 216
    about Chinese immigrants   237
    defining   188
    popularity of   219
    in Tin Pan Alley   219–20, 225, 239, 242
ethnic songs about, Italian immigrants   216–7
Europe, James Reese   104, 112
"Everything in America Is Ragtime"   205
exceptionalism, American   20, 62
    in patriotic songs   81

*Face the Music*   72
Faye, Alice   175
feminism   84, 147
*Fiddler on the Roof*   251
Fields, Dorothy   7, 122
Fields, W. C.   118
Fifteenth Amendment, U.S. Constitution   130
*Fifty Miles from Boston*   212
*Finian's Rainbow*   184, 186, 187
Fitzgerald, Ella   10
*Flahooley*   184
*The Flapper* (film)   244
Fogerty, John   283–4
folk songs   83–84, 260–1
"For A'That"   128
Forbes, Camille A.   117
"Foremother's Hymn"   134
Fortney, W. G.   130
Fort Sumter   25
Foster, E. W.   61
Foster, Stephen   18, 48, 106, 170
    African Americans portrayed by   153–5
    writing for minstrel shows   150–1
Fourteenth Amendment, U.S. Constitution   94
Francis, Arthur   42, 43
"Free at Last"   186
Frishberg, Dave   24

Frost, Robert  255, 290
Fry, Christopher  196
Furia, Philip  36

Gandhi, Mahatma  125, 180
Gannon, Kim  75
Gardner, Oscar  242
Garfunkel, Art  287
Garland, Judy  75–6, 111
Garrison, William Lloyd  128
Gaskill, Clarence  215
*George Washington, Jr.*  38
Gerber, Alex  189, 218
Germany  43
Gershwin, George  34, 41–3, 59, 196–8
    on American sound  53
Gershwin, Ira  42, 59
"Get Off the Track"  90
Gettysburg Address  24, 132
Gibbons, James  28–9
G.I. Bill  168
Gideon, Melville  234
"The Gift Outright" (Frost)  255
Gilbert, David  105, 113, 115
Gilbert, L. Wolfe  193, 221
Gilbert, W. S.  184
"Gimme de Leavin's"  110
"Gimme Ma Money"  160
Giovanni, Nikki  86, 92, 165–6
"Give Me Liberty or Give Me Love"  60
"Give Peace a Chance"  84
"God Bless America"  9, 10, 21, 75, 83, 171, 204
    Guthrie critiquing  71–2
    writing of  69–70
"God Blessed America for Me"  71
"Go Down, Moses"  88
"God Rest Ye, Merry Gentlemen"  74
"Goin' Down the Road Feeling Bad"  267
"Going Home Train"  64
"Going to the Polls"  137
*Gold Diggers of 1933*  44, 249
"Golden Slippers"  165
Goldenthall, Jacob  188–90
"Good by Alexander, Good bye Honey-Boy"  167

"Good-Bye-Broadway, Hello France"  247–8
Goodman, Benny  10, 103, 113
Goodman, Joe  161
Goodman, Steve  285–6
Goodman, William  262
Goodwin, Joe  141, 231
Google Maps  252
Gorney, Jay  44
Gottler, Archie  56
Graff, George, Jr.  227
Graham, Roger A.  104
Grainger, Porter  96–7
*Grease* (film)  7
Great American Songbook  5, 13, 156, 170
Great Depression  9–10, 43, 60, 62, 244, 266, 279
Great Migration  50
Green, Eddie  12
Green, Stanley  224
greenhorns  188–9
"Grizzly Bear Rag"  176
Gross, Terry  80–81
Guthrie, Woody  63–8, 76, 84, 99, 252, 268
    on "God Bless America"  71–2
    lyrics of  267–8
*Guys and Dolls*  249–51
*Gypsy*  250

Haggard, Merle  119, 272
"Hail, Columbia"  23, 24, 31
Hajdu, David  97–8
Hall, Adelaide  121
*Hallelujah I'm a Bum* (film)  279–80
"Hallelujah Song"  136
Hamm, Charles  196, 204
Hammerstein, Oscar, II  19, 169, 181–4, 264, 283, 288–9
Hammond, George P.  176
Hanby, Benjamin  149–50, 156
Handy, W. C.  114
Hanley, James F.  222, 224
"Happy Days Are Here Again"  62
Harburg, E. Y.  5–6, 9, 12, 169, 185, 187, 196
    political engagement of  184–5

"Hard Times Come Again No
    More" 34–5
"Hard Travelin'" 268
Harlem 10
Harlem Hellfighters 114
"Harlem on My Mind" 125, 178
Harlem Renaissance 87, 102, 122, 161,
    171
Harlin, Byron G. 174
Harnick, Sheldon 250–1
Harper, Ellen 13
Harrigan, Edward "Ned" 210–2
"Harrigan" 213
Harris, Charles K. 19
Harris, Marlon 104
Harrison, William Henry 61
Hart, Lorenz 61, 280
Hart, Moss 61, 72, 123, 180
Hartman, Saidiya 102
Harvey, Eleanor J. 18
Hasse, John Edward 12, 40
"The Hat My Father Wore Upon St.
    Patrick's Day" 193
Hauptman, William 185
"Have Yourself a Merry Little
    Christmas" 11, 75
Havez, Jean 57
Hayes, Lee 84
Hayes, Rutherford B. 61
Hazard, Rebecca N. 146
"Heat Wave" 125
Hein, Silvio 239
Helf, Fred 217
Henderson, Fletcher 103
Henry, Patrick 16
Herbert, Elizabeth Boynton 138
Herbert, Victor 36
Herman, Jerry 250
Hermann, Steven 254
Hess, Cliff 206
*High, Wide, and Handsome* 288
Higley, Brewster M. 262–3
Hill, Billy 265
Hitler, Adolf 69, 70
"Hobo's Meditation" 271
Hochberg, Isidore 196
Hodges, Catherine T. 14

Hoffman, Aaron S. 236
"Ho! For California!" 261
Hogan, Ernest 158–9
Holden, Stephen 8
"Hold the Fort" 132
Holiday, Billie 124
*Holiday Inn* 177
Holly, Buddy 85–6
Hollywood 6, 168
Holton, J. W. 140
"Homeward Bound" 286
"Honeysuckle Rose" 122
Hooker, John Lee 95
Hoover, Herbert 45, 125, 180
Hopkinson, Joseph 23
Hopper, Edward 53–4
Horne, Lena 10, 178, 179
*Hot Chocolates* 123
Hotel Marshall 100–1
"Hottest Coon in Dixie" 106
Howard, Alan 86
Howard, Joe E. 144, 145
Howard University 164
Howe, Julia Ward 27
Hubbell, Raymond 143, 144
Hudson, Henry 258
Hudson River School 3
Hunter, Alberta 98
Hutchinson, Anne 246
Hutchinson, Jesse 62, 261
Hutchinson Family Singers 30, 90
Hymer, John B. 238
hymns 26

"I Ain't Got Nobody (Much and Nobody
    Cares for Me)" 104
identity, American 3, 238–9
    Broadway and 247–8
    ragtime shaping 47–8
    vaudeville and 215–6
"I Don't Care" 217
"I Don't Want to Walk without You" 44,
    73
*I'd Rather Be Right* 61
"If It Wasn't for the Irish and the
    Jews" 195
"If I Were President" 61

"If You've Never Been Vamped by a Brownskin" 121
"I Got De Headache Now" 117, 118
"I Heard What You Said About Me" 93–4
"I Just Can't Make My Eyes Behave" 142
"I Just Met the Fellow Who Married the Girl That I was Going to Get?" 141
"I'll Be Home for Christmas" 10–11, 75
"I'll Walk Alone" 44
"I'm a Jazz Vampire" 51
"I'm Always Chasing Rainbows" 141
"I'm Gonna Pin a Medal on the Girl I Left Behind" 57
"I'm Just Simply Full of Jazz" 51
immigrants and immigration 21, 30–1, 46, 141–2, 197. *See also specific topics*
   assimilation of 192, 198–9, 218
   in Manhattan 209
   Nationalization Act of 1870 236–7
   patriotism and 206–7
   population of, in U.S. 189
   stages of immigration 192
   vaudeville and 215
   waves of 206–7, 245
   women 218
Immigration Quota Law 245
"Immigration Rose" 225–6
improvisation 93
"I'm Tired of Eating in Restaurants" 117
"In Blinky, Winky, Chinky, Chinatown" 240
individuality and individualism 246–7
   jazz and 12, 50
Industrial Revolution 33
inflation 23–4
"In Honeysuckle Time" 121
injustice 83
"In My Merry Oldsmobile" 142
Inskeep, Steve 79–80
"In the Evening by the Moonlight" 165
"In the Heart of the City That Has No Heart" 275
*Irene* 243–5
Irish immigrants 192
   in Manhattan 208–11
   stereotypes of 210, 212, 215, 227
   women 228–9
"The Irish Suffragette" 145
Irving, Washington 2
Irwin, May 107
"I Should Worry and Get Wrinkles" 143–4
"Is It Right?" 130
Iskowitz, Israel. *See* Cantor, Eddie
isolationism 70–1, 161–2
"Italian Girl" 231–2
Italian immigrants 192–3, 198–9
   ethnic songs about 216–7
   stereotypes 222–3
*It Happened One Night* (film) 279
"It's All Been Done Before but Not the Way I Do It" 217
"It's a Long Way to Tipperary" 140
"It Was Good Enough for Grandma" 185
"I've Been Working on the Railroad" 284
"I've Got Troubles of My Own" 108
Ives, Burl 273
"I Want to Go Back to Michigan (Down on the Farm)" 277
"I Wish That You Was My Gal, Molly" 229

Jacobs, Jim 7
James, Henry 207
Jane, Lucy 159
January 6 insurrection 291
Jasen, David 219
jazz 133
   history of 49–51, 102–3, 114
   individuality and 12, 50
   in New Orleans 49–50
   popularity of 50–1
*The Jazz Singer* (film) 195
Jefferson, Blind Lemon 52, 96
Jefferson, Thomas 31, 61
Jennings, Waylon 79
Jerome, William 163, 194, 195
Jewish Americans 71, 193–4, 198–9
   as blackface performers 160–1
   stereotypes 200–1, 222
   women 232–4

Jim Crow laws   14, 40, 100, 130, 153, 177–8
"John Brown's Body"   26–7
"John Henry"   93
Johnson, Alphonso   52, 109
Johnson, Billy   108
Johnson, James Weldon   22, 104, 107, 108, 117, 121
  on "coon songs"   109–10
Johnson, J. Rosamond   104, 107–11
*The Jolly Bachelors*   201
Jolson, Al   160, 193, 195, 197, 219
Jonah Man (character)   107, 110, 116, 118
"The Jonah Man"   107
Jones, Johnny   36
Joplin, Scott   196
Josephson, Barney   124
"Jump Jim Crow"   149–50
"Just A-Wearing for You"   35

Kaatskill Mountains   2
Kahn, Gus   193, 241, 277–9, 288
Kander, John   248
Kaplan, James   102
Kauffman, George S.   59, 61, 184
Kay, Buddy   61
Kelly, Daniel E.   262, 264
Kendall, Marguerite   240
Kennedy, John F.   45, 62
Kent, Walter   75
Kern, Jerome   19, 181–2, 231, 283, 288
Key, Francis Scott   21
Kimball, George   27
King, Martin Luther, Jr.   45
"Kingdom Coming"   155, 156
"King of the Road"   272–3
Kirk, John   147
Kirschner, Elliott   1, 14
Kittredge, Walter   30
"Kitty the Telephone Girl"   230
"K-K-K-Katy"   58
Koehler, Ted   122, 178
Krasner, David   108
Krehbiel, H. E.   115
Ku Klux Klan   71

Kun, Josh   11
Kushner, Tony   196

*Ladies First*   42
Lamb, Arthur J.   19
Lamb, Joseph F.   196
Lampell, Millard   84
"The Land of Beginning Again"   251
Lane, Burton   186
Lang, Eddie   102
Lange, Arthur   218
LaRocca, Nick   103
"The Last Round Up"   265
Lauders, Gustave   143
Lawlor, Charles B.   209
Layton, Turner   167
Lazarus, Emma   204
Leadbelly   94
League of Nations   43
*Leatherstocking Tales*   252
Lee, Peggy   10
Lee, Robert E.   24
Lehar, Franz   36
Lehman, David   5
Lennon, John   84
Leslie, Edgar   56, 206, 232
*Letters from an American Farmer* (St. John)   17, 203
Lewis, Andy   236
Lewis, Meriwether   258
"Liberty"   133
Library of Congress Archive   268
"Lift Every Voice and Sing"   21, 22
Lincoln, Abraham   5, 24–6, 28–9
Lincoln, C. Eric   94
Lindsay, Howard   72
*Little Johnny Jones*   36, 37
Livernash, Will L.   39
"Livery Stable Blues"   103
"Liza Johnson Joins De Sufferjets"   142
Locke, Alain   87
Loesser, Frank   249, 250
Lomax, John A.   93, 260, 263
"The Lost Chord"   35
Loudermilk, John D.   285
Louisiana Purchase   31, 75
"The Lovely Ohio"   262

"Love Me To a Yiddisha Melody"   221
love songs   5–7
    from Tin Pan Alley   73
"Lullaby of Broadway"   248, 249
Lunceford, Jimmie   103
*Lusitania*   63
lynching   123, 179

MacArthur, Douglas   45
Macauley, F. E. M.   131
Macdonald, Ballard   216
Macy, William Hussy   135
*Madame Butterfly* (Puccini)   239
Madden, Edward   241
Maeble, E. S.   192
Magee, Jeffrey   171
"Mammas Don't Your Babies Grow Up To Be Cowboys"   264
"Mammy's Choc'late Soldier"   166
Mancini, Henry   280–1
"Mandy"   172
Manhattan: African American population in   100–1
    immigrants in   209
    Irish immigrants in   208–11
"Manhattan Madness"   256
Manifest Destiny   31
Mantle, Mickey   7
"Marching Through Georgia"   154
"Marie from Sunny Italy"   172
Marion, Francis   244
"(Mariutch Make-a the Hootch-A-Ma-Kooch) Down at Coney Isle"   232
Marsalis, Wynton   12
Marshall, Davel   269
Marshall, Donald   244
Martin, Hugh   75–6
Marx, Minnie   214
Marx Brothers   5, 214
"Materna"   32
Matthews, Chris   82
Matthews, Lewis W.   168
"Maybe You Think I'm Happy"   221
McAllister, Marvin   104
McCarron, Charles   277
McCarthy, Joe   141, 184

McGlinn, John   181
McHugh, Jimmy   7, 122, 225–6
McLean, Don   85–6
McWhirter, Christian L.   29
Meeropol, Abel   123, 124, 179
*Meet Me in St. Louis* (film)   75, 111
Melnick, Jeffrey   171
melodrama   18–20, 150
Melting Pot   14, 189, 191, 196, 203, 239, 245
"The Melting Pot"   191–92
*The Melting Pot* (Zangwill)   203–4
"Men of Harlech"   131–2
Mercer, Johnny   53, 280–1
Mesta, Perle   72
Metz, Theodore   159
Mexican-American War   261
Meyer, George W.   141, 161, 231
Miles, Rufus E.   3
Miles's Law   3
Miley, Bubber   12
*Milk and Honey*   250–1
Miller, Elizabeth Smith   128
Miller, Marilyn   180
Miller, Roger   185, 186, 272, 283
Mills, Florence   121
"Mind the Baby, I Must Vote Today"   145
minstrel shows   40–1, 101–2, 104–5, 156, 164, 219
    Berlin on   170–1
    Foster, S., writing for   150–1
*Miss Liberty*   204
"Miss Lucy Neale"   150
modernism   105
modernity, ragtime and   114
Mohr, Halsey K.   232
Monaco, James V.   58
Moody, Richard   210
Moon, Krystyn R.   108, 237–8
"Moon River"   280–1
Moore, Fred D.   242
Moran, Ed   217
Morrissey   83
Morse, Theodore F.   241
Morton, Jelly Roll   103
Mott, Lucretia   127
Mountain, Margaret   142

"Muddy Water"   283
Mullaly W. S.   236
*The Mulligan Guard Ball*   212
Munich Pact   70
*My Antonia* (Cather)   169
"My Country, 'Tis of Thee"   21, 23, 24, 31, 38
"My Country Used to Be"   24
"My Grandfather Clock"   154
"My Hometown"   287
"My Irish Suffragette"   144
"My Little Hong Kong Baby"   240
"My Little Yiddisha Queen"   234
"My Mammy"   195–6
"My Old Kentucky Home"   106, 152
"My Sweetheart Is Somewhere in France"   58
Myth of the Garden   20–1, 31

NAACP. *See* National Association for the Advancement of Colored People
Nashville   6
National Association for the Advancement of Colored People (NAACP)   22
nationalism, patriotism v.   2, 3, 14
National Public Radio   79
Native Americans, genocide of   68–9
nativism   207
Naturalization Act of 1870   26
Nazi Party   71
Nelson, Julia B.   137
Nelson, Willie   252
"The New America"   138
"The New Colossus" (Lazarus)   204
the New Negro   116, 117
New Orleans   47
  jazz in   49–50
*Nice People*   244
Nichols, Anne   220, 238
Nineteenth Amendment, U.S. Constitution   127, 129–30, 140
"Nobody"   119, 120
"Nobody Knows the Trouble I've Seen"   94
"No Irish Need Apply"   208

Norton, George A.   114
Norworth, Jack   201, 229
"Now That the Buffalo's Gone"   69
Noyes, Frances F.   133
Nysewander, Benjamin F.   136

Obama, Barack   170, 287–8
Obomsawin, Mali   68
O'Brien, Margaret   75, 111
*Of Thee I Sing*   59
"Oh! How I Hate to Get Up in the Morning"   171
"Oh! Susannah"   151, 172
Oklahoma   2–3
"Oklahoma!"   290
Olcott, Chauncey   227
"The Old Arm Chair"   35
"Old Folks at Home"   152, 154, 156, 172
"The Old Granite State"   90
"Old Rosin the Bow"   62
"The Old Settler's Song"   260
"The Old Ship of Zion"   91
Old Testament   88
*The Old Town*   143
"Old Uncle Ned"   150
*Olive Oyl for President*   61
Oliver, King   103
"Ol' Man River"   182–3, 283
Onkey, Lauren   79
Ono, Yoko   84
*On the Avenue* (film)   126
"On the Road Again"   252
"On the Sunny Side of the Street"   7
"Onward Christian Soldiers"   28, 138
opium   240–2
optimism   7
  in song   2
Original Dixieland Jazz Band   102, 103
"Over the Rainbow"   9, 186

Pacific Railway Act   284–5
Packard, Winthrop   129
Park, Robert   192
Parkhurst City Vigilance League   176
Parkman, Francis   254
parlor ballads   35
"Pastures of Plenty"   67

patriotic songs  4
   American exceptionalism in  81
"Patriotic Voting"  139
patriotism  8
   of African Americans  112, 171–2
   of Berlin  69–72
   of Cohan  38
   defining  1–2
   immigration and  206–7
   inclusiveness of  189–90
   nationalism v.  2, 3, 14
   racism v.  148
   ragtime and  205
   reclaiming  1–2
   Smith, S., on  3–4
   in Tin Pan Alley songs  56–7
   during World War I  166–7
Paul, Alice  126
Payne, John Howard  11
Peace Corps  82–83
Pearl Harbor  43, 73
Pelham Bay Café  173, 176, 205
Phile, Philip  23
Piantadosi, Al  140–1
Piazza, Tom  269
Pike's Peak  31–2
Pilgrims  252
"Pinky Panky Poo"  236
"Pipe Dream Blues"  240
"The Police Won't Let Mariuch-a Dance (Unless She Move-Da-Feet)"  232–3
Pollyanna songs  7, 22
Poole, John F.  208
"Poor Uncle Tom, Good Night"  152
popular songs  3
   affective content of  4
   in America  6
   Berlin on  5
   contemporary sentiments expressed by  8
Porter, Cole  248, 256
potato famines  208
"The President's March"  23
Progressive Era  193
Prohibition  244
Protestantism  138

protest music  83, 95
   the blues as  99
   work of Williams, B., as  118–9
"Proud Mary"  283–4
"Prove It on Me"  95
Pryor, Arthur  40, 113
public discourse  8–9
Puccini, Giacomo  239
Purcell, Sarah J.  4
"Put It Right Here (Or Keep It Out There)"  12, 96
Putnam, Claude, Jr.  292

race-mixing  175
racism  104, 108, 168
   against African Americans  40–1, 102, 186
   critiquing  187
   in nineteenth century  149
   patriotism v.  148
   in suffrage movement  130
Radford, Dave  276
radio  10
*Rags*  45
ragtime  18, 101, 105, 170, 175
   American identity shaped by  47–8
   Berlin popularizing  176–7
   condemnations of  175–6
   "coon songs" in  206
   dances and  49
   history of  113–4
   modernity and  114
   patriotism and  205
   popularity of  161
*Ragtime* (Doctorow)  46
"Ragtime Laundry"  242
"The Ragtime Soldier Man"  57
Rainey, Gertrude "Ma"  95, 98
Rainger, Ralph  60, 248
"Ramblin' Fever"  272
Rather, Dan  1, 14
Razaf, Andy  122, 123
Reagan, Ronald  80
"The Real American Folksong (Is a Rag)"  42–3
Reconstruction (historical period)  14, 94, 291

*Index*

"Remember My Forgotten Man" 44–5, 267
"Remember Pearl Harbor" 43–4
Remington, Frederick 266
Rice, Thomas Dartmouth 148–9
Riis, Thomas L. 108, 109
*Rilla of Green Gables* 57
Rimler, Walter 42
"Rip Van Winkle" (Irving) 2
"Rise Up Women!" 135
"Rising High Water Blues" 52
Robeson, Paul 121
Robin, Leo 60, 248
Robinson, Harriet H. 132
Robinson, Jackie 7
Robinson, J. Russel 240
Robinson, Mark 185
Rodgers, Jimmie 268–72
Rodgers, Richard 61, 182, 264, 280
Rogers, Alex 119
Rogers, Howard E. 58
Rogin, Michael 161
Rome, Harold 64
Roosevelt, Eleanor 63
Roosevelt, Franklin Delano 61
Roosevelt, Teddy 36
Root, George Frederick 25–6, 29
Rosenberg, Deena 9, 187
Rothafel, Samuel L. 48
Route 66, 259, 269
Roxy Theater 48
Ruby, Harry 69–70
Ryskind, Morrie 59

Sabatella, Matthew 268
"Sadie Salome (Go Home)" 200, 218, 220, 231
Sainte-Marie, Buffy 68–69
St. John, John Hector 16–7, 203
*Sally in Our Alley* 111
Salter, Mike 173
Sans Souci 104
satire 184, 187
Sayre, Jemmy 140
"School Days" 142
Schuller, Gunther 114
Schultz, Dutch 122
Schurz, Carl 20–1

Schwartz, Jean 163, 193–5
Schwartz, Stephen 45, 46
Scott, James 196
Scott, Randall 266
"Second Hand Rose" 222, 224
Seeger, Pete 67, 84, 95, 260, 273
"Semper Fidelis" 40
Seroff, Doug 157, 161
"Settle Down in a One-Horse Town" 276
Shafee, Layal 268
"Shall We Gather at the River?" 26
sharecropping 186
Sharples, Winston 61
Shaw, Artie 103
Shaw, George Bernard 184
sheet music 10, 19–20, 132–3
Shields, Ren 230
"Shillington" (Updike) 254
Shipp, Jesse A. 119
Shipp, Thomas 123–4
"The Ship That Never Returned" 154
*The Shootist* (film) 257
Short, Hassard 239
"Should to Shoulder" 132
*Show Boat* 19, 181–4, 283, 296 n.6
"Shuck that Corn Before You Eat" 92
*Shuffle Along* 120–1
"The Sidewalks of New York" 208–9
Silber, Irwin 126
Silver, Abner 189, 218
Silver, Frank 219
Silverstein 15
Simon, Paul 76–7, 287
Simone, Nina 119, 166
Sinatra, Frank 10
"Sing Me to Sleep, Mammy Dear" 121–2
Sissle, Noble 51, 114, 121
*Sister Carrie* (Dreiser) 275
"The Skidmore Guard" 212
slavery 21, 41, 152–3, 164
 Emancipation 86–7, 92–3, 155
 work songs and 92–3
"Slavery Is a Hard Foe to Battle" 91
"Slumming on Park Avenue" 126
Smith, Abram 123–4
Smith, Bessie 52, 98, 174–5
Smith, Mamie 97–8, 121

Smith, Steven B.   1
  on patriotism   3–4
Smith, Trixie   98
Smith, Willie "The Lion"   101
Smithsonian American Art Museum   18
Snyder, Robert   214
Snyder, Ted   173, 229
social justice   83–5
"So Long, It's Been Good To Know Yuh"   268
"Somebody Loves Me"   41
"Sometimes I Feel Like a Motherless Child"   94
Sondheim, Stephen   78, 250
"Song of Freedom"   171
"Song of the Free"   88
"The Song of the 'Metis' Trapper"   261
"Sonny Boy"   195–6
Sousa, John Philip   5, 37, 40, 113
Sowell, Thomas   207
Spanish-American War   31
spiritualism   27
spirituals (songs)   87–8, 106
  the blues and   94
Springsteen, Bruce   45–6, 79–81, 287
Stamper, Dave   191, 192
Stanbury, Douglas   48–9
Stanton, Elizabeth Cady   127
Staples, Mavis   35
"The Stars and Stripes Forever"   5, 24, 40
"The Star-Spangled Banner"   21, 38
Statue of Liberty   49, 204
Stebbins, Catharine F.   139
stereotypes: of African Americans   102, 109, 152–5, 166
  of Chinese immigrants   241–2
  of Irish immigrants   210, 212, 215, 227
  of Italian immigrants   222–3
  of Jewish Americans   200–1, 222
  in Tin Pan Alley songs   191
Sterling, Andrew B.   218
Stern, Jack   234
Stewart, James   266
St. Louis   47
Stone, Henry   29
Stone, John A.   261
"Stormy Weather"   178

"Strange Fruit"   123–4, 179
Strauss, Richard   200
"Strike for Liberty"   131
Strouse, Charles   45, 46
Styne, Jule   250
Subotnik, Rose Rosengard, on Tin Pan Alley   12–13
"Sue Me"   250
"The Suffrage Flag"   134
suffrage movement   127–9, 132–3, 135–6
  racism in   130
  Tin Pan Alley and   142–6
*Sullivan's Travels* (film)   279
"Supper Time"   125, 179
Sutton, Willie   198
Swanstrom, Arthur   51
"Sweet Rosie O'Grady"   228
swing   12
syncopation   48, 52, 170, 197

"'Tain't Nobody's Business If I Do"   96
"Take Me Out to the Ballgame"   10, 71
"Take This Hammer"   93
talking blues   99
"Talking Blues"   99
"Talking Dust Bowl Blues"   99–100
Tanguay, Eva   217
"Taxation without Representation"   130
"Taxation without Representation Is Tyranny"   136
"Teddy Da Roose"   217
the Tenderloin, Manhattan   100–1
"Tenting on the Old Camp Ground"   30
"That International Rag"   205
"That Kazzatsky Dance"   233
"That Ragtime Suffragette"   144
"There's a Little Bit of Irish in Sadie Cohn"   234
"They're All Good American Names"   194
*This Is the Army*   171
"This Is the Life"   275, 276
"This Land Is Your Land"   68, 69, 71–2
Thomas, J. R.   192
Threat, Charissa   168
Thurman, Howard   85
Tierney, Dominic   28
Tierney, Harry   243
"Tiger Rag"   103

Tillis, Mel   273
"Till We Meet Again"   58
"Tin Cup Blues"   96
Tin Pan Alley   6, 11–2, 18, 20, 34, 41, 159
   dances and   49
   ethnic songs in   219–20, 225, 239, 242
   love songs from   73
   patriotism in   56–7
   stereotypes in songs of   191
   Subotnik on   12–13
   suffrage movement and   142–6
   women in   223–5
*Tintypes*   46
"To Anacreon in Heaven"   21
Tocqueville, Alexis de   16
"To His Mistress Going to Bed"   253
"Tony Spagoni's Cabaret"   215
"Toot Toot Tootsie"   195–6
*Torch Song*   60
train songs   284–5
"Train Whistle Blues"   270
trickster archetype   115
*A Trip to Coontown*   108
triumphalism   20–21, 23, 28–9, 38, 62, 261
Truman, Harry S.   72, 168
Trumbauer, Frank   102
truth-telling   76
Tubman, Harriet   89, 91
Turner, Nat   87
Twain, Mark   185

Ukraine   23
"Uncle Joe's 'Hail Columbia'"   155
"Uncle Sam's Daughter"   135
*Uncle Tom's Cabin*   152
Underground Railroad   89, 154–5
"Under the Bamboo Tree"   111
Union army   24, 29–30
"Union Maid"   84
United States Marine Band   40
Updike, John   254
urban life   274–5

Valens, Ritchie   86
Van Alstyne, Egbert   241
vaudeville   196–7, 214
   identity, American and   215
   immigrants and   215

"Vietnam"   80
Vietnam War   28
Vincent, Theodore   107
Von Tilzer, Albert   57, 277
Von Tilzer, Harry   19, 232

"Waitin' for the Robert E. Lee"   193
"Waiting for a Train"   270–1
Walker, George   115–6
Waller, Thomas "Fats"   122, 123
"Waltz Me Around Again, Willie"   229–30
"Wanderin'"   259
wanderlust   246–7, 268–70
Ward, Samuel A.   32
Warren, Harry   44, 248, 256
Washburn, Henry S.   25
Washington, George   16, 23, 69
"Washington Post"   40
Waters, Ethel   98, 125, 180
   Berlin and   178–9
Wayne, John   266
"We All Fall"   141
Webb, Clifton   180
Webb, E. H.   145
Webster, Daniel   285
"The Wedding of the Chinee and the Coon"   108–9
"We Did It Before"   43–4
"We Don't Have No Payday Now"   93
Weeks, Harold   238
Wellesley, College   31
Wellman, Judith   128
West, Eugene   225–6
West, Paul   231, 240
the West, American   2–3, 257–9, 265–6
*West Side Story*   78
"What the Well-Dressed Man in Harlem Will Wear"   171–2
Wheeler, L. May   135, 136
"When Alexander Takes His Ragtime Band to France"   205–6
"When Irish Eyes Are Smiling"   227–8
"When Mose with His Nose Leads the Band"   215
"When the Midnight Choo-Choo Leaves for Alabam"   277
"When the Swallows Homeward Fly"   35
"When the World's on Fire"   67

"When Women Cast the Ballot (The Important Question)" 136
"When Yankee Doodle Marches Thro' Berlin, There'll Be a Hot Time in the U.S.A." 39
"Where the Black-Eyed Susans Grow" 276–7
"While the Band Played an American Rag" 205
Whitcomb, Ian 200
White, George 143
"White Christmas" 10, 75, 177
    writing of 73–5
Whiting, Richard A. 59, 276
Whitman, Walt 3, 254
"Who Dat Say Chicken in Dis Crowd" 106
"Wild Cherries Rag" 173
Wilder, Alec 164
Williams, A. S. "Clubber" 100
Williams, Bert 104, 110, 115–6, 122
    protest music of 118–19
Williams, H. A. 8
Williams, Harry 144
Williams, Roger 246
Williams, Spencer 104, 240
Williams, William B. 10
Wilmerding, John 2
Wilson, Edith 123
Wilson, Woodrow 63, 126
*Winesburg, Ohio* (Anderson) 253–4
Wisconsin Territory 259
Witmark, Isadore 106
Wollstonecraft, Mary 135
"The Woman's Cause Is Right" 139
women: equality of 84–5, 98
    immigrant 218
    Irish immigrants 228–9
    Jewish 232–4
    in Tin Pan Alley 223–5
"Women's Ballot or 'Whosoever Will'" 137
Women's Christian Temperance Union 139
"The Women's Marseillaise" 131
Women's Political Union 131
Women's Rights Convention 127

Wood, Ina 84
Woods, Harry 288
Work, Henry Clay 62–3, 154, 155, 284
work songs 92–93
World War I 11, 38–9, 43–4, 70, 112, 161–2, 243–4
    African Americans in 166–7
    armistice 251
    patriotism during 166–7
World War II 25, 43–4, 67, 99–100
    African Americans in 168
Wright, Robert 281

Yale Glee Club 154
Yang, Jia Lynn 191
"Yankee Boy" 46
"Yankee Doodle Blues" 41, 42
"Yankee Doodle Boy" 37, 199
"A Yankee Doodle Boy Is Good Enough for Me" 39
*Yankee Doodle Dandy* 36–7
"Yankee Doodle Dandy" 36–7
"Yankee Doodle Rhythm" 42
Yankee Doodle songs 24, 46
"Yankee Shuffle" 40
"The Year of Jubilo" 155
Yellen, Jack 62
"Yes, We Have No Bananas" 219
"Yes Sir, That's My Baby" 194
"Yiddle, on Your Fiddle, Play Some Ragtime" 235
Yip, Harburg 9
*Yip Yip Yaphank* 69, 70, 171
yodeling 269–70
Yoelson, Asa. *See* Jolson, Al
"You Made Me Love You" 141
"Young America" 201
"You're a Grand Old Flag" 38
"You're a Grand Old Rag" 38
"You're Easy to Dance With" 177

Zangwill, Israel 203
Ziegfeld, Florenz 115, 143
*Ziegfeld Follies* 115, 117
"Zip Coon" 159, 160
zoot suits 171–2